POLICE
WITHOUT BORDERS

The Fading Distinction Between Local and Global

International Police Executive Symposium Co-Publications

Dilip K. Das, *Founding President-IPES*

Global Trafficking in Women and Children
By Obi N.I. Ebbe and Dilip K. Das
ISBN: 978-1-4200-5943-4

Contemporary Issues in Law Enforcement and Policing
By Andrew Millie and Dilip K. Das
ISBN: 978-1-4200-7215-0

Trends in Policing: Interviews with Police Leaders Across the Globe, Volume Two
By Dilip K. Das and Otwin Marenin
ISBN: 978-1-4200-7520-5

Criminal Abuse of Women and Children: An International Perspective
By Obi N.I. Ebbe and Dilip K. Das
ISBN: 978-1-4200-8803-8

Urbanization, Policing, and Security: Global Perspectives
By Gary Cordner, Dilip K. Das, and AnnMarie Cordner
ISBN: 978-1-4200-8557-0

Global Environment of Policing
By Dilip K. Das, Darren Palmer, and Anthony L.Sciarabba
ISBN: 978-1-4200-6590-9

Trends in Policing: Interviews with Police Leaders Across the Globe, Volume Three
By Dilip K. Das and Otwin Marenin
ISBN: 978-1-4398-1924-1

Police Without Borders: The Fading Distinction between Local and Global
By Cliff Roberson and Dilip K. Das
ISBN: 978-1-4398-0501-5

Terrorism, Counterterrorism, and Internal Wars: Examining International Political Violence
By Austin Turk, Dilip K. Das, and James Ross
ISBN: 978-1-4398-2104-6

Effective Crime Reduction Strategies: International Perspectives
By James F. Albrecht and Dilip K. Das
ISBN: 978-1-4200-7838-1

Strategies and Responses to Crime: Thinking Locally, Acting Globally
By Dilip K. Das, Mintie Das, and Larry French
ISBN: 978-1-4200-7669-1

Justices of the World: Their Views, Opinions and Perspectives
by Cliff Roberson and Dilip K. Das
ISBN: 978-1-4200-9978-2

Cross Cultural Profiles of Policing
By Dilip K. Das and Osman Dolu
ISBN: 978-1-4200-7014-9

POLICE WITHOUT BORDERS

The Fading Distinction Between Local and Global

Edited by
Cliff Roberson
Dilip K. Das
Jennie K. Singer

International Police Executive Symposium
Co-Publication

CRC Press
Taylor & Francis Group
Boca Raton London New York

CRC Press is an imprint of the
Taylor & Francis Group, an **informa** business

CRC Press
Taylor & Francis Group
6000 Broken Sound Parkway NW, Suite 300
Boca Raton, FL 33487-2742

First issued in paperback 2019

ISBN-13: 978-1-4398-0501-5 (hbk)
ISBN-13: 978-0-367-86503-0 (pbk)

Visit the Taylor & Francis Web site at
http://www.taylorandfrancis.com

and the CRC Press Web site at
http://www.crcpress.com

Table of Contents

Preface

Police without Borders: The Fading Distinction Between Local and Global was the goal of the Fifteenth Annual International Police Executive Symposium held in Cincinnati, Ohio, USA in 2008. This annual IPES meeting focused on policing without borders, the need for international and national cooperation among policing agencies, and the need for cooperation between the police and the academic community, private policing agencies, and the general public. Distinctions between local practices in relationship to global policing practices were highlighted in the myriad papers presented. This conference was hosted by the Cincinnati Police Department and the Ohio Association of Chiefs of Police and was organized by the Home Office of the United Kingdom.

Sixty-five police executives, government officials, academics and researchers from forty-two countries, representing most of the continents, made presentations that focused on themes that addressed all aspects of policing in a global community. Selected papers presented at the symposium were chosen to become book chapters, and feedback from the symposium participants facilitated the collaboration with the papers' authors to fully assimilate the current research in each area. The papers chosen were supplemented with a few papers not presented at the IPES conference in order to provide a more complete discussion of the themes involved in policing without borders.

The wide forum of countries and scholarly members from the field of policing all share the goals of practicing evidence-based policing, expanding international policing research, and working to create a collaborative global community of police agencies. The collaboration between scholars and practitioners created the unique information presented in this book regarding the ways in which communication between international police communities can create policing without borders.

About the Editors

Cliff Roberson is the academic chair of the Graduate School of Criminal Justice, Kaplan University, and editor-in-chief of *Professional Issues in Criminal Justice Journal* (www.picj.org). He is also an emeritus professor of criminal justice at Washburn University and a retired professor of criminology, California State University, Fresno. His previous academic experience includes professor of criminology and director of the Justice Center, California State University, Fresno; professor of criminal justice and dean of Arts and Sciences at the University of Houston, Victoria; associate vice president for academic affairs, Arkansas Tech University; and director of programs for the National College of District Attorneys, University of Houston.

His nonacademic legal experience includes heading the Military Law Branch, U.S. Marine Corps; Trial and Legal Services supervisor, Office of State Counsel for Offenders, Texas Board of Criminal Justice; private legal practice; judge pro tem in the California courts; trial and defense counsel and military judge as a marine judge advocate. Dr. Roberson is admitted to practice before the U.S. Supreme Court, Federal Courts in California and Texas, the Supreme Court of Texas, and the Supreme Court of California.

Dr. Roberson's educational background includes a PhD in human behavior, U.S. International University; LLM in criminal law, criminology, and psychiatry, George Washington University; JD from American University; BA in political science, University of Missouri; and one year of post-graduate study at the University of Virginia School of Law.

Cliff has authored or co-authored numerous books and texts. His recent texts on criminal justice subjects include:

- *Constitutional Law and Criminal Justice* (Taylor & Francis, 2009)
- Roberson and Das, *An Introduction to Comparative Legal Models of Criminal Justice* (Taylor & Francis, 2008)
- *Identity Theft Investigations* (Kaplan Publishing Co., 2008)
- Birzer and Roberson, *Police Operations* (Pearson, 2008)
- Birzer and Roberson, *Policing Today and Tomorrow* (Prentice Hall, 2006)
- Wallace and Roberson, *Principles of Criminal Law*, 4th ed. (Allyn and Bacon, 2008)

- *Criminal Procedure Today: Issues and Cases*, 2nd ed. (Prentice Hall, 2000)
- Roberson, Wallace, and Stuckey, *Procedures in the Justice System*, 9th ed. (Prentice Hall, 2009)
- Roberson and Wallace, *Introduction to Criminology* (Copperhouse, 1998)
- *Introduction to Criminal Justice* (Copperhouse, 1994; 2nd ed., 1998; 3rd ed., 2000).
- Masters and Roberson, *Inside Criminology* (Prentice Hall, 1996)
- Birzer and Roberson, *Introduction to Private Security* (Pearson, 2008)

Dr. Dilip Das served as a police chief before joining academia. He is the founding president of the International Police Executive Symposium (IPES; www.ipes.info), which brings police researchers and practitioners together to facilitate cross-cultural, international, and interdisciplinary exchanges for the enrichment of the profession. Professor Das also serves as the founding editor-in-chief of *Police Practice and Research: An International Journal*, which is affiliated with the IPES. His publications include more than 24 books and numerous articles. He is a professor of criminal justice and a human rights consultant to the United Nations.

Jennie K. Singer, PhD, is a clinical forensic psychologist with experience in a variety of correctional settings. Dr. Singer is an assistant professor at California State University, Sacramento in the Division of Criminal Justice. She has done research on sex offender recidivism and on sex offender management practices for the California Sex Offender Management Board. She is currently working as editor for a book on trends in international corrections with Dr. Dilip Das.

Contributors

Viviana Andreescu, PhD, is assistant professor of criminal justice at the University of Louisville, Kentucky, USA. Her publications include studies focusing on violent crimes, fear of crime and victimization in Europe, criminal justice issues related to social minorities, and attitudes toward the police in Eastern Europe.

Jessica Li Chi-mei is a lecturer at the Department of Applied Social Studies, City University of Hong Kong. She received her BA in social work, a PhD from the City University of Hong Kong, and an MPhil in criminology from Cambridge University, UK. Before teaching at the City University of Hong Kong, she was a social worker for 15 years providing services to young offenders and their families. Her research interests are in the fields of community policing, private policing, situational crime prevention, and rational choice theory. In recent years, she has worked on local and overseas projects related to juvenile offenders, workplace violence prevention, female drug abusers, juvenile theft, and domestic violence. Her recent book, *Theft and Delinquency: Juvenile Crime Prevention Theories and Practice*, was published in 2008.

John A. Eterno, PhD is the chairperson and associate dean and director of the graduate program in criminal justice at Molloy College, Rockville Centre, New York. He is a retired captain from the New York City Police Department and managing editor of an international peer-reviewed criminal justice journal, *Police Practice and Research.* He is the author and coauthor of many peer-reviewed journal articles that have appeared in *Criminal Law Bulletin, Women and Criminal Justice; Policing, An International Journal of Police Strategies and Management, Professional Issues in Criminal Justice*, and *International Journal of Police Science and Management.* His books include *Policing within the Law* (Praeger), *Police Practices in Global Perspective* with Dilip Das (Rowman & Littlefield), and his newest, *Unveiling Compstat: The Naked Truth* with Eli Silverman, which will be published by CRC Press/Taylor & Francis Group: London in 2011.

Raymond Kendall is currently honorary secretary general of Interpol and chairman of the Centre of Excellence on Public Security's Senior Advisory Board. He is an international expert on crime and security. Mr. Kendall served as secretary general of Interpol from 1985 to 2000. Prior to that, he was deputy assistant commissioner of the London Metropolitan Police. In 1971, he became assistant director of drugs at the International Criminal Police Organization and was promoted to director four years later. More recently, he served as chairman of the Supervisory Committee of the European Anti-Fraud Office. Mr. Kendall as been awarded many honors including *Chevalier de la Legion d'Honneur* (France), the Queen's Police Medal for Distinguished Police Service (United Kingdom), and Bearer of the Saint Martyr Triphon Order, First Class (Russia).

Lucille Dunn Kratcoski, MA, research associate with Kratcoski Research, has completed research in many criminal justice areas, including corrections, community corrections, juvenile delinquency, and policing. She is the author or coauthor of many journal articles and papers presented at professional meetings that dealt with these topics. She is coauthor of *Juvenile Delinquency, 5th edition*, 2004, also published in a Chinese language edition in 2009. She has assisted with the official recording of the International Police Executive Symposium and currently serves as the IPES archivist.

Peter C. Kratcoski, PhD, emeritus professor of justice studies, Kent State University, Ohio, USA and adjunct professor of justice studies at Kent State University's regional campuses, served as chairperson of the Department of Criminal Justice Studies at Kent State. He completed research and served as a consultant for numerous juvenile justice and social service agencies. He has authored a number of books, written numerous book chapters and articles for professional journals, and presented many papers at national and international professional conferences. He served as editor of *The Journal of Crime and Justice* and currently is North American editor of Police Practice and Research. He is the official recorder for the International Police Executive Symposium and has authored a number of articles and book chapters based on the topics that were the focuses of the IPES meetings. He is the coauthor with Dilip K. Das of *Meeting the Challenges of Global Terrorism* (2003) and *Police Education and Training in a Global Society* (2007). His current research and writing focus on juvenile justice, school violence, and international policing.

David Lowe is a professor at and a principal lecturer running the law degree program at Liverpool's John Moores University, UK. He recently completed a PhD researching the role of the Imperial Security Bureau

(ISB) in counterterrorist investigations. His main research interests are terrorism, human rights. and policing. He served 27 years with a UK police force, including two postings to the ISB as a detective constable and as a detective sergeant, Most of his police service was mainly as a detective in the Special Branch where he was involved in counter-terrorism ranging from the activity of Irish groups such as the Provisional IRA to Islamic-based groups including Al Qaeda.

Odd Berner Malme is a police counselor at the Permanent Mission of Norway to the United Nations. As the deputy national commissioner of the Norwegian Police, Mr. Malme developed strategies to prevent and combat organized and transnational crime.

Darko Maver, PhD, is a professor at the faculty of criminal justice and security, University of Maribor and at the faculty of law, University of Ljubljana, Slovenia. The former director of CID at the Ministry of the Interior, Republic of Slovenia; he is also the former dean of the college of police and security studies at the University of Ljubljana and is currently the editor-in-chief of *Revija za kriminalistiko in kriminologijo.*

Gorazd Meško, BA, MA, PhD, is professor of criminology and dean at the faculty of criminal justice and security at the University of Maribor, Slovenia. He was a visiting scholar at the Institute of Criminology in Cambridge, UK in 1995 and 2001 and at the Centre for Criminology at the University of Oxford in 1996 and 1999. He conducted his postdoctoral research on crime prevention at the Institute of Criminology in Cambridge in 2001 (OSI–HESP grant). His research includes criminal careers, crime prevention, policing, fear of crime, and crimes against the environment. His recent works include *Policing in Emerging Democracies: Critical Reflections* (ed., 2007), *Crime, Media and Fear of Crime* (ed., 2009), and *Crime Policy, Crime Control and Crime Prevention: Slovenian Perspectives* (ed., 2009).

Nahanni Pollard is the strategic planning and policy advisor within the Planning, Research and Audit Section of the Vancouver Police Department. She is also a PhD candidate in criminology from Simon Fraser University, where she also obtained her BA (2003) and her MA (2004) in criminology. Ms. Pollard is the recipient of two Chief Constable Unit Citations for her work on the VPD operational review and research surrounding chronic offenders.

Victor N. Shaw, PhD, is a professor of sociology at California State University–Northridge. Dr. Shaw is interested in the study of crime, deviance, social control, organizational behavior, higher education, academic careers, and public policy, and has published widely in those areas. His recent books include *In View of Academic Careers and Career-Making Scholars: Innovative Ideas for Institutional Reform* (2008); *Crime and Social Control in Asia and the Pacific: A Cross-Border Study* (2007); *Career-Making in Postmodern Academia: Process, Structure, and Consequence* and *Substance Use and Abuse: Sociological Perspectives* (2002).

Ruben Sorge began his policing career in 1989 with the Vancouver Police Department. He was promoted to sergeant in 2000 and staff sergeant in 2008. He is currently assigned to the Operations Investigative Section, where he oversees more than 80 officers and civilians focusing on special investigations and crime analysis. S/Sgt. Sorge is a graduate of Simon Fraser University with a BA in criminology and has received numerous awards during his career, most recently including a Meritorious Service Award from the Governor General in 2009, and a Chief Constable's Commendation in 2008.

Adki Surender is a reader and head of the Department of Public Administration at Vivek Vardhini College of Arts, and Commerce (AN), celebrating its Golden Jubilee year, and affiliated to Osmania University, Hyderabad, Andhra Pradesh, India. He received his MPhil in police housing and PhD in administration of urban traffic police from Osmania University, Hyderabad in the Telangana Region of South India. His research interests include urban traffic and transportation, women police, urban poverty and urban waste management. He has contributed a number of articles for various journals and magazines and participated in and presented a number of papers at international and national seminars, workshops, and conferences on various aspects of public administration, police administration and urban administration. He is a member of various professional bodies and a member of the Board of Studies in the Department of Public Administration at Osmania University.

Kam C. Wong is visiting professor of law at the City University of Hong Kong and chairman and professor at Xavier University. He earned a BA (Hons.) and JD from Indiana University, a diploma (N.I.T.A.) from Northwestern University, and both an MA and a PhD from the State University of New York at Albany. He was vice chair of the Hong Kong Society of Criminology (1999–2002); associate fellow at the Center of Criminology, University of Hong Kong, vice president (2001–2002), president (2002–2003) of the Asian Association of Police Studies (AAPS), and director of the Chinese Law Program, Chinese University of Hong Kong (1997–2002). His writings have appeared in *Criminal Law Bulletin, Georgetown Journal of Law and Public*

Policy, Columbia Journal of Asian Law, British Journal of Criminology, Journal of Information Law & Technology (JILT), Pacific Rim Law & Policy Journal, International Journal of the Sociology of Law, Australian Journal of Law and Society, Australian and New Zealand Journal of Criminology, and *John Marshall Journal of Computer and Information Law*, and others. His latest books are *The Impact of USA Patriot Act on American Society: An Evidence Based Assessment* (2007) and *The Making of USA Patriot Act: Legislation, Implementation, Impact* (2008 in Chinese).

Minoru Yokoyama completed his BA in law and MA in both criminal law and sociology at Chuo University in Tokyo. He is a vice president of Kokugakuin University, a professor and the former dean of the faculty of law, and the chairperson of the International Exchange Committee of Kokugakuin University in Tokyo. He is the former second vice president of the Research Committee for the Sociology of Deviance and Social Control of the International Sociological Association, a member of the board of directors and former president of the Japanese Association of Sociological Criminology. Currently, he is a member of the board of directors of the Japanese Association of Social Problems, president of the Tokyo Study Group of Sociological Criminology and serves as a vice chair of the Local Arrangement Committee for 16th World Congress of the International Society for Criminology to be held in Kobe in 2011. He has presented numerous papers at national and international conferences and symposia, and has published many articles in professional journals.

Introduction

Policing Without Borders: The Fading Distinction between Local and Global emphasizes the rising need for a cohesive international policing community. As crimes become more transnational in scope, the need for systematic communication between national police agencies becomes increasingly apparent. Various methods of collaboration need to address ways to institute global police communication. The chapters of this book focus on the theme of how local and global police practitioners and researchers can better collaborate on the mission of viewing policing with a global focus.

As stated by Peter and Lucille Kratcoski in Chapter 1, many organized crimes such as international trafficking in drugs, weapons, and humans affects numerous countries. Each has a vested interest in breaking these crime rings and preventing continued or escalating international crime. Others, such as cybercrimes and international money laundering, also affect numerous nations and can best be solved with a transnational approach. One concern presented by the Kratcoskis is that stronger, more powerful nations may exploit less powerful, developing nations. The Kratcoskis find it imperative that well-crafted agreements and treaties between nations avoid such exploitation and increase the ease and ability for nations to collaborate in a policing mission.

The chapters in this book create a scenario of the global policing community. The authors discuss many issues in countries around the world to explore a variety of policing methods as well as cultural and historical information to paint a vivid view of the different countries' textured policing styles and programs. In Chapter 2, Raymond Kendall, the Honorary Secretary General of Interpol, discusses policing activity and human rights. Kendall states that despite numerous international documents proclaiming the importance of human rights in policing practice, corrupt police agencies throughout the world have a long history of human rights violations. Officers who perform their duties with a strong interest in doing what is legally specified may fail to grasp the underlying premise of acting in a humane fashion. He calls for established countries to aid developing countries in policing practices that focus on human rights.

In Chapter 3, Professor Victor Shaw examines the issues involved in keeping order in a time of dynamic change and social control in Asia and the Pacific. He points out the bigger picture of change in ideology and government in police organizations: If both the stronger and weaker nations are able to collaborate and communicate what works for a variety of nations' police systems, then the global community can learn and select the best from traditional and contemporary practices, Eastern and Western views, and socialist and capitalist societies. Ideally, strong nations with working police practices can serve as models for less organized police agencies throughout the world.

In Chapter 4, Professor Surender Adki discusses the growth and development of women police in India. He provides information and statistics regarding the lack of power and the low percentage of female officers in India, introducing an international perspective by comparing the growth and strength of female officers in other countries. Adki states that women can play a vital role in policing, particularly because their work adds depth and quality to a mostly male profession. As female victims and perpetrators increase worldwide, the issue of increasing the presence and utility of women police officers is a global concern.

In Chapter 5, police officers Gorazd Meško and Darko Maver examine the challenges and obstacles in policing in Slovenia. In discussing Slovenia's quest for achieving police professionalism and adapting its agency's methods to a more modern world society, the broader issue of police ethics is explored. By studying one country, issues affecting many countries come into focus. Like Slovenia, many countries have police agencies in which cynicism and prejudice against marginalized groups are impediments to a higher ethical standard in policing. Meško and Maver suggest that having international support and global public pressure placed on the world's police agencies would aid nations in valuing and creating training and programs teaching police ethics. Creating a global code of police ethics or a European code of police ethics, as the authors suggest, would be a key method of propelling the idea of police without borders.

The study of policing in China by Professor Kam Wong is examined in Chapter 6. Wong discusses the history of research on policing in China, citing difficulties with applying Western framework and theories to a nation with a unique cultural context, history, and complex political circumstances. Wong cites the need for Chinese researchers to build the knowledge and theoretical constructs of their society despite the many obstacles to obtaining complete and correct data in a culture of restricted access to information. Wong speaks about the difficulties in obtaining information in China and suggests ways to overcome this problem. Despite the lack of police research by Chinese scholars, these studies must take place to create the necessary research and theory to inform policy and practice. These issues are relevant and vital in understanding how to use this methodology in creating research and theory in areas of the world where public access has been limited by governmental policy. All nations have unique cultural circumstances, some of which can present difficulties in completing necessary research. The applications of the research ideas presented in this chapter imply that other countries could benefit from similar methodology.

Chapter 7 is a discussion by Professor Minoru Yokoyama of the development of guidance activities by the Japanese police for the prevention of juvenile delinquency. Yokoyama presents information on the waves of juvenile crime since World War II and expands on the way Japan has handled juvenile delinquents over the years. A special point concerns the ease with which Japanese juveniles cross borders with the advent of numerous modes of transportation. With border crossing, juvenile crime takes on a more global framework and nations must work together to ensure that young criminals are brought to justice in their own countries.

In Chapter 8, Professor Li Chi-mei shares an innovative police project that tackled the youth crime problems in Hong Kong. She notes that despite Hong Kong's reluctance to embrace the sound and popular philosophy of community policing, their "Operation Breakthrough" borrowed the methods of a similar program in Southern Australia where community policing is routinely practiced. Positive change that results from creative and cross-cultural police research is another reason such cross-national communication can be so successful. Proactive methods that work to reduce crime are particularly needed across the globe.

Police officers Ruben Sorge and Nahanni Pollard discuss a form of modern banishment in Canada involving non-returnable arrest warrants in Chapter 9. Difficulties arise from the legal murkiness and cost of transferring a Canadian fugitive back to his local jurisdiction. The authors address legal and methodological ways to create a better system that ensure those arrested face justice. The chapter presents a microcosm of the global issue regarding those who flee borders and jurisdictions to escape the courts. Creating a system of extradition to bring offenders wanted in another state or country into custody where the fugitive's original crime was committed is another way to establish a global policing community. Although this chapter focused on issues specific to the Canadian provinces, examining the positive results of cooperation between local agencies working together implies that cooperation between national agencies would create the same positive change from a global viewpoint.

In Chapter 10, Professor David Lowe describes his covert participant observer research while working in the United Kingdom's Integrated Special Branch, an intelligence unit. Lowe discusses the hardships and successes of his covert research as a valid method of conducting worldwide research on the inner workings of clandestine police agencies in charge of counterterrorism. It is important for international researchers to share and explore the best methods of researching sensitive police organizations. Although Lowe describes his specific methodology used in the United Kingdom, the broader application of his research methods could be helpful and relevant to nations wishing to study counterterrorism units.

In Chapter 11, Viviana Andreescu and Odd Berner Malme discuss virtual organized crime groups that utilize cyberspace to commit global fraud and trafficking crimes. The authors maintain that organized crime is a global phenomenon requiring international cooperation to solve heinous crimes such as the trafficking of drugs or human beings. The Nordic countries are among the most successful and highly educated nations in the world yet, despite the human trafficking they experience due to the legalized sex trade and affluence of their citizens, they are also known for high levels of peace and safety. Although not an actual member of Europol, Norway participates in international agencies, such as Europol and Interpol. The positive changes Norway is making in combating global organized crime are on both local and global levels. Andreescu and Malme discuss the specific steps Norway is making at this time, implying that all nations can make similar changes to thwart the hold that virtual organized crime groups have on the global community.

In Chapter 12, retired NYPD Captain and Professor John Eterno reviews a public housing safety initiative in the Eastern District of New York, presenting the methodology that the public housing initiative used to pick two housing developments needing crime prevention and reduction methods. With the aid of a steering committee and collaboration between federal, state, and local agencies and community leaders, residents and outreach agencies created, implemented, and evaluated the results of their coordinated efforts. Eastern New York's project serves as a relatively successful model for other communities and nations to review and potentially modify for use in their own locations.

As these chapters demonstrate, viewing local and national policing methods with a global perspective and a cross-national approach can truly reduce the effect of national borders while increasing the knowledge, research and practical approaches to policing in the world community.

Jennie K. Singer, Dilip K. Das, and Cliff Roberson

Police Without Borders
An Overview

1

PETER C. KRATCOSKI AND
LUCILLE DUNN KRATCOSKI

Contents

Introduction

The concept "policing without borders" can elicit a number of interpretations of its meaning. Generally, the concept is used to denote changes in policing in the present global society, where the borders of nations have been virtually eliminated because of the cooperative agreements made between nations for mutual assistance and aid.

Other, more general meanings associated with the concept include the changes brought about by the use of electronics to transmit information and intelligence regarding various types of crimes across national borders and even worldwide, without being concerned with the national borders of the countries. Since much of criminal activity, especially that associated with organized crime and terrorism, crosses national borders, there is a need for a more standardized response to it. Examples of attempts to establish standardized methods of responding to international crime include the enactment of new laws, the use of electronic techniques for international investigations, and even a more standardized approach to police officer training and education. In this regard, we see large, powerful countries providing equipment and training materials for the police of smaller, less developed countries. This assistance focuses on concern for human rights. Respect for human rights is a key principle of the notion of "rule of law," and respect for human dignity is central to the concept of policing without borders. The goal of this activity is to help underdeveloped countries produce professionally trained police forces that are comparable to those of the countries providing the training.

Another broadly based notion related to the concept of policing without borders centers of the fact that the police agencies are no longer closed institutions. In the past, police administrators could more or less establish the operational policies, rules, and procedures for the agency they were administrating without having to be concerned with outside forces such as the mass media, citizen oversight groups, legislators, or academics. Policies and procedures generally were based on tradition, and administrators followed the traditional ways even when there was considerable evidence that their methods were not always the most effective. Often the standard traditional approach to police administration did not consider the different needs and rights of the personnel within their own organization, and persuasion from police professional organizations was needed before police administrators were convinced that changes in policies would be beneficial to the organization. In a similar vein, input from citizen action groups helped focus on the necessity to address some of the specific problems of certain members of the community. The police administrators were only concerned with their own jurisdiction and did not see the need to join in cooperative ventures with other policing agencies. Several traumatic events preceding the 9/11/2001 terrorist attack on the World Trade Center and other targets in the United States had stimulated the need for policing agencies to cooperate with each other on national and international levels, but this single event, more than any other, triggered the urgency for such cooperation.

The Fifteenth Annual International Police Executive Symposium held in Cincinnati, Ohio, U.S. (2008), focused on policing without borders, the need for international and national cooperation among policing agencies, and the need for cooperation between the police and the academic community, private policing agencies, and the general public. This conference was hosted by the Cincinnati Police Department and the Ohio Association of Chiefs of Police and was organized by the Home Office of the United Kingdom.

Sixty-five police executives, government officials, academics, and researchers from 42 countries, representing most of the continents, made presentations at the sessions and took part in formal and informal discussions that focused on the following themes:

- Factors that inhibit effective policing in a global society such as national territorial boundaries, notions of sovereignty, and laws, and the methods that are used to bring about the changes needed to reduce these barriers;
- The uses of technology, including the Internet, by criminal and terrorist organization to foster international and national crimes, and the ways policing agencies use these technologies to combat international and national crime;
- The cooperative efforts of police at the national level to reduce the communication gaps between national, state, and local policing agencies for the purpose of making them more effective;
- The need to develop global standards for human rights to ensure that the rights of people will be protected regardless of their national citizenship;
- Factors that create borders between the administrators of policing agencies and the personnel of these agencies representing various constituencies, the consequences these barriers produce, and the methods used to reduce the borders to increase the effectiveness of policing;
- The methods used to address the barriers brought on by prejudicial and differential policing, resulting in some segments of the population feeling that they are being treated unjustly by the police (Kratcoski and Kratcoski, 2008).

In the following discussion, emphasis will be placed on the need for cooperation, coordination, and integration of policing agencies, both on the national and international levels.

The Globalization of Crime and Terrorism

A nation can no longer rely exclusively on its own security forces and resources to protect its citizens from crime and terrorism. The sources of the threats to the security of a country often are external to the country and can only be controlled through cooperative ventures with other countries. For example, a National Institute of Justice Report (see Sedgwick, 2008:5-6) titled *Methods and Motives: Exploring Links between Transnational Organized Crime and International Terrorism* indicates that the relationships between organized crime groups and terrorist organizations are becoming regular and permanent.

Using information from several research reports on the topic of international organized crime, Sedgwick (2008:8) noted that internationally organized criminal groups are involved in the following types of crimes:

- Energy and strategic materials markets;
- Smuggling and trafficking of goods and people;
- Money laundering;
- Fraud;
- Cyber-crime; and
- Terrorist operations and foreign intelligence.

In order to mount a successful counterattack against international crime and terrorism, a global strategy is needed. The action plan requires cooperation and involvement from strong, powerful nations as well as from nations that have few resources to contribute. The global strategy developed to respond to international crime and terrorism must be based on a world systems theory.

World Systems Theory

This theory is grounded in the assumption that every nation is part of a world economic system. If one nation suffers some traumatic economic or political upheaval, all of the other countries of the world are affected in some way (Onwudiwe, 2002:1-27).

The same analysis can be applied to crime and terrorist activity. For example, the repercussions of the organized criminal activities related to drug trafficking that originated in one country will be felt in all of the countries throughout the world in which the drugs are trafficked. The 9/11/2001 terrorist attacks on the World Trade Center and other targets in the United States affected most countries of the world either economically or psychologically. The specific effect international crime and terrorism has on a country is closely related to the amount of wealth and resources a country possesses. In a very poor country with a weak government, the activities of organized criminal groups and terrorists can destroy a nation if it does not receive assistance from other nations that are part of the world economy.

In the world economy, nations are not equal in power or wealth, and stronger nations can exploit weaker nations if some forms of mutual aid agreements are not put in place to counteract the imbalance of power among the nations. Onwudiwe (2002:1-27) placed the nations of the world system into three categories: controlling, semi-controlling, and exploited. *Controlling nations* are the most powerful nations in the world system. They have the power to exploit the weaker nations, but often will provide assistance to the weaker nations rather than exploiting them because in the long run it will serve their best interests if the weaker nations become stronger, gain political and economic independence, and become committed allies. The *semi-controlling nations* have sufficient resources to exert some control over weaker nations, but are themselves vulnerable to exploitation from stronger nations, and thus generally join the stronger nations in mutual aid agreements designed to provide protection to all of the nations, weak or strong, who participate in the mutual aid agreements. The *exploited nations* are generally in a developmental stage. Their economies are weak and they may have gone through a dramatic change in their political structure. Since the governments are often unstable, the economies are weak, the leaders are often corrupt, and the citizens are often discontented and willing to take any opportunity to improve their welfare. As a result, these countries are very vulnerable to infiltration and exploitation by organized crime and terrorist organizations.

The strategies followed by many countries of the world to combat international crime and terrorism are grounded in the world system theory. The stronger, controlling countries have invested huge amounts of money and other resources, including human resources, into assisting weaker nations in the development of their economies, governments, and justice systems. Most of this assistance is provided through the establishment of various types of agreements and treaties.

Types of International Agreements

Using a model developed by Benyon (1997:107), international cooperative agreements used by governments to control international crime can be characterized as consisting of the following:

- Macro-level agreements. These consist of constitutional and international legal agreements that are designed to harmonize national laws and regulations.
- Meso-level agreements. These consist of agreements pertaining to the operational structures, practices, and procedures of the police and other justice agencies when several nations are involved in international policing ventures.
- Micro-level agreements. These consist of matters pertaining to specific offenses and the control of a specific type of crime.

Das and Kratcoski (2001) note that global treaties signed by members of the United Nations, such as those pertaining to war crimes, the extradition of criminals, or the involvement of nations in crisis management, are examples of macro-level agreements. The exchange of information by several countries relating to criminal matters would be a good example of meso-level agreements. Micro-level agreements generally consist of reciprocal cooperative ventures on specific criminal matters by two or more countries. A multi-nation drug trafficking task force would be a good example.

The United Nations

Several of the presentations at the Fifteenth Annual Police Executive Symposium illustrated how systems theory is being applied through various forms of international cooperative agreements. For example, as many countries in Europe, Africa, and Asia experienced civil and political unrest, and blatant violations of human rights by political leaders and the police were observed, the United Nations (U.N.) became more actively involved and established crisis management missions in some of the countries in which internal conflicts were the most pronounced. The U.N. Congress on Crime Prevention and Control served as the platform for establishing several U.N. Commissions, including the Organized Crime Commission and the Commission on the Trafficking of Narcotics and the Trafficking of Humans. The United Nations Program on Crime Prevention and Criminal Justice developed the mechanisms for the United Nations to become involved in peacekeeping missions, conduct police training seminars, and establish police training centers that focus on international crime control. The training of the police in using policing methods that protect the human rights of citizens is central to all of the programs sponsored by the United Nations (Das and Kratcoski, 2001:22).

The United Nations Police (UNPOL) is administered under the United Nations Police Division (UNPD). The Department of Peacekeeping Operations places peace officers from various countries in countries from which a request for assistance has been received. Carpenter (2008) notes that UNPOL missions consist of three phases. The UNPOL first provides security for the citizens. Often the country is in a state of crisis when UNPOL is summoned, and restoring some type of order is an immediate task. This task may require UNPOL to assist in maintaining crowd control, making arrests, holding law violators in detention, protecting property, and protecting U.N. personnel. After a degree of stability has been achieved, the second phase begins. This entails rebuilding the justice system by reforming and restructuring the justice agencies. During this phase, UNPOL assists in the recruitment and training of police and other personnel. If UNPOL is successful during phases one and two, the third phase of its involvement in a peacekeeping mission centers on a gradual return of the responsibilities for keeping the peace back to the country's justice agencies. The mission is accomplished when UNPOL withdraws.

According to Carpenter (2008:6) requests for U.N. police missions have increased and the qualifications needed for police officers recruited for these missions have changed. In addition to the need for line officers, there is now a greater need for police leaders, managers, and specialists.

United Nations Peacekeeping Missions' Human Rights Emphasis

The United Nations' success in what is now Bosnia and Herzegovina illustrates how a peacekeeping mission can bring stability to a war-torn country. Matijevic (2008:12) reports that during the Bosnia-Herzegovina War, almost 100,000 people were killed, several millions were forced to leave their homes, and there was mass destruction of property. The police were generally helpless in protecting the people's human and civil rights. Matijevic (2008:12) notes that during the war the general security of the country and the protection of human rights and freedoms were at their lowest level. After the signing of the Dayton Peace Agreement and with the help of the United Nations, peace and order and a respect for human rights have been established in Bosnia and Herzegovina. Matijevic (2008:16) attributes this stability to several factors. First, the police structures in Bosnia and Herzegovina are now a key institution of the state with authority to provide a stable and safe environment for the citizens and property, as well as respect of human rights and freedoms. Second, high professional standards in the police organizations are expected. Third, the police have made a concerted effort to gain the trust and confidence of the citizens. This has been accomplished through a community policing approach, with emphasis on providing service to the people, rather than to a political head of state.

The International Network to Promote the Rule of Law (INPROL) has contributed to a number of United Nations Peacekeeping Missions. This project relies on the professionals and practitioners within the cooperating organizations to connect with each other and to provide information, training, and research on matters related to police law, witness protection, interim prison security, and the education of the public on the role of the police in a democratic society. In addition, INPROL assists in the identification of highly qualified individuals to be considered for senior positions in U.N. international policing projects (Dziedzic 2008: 3,10).

International Policing Within the European Union

The 27 members of the European Union are bound by a number of international agreements developed under the Common Foreign and Security Policy. The European Security and Defense Policy direct the military and civilian crisis management missions of the European Union (White, 2008). Crisis management missions involve providing assistance to a nation in crisis by giving assistance in policing, establishing law and order, handling crises such as controlling mobs, and protecting property. White (2008:10) used the crisis management mission in Iraq to illustrate the role of EUJUST LEX. Several of the specific goals of EUJUST LEX during this mission included:

- Training senior police administrators, judges, prosecutors, and prison administrators in administrating justice following the rule of law;
- Using methods of policing that promote a respect for human rights;
- Promoting teamwork and collaborative relationships among justice agencies; and
- Developing professionally trained officers who will be respected by the people.

Plywaczewski and Plywaczewski (2008) described several other programs under the auspices of the European Union that are designed to promote efficiency and effectiveness and to ensure that the interests of the weaker nations within the European Union are protected. Europol (Plywaczewski and Plywaczewski, 2008:1) promotes cooperation among the members of the European Union to increase the effectiveness in combating terrorism and all forms of international crimes. It gathers, collates, analyzes, and distributes information on criminal matters to the member nations. EUROJUST was developed to facilitate the execution of mutual aid agreements created by the member states of the European Union.

Malme (2008:8) reported on the trends of crime in Norway and how the Schengen Border Control Agency, FRONTEX, created in 2005, assists in combating international crime. He notes that organized crime has become more international, with drug trafficking, trafficking in humans, and money laundering being the most serious of the crimes confronting Norway. The Schengen Cooperative, consisting of 24 countries from Northern Europe, created FRONTEX to coordinate the field management of the external border patrol of the member nations of the European Union that have borders with nonmember nations. According to Laitinen (2006:6) the activities of FRONTEX are critical to the development and functioning of the European Union Integrated Management System.

Several other programs under the auspices of the European Union were developed to specifically combat the increasing involvement of organized crime and terrorist groups in international criminal activities. The European

Anti-Fraud Office was created when research revealed that corruption and fraud were becoming major problems for some countries within the Union. The Task Force on Organized Crime in the Baltics investigates the criminal activities of organized crime units pertaining to illegal immigration, trafficking in humans, drugs, weapons, and environmental crimes (Plywaczewski and Plywaczewski, 2008:9).

Bolesik (2008) discussed the specific problems Hungary experiences with international crime. Hungary, a member of the European Union, is surrounded by a number of Central and Eastern European nations. The Hungarian Police and various justice agencies play a vital role in ensuring that the programs such as EUROJUST, EUJUST LEX, and FRONTEX, developed under the Common Foreign and Security Policy of the European Union, operate in accordance with the goals established for these programs. In addition, Hungary participates with neighboring countries in joint task forces to investigate specific international crimes such as drug trafficking. The International Law Enforcement Academy (ILEA) was established in Budapest in 1995 to provide advanced police training for Eastern European countries. This academy is jointly administered and funded by the U.S. Federal Bureau of Investigation and the Hungarian government. According to a personal interview with Max Edelbacher and Peter Kratcoski, the training is modeled after the training Federal Bureau of Investigation (FBI) agents receive at the National Training Academy. The standardized universal approach to police training focusing on international crime and terrorism provided at the ILEA is an important method for narrowing the differences in policing created by the different cultures, languages, and laws of the countries involved.

The Organization for Security and Cooperation in Europe (OSCE) was established in 1995 to develop cooperative operations among the various countries of Europe and cooperative ventures with other countries of the world. The goals of the OSCE include conflict prevention, crisis management, and post-conflict rehabilitation. The activities of the OSCE include cooperative ventures relating to preventing trafficking in humans, combating terrorism, conflict prevention, gender equality, economic and environmental protection, and external cooperation in policing and police training (http:www.osce.org:1). The OSCE training strategy "is based on a joint management and staff-owned approach. It seeks to enhance the co-ordination of training policies and activities, as well as the development of synergies, and favors co-operation with participating States, other international organizations and training institutions" (hhtp:www.osce.org:1). The OSCE training coordinator is based in Vienna, Austria.

North American Efforts to Close the Borders to Crime and Terrorism

Several of the recommendations for U.S. counterterrorism strategies that came out of the 9/11 Commission Report were:

- To assist countries with their economic, technological, and educational development, political reform, and law enforcement;
- To increase and improve cooperation and communications among local, national, and international law enforcement agencies nationally and internationally; and
- To include the private sector in the strategies and costs related to national security and terrorist prevention (9/11 Commission, 2002:361-398).

Sedgwick (2008) reported that in 2007 all of the five U.S. government departments—Justice, Defense, Homeland Security, Treasury, and State—were involved in cooperative programs with 90 countries directed toward curtailing organized crime and terrorism. In addition, the federal investigative and policing agencies cooperated with many of the 18,000 local and state policing organizations by establishing task forces directed toward organized crime and terrorism. One of the changes that came out of 9/11/2001 was the establishment of Regional Information Sharing Centers.

These centers provide:

- Investigative support and training;
- Analytical services;
- Specialized equipment;
- Secure information-sharing technology;
- Encrypted e-mail and communications capabilities; and
- An automated system that enables access by the private sector and non–law enforcement agencies. (Sedgwick, 2008:10-11).

The International Criminal Investigative Training Assistance Program (ICITAP) is coordinated with the U.S. Department of Justice's Overseas Prosecutorial Development, Assistance, and Training Office (Kratcoski and Henry, 2001:462). Ducot (2008:4) reported on the mission of ICITAP, which is "to work with foreign governments to develop professional and transparent law enforcement institutions that protect human rights, combat corruption, and reduce the threat of transnational crime and terrorism." Currently, ICITAP has 17 field offices attached to U.S. embassies and has established programs in almost 50 countries located in various parts of the world.

The countries selected for ICITAP programs are generally in a transitional stage. Before a country is selected, there has to be some evidence that the country can sustain institutional development and that its government will consist of some form of democracy. The staff members selected to provide the training are recruited from various countries, generally from those countries that have cultures similar to the country in which they are placed. The programming used is based on a problem-oriented policing model, that is, to establish a goal, assess the situation, plan the activities, implement the plan, and evaluate the outcome. Beinhart (2008) emphasized that the training provided must be tailored to the skills and needs of the officers of the host country. Generally, "hands-on" training rather than formal classroom training is provided. Beinhart (2008:5) notes that "[r]espect for human rights and human dignity is interwoven throughout all ICITAP training."

As a result of the terrorist attacks of 9/11/2001, the U.S. Departments, having the responsibility to protect the security of the nation, expanded their international programs, changed the focus of many of their programs to combating terrorism, and increased the number and types of international agreements.

The FBI has more than 50 Legal Attaché Offices (Legats) located in U.S. embassies and consulates throughout the world. The FBI agents assigned to these offices work with the police of the host countries in coordinating international investigations, linking U.S. and international resources in critical criminal areas, and providing training in specialty areas such as counterterrorism, cyber-crime, forensic techniques, and human trafficking. The rules for the joint activities and information sharing are set by formal international agreements between the host country and the United States (Federal Bureau of Investigation [FBI], 2007:1).

The U.S. Drug Enforcement Administration has 86 foreign offices and, in conjunction with foreign law enforcement agencies, conducts investigations into the criminal activities of international drug trafficking. These investigations involve gathering intelligence and assisting the host countries in providing training, technical assistance, and equipment (Drug Enforcement Administration [DEA], 2007:1).

The U.S. Department of Homeland Security (DHS) was created in 2003 by the U.S. Congress. The thrust of this legislation was to unite and integrate 22 existing agencies into the DHS structure. In addition, other federal agencies were directed to develop cooperative relations with the DHS to ensure that U.S. national security will be protected. Several of the key features of the mission of the DHS are:

- To protect air, sea, and land transit systems that transport people and goods into the United States;

- To expand the tasks of Customs agents and refocus the role of federal agencies such as the FBI; the Bureau of Alcohol, Tobacco, and Firearms (ATF); and the DEA;
- To develop more extensive contacts and cooperative relations with international information- and intelligence-sharing agencies such as Interpol, Europol, and the United Nations;
- To develop and coordinate counterterrorist planning and programs; and
- To develop liaisons with the FBI, Central Intelligence Agency (CIA), and the State Department that focus on defending the United States against internal and external threats to its security (Department of Homeland Security [DHS],).

Several of the presentations at the Fifteenth International Police Symposium illustrated the programs that were based on the 9/11 Commission Report recommendations. Morckel (2008) reported on the types of training and technical assistance provided by Data-Driven Approaches to Crime and Traffic Safety (DDACTS), a coordinated cooperative venture between the National Safety Administration and the Bureau of Justice Assistance. This involves a systematic approach to identifying the most difficult crime and traffic problems facing a community, the collection of timely and accurate data, analyzing the data, and developing the most efficient and most-likely-to-work plan for responding to the problem. Morckel emphasized the use of strategies that have already been proven effective by law enforcement agencies and inclusion of a coalition of local partnerships in the solution plan. The local community and law enforcement never lose control of the operations designed to solve the crime problems facing the community. Federal agencies provide training, resources, technical assistance, and evaluation to the programs developed through the cooperative efforts, but do not assume the power to make policies.

Allison Henry-Potts (2008) discussed the methods used by the U.S. State Department's Office of Civilian Police Programs and Rule of Law when it enters into a United Nations Policing Mission or when the United States establishes a bilateral agreement with another nation to assist in bringing civil order and rule of law to a war-torn country.

The civilian police enter the country after some degree of stability and order has been established by the U.N. military contingents. The primary mission of the civilian police is to assist the local police in establishing law and order based on the rule of law. Henry-Potts emphasized that the military should not be involved in training police, since the military and the police have different missions. The officers selected for the program follow a holistic approach. It is very important that the right officers are selected and that they have the proper types of equipment. The U.N. or U.S. police officers must be sensitive to the culture of the country being assisted, give attention to the resources available, and avoid political entanglements and actions that could lead to considerable negative sentiment toward the police officers assigned to the mission. However, the mission can be an instrument of change. For example, one of the special goals of the Afghanistan mission is to train female police officers to fill higher-level positions within the police organization.

Cordner and Shain (2008) reported on a conference held at Eastern Kentucky University, U.S.A., where government and non-government representatives from several countries discussed issues pertaining to rule of law, criminal justice reform, and protecting human rights as they apply to the Republic of Uzbekistan. The conference was funded by grants from the Institute for New Democracies, a program under the auspices of the U.S. State Department and the Regional Policy Foundation, an independent, non-government organization dedicated to protecting the national interests of the Republic of Uzbekistan. The government and non-government representatives attending the conference came to an agreement on a number of recommendations relating to methods that can be used to protect human rights in a developing country, the importance of criminal justice reform, new legislation needed, and how community policing can be used to help build a trusting relationship between the people and the police (Cordner and Shain, 2008:13-14).

Canada has a long history of having developed international cooperative agreements to protect its national interests, especially with the United States. These agreements pertain to immigration, border security, and, most recently, illegal trafficking of drugs, weapons, humans, and other goods that can be sold on the open market. Many of these agreements were ad hoc. Canada had experienced several major attacks by terrorists on its homeland, and the 9/11/2001 attacks on the World Trade Center and other targets in the United States drew attention to Canada's own vulnerability from both domestic terrorism and international terrorism. Hataley (2007) notes that the 32-Point Smart Border Declaration and Action Plan, which created Integrated Border Enforcement Teams consisting of U.S. and Canadian policing agents who focus on preventing drug trafficking, the trafficking of weapons, and terrorist activities, was the result of the increase in organized crime and terrorist activity Canada was experiencing.

Lemieux (2008) completed research on the effectiveness of international drug trafficking investigations in which Canadian policing agencies participated. Using data provided by the U.S. Department of Justice and the Drug Enforcement Administration on 61 major investigations completed between 2005 and 2008, he sought to determine why the outcomes of some investigations were successful and led to arrests and prosecutions while others did not have very positive results. He found that there were 58 countries involved in one or more of the investigations of drug trafficking. He discovered that the successful operations were associated with the number of countries participating in the investigation and the "professionalization" of the police cooperation. The investigative teams performed best when they were together for a long period of time and possessed common professional traits such as training, investigative skills, and dedication to adhering to high international professional standards (Lemieux, 2008:13).

The Civilianization of Police Work (Narrowing the Gaps Between Police, Private Enterprise, the Academic Community, Social Service Agencies, and the Citizenry)

It has long been recognized by police administrators that police work is dependent on other agencies and organizations, both public and private, within the community. Police organizations in an open society are influenced by and often dependent on the national and state legislatures, the judiciary, the mass media, social service agencies, commercial enterprise, educational institutions, and the public. The dependence is often direct, as in the case of private enterprise building the communication equipment and hardware that police need in the modern age of electronics, or relying on the work of scientists when completing DNA testing related to a criminal investigation.The influence can also be indirect, such as the citizenry being critical of police practices and the police needing to change practices. Specific examples of the closing of the gap between the police and other institutions in society through cooperation, mutual dependence, and the sharing of resources and personnel include:

- Many police organizational and management models are adaptations of models for administrative use in large corporations, government bureaucracies, and public service institutions. These administrative models, such as total quality management and management by objectives, were often developed by research institutes connected to universities. They eventually were applied to police organizations in modified forms. COMSTAT was developed in this way.
- Police and social scientists, such as sociologists, psychologists, and political scientists, collaborate on developing, administrating, and evaluating community action programs such as community policing projects.
- Civilians now fill many of the positions within the police organization that were filled entirely by police officers in the past. These include computer programmers, crime statistics analysts, lawyers, accountants and comptrollers, and public affairs managers. In

addition, civilians fill the relatively new positions within the departments such as police psychologist.

- Educational institutions offer academic degrees in criminal justice and some institutions of higher learning offer basic and advanced police training programs. In reverse, police training academies often use academics to provide instruction in specialized topics such as law, human relations, and juvenile justice.
- Police administrators and line officers have obtained advanced degrees in administration, public administration, and criminal justice. Many senior-level police officers have taken academic positions on their retirement from the police. Because of their police experiences they are able to integrate the theoretical with the applied in their classroom instruction.
- Private security agencies and auxiliary police now assume many of the specific tasks that were the responsibility of public police in the past. In addition, these private agencies often assist the public police in matters such as investigations of insurance fraud, arson, missing persons, and other types of investigations in which a solution would benefit both the private and public policing agencies.
- Private commercial organizations provide the police with equipment specially made for police use, such as armor, tasers, communications equipment, computer software, weapons, and other paraphernalia.
- Police leaders have become involved in academically oriented professional organizations. The contacts with academics made through these organizations have led to collaborative research and publications.

Several of the presenters at the Fifteenth International Police Executive Symposium (2008) used material to illustrate how the gap between the police and other institutions in the community is closing as the result of interaction, collaboration, and mutual support. The administrators of policing agencies have long realized that effective policing in a global society is a complicated endeavor and, to be effective, officers must be professionally trained and understand how to utilize the talents, skills, and experiences of professionals working outside of the police organization. Kratcoski (2004) notes that the present-day challenges facing police are so extensive that those seeking careers in police work must prepare themselves by obtaining an education that will help them understand, conceptualize, and critically analyze the situations and crime-related problems they will encounter, as well as assist them with developing the skills needed to accomplish the immediate tasks and goals of police operations. In addition, the education and training received by officers, regardless of the specific country in which the training is received, must focus on obtaining the knowledge and skills that will be useful in policing at the local level as well as internationally. Present-day police officers are challenged with developing an understanding of how sophisticated technology is used by criminals, and how organized criminal and terrorist networks operate, how the development of cross-border trade and economic systems stimulates criminal activity, and how movements of people across borders can create conflict as well as crime.

Tong (2008) remarked that the academic preparation of police should be theoretical and include information gathered from a variety of disciplines. Students preparing for police work should interact with students and professors from a wide range of disciplines, rather than be isolated in programs involving specific preparation for police work. Bryant (2008) emphasized the need for police, especially those who are administrators, to understand the scientific method and how it is used to formulate hypotheses, apply inductive and deductive logic, verify the validity of research outcomes, and be able to test theories relating to crime. In this regard, most of the police agencies that require some academic preparation in addition to basic skills development in their police training programs should require a course in research methods.

The transplanting of police officials into academic settings and academics into police organizations is becoming more prevalent. Academics are found teaching in police academies, completing collaborative research with police officials, and making presentations before police organizations, such as the International Chiefs of Police Association. The Commission on Accreditation for Law Enforcement Agencies (CALEA) was established to create professional standards for police agencies. Since the inception of CALEA, this independent organization has accredited almost 1,000 police agencies, police training academies, and communication centers in the United States, Canada, and Mexico (Cordner, 2008). Police professionalism is also demonstrated by the fact that police officers are earning advanced academic degrees, teaching in universities, making presentations at the meetings of professional associations, and writing for and having their work published in professional journals.

Palmiotto (2008:2) notes that the International Police Executive Symposium, founded by Dr. Dilip Das, has brought together academics and police practitioners who are also researchers to facilitate cross-cultural, international, and interdisciplinary discussions, and to provide a forum for disseminating information on the findings of their research and identifying and describing police practices that are effective. Das (2008) emphasized the need for police leaders to share their knowledge with others by publishing in professional journals as well as in trade journals.

The importance of the police in becoming professionally involved with academics in research and the development of policies pertaining to police operations was illustrated by several of the speakers at the Fifteenth International Police Executive Symposium. After Slovenia gained its independence, the Ministry of the Interior established a goal for the Slovenian

Police to become professional on a scale comparable to the more recognized police organizations throughout the world. In order to determine if this goal was being achieved, Tong financed research that focused on police professionalism, organization, standards, and practices. Currently, academics and police practitioners are working together on research projects pertaining to police development and training and police culture. They have attended international conferences, shared the findings of their research, and collaborated with academics and researchers from other countries. The findings of their research have been used by political administrators to justify changes in the organization of the Slovenian Police (Mesko and Maver, 2008).

Many times in the past, police agencies would establish new policies, develop new organizational structures, or implement new programs without sufficient planning for setting up ways of measuring if the changes, once made, accomplished what was intended. When the changes were eventually evaluated, it was often discovered that they had not resulted in the accomplishment of the desired goals. Police administrators often justified implementing programs without research input by saying that the information provided by the academics through their research was either not relevant or that the findings were not made available until long after there was a need for them. William J. Bratton, the past New York City Police Commissioner, when asked how important academics have been to the day-to-day practice of managing a police agency, responded,

> ... I really do not use, to any great degree, the work of academics.
>
> There are several reasons. One, many academics write for each other, not for practitioners, and when you attempt to read many of their studies, they are literally not readable. Two, oftentimes their studies are dated. It always infuriates me that we're usually reading studies about events and issues of three or four years back. Policing is much more contemporary than that, and if there was one lesson in policing in the 90s it is (that) you need to be timely. (Henry, 2000:560-561)

Bratton's criticism of the effect the research of academics has on police practices and policies is perhaps rather harsh. Some problems and issues relating to police practices and policies such as corruption, selection of personnel, developing objective standards for promotions, and researching questionable practices such as racial profiling do not need an immediate response. It may take months or even years of data collection, using a scientific methodology, to determine if there is a problem and, if so, how it can be solved. However, Bloss (2008:18) emphasized the importance of having ongoing relations in place between police organizations and academic research collaborators during the planning and initiation stages of any new project, policy implementation, or organizational change. He stressed that this collaboration should continue throughout the process and include analysis of the effectiveness of the changes after the project is completed.

The Cincinnati Initiative to Reduce Violence is an example of this type of police–academic researcher coordination. With the goals of reducing gun violence and gun-related homicides in the city, law enforcement agencies gathered intelligence on violent street groups. After academic researchers mapped the patterns of violent interaction, teams made up of probation officers, parole officers, and social service and community service workers made contact with the members of the violent groups and confronted them with the consequences of continuing to engage in violent behavior. The academic researcher who evaluated the results found reductions in gun-related violence, strong increases in the number of these identified offenders who requested and received social services, and improved police-community relations (Engel, Streicher, Whalen, and Baker, 2008).

In two public housing projects in New York, a collaborative practitioner–academic researcher project involving representatives of numerous community agencies and a local researcher used steering committees to set up safety initiatives. Using a problem-oriented policing model, the practitioners and academics identified the needs of the project residents and the possibilities for cooperation and success. They decided to develop action programs in the public housing setting. These programs included undercover narcotics investigations, a gang prevention program, a Youth Court, and a prison parolee community re-entry program. The effectiveness of the programs was systematically evaluated through the use of field observations, a specially designed questionnaire given to the residents, and analysis of crime statistics (Eterno, 2008).

Yokoyama (2008:3-35) reported on the cooperative programs that were established in Japan for dealing with the drastic increases in juvenile crime that Japan experienced in the second half of the 20th century. The changes in the lifestyles of youths in present-day Japan, especially their increased mobility and their acceptance of the values and cultures of Western civilization, resulted in a need for the police and other youth-serving agencies to develop new approaches for dealing with deviant youth. Programs were established in Japan that required input from the police, social service agencies, and volunteers from the community. In 2002, the National Public Safety Commission of Japan authorized the establishment of juvenile support centers throughout Japan. The police officers and counselors who work at these centers focus on changing the behavior of youths who have committed less serious offenses by diverting them out of the formal justice system and thus avoiding the institutionalization of these youths. In addition, an evaluation of these programs is completed to determine if they are effective.

Li Chi-mei (2008) reported on the results of Operation Breakthrough, a camp established in Hong Kong by the police and social service agencies for delinquent youths who were at a high risk of reoffending. The youths sent to this camp, modeled after the "boot camps" found in the United States, are required to engage in a rigorous program of physical fitness and other activities geared toward having them change their behavior, attitudes, and values. An evaluation of the program, completed by professors from the University of Hong Kong, revealed that the youths who completed the Operation Breakthrough program improved in self-confidence, physical fitness, attitudes, and personal values.

Narrowing the Gap Internally: Issues Relating to the Recruitment, Training, Retention, and Promotion of Police Officers

Kratcoski (2007:4) noted that the challenges faced by police agencies in the 21st century can be placed into two major categories. The first relates to police responses to changes in the social and cultural climates of their own countries. These changes may have been the result of significant threats to the security of the countries brought about by terrorism or crime, political upheaval and unrest, as well by increases in international crime that are related to its globalization. The second category relates to structural and policy changes within the police organizations. These changes may be partially a result of the growing need to employ more professional, technically trained police officers who can respond to the types of crime problems that have emerged in the global society. Structural and policy changes within the police organizations must be made to address ongoing institutional discrimination; changes in police priorities demanded by the community, including accountability and oversight procedures; new laws affecting police practices; the need to interact and cooperate with local, national, and international criminal justice agencies; and requests for changes coming from groups or organizations within the police structure such as police unions and organizations representing the interests of female police officers.

Palmer and Whelan (2008) suggest that the "new federalism" in Austria, brought about by the perceived threat of terrorism, resulted in more federal police involvement in internal matters and the development of cooperative ventures between the federal and the local police in counterterrorism strategies. According to King and Sharp (2007:387), the term "securitization" is useful in illustrating how there has been a significant merging of internal and external security in the United Kingdom. They contend that legislation and policy shifts have resulted in changes in police priorities, with a gradual replacement of the local policing concerns with national priorities.

Other police organizational changes have been brought about by the expansion of the powers of police unions and the efforts of other organizations seeking more equitable treatment for minorities and women engaged in police work. The powers of police labor unions have expanded beyond those traditional areas of negotiating with management to include matters pertaining to recruitment of personnel, salaries, seniority, benefits, and work assignments into areas that have been considered to be exclusively in the realm of management, including issues relating to oversight, accountability, policy development, and changes in the organizational structures. Fantino (2008) noted that the police must appreciate the diversity in ages, gender, race, socio-economic status, religions, and cultures that exist in most communities and countries throughout the world and develop a way of responding to this diversity. The barriers of mistrust and hostility between the police and the citizenry that were created as a result of racism and discrimination can be broken down if the police respond to and interact with the public with respect and trust. Wong (2008:1) suggested that police should be considered a depository for social resources, with their effectiveness in solving community problems determined by the amount of time, materials, skills, ideas, and knowledge they possess. In this regard, the more skills and knowledge they have to deal with a multicultural society, the more effective they will be in their work.

In a similar vein, as police organizations become more diverse in terms of the racial, cultural, and gender composition of their employees, some of the "good old boys" practices must be replaced with policies and practices that are equitable for all concerned. Many instances of inequities in the recruitment, retention, and promotion of police based on race and gender have been documented. For example, Surender (2008:1) reported that, while changes have occurred in India and some women have reached high positions as police chiefs, nevertheless, less than 4% of the police in India are women, and of these, 89% are employed in the lower ranks. In addition, the large majority of female officers are assigned to work with women and children or on traffic details. Other research has revealed that female officers who ask for part-time work assignments because of family responsibilities frequently find that their opportunities for new training and advancement in the organization become limited (Charlesworth, 2008). Charlesworth and Harwood (2008) revealed that efforts to develop flexible work practices and part-time work assignments in several police organizations in Australia met with considerable resistance from middle- and senior-level management.

Harwood (2008) stated that, worldwide, women are underrepresented in key decision-making positions in police organizations. She concluded that female officers are not found in the senior-level management positions to the extent one might expect based on their numbers and experiences because of problems related to changing the cultures of the police organizations to make them more open for female officers to succeed.

In many countries, a major reason for the under-representation of racial and ethnic groups and women in the upper levels of police management is that members of these groups are not motivated to enter police work to the extent one might expect. Often *perceptions* of a lack of opportunities in the police profession or few possibilities for success in a police career may be the most important factor in determining if members of certain groups choose the police profession as a career. When this occurs, women and members of certain racial groups may not be under-represented in the police organizations as a result of discrimination, but because they excluded themselves.

Kaur (2008) compared the proportion of women police officers in the United States, Germany, and India. She discovered that the percent of police officers who are women is increasing in India, decreasing in the United States, and remaining stable in Germany. She attributed these findings to the fact that women in India are motivated to enter police work because it is viewed as a powerful profession, while in the United States women are reluctant to enter police work because it is viewed as a dangerous job. In Germany, women motivated to enter police work were impressed with the opportunities for a secure job with benefits. Kaur (2008), Burns, Mayberry, Wietinger, Boniface, and Robertson (2008) provided information on problems women in police work have experienced relating to sexual harassment, perceptions by male officers that the female officers were not as competent as male officers, and other prejudices toward female officers, including discrimination in promotions, a general distrust of female officers by some administrators, and a lack of flexibility of some administrations to consider the special needs of the female officers.

Summary

In this discussion, we have attempted to demonstrate that the concept "policing without borders" can have a variety of meanings in addition to the one that is most commonly understood in reference to the geographical and territorial borders that create national physical divisions of countries. The need for countries to develop international agreements to combat crime and terrorism and to promote a better way of life for all nations was stressed. In our global society, the importance of having stronger, more economically secure countries, and assisting those countries that are in various stages of economic and political development cannot be overemphasized.

Borrowing from the motto used by Alexander Dumas (1910) in *The Three Musketeers*, "One for all, all for one," each country in the world system is dependent on all countries in some way, just as all countries are dependent on each individual country.

The interdependence of nations in seeking solutions to the problems created by international crime and terrorism has also been highlighted here. Pacts ranging from bilateral, multi-national, and global agreements; treaties; and commissions formulated by the United Nations and the European Union, to informal agreements between two nations are developed for the purpose of implementing more effective means to combat crime. The police must rely on international cooperation to combat such criminal activities as international money laundering, cyber-crime, and international trafficking of drugs, weapons, and humans, since these crimes transcend national boundaries.

The discussion presented here also revealed that, as the police and justice agencies of various countries communicate with each other, cooperate on police matters, share their expertise, and engage in similar types of training, they learn that their differences in cultures, skills, and policing objectives are not as great as they may have supposed. Generally, those employed in police work want to be professional and effective in the performance of their policing tasks. This is true regardless of the economic status of the country in which they are employed; the type of policing agency, local or national, in which they work; or their position within the organization (administration, supervisor, or line officer). Also, in keeping with the notion of professionalism, they want to be justly compensated and rewarded for their work. This requires that their work output be evaluated solely on the basis of merit and that the evaluation be free from prejudices and biases on the part of those completing the evaluations.

The notion of police professionalism implies that officers will utilize the technology, information, and input from other professionals that will be useful to them in their work. It has been shown that police can become more effective if they interact and cooperate with other professionals. Several projects were cited in which the police and academics collaborated in the planning, implementation, and evaluation of crime prevention programs.

Some police agencies are struggling to reach the high standards of professionalism that have already been established by other agencies. For a national police agency, the reasons for the lack of police professionalism may be related to the overall poverty existing in the country, a lack of stability or corruption in the government, or to a deficiency in the police organization resulting from inadequate funds and resources to support a professional police organization. For a local police organization, the deficiency may be related to poor administration or insufficient resources and funding. Several programs described here illustrate how representatives of police agencies in stronger, more prosperous countries assisted developing countries with resources, information exchanges, and the training of police officers.

One can expect more cooperation, better communications, and the development of common standards for police work as the gaps in understanding and commitment between nations, professions, the police, and the communities continue to narrow in the future.

References

Beinhart, E. (2008), "Democratic Policing in an Emerging Democracy," Panel Discussion at the 15th Annual International Police Executive Symposium, Cincinnati, May 12–16.

Benyon, J. (1997), "The Developing System of Police Cooperation in the European Union" in W. F. McDonald, ed., *Crime and Law Enforcement in the* Global *Village,* Cincinnati: Anderson.

Bloss, W. P. (2008), "Bridging Book and Badge: Developing Sustainable Police-Academic Research Partnerships," Presentation at the 15th Annual International Police Executive Symposium, Cincinnati, May 12–16.

Bolesik, Z. (2008), "Characteristics of Cross Border Investigations in Hungary," Presentation at the 15th Annual International Police Executive Symposium, Cincinnati, May 12–16.

Boniface, G. (2008), "Police Reform: Making it Happen and Making it Last," Presentation at the 15th Annual International Police Executive Symposium, Cincinnati, May 12–16.

Bryant, R. (2008), "Toward a Theory of Intelligence," Presentation at the 15th Annual International Police Executive Symposium, Cincinnati, May 12–16.

Burns, G. (2008), "Police Reform and Managerialism," Presentation at the 15th Annual International Police Executive Symposium, Cincinnati, May 12–16.

Carpenter, A. (2008), "International Policekeeping: The Thin Blue Line," Presentation at the 15th Annual International Police Executive Symposium, Cincinnati, May 12–16.

Carpenter, A., S. Charlesworth, G. Burns, L. Mayberry, E. Wietinger, G. Boniface, and D. Robertson (2008), "Gender Equality/Cultural Reform in Policing," Panel Discussion at the 15th Annual International Police Executive Symposium, Cincinnati, May 12–16.

Charlesworth, S. (2008), "Policing, Gender, and Working Time: The Case of Part-time Detective," Presentation at the 15th Annual International Police Executive Symposium, Cincinnati, May 12–16.

Charlesworth, S. and S. Harwood (2008), "Foundering at the Border: Flexible Work Policies and Practices in Police Organizations," Presentation at the 15th Annual International Police Executive Symposium, Cincinnati, May 12–16.

Cordner, G. (2008), "CALEA: Police Agency Accreditation," Presentation at the 15th Annual International Police Executive Symposium, Cincinnati, May 12–16.

Cordner, G. and C. Shain (2008), "Human Rights—The Rule of Law, Terrorism and Community Policing," Presentation at the 15th Annual International Police Executive Symposium, Cincinnati, May 12–16.

Das, D. K. (2008), "Police Leaders as Thinkers," Presentation at the 15th Annual International Police Executive Symposium, Cincinnati, May 12–16.

Das, D. K. and P. C. Kratcoski (2001), "International Police Cooperation: A World Perspective," in D. J. Koenig and D. K. Das (eds.). *International Police Cooperation: A World Perspective.* New York: Lexington Books.

Department of Homeland Security (DHS), http://www.dhs.gov/xabout/structure/
Drug Enforcement Administration (DEA) (2007), DEA Office Locations and Foreign Cooperative Investigations. http:/www.dea.gov/ptograms/fci.htm
Ducot, G. E. (2008), "Democratic Policing in an Emerging Democracy," Panel Discussion at the 15th Annual International Police Executive Symposium, Cincinnati, May 12–16.
Dumas, A. (1910), *The Three Musketeers.* New York: The F. M. Lupton Publishing Company.
Dziedzic, M. (2008), "The International Network to Promote the Rule of Law," Presentation at the 15th Annual International Police Executive Symposium, Cincinnati, May 12–16.
Engel, R. S., T. H. Streicher, J. L. Whalen, and G. Baker (2008), "Cincinnati Initiative to Reduce Violence (CIRV)," Panel Discussion at the 15th Annual International Police Executive Symposium, Cincinnati, May 12–16.
Eterno, J. A. (2008), "The Public Housing Safety Initiative in the Eastern District of New York: A Collaborative Researcher and Practitioner Program," Presentation at the 15th Annual International Police Executive Symposium, Cincinnati, May 12–16.
Fantino, J. (2008), "Policing a Multicultural Society and the Drive to Keep Pace with Changing Communities," Keynote Address at the 15th Annual International Police Executive Symposium, Cincinnati, May 12–16.
Federal Bureau of Investigation (FBI) (2007), Legal Attaché Offices. www.FBI.Gov.
Harwood, S. (2008), "Crossing the Gender Border," Presentation at the 15th Annual International Police Executive Symposium, Cincinnati, May 12–16.
Hataley, T.S. (September 2007). Catastrophic terrorism at the border: The case of the Canada-United State border. Homeland Security Affairs, Supplement no 1. http://www.jsaj.org/?Specialarticle=Supplement.1.1.
Henry, V. (2000), A conversation with William J. Bratton, *Police Practice and Research, 1*(4):559–580.
Henry-Potts, A. (2008), "Democratic Policing in an Emerging Democracy," Panel Discussion at the 15th Annual International Police Executive Symposium, Cincinnati, May 12–16.
Kaur, P. P. and H. Hoffman (2008), "Women Police: A Comparative Study of the United States, Germany and India," Paper presented at the 15th Annual International Police Executive Symposium, Cincinnati, May 12–16.
King, M. and D. Sharp (2006), Global security and policing change: The impact of Securitisation on UK policing at the national and local level, *Police Practice and Research: An International Journal, 7*(5):379–390.
Kratcoski, P. C. (2004) "The Challenges of Police Education and Training in a Global Society" in Kratcoski, P. C. and D. K. Das (eds.). *Police Education and Training in a Global Society*. New York: Lexington Books.
Kratcoski, P. C. (2007), "Police Role and Issues in the 21st Century: An International Perspective." Unpublished paper.
Kratcoski, P. C. and L. D. Kratcoski (2008), "Police Without Borders: The Fading Distinction Between Local and Global," Executive Summary of the Fifteenth International Police Executive Symposium. Unpublished manuscript.
Kratcoski, P. C. and V. E. Henry (2001), "A Conservation with Patrick H. Lang: Reflections on His Justice Career," *Police Practice and Research: An International Journal, 2*(4):461–471.

Laitinen, I. (2006), "Statement of Executive Director of FRONTEX," FRONTEX Annual Report.
Lemieux, F. (2008), "Assessing the Effectiveness of International Police Cooperation Systems," Presentation at the 15th Annual International Police Executive Symposium, Cincinnati, May 12–16.
Li Chi-mei, J. (2008), "An Innovative Police Project to Tackle Youth Crime Problems in Hong Kong: The Operation Breakthrough," Paper presented at the 15th Annual International Police Executive Symposium, Cincinnati, May 12–16.
Malme, O. B. (2008), "Transnational and Organized Crime, A Perspective from the Northern Hemisphere," Presentation at the 15th Annual International Police Executive Symposium, Cincinnati, May 12–16.
Matijevic, M. (2008), "Functionality of Bosnia and Herzegovina Police in the Post-War Period, with Particular Review on Protection of Human Rights and Freedom," Presentation at the 15th Annual International Police Executive Symposium, Cincinnati, May 12–16.
Meini, B. (2008), "Implications for Law Enforcement, Public Safety and Policing in South Africa," Presentation at the 15th Annual International Police Executive Symposium, Cincinnati, May 12–16.
Mesko, G. and D. Maver (2008), "On Police and Policing in Slovenia—Obstacles or Challenges," Presentation at the 15th Annual International Police Executive Symposium, Cincinnati, May 12–16.
Morckel, K. (2008), "Data Driven Approaches to Traffic Safety," Presentation at the 15th Annual International Police Executive Symposium, Cincinnati, May 12–16.
9/11 Commission (2002), *The 9/11 Commission Report*, New York: W.W. Norton and Company.
Onwudiwe, I. D. (2002), *The Globalization of Terrorism.* Hampshire, England: Ashgate.
Palmer, D. and C. Whelan (2008), Counterterrorism across the policing continuum, *Police Practice and Research: An International Journal, 7*(5):449–465.
Palmiotto, M. (2008), "The Mission of the International Police Executive Symposium," Presentation at the 15th Annual International Police Executive Symposium, Cincinnati, May 12–16.
Perras, C. (2008), "Targeting Groups Instead of a Particular Crime: A Better Way of Doing Transnational Investigations," Presentation at the 15th Annual International Police Executive Symposium, Cincinnati, May 12–16.
Philipson, C. and J. Lundalv (2008), "Police Vehicle Collisions in Sweden: How Do We Reduce the Possibility of Deaths and Injuries by Police Cars?", Presentation at the 15th Annual International Police Executive Symposium, Cincinnati, May 12–16.
Plywaczewski, E and W. Plywaczewski (2008), "International Police Cooperation from the European Union Perspective," Presentation at the 15th Annual International Police Executive Symposium, Cincinnati, May 12–16.
Sedgwick, J. L. (2008), "International Challenges to Law Enforcement: Policing in the Global Age," Keynote address at the 15th Annual International Police Executive Symposium, Cincinnati, May 12–16.
Surender, A. (2008), "Growth and Development of Women Police in India," Presentation at the 15th Annual International Police Executive Symposium, Cincinnati, May 12–16.

Tong, S. (2008), "Development in Initial Police Training: A University Perspective," Presentation at the 15th Annual International Police Executive Symposium, Cincinnati, May 12–16.
White, S. (2008), "Democratic Policing in an Emerging Democracy," Panel Discussion at the 15th Annual International Police Executive Symposium, Cincinnati, May 12–16.
Wong, K. (2008), "The Study of Policing in China," Paper prepared for the 15th Annual International Police Executive Symposium, Cincinnati, May 12–16.
Yokoyama, M. (2008), "Development of Guidance Activities by Japanese Police for Juveniles," Presentation at the 15th Annual International Police Executive Symposium, Cincinnati, May 12–16.

Policing Activity and Human Rights

2

RAYMOND KENDALL

Contents

Introducing Human Rights and the Police

British police organizations in the 1950s and 1960s did not mention the modern idea of human rights as inherent ethical principles. Training focused on the legal requirement to inform persons who were arrested of the reason for their arrest and their right to remain silent. The link was not made between the legal requirement and the human rights aspect. This distinction is important because it tends to establish why police officers act the way that they do, generally, in application of the law rather than in consideration of human rights, and I shall return to this later. In 1948, the Universal Declarations of Human Rights was established as the primary global expression of rights to which all human beings are inherently entitled, asserting the recognition of human dignity of all people as the foundation of justice and peace in the world.

It was the first time in history that the international community embraced a document considered to have universal value, "a common standard of achievement for all peoples and all nations." Its preamble acknowledges the importance of a human rights legal framework to maintaining international peace and security, stating that recognition of the inherent dignity and equal and inalienable rights of all individuals is the foundation of freedom, justice, and peace in the world.

Specifically relating to the police is the 1979 UN Code of Conduct for Law Enforcement Officials, which states that police officers will respect and protect human dignity and maintain and uphold the human rights of all persons, and that force should be used only when strictly necessary and to the extent required for the performance of their duty.

The Council of Europe within its Human Rights Division has greatly contributed to the establishment and recognition of human rights in general, and particularly to the role of police as a pivotal point in the judicial system of a state which aspires or claims to be, a democracy. In 1997, the Council launched a program called Police and Human Rights 1997–2000. Because the police conduct inquiries into suspected crimes and in certain circumstances execute judicial sanctions that bring them into constant contact with the citizens of their country, police behavior should symbolize the respect of human rights and their protection on its territory. The way in which police organizations carry out their duties represents an infallible indicator of the level of quality of a democratic society and the way in which the state of law is respected. The continuity of the program was assured by the creation of a new program, Police and Human Rights Beyond 2000, whose aim was to train police officers in standards of human rights and instill in them the knowledge that would permit them to apply the standards in their daily work.

In April 2005, the Council organized a conference of Police and Human Rights coordinators in Strasbourg and, without going into the detail of the proceedings, some of its conclusions, among others, are worthy of note.

Protecting Human Rights Is the Core Function of Policing

It is of paramount importance to foster a culture in police organizations for protecting and respecting human rights. The organizational culture has to be grounded on human rights standards as a fundamental value. Human rights components have to be an integral part of police training, both theoretical and practical.

In September 2001, the European Committee of Ministers adopted the Code of Police Ethics, which contains a number of important provisions of application of human rights principles. There are many different initiatives, and there are many others, often inspired by the action of non-governmental organizations (NGOs), which show that the issue of human rights has now become an inevitable part of our societal way of life and that we have a responsibility to ensure that the Universal Declaration of Human Rights is truly universal.

The recent space shuttle carried on board a copy of the Universal Declaration and one member on board cynically said to another, "Perhaps before we take this we should ensure that it is applied as it should be on earth."

The Broader Context

The police are only one aspect of a broader public security context. Focusing on the police and human rights may blinker the human rights discourse from wider human rights abuses that arise from a lack of security.

The International Council on Security and Development, formerly known as the Senlis Council, has worked on drug and policy issues, opium cultivation in Afghanistan, and public security policy in Brazil. In both Afghanistan and Brazil, I think Europe has an important role to play in sharing the expertise and knowledge it has built up over the past decades in terms of the best practices of policing and how they relate to public security and human rights. Within the framework of the European Union, we are already implementing programs that try to tackle the problem of public security in Afghanistan and Brazil through collaborative projects focusing on technical assistance and sharing of best practices.

The European Union launched an EU Police mission (EUPOL) in Afghanistan in June 2007, which combined the knowledge of a great number of European countries in terms of policing. This EUPOL mission aimed to help Afghanistan establish sustainable and effective civilian policing arrangements under Afghan ownership and in accordance with the best international policing practices and international human rights standards. The project built on experiences elsewhere such as the European Union police missions in the Palestinian Territories and in the Congo. Progress, of course, takes time, but in Afghanistan there is already more attention paid to human rights within the work of the police.

A small, concrete example of increased human rights is the way the Afghan police is stopping cars. They are friendlier toward drivers when talking to them and asking them about searching the car and seeing their driving license. However, at the institutional level, a lot remains to be done, as there are many uncertainties about the lack of control the Karzai administration has over the police force. In addition, corruption is rife because of the relatively low salaries the police officers receive. Sometimes, the uniformed police themselves commit crimes.

As a result, local communities have occasionally chosen to support Taliban as an alternative to the corrupt police force that continues to carry out arbitrary arrests and to demand bribes. This shows that training the police on human rights and best international policing practices can become an empty shell if the security and development parameters of the country are highly problematic. The same holds true for Brazil, although the security and development parameters are, of course, rather different. Rio de Janeiro is a salient example, famous for summary executions, police corruption, and ruthless drug-trafficking gangs as a way to explore the subject of human rights and policing, a subject that is of a somewhat different perception than here in the North, compared to conditions where our notion of democracy seems difficult in its application.

The Example of Rio de Janeiro—The Public Security/Human Rights Impasse

In Rio, the police have developed a culture that may be described as hating human rights. During protests it is not uncommon for police to pose with baseball bats with *direitos humanos* scrawled down the side of them. The police simplistically associate the concept of human rights with the action of antagonistic NGOs that seem to protect criminals, giving them impunity to commit criminal acts, while punishing hardworking police officers who put their lives on the line for society.

At the same time, human rights NGOs and the UN Human Rights Commission denounce the police of Rio de Janeiro for committing human rights abuses en masse on the urban poor through belligerent public safety policies. Executions and corruption are rife, and the police contribute significantly to the city's high murder rate. How can we understand this antagonism between the police and human rights?

Politics and the Human Rights Discourse in Rio

This resistance to and political polarization of human rights is a result of the way the discourse has been employed historically in Rio over the last 30 years as a political instrument, which strongly influenced public security policies. Toward the end of the period of "military rule" in 1978, pro-democracy groups employed an antagonistic human rights agenda as a central component of the pro-democracy reform platform.

In the immediate post-military regime period of the early 1980s, the police, stigmatized as oppressive remnants of the dictatorship, were given restrictions in what they were allowed to do in carrying out their normal duties. It is clear that this was a reaction to the brutality of the police during the period of military rule. Newspaper reports from the time openly admit the use of torture as an investigative technique; for example, in one article, a policeman explained with pride that he had already extracted 15 confessions from one suspect. He thought that he could get at least five more confessions with another hour or two of beating, comparing the suspect to a squeezed orange in which there is always a last drop to be squeezed out if one works hard enough.

Additionally, the police's form of operating in the poor urban areas demonstrated a complete lack of respect for individual rights. A *foot in the door* policy was employed in poor areas, with police kicking down doors and demanding work registration documents. In this situation, the police were fully associated with the most repressive aspects of military rule, and the new democracy felt it a priority to curb the actions of the police force. During the 1980s, Public Security policy was marginalized in favor of human rights–based measures. New rules were brought in that forbade the police to enter into the favelas (shanty towns), ostensibly as a way of preventing the police from committing human rights abuses on the urban poor.

However, this lack of police presence created a vacuum and allowed criminality and alternative power structures to develop within these areas, contributing to the territorial dominance of criminal groups instead of the state. This was a result of policy makers' lack of attention to Public Security policy, and a political rather than functional understanding of the police. It is also a fact that the democratization in Brazil in 1978 was accompanied by a rise in criminality, especially of homicides among young men. In interviews with both Rio's police and Public Security experts, there is a consensus of opinion that this historical turning point is one of the main reasons for the entrenchment of drug-trafficking gangs in Rio's favelas.

This history also goes some way to situating Rio Police's disparaging attitude toward human rights. They perceive that the human rights arguments gave criminals impunity and enabled them to dominate wide areas of the city.

Introducing Rio's Security Context

Many security dynamics were at play in Rio in order to give some context to contemporary Public Security issues in Rio de Janeiro. Drug-retailing gangs are locked into a brutal market competition with each other for control of strategic locations from which to sell drugs. Factional competition led to the necessity for weapons with which to defend and acquire strategic locations from rivals and state authorities. Guns easily find their way into the city, given Brazil's porous border with Paraguay where, for example, guns can be bought and sold in illegal street markets.

This situation has led to a virtual territorial stalemate in the city, where entrenched drug-trafficking gangs have full domination over almost all of the 700 favelas in the region, and public security forces do not have the resources to reclaim this territory. State forces conduct sporadic military-style mega-operations designed to capture specific individuals, or operations to reduce drug-trafficking organizations' arsenals of drugs and guns within the favelas. However, these operations are incursions into foreign territory, and do not have the aim of bringing this area under state jurisdiction, as this would require resources that are not available.

Police relationships with drug factions are characterized by extreme violence. Police and drug factions confront each other using war-grade weaponry, employing calibers such as 7.62, 556, or bigger, as well as grenades and mounted machine guns. The police also use armored cars in operations so as to transport police safely from one area to another, and helicopters to provide covering fire. These operations often result in the death or arrest of faction members and the police, as well as the apprehension of weapons and drugs. These confrontations take place in Rio's favelas, areas of high population densities and weak housing structure with a history of the criminalization of the poor. Often, innocent people get caught in the crossfire, as high-caliber bullets easily pass through the thin walls of favela residences.

The Criminal Justice System

The criminal justice system is an important factor in understanding human rights and the police in Rio. Inefficiencies in the criminal justice system have a perverse effect on the ways both the police and criminal factions operate. Both the gangs and the police operate brutally because of certain aspects of the way the justice system functions. They are frustrated and have the feeling that they are not part of a structured judicial system and, in fact, have the impression that they are the only force of intervention that can protect the citizens.

The Effect of the Justice System on the Drug Factions

The shortcomings of the criminal justice system act as a perverse incentive for members of criminal gangs to increase their brutality and ruthlessness. Given the prevalence of corruption, and loopholes in the law, the more individuals demonstrate their worth to the faction, the more likely the organization is to either:

1. Upon arrest, pay the bribe to arresting officers to let the captured individual go free, or

2. At trial, employ a good lawyer to defend the individual. Loopholes in the criminal justice system mean that the individual has a relatively high chance of acquittal with the defense of an experienced lawyer.

The prosecution system is also very inefficient and fosters a climate of impunity and incentive to commit crime. For example, one study showed that in the mid-1990s in Rio de Janeiro, of 4,227 records of homicide occurrences registered with the Civil Police, only 4.6% of them had the perpetrator and motive established. Another study found that 92% of homicide cases presented by the police were dismissed for lack of sufficient proof to go to trial. In addition, The Statute of The Child and The Adolescent states that children under 18 years old cannot be tried for adult crimes and must be sent to juvenile rehabilitation centers. This means that even for a crime such as murder, minors will only serve until age 18 and then be released and have their criminal records erased. The perverse effect of this legislation is that criminal factions are encouraged to recruit minors, as they can act with a higher level of impunity. Thus, the weakness of the justice system thus encourages impunity, the recruitment of children in criminal factions, and a culture of brutality within criminal factions.

The Police Perspective

Mirroring the brutalizing effect of the justice system on criminal factions, it also exercises a perverse effect on the way the police engage with drug-trafficking gangs. Police officers do not have confidence in the criminal justice system, and are revolted by the apparent impunity that the weakness of the justice system confers to criminal factions. Police officers know that once arrested there are many instances where drug faction members can escape the full application of the law:

- Arresting officers may release them in return for a bribe.
- A lawyer exploits loopholes in the law, leading to a short sentence or acquittal.
- Once in prison, early release could be petitioned by lawyers.
- Homicides are rarely investigated thoroughly, or rarely reach trial.
- Minors will serve only up to the age of 18.

Police are almost given the incentive to kill drug faction combatants because they are aware of the slim chance that the justice system will yield "justice." This is a matter of brutal pragmatism for the police engaged in guerrilla warfare with the drug factions. From a militaristic perspective, they know that if they do not kill the individual when they have the opportunity, they face the risk of being shot at by the individual at a later date.

From these brief examples, we can conclude that overhauling the justice system would have the effect of reducing human rights violations. Because the police lack faith in the system, they take matters into their own hands, and criminal factions are encouraged in their activities as the justice system seems to allow them to act with impunity. Under these conditions it is difficult to know where to begin in our exercise to establish and control the application of human rights principles.

The United Nations' Perspective on Human Rights and the Police in Rio

In 2007, Human Rights *rapporteur* Phillip Anston visited Brazil and compiled a report that concluded that Rio State frequently violates human rights in the incursions to favelas designed to combat narco-trafficking. In his report Anston notes that Rio's police on average kill three people per day, and are responsible for 18% of the state's murder rate.

The Case of Complexo de Alemao

In his report, Anston cited a police "mega-operation" that took place in June 2007, in which more than 1,000 police officers participated, as an example of Rio Police's human rights abuses. The operation, designed to reduce the faction's arsenal, took place at *Complexo Alemao*, a huge conjunct of 16 favelas and headquarters of Rio's largest drug faction, *Commando Vermelho*. Anston criticized the operation for putting innocent people's lives at risk, and for stopping thousands of local children from going to school. He was also very critical of reported summary executions by the police, presenting data from coroners' reports which showed that of the 26 people killed, 14 were shot in the back and six had point-blank entry wounds to the face.

He concludes that:

> It appears that if someone is a drug trafficker, then killing him is justifiable, when there is no justification for killing anyone. If a person sells drugs the procedure should be to arrest him … If there is the policeman's life or somebody close to him at risk, this justifies the use of force, but not killing.

From a human rights perspective, there is no doubt that the police are guilty of human rights abuses as well as criminal offenses. We encounter a "Dirty Harry" syndrome reality, where "dirty" means (i.e., executions) are employed toward a "clean" end, the ending of the drug faction's tyranny over a community. In effect, the police have taken the law into their own hands. However, if we amplify our understanding of the rights discourse, then we can also conclude that a state allowing criminal factions to dominate state territory is also an abuse of a citizen's fundamental human rights.

The Importance of the Right to Security

Security is essential for the successful democratic development of society. It is a prerequisite for democratic engagement, economic development, and social cohesion. For example:

- In the absence of security, there are no conditions for civil society engagement. Without it, civil society organizations cannot flourish, civil leaders do not emerge, and only crime flourishes.
- Security is a prerequisite for the establishment of economic networks. Without security, businesses cannot grow.
- Security is essential for social cohesion, and the teaching of solidarity with society. Without security, teachers have to mediate their messages, or put their lives in danger.

From this example, it is clear that without security, human rights are also inhibited. If we revisit the previous example of *Complexo de Alemao*, we can see that the lack of security inhibits the human rights of local residents.

In a confidential report from Rio's *Disque Denuncia* (Brazil's Crime Stoppers organization) for the month prior to the operation in *Complexo Alemao*, the following human rights abuses were observed:

- Faction members in the area obliged residents to give them food, turn their houses into drug-selling points or artillery positions, and hide weapons, or face expulsion.
- Faction members shot residents so as to incriminate the police, and local community leaders delivered false denouncements of human rights abuses and executions by the police to human rights lawyers.
- Faction members beat residents, angry with police presence in the area.
- The water supply was cut off as an incentive for residents to protest against police presence in the area.

From these few examples it is clear that drug-dealing factions commit many human rights abuses, and their removal from territorial control of territories is essential for guaranteeing human rights of local residents. The state's lack of control over its territory allows non-state actors to perpetuate human rights abuses, and denies local residents the fundamental right to security. Therefore, the state must reclaim this territory; however, the state must demonstrate a permanent presence in these areas, and not rely on punctual guerilla-like incursions. Also, the positive dimension of the state must be demonstrated through social policies, bringing health, education, and opportunity to marginalized areas.

Toward Breaching the Impasse

The impasse between an antagonistic, anti-police human rights discourse and repressive police actions needs to be readdressed. In the case of Rio, the basic principles of human rights need to be reestablished as a constructive bridge-building discourse between the police and society. The police's only notion of human rights is in a negative context, where they are the enemy. This leads to a reactive attitude of disparagement of human rights among the police. For them, the human rights discourse only serves to give impunity to bandits, and indict zealous police who are defending society.

The police aim to be rights providers, risking their lives trying to provide the fundamental right of security for society. The importance of human rights for the police must be understood from a strategic perspective, in that demonstrating respect for human rights is strategically advantageous. The police must understand that persistent cases of violence and corruption, and the perceived impunity of the police to commit human rights abuses, contributes to a lack of confidence in the police. This distances the population from the police, resulting in low levels of public-police collaboration, and the growth of private security initiatives.

The human rights and police discourse must be amplified to include human rights abuses that are perpetuated because of a lack of police presence. Human rights advocates must forge alliances with the police in order to encourage them to become human rights defenders. Regarding summary executions, the environment of the justice system must be the focus for intervention. Legal loopholes, inefficiencies, and corruption must be addressed from the principle of providing justice, reducing the incentive for police officers to resort to their own interpretations of "Dirty Harry"-style justice. The Rio example because I am now familiar with the situation there despite its complexities, but also because it illustrates the difficulties that exist between establishing principles on the one hand and applying them on the other. If there is not a strong political will to achieve an objective, nothing will be achieved. Fortunately, in Brazil, the political will seems to have been established and a five-year plan of action has been embarked upon with a multifaceted approach and with appropriate financial resources, so hopefully the future will be optimistic.

In conclusion, political will is important because it is at the level of government that law is established, and it is impossible not to evaluate this aspect when one is considering the subject of human rights and the police. The police act in accordance with the law, and it is the law that establishes the conditions in which they operate.

Examing the question of human rights is important. There is a major issue of contention is that of non-respect of basic human rights in as far as the treatment of suspected persons and prisoners is concerned.

We are fortunate in our democracies, and particularly in Europe, that we have established internationally applicable principles in relation to human rights, but also a control mechanism to enable us to establish that these principles are being applied. In the European context, representatives of the European Commission on Human Rights, as well as other professional bodies who produce reports and recommendations on human rights issues, make regular visits, with the consent of state governments. These recommendations are designed to ensure that the right conditions are created for human rights to be as fully respected as possible. This is important to establishing the conditions in which police are to operate, bearing in mind what I said in the beginning with my remarks about police operating within the respect of the law.

The International Commission of Jurists in a report in October 2008 found, for example, that incommunicado detention, even where judicially supervised, cannot adequately protect the safety of detainees. Further, that in order to reliably protect rights the principle of immediate access to a lawyer to consult in confidence is indispensible. Likewise, access to information to help in preparing a defense should not be restricted. These are just examples of issues that could easily be resolved by simple changes in legislation, and that would go a long way to creating conditions of transparency and clarify and justify police action. I repeat that police take action within the limits that are placed upon them by law and, as far as the public is concerned, justice must be done but also be seen to be done.

Six principles were established by the Association of Chief Police Officers of the United Kingdom after the adoption of the Human Rights Act in October 2000. These principles are applicable to each area of policing to reach compliance with human rights:

1. *Legality*—Is there a legal basis for police actions? Is that legal basis in statute, regulations, or case law, and is it available to a member of the public?
2. *Proportionality*—Can the police demonstrate that actions taken were "proportionate" to the threat or problem it sought to prevent?

3. *Relevance/Necessity*—Was the police action strictly relevant to the particular threat/problem?
4. *Subsidiarity*—Was the police action the best "force/intrusive" available?
5. *Equality of Arms*—In any trial process did the defendant have the same information and access to information as the police/prosecution?
6. *Remedy*—Is there an independent public remedy available to the citizen?

It was added in conclusion that it is hoped that the Human Rights Act will help to create a society in which the rights and responsibilities of individuals are properly balanced.

Much progress has been made regarding human rights, but there is still a long way to go before we can assume that the Universal Declaration of Human Rights is universally applied, and we must also remember that this is essentially a question of human behavior which cannot be resolved by legislation alone.

Keeping Order in a Time of Dynamic Change and Exchange

3

Social Control in Asia and the Pacific

VICTOR N. SHAW

Contents

Introduction

Asia and the Pacific is a dynamic region of expanding economic development, deepening political reform, and sweeping cultural transformation in the world. Amid rapid, drastic, and multifaceted social change, crime, deviance, and social problems occur in unprecedented volumes, forms, and complexities, posing serious challenges to social control systems in countries throughout the region. It is obviously not enough to expand the old social control system. It is more important to modernize the whole system so that it is able to deal with new situations more effectively and efficiently (Xu, 1995; Shaw, 1996; Marx, 1997; Newman, 1999; Du Guerny & Hsu, 2002; MacMichael, 2003; Nagel, 2003; Davis, 2006; Deflem, 2006; Sung, 2006; Bakken, 2007; Chan, 2007; Terrill, 2007; Melossi, 2008; King, 2009).

This chapter focuses on change of control ideologies, transfer of control technologies, professionalization of control forces, and modernization of control systems as four critical areas of challenge, opportunity, and promise facing social control in Asia and the Pacific. Each area is examined with a review of historical background, an analysis of opposing forces, and a proposal for synthetic integration.

Change of Control Ideologies

While it remains an open question whether control arrangements determine control ideas, or vice versa, it takes courage and a change of ideology to reform any existing social control system.

Historical Background

The idea of social control appears as early as the time of Aristotle when scholars began to reflect upon the nature of human social life (Roucek, 1978). In sociology, Edward Ross (1901) first elaborated social control in relation to law, public opinion, education, religion, custom, ceremony, art, enlightenment, illusion, and morality.

After Ross, social control took on a variety of interpretations in the literature (Janowitz, 1975). Macrosociological perspectives examine how laws and the criminal justice system inhibit rule-breaking behavior as well as foster oppression and alienation in society. Microsociological perspectives, on the other hand, explain how people conform by internalizing the external control through an individual socialization process (Davis & Anderson, 1983; Cohen & Scull, 1983).

Reiss (1951) was one of the first sociologists to study the relationship between personal and social controls. He argued that juvenile delinquency results from a failure to internalize socially prescribed norms of behavior. Toby (1957) observed that only a few among many youths in socially disorganized neighborhoods committed crimes. He attributed the difference to the individual's own stake in conformity to society's normal standards. Reckless (1961) presented an even broader analysis of how personal factors interact with social control in his containment theory. According to him, for every individual there exists a containing external structure and a protective internal structure, both of which provide defense, protection, and insulation against deviant behavior.

Matza (1964) assumed that adolescents normally feel a moral obligation to abide by the social "bind" between a person and the law. They drift into delinquency not because of an involuntary failure of their inner and/or outer containment, but rather because of a voluntary development of defense mechanisms that release them from the constraints of convention. For example, they use denial of responsibility, denial of injury, denial of the victim, condemnation of the condemner, and appeal to higher loyalties as defenses to rationalize particular delinquent acts, neutralize their inner sense of guilt, and ward off possible social attacks (Sykes & Matza, 1957).

Hirschi (1969) shifted focus from individual motivations to commit delinquency to individual determinations to observe social norms. To explain conformity, he identified four social bonds. First is attachment: how closely a juvenile is tied to his or her parents, school, and peers. Second is commitment: whether a juvenile aspires to educational excellence and vocational success. Third is involvement: how much time and energy a youth invests in activities that promote the interests of society. The last is belief: whether a youth shares social values that entail respect for law and order.

Outside the functionalist tradition that centers on socialization, personal control, and social bonds, Gibbs (1981) defined social control as an attempt by one individual(s) to manipulate the behavior of another individual(s). In an interactionist perspective, he identified five types of social control: referential, allegative, vicarious, modulative, and prelusive. Black viewed social control as "all of the practices by which people define and respond to deviant behavior" (1984: xi). Horwitz (1990) developed a systematic typology of social control in terms of style, form, and effectiveness.

More recently, Shaw (1996, 2002) explained social control as any mechanism for securing individual compliance, maintaining collective order, or dealing with problematic situations. He explored the West versus the Third World, formal versus informal, primary versus secondary group, social versus organizational, regulative versus suggestive, and external versus internal dimensions of social control in Chinese work units. He also examined control with regard to its source, dimension, degree, substitution, and restoration in the field of substance use and abuse.

Opposing Forces

The ideology of social control centers on such fundamental issues as to whom control is applied, how it is exercised, and what purpose it serves. Formally, social control ideology manifests in the organization of a state and its policies and practices toward crime, deviance, or social problems. Informally, it takes root in public opinion, social sentiment, and cultural activities.

In Asia and the Pacific, there exist three major contradictions in social control ideology. First, between traditional and contemporary forces, where the former emphasizes conscience, self-discipline, kinship, and community as primary sources in socialization, peacekeeping, and conflict resolution. The contemporary force, in contrast, stresses the importance of legal codes, justice systems, social organizations, and governmental apparatuses in educating the young, correcting the wayward, and maintaining order in society. Almost every developing country in the region, whether it is India, Papua New Guinea, or Peru, experiences a certain degree of tension, sometimes open struggle, between existing authorities embedded in tradition and the emerging forces of modernization.

The second contradiction is between socialist and capitalist systems. The socialist system advocates collectivism, a unified national ideology, one-party control, an organized social deterrence system, repentance through thought reform, and correction by way of productive labor; whereas the capitalist system embraces individualism, open media, multi-party rule, specific reactions by specialized professionals, freedom of belief, doing-time imprisonment, and just-desserts punishment (Shaw, 1996; Barlow, 2000; Melossi, 2008; King, 2009). Conflict between social systems constantly figures in international dynamics and occasionally escalates into ideological warfare across territorial borders, when capitalist nations criticize socialist states for power abuse, political repression, and human rights violations, and when socialist countries admonish capitalist societies for drug epidemics, racial tensions, and rampant criminality on the streets and in organizational settings.

The third contradiction is between Eastern and Western civilizations. In the East, people are cultivated to observe the unity between mind and body, between individuals and society, and between society and nature. Individuals who strive for inner peace do not expect to be forgiven for their wrongs. Instead they remain ready to admit guilt, to receive punishment, and to change themselves through serious effort. In the West, on the other hand, people are warned of the essentially adversarial relationships they have with their fellow humans, social institutions, and natural environments. Individuals who aspire for self-actualization would mobilize every possible resource they have to defend themselves against a charge. They will not admit guilt even they are indeed guilty of a crime until they fully explore procedural technicalities in a court of law.

Besides the three major contradictions, there are other critical clashes in Asia and the Pacific. Just as Muslim countries have to balance the dictates of Islamism with the demands of a secular social order, societies with a history of colonialism need to reconcile the influence of colonizers with the mandate of self-rule. Most important, countries in transition from traditional to contemporary, socialist to capitalist, and/or Eastern to Western forms of social control often experience an inevitable state of ideological ambivalence and practical disorganization. On the one hand, they question older social control philosophy and lament the declining influence of existing measures. On the other hand, they remain suspicious about new social control ideas and have yet to see the effect of a different approach upon application. In China, for example, the control system wrestles with various contradictions between communist ideology and social reality. The long-held explanation that crimes are historical residues of feudalism, capitalism, and imperialism from an older society no longer seems plausible to the general public. There is also a reluctance to apply Western theories to the new social situation of economic development. The result is a contradictory ideological system. Under it, socialization of children becomes problematic. Mobilization of public support for preventing and fighting crime is in limbo (Xu, 1995; Shaw, 1996; Liu, Zhang, & Messner, 2001; Bakken, 2007).

Synthetic Integration

In Asia and the Pacific, while there is a general movement from traditional, socialist, and Eastern to modern, capitalist, and Western forms of social control, there are both ideological and practical needs to bring seemingly opposite developments into a synthesis for the greater good of justice, cohesion, and stability (Xu, 1995; Marx, 1997; Inglehart & Baker, 2000; Goldsmith & Dinnen, 2007; Clements, 2008).

Change begins with a bottom-line agreement that no one side should ever be singled out to bear the whole blame of deviance, crime, and social problems in a society. Tradition sanctions the force of inhibition but fosters ignorance, neglect, and negligence. Modernity unleashes the energy of freedom but spreads arrogance, extravagance, and exploitation. Socialism engenders individual laziness, managerial ineffectiveness, and political corruption while emphasizing collective unity. Capitalism brings about egoistic selfishness, organizational manipulation, and economic cruelty while stressing entrepreneurial prosperity. Eastern culture experiences favoritism and nepotism as it emphasizes strength of family, balance of groupings, and harmony of community. Western civilization witnesses individualism and bureaucratism when it commits to self-actualization, procedural formality, and organizational standardization. Each side has its pros and cons: creating problems in some areas while providing defense against deviations in other dimensions.

With a no-blame clause in sight, there then can be a no-incompatibility view of social control and its measures. Specifically, are measures inherited from history, socialism, or Eastern civilizations compatible with those that have emerged in modernization, capitalist development, or the process of institutionalization? There used to be absolute rejection of the other side's ideas, especially during the Cold War. For example, socialist countries attacked due process and other justice procedures in capitalist societies as political ploys by the rich, the powerful, and the educated to manipulate the poor, the powerless, and the illiterate. Capitalist nations condemned collective surveillance, thought reform, and correctional labor in socialist states as grave violations of civil liberties by government against the citizenry. Within socialist camps, patriarchal order and kinship-based restraints were criticized as backward or even reactionary. Between the East and the West, the "clashes of civilization" debate speculated an imaginative infusion of Confucianism with Islam as the realistic threat to the dominant Western civilization (Huntington, 1993). Now with the Cold War as history, it is time for one side to look into the other openly and honestly. Indeed, for any nation-state to tackle deviance, crime, and social problems effectively within and outside its borders, it must incorporate every useful element from both tradition and modernity, both socialism and capitalism, or both Eastern and Western cultures into its overall social control system.

A recognition that social control measures from opposing sources can be brought to work side by side further entails that no workable control approach shall be sanctified as a panacea for any single or set of social problems. In fact, each control practice works with specific people within their environment. When it is stretched beyond capacity, it will lose effect and may even pose a danger to what it is supposed to serve. For example, communal surveillance serves as a customary measure of neighbor reminding neighbor, relative correcting relative, colleague motivating colleague, or friend helping friend when it takes place informally in traditional, socialist, or Eastern cultural settings. However, it can lead to mutual distrust and distancing if it is imposed upon the community by governmental authority as a formal form of social control. Similarly, due process ensures openness and fairness in law and its application in modern, capitalist, or Western social conditions. But it may cause bureaucratic stalemate or legal impasse and, much worse, may even let loose serious criminals when it is pursued as sheer formality rather than substantive safeguard. The "no panacea" clause is especially important for developing societies as they look for sets of preventive measures or a system of interventional control that would ideally take care of all their problems once and forever.

At a global level, there should be an ideological consensus that no country, no matter how strong or successful it is, can serve as an example for the rest of the world to follow. In some stereotypical views, one country is considered as mired in traditional forces or burdened by a culture that does not facilitate social progress, whereas another is celebrated as a supermodel or superpower possessing everything that is key to order, justice, and prosperity. Now as traditional, socialist, and Eastern forces mingle with modern, capitalist, and Western factors across the globe, it is important to understand that no country symbolizes only one side of a contrast. In Asia and the Pacific, China is no longer an undisputable representative of tradition, socialism, or Eastern culture. Nor is the United States an identifiable model of the best of modern capitalism or Western civilization. With a no-model clause, developing societies can then learn useful lessons from many of their developed counterparts, not just one dominating player such as the United States. Similarly, developed nations can turn to different developing countries, not just China or India, for critical insight.

On the new ideological basis of no blame, no incompatibility, no panacea, and no model, there seems to be one natural outcome: a synthesis of thesis and antithesis. Specifically, social control must build upon and move beyond opposing forces to face an increasingly dynamic reality. Population in most nation-states is no longer homogenous in terms of ethnicity, education, ideological orientation, and political affiliation. In developing countries, trained managerial or technical personnel from multinational corporations mingle with illiterate migrant workers from hinterland villages. In developed societies, immigrants from the Third World disperse in affluent middle-class households as domestic workers. The community is no longer closely knit. People come and go. In their sojourn, they leave for work before dawn and return home at dusk. Nor is any community a sheer disarray of unrelated people and events. Residents still share common concerns and often comfort one another in times of difficulty. Social control, therefore, needs to be more flexible, specific enough to attend the needs of individual groups but general enough to maintain universal standards; quick enough to bring under control a particular troubled situation but gradual enough to gain understanding from the community; or informal enough to connect to the prevailing sentiment of its clientele but formal enough to demonstrate the soundness of the whole system.

Given the fact that tradition, socialism, and Eastern culture are losing ground to modernity, capitalism, and Western ways of life around the world, it is important that modern, capitalist, and Western forms of social control conscientiously learn from their traditional, socialist, Eastern counterparts in both general philosophy and specific approaches. In the United States, for example, leaders in both political parties have advocated social equality and universal justice, a cause that has much in common with socialism. Recently, conservative politicians have joined religious groups to emphasize the value of family and community in rearing the young. Community policing is gaining popularity in cities across the country (Barlow, 2000; Peak, 2006). The Office of National Drug Control Policy is working on a unified message through the mass media against drug use. In dealing with immigrants from Asian societies and former socialist countries within their ethnic enclaves, American law enforcement and court officials are learning to become more sensitive to the concept of cultural, religious, and social congruence. Hopefully, most of them will be able to apply the law in a way that is not simply professional but clearly humanistic, not just procedurally formal but somehow familiar to immigrants who come from different cultural, economic, and political systems.

Transfer of Control Technologies

In social control technology, hardware includes weapons, vehicles, communication devices, test instruments, and other high-tech equipment used in crime control. Software, on the other hand, may involve ideas about organization of a justice system, recruitment of police officers, training of correctional personnel, institutionalization of a legal procedure, adoption of certain prosecuting strategies, or implementation of new prevention or rehabilitation programs. In Asia and the Pacific, while many developing countries have yet to modernize their antiquated social control system with technology, developed nations need to overcome self-satisfaction, break away from the overuse of equipment, and look for continuing innovation in technology useful in social control.

Historical Background

Social control grows in technical complexity as forensic science expands its application of technology to criminal and civil laws enforced throughout the justice system. Forensic science begins literally with fiction when Sherlock Holmes was portrayed as having used techniques of serology, fingerprinting, firearm identification, and document examination in his criminal investigations (Berg, 1970). In real life, Mathieu Orfila established forensic toxicology as early as 1814. Alphonse Bertillon devised a systematic procedure of body measurements in 1879. Francis Galton published *Finger Prints* in 1892, while Albert Osborn put in print his book, *Questioned Documents*, in 1910. A simple procedure was developed by Leone Lattes in 1915 to determine the blood type of a dried bloodstain, while firearm examination techniques were refined by Calvin Goddard in the 1920s by the use of the comparison microscope (Inman & Rudin, 2000).

As specific techniques developed, Hans Gross coined the word *Criminalistics* and, for the first time, detailed the assistance that criminal investigators could draw from various scientific disciplines, such as anthropometry, fingerprinting, microscopy, botany, chemistry, physics, and zoology. On the practical side, Edmond Locard worked to build a crime laboratory in the police force so that scientific methods could be used in aid of real-world crime detection. With his phenomenal success in France, crime laboratories sprang up in countries across Europe, from Austria, Finland, Germany, and Holland, to Sweden, following World War I (Thorwald, 1967; Inman & Rudin, 2000).

In the United States, the first forensic laboratory was created in 1924 at the Los Angeles Police Department. A few years later, the Federal Bureau of Investigation (FBI) organized a comprehensive national laboratory that aimed to offer a full spectrum of forensic services to all law enforcement agencies in the country. Following the FBI model, a crime laboratory now typically includes such departments as those for physical science, biology, photography, firearms, and document examination, and various special units ranging from toxicology, latent fingerprint, polygraph, and voice print analysis to evidence collection. In 1981, the FBI opened its Forensic Science Research and Training Center to develop cutting-edge technologies and provide crime laboratory personnel with state-of-the-art training in forensic methods (Inman & Rudin, 2000; Theoharis, 2004; Melossi, 2008).

Another important development was the opening of the National Law Enforcement and Corrections Technology Center in 1994. Sponsored by the National Institute of Justice, the Center provides five critical services, bridging science with law enforcement and correctional practice. The first is to offer technological assistance in communications systems, evidence analysis, information-led policing, and school safety. The second is to develop performance standards and testing methods for public safety equipment. The third is to introduce emerging technologies to those who can use them through special events and demonstrations such as the Mock Prison Riot. The fourth is to address equipment needs by making federal surplus property available to local law enforcement agencies and correctional facilities for little or no cost. The fifth is to bring the research community and private industry together to put technologies into the hands of public safety officials. The Center now keeps a pool of product managers, engineers, and market research specialists who develop, manufacture, and distribute new products for the ever-changing needs of public safety practices.

Opposing Forces

As societies vary widely in socioeconomic development across Asia and the Pacific, social control exhibits a full spectrum of technological complexity: lack of technology versus a plethora of technology, low-level technology versus high-level technology, commonsensical wisdom versus artificial intelligence, and developing context versus developed environment.

First, the advantages of the system that has all necessary technology over the other's lack of technology are obvious: when police officers have to walk on foot to patrol a limited area while traffickers use vehicles, sea boats, or even airplanes to transport stowaways or contrabands over a long distance; and when social control agents in one country have to use their natural senses to check people and materials for entry from another country with advanced technology, where outflow of human and nonhuman cargos is fast processed by electronic devices. There are also disadvantages for the side that has a great deal of technology compared to its counterpart that lacks technology. For example, in the country lacking modern technology, a diligent investigator works with a criminal suspect to make the suspect confess, while in the country possessing advanced technology a polygraph machine may let go a lying offender. In the former country a responsible correctional officer keeps every inmate under his or her watchful eyes while in the latter country an electronic surveillance system may fail to detect an inflow of controlled substances or even the escape of a convict. At a general level, technology brings swiftness, effectiveness, and efficiency to social control, all of which make it natural for people to apply technology as fully as possible. However, since technology is not always dependable and use of technology tends to cultivate a state of dependency, no or little technology does not necessarily represent a complete loss of social control.

Second, the contrast of low-level technology versus high-level technology is probably more prevalent because the use of technology has expanded to almost every corner of the world. At centers of technological innovation there is a greater presence of technology and its higher-end products, whereas in various backwater regions of modernization there are remnants of older technology and its lower-end relics. For example, in rural areas police officers ride bicycles, carry old-style rifles, or depend on wired phone services, whereas in cities law enforcement agents bear high-precision firearms, patrol in well-equipped vehicles, and use wireless communication devices. Similarly, some transnational crime groups often outperform local law enforcement agencies because they have outspent their opposition on high-tech equipment. Low-level technology builds on mechanics. It aids but does not necessarily replace humans in substantive functions. With low-level technology, social control agents may still be able to activate their commonsensical responses whenever necessary. On the other hand, high-level technology develops from electronics. It does not just assist but oftentimes replaces humans altogether in major aspects of job performance. In a high-tech environment, agents of social control may end up depending solely upon external devices in their work.

Third, the contrast of commonsensical wisdom versus artificial intelligence figures in the debate because an absolute absence or a differential presence of technology not only defines the setting in which crime takes place but also determines the way by which social control reacts to crime. Technological products reflect human intelligence. In the sense that intelligence contained in technological equipment is external to and feeds back on any live agent who acts out of his or her natural intelligence, the former can be considered artificial. Obviously, artificial intelligence represents shared and externalized human knowledge. It frees people from hard labor or makes people effective in their job functions. Commonsensical wisdom, on the other hand, is what individuals possess and exercise in life. Although it is limited in scope, it connects people to their environment with all necessary sensitivity. As for social control, commonsensical wisdom is indispensable because it reminds agents of the human and social aspects of their work.

Despite all the technological devices they may have in hand, they still need to make active use of their everyday insights while working with people. Most important, in social settings where technology has yet to take root, artificial intelligence may alienate people from participation in first-line defense programs. With commonsensical wisdom, law enforcement officials do not just hide in armored vehicles; instead they stay in tune with the populace as fellow guardians. They do not just monitor people by high-tech devices; instead they join with common citizens hand in hand on day-to-day social interactions.

Finally, the contrast of developing versus developed environment is critical because it affects the first three comparisons. In a developing society, technology is likely to be either nonexistent or at a low level. There can be acute needs for technology and its higher-end products. Or there can be no need for technology at all. Resources for the acquisition of technology are likely to be lacking, while infrastructure for the use of technology remains inadequate. For example, many large cities in Asia and the Pacific struggle financially to meet their growing need for social control technology, especially high-tech equipment. The developed environment, in contrast, serves as the center for technological innovation in the first place. Infrastructure supports the application as well as a continuing upgrade of technology. Cost for technology is integrated in the budgetary process. Social control agents are tuned to the operation by way of technology. In fact, as technology is widely available and criminal elements are often savvy in the application of the most recent inventions, law enforcement functions properly only with adequate aid from technology and its higher-end products.

Obviously, it is most problematic when a social control system of no or low-level technology is overwhelmed by criminal groups who have access to higher-end technology. It is no less problematic, however, when law enforcement agents who depend upon technology are caught off guard by perpetrators who appeal only to commonsensical wisdom in their criminal undertakings. For instance, a police force entrenched in automobile patrol may suddenly lose its ability to pursue a suspect who abandons his or her vehicle and runs on foot into a forest. Or what aid can a surveillance system offer when offenders wear veils or whisper in each other's ear?

Synthetic Integration

Across Asia and the Pacific, a large number of developing societies are in urgent need of importing such hardware as weapons, communications devices, laboratory instruments, and other high-tech products used in crime control (Pawar & Goyal, 1994; Inman & Rudin, 2000; Wong, 2007; King, 2009). Regarding software, both developing and developed countries need to learn new training methods, apply new codes of conduct, institute new legal procedures, adopt new prosecuting strategies, and implement new prevention or rehabilitation programs for a social control system of high efficiency and integrity (Theoharis, 2004; Welsh & Harris, 2004; Benekos & Merlo, 2006; Goldsmith & Dinnen, 2007; Clements, 2008; Melossi, 2008).

The importance of technology is most apparent in emerging societies because (a) emerging societies are faced with rising deviance, crime, and social problems; (b) they do not have much technology to begin with; and (c) technology is at the center of their socioeconomic emergence. To interdict organized crime groups from smuggling aliens or contrabands, coast guards, customs officials, and border patrols need to make use of high-speed sea boats, four-wheel-drive vehicles, and high-tech surveillance devices. Watching with the naked eye or chasing on foot becomes inadequate to handle the increasing flow of people and materials in and out of border crossings, and to respond to well-equipped criminal operations. To contain social unrest upon rising unemployment and widening social gaps, law enforcement officers need to specialize in applying mass deterrence or dispersal measures such as high-pressure water and tear-gas grenades. Most important, police officers, prison guards, and social workers need to be educated about civil liberties so that they treat subjects professionally while staging a necessary intervention. In China, more and more police stations are switching from foot patrolling and bicycle policing, procedures which are still used in established neighborhoods in Japan, to American-style automobile patrols for more effective crime control in sprawling industrializing metropolises (Bayley, 1991; Bakken, 2007). In prisons, reeducation shifts from thought reform to vocational training. The correctional system as a whole is becoming more open to successful rehabilitation programs around the world (Shaw, 1998; Terrill, 2007).

Importing and learning bring different sides closer, making social control systems more similar across the world. First, "borrowers," "lenders," "importers," "exporters," "learners," and "teachers" are relative terms. Countries that borrow technology offer sites or lend space for technological application. Nations that import technology provide funds or export capital for technological replication, and further, technological innovation. Societies that learn technology contribute feedback or teach how technological products can be modified for different users or improved for different operational conditions or social environments.

Specifically, borrowers, importers, or learners need to know the past, the present, and the future when they decide what and how much technology they can incorporate in their social control system. They ought to remember that there were positive social mechanisms in place to keep crime low in older times before they contemplate a wholesale installation of technology. In the meantime, they should recognize that there are inevitable social forces on the horizon to drive up crime in the new era when they lean toward downplaying technology as a wasteful luxury. In fact, technology has become so intertwined with crime that it is impossible to fight crime without technology. Most important, learners must take an active role in the process of learning. They must learn to command and invent rather than be commanded and changed by technology in social control operations.

Lenders, exporters, or teachers, on the other hand, need to overcome a general sense of advantage they feel they have over their counterparts. They must admit that technology, high technology, or artificial intelligence can learn from no technology, low technology, or commonsensical wisdom. They also need to understand that it is difficult for technology to take root in a changing society. Most important, they should refrain from using technology as a weapon to break into a market for usurious profits, as an excuse to interfere in the internal affairs of a society, or as a bargaining chip to gain preferential treatments in bilateral dealings. Indeed, only when they move beyond individual interests can they share state-of-the-art technology or donate their phased-out, yet still well-functioning, equipment for use in undeveloped or developing environments for the common good of mankind. In the real world, it is often the lender, exporter, or teacher who stands in the way as the first barrier to technology transfer. For instance, between developing socialist states and developed capitalist countries, the latter enforces a technological blockade from time to time so that the former does not benefit from the most advanced technology in national defense and social order maintenance. Between India and Japan, the latter may set the price of a technology so high that the former just cannot afford to import it for use in social control. Between Mexico and the United States, if the latter is modest in its international manners, the former may feel comfortable in cooperating with the latter or may even receive excess technology and surplus equipment from the latter for use in joint control operations along the border.

Professionalization of Control Forces

Professionalization involves both individual members and system components. On the part of individual members, they need to meet basic educational requirements, master essential knowledge and skills, internalize occupational codes of conduct, and specialize in a line of duty with professional competency. Within the social control system, professionalization means that a division of labor is maintained, roles and ranks are differentiated, and procedural restraints are instituted to ensure that control organizations and operations run with autonomy, effectiveness, efficiency, and integrity. In Asia and the Pacific, professionalization of control forces seems inevitable when new ideas are introduced and new technologies are applied in different social control settings.

Historical Background

Professionalization of social control begins with the regularization of the police. In English history, members of a tithing formed the "frankpledge" in the eleventh century to keep order in their community. The system gained strength later with the assignment of a king's representative, the *reeve*, in each shire or county. The shire reeve, or sheriff, drew assistance from a *posse comitatus* composed of able-bodied citizens when he executed summonses, enforced the laws, and presided over the court. As the population grew into larger towns, more control titles such as constables, night watchmen, and justices of peace arrived on the scene. However, it was not until the industrial revolution that a system of professional police force came into being in England.

As in England, colonial America saw social order or disorder placed in the hands of county sheriffs, town marshals, constables, and *posses* composed of civilians. Uniformed police forces appeared late in American cities in the nineteenth century when immigration fueled growing hostility toward minorities, resulting in mob violence and social unrest. For decades after the establishment of various municipal police forces, however, law enforcement in the United States was disappointedly mired in politics. Officers were admitted to the force without explicit standards. They received little training and supervision, and tended to be corrupt and abusive on the job (Walker, 1992; Melossi, 2008).

The chronic problem of untrained and corrupt police generated pressure for serious reform. Early in the twentieth century, progressive reformers started to work on the professionalization of the police force around the country. August Vollmer, a pioneer in the reform movement, argued that a professional police force should take crime fighting as its primary responsibility. To fulfill its professional duty, it needs to be nonpolitical, well recruited, well trained, well disciplined, and equipped with technology. Vollmer's student, Orlando Wilson, also made significant contributions to modern policing in the area of management and administrative techniques (Walker, 1992).

Opposing Forces

Professionalization is inherently connected to secularization. On the one hand, social control agents have a vested interest in gaining occupational prestige by becoming trained with systematic knowledge, comprehensive skills, sophisticated protocols, and advanced technology. Members of the populace have a desire to expect fair treatment and secure protection from a police force that looks professional in their eyes. On the other hand, social control agents need to connect to the community to the extent that they are part of rather than above the local society. People in the general public want to relate to social control personnel to a degree that they do not just revere them as crime fighting professionals, but also can count on them as community service agents. In Asia and the Pacific, while in some developed contexts social control falls into the professional cage as an alienating force to its serving public, in some developing or undeveloped environments social control is so mired in the masses that it is often unable to distinguish itself for routine functions. For example, in the United States there is often community uproar over excessive force used by the police, whereas in an economically depressed country there may be public lootings in which police officers join street mobs in taking others' properties for their own use or possession.

Within the sphere of professionalization exist four pairs of focal interests. Professionalization in form emphasizes uniform, equipment, procedure, and physical layout. Grounded in materialism, it believes that a social control force takes a professional outlook when its members wear standard uniforms, bear advanced firearms, and follow explicit procedures, or when it as a whole is housed in an awe-evoking building complex and armed with state-of-the-art equipment. For example, China has made a national effort to put all its police officers, prosecutors, judges, and correctional guards in standard uniforms so that they all stand out from the crowd as professionals in social control. Professionalization in content, on the other hand, focuses on knowledge, skills, rules, and cultural norms. Drawing from idealism, it argues that a social control force becomes professional only if its members command expert knowledge, master specialist skills, and are competent in each specific area of their duty, or if it overall is tempered with institutional restraints, is separated from partisan politics, and resonates with the general public. In some Asian countries, motorists sometimes can buy their way out of a traffic violation by submitting to the examining officer their driver's license with cash inside or underneath it. The officer may look professional in every physical aspect. However, when he or she takes bribes on duty, people can only wonder what is left professionally under his or her seemingly professional cloak. Indeed, form is empty without content.

In another dimension, technological professionalization concerns what and how much members of a social control force know about their profession, its recent developments and essential techniques, or whether the entire force itself keeps pace with scientific process. The test of its technological capacity is the readiness with which a control system reacts to changing dynamics in crime, deviance, and social problems. Moral professionalization, in contrast, regards what ideology a social control force upholds, which party it protects, and how committed it is to its cause. As for individual members, moral professionalization requires that they follow a code of conduct and serve as role models for the general public. For example, in capitalist countries law enforcement agents pledge to be loyal defenders of democracy, whereas in socialist states social control professionals vow to be humble servants of the people. In both capitalist and socialist contexts across Asia and the Pacific, technological professionalization proceeds often after moral professionalization is on track. Obviously, police officers would not explore far into a technology that shields them from ordinary people if they are taught to be of the people and for the people on their job. Similarly, they would learn ways of connecting to the people when community policing is touted as a moral guideline.

Still another dimension is organizational versus operational professionalization. The former eyes the way the social control force is set up, its recruitment procedures, training protocols, evaluation processes, disciplining policies, and even facilities or equipment, especially as to whether the overall appearance gives the public a sense of organizational efficiency and sanctity. The latter, in contrast, measures the degree of effectiveness with which the social control force operates amid its professional tasks, from fighting crime to containing social disorder to dealing with an emergency. In Asia and the Pacific, while some social control forces are so bureaucratized that they often fail in the face of a large-scale attack or disaster, some law enforcement agencies are so agitated to respond to social contingencies, one after another, that they rarely settle into their everyday functions.

Finally, professionalization for impression is outwardly oriented to the public and public image of the social control force. When individual members behave professionally on their duties, they earn a favorable reputation of competency, dependability, and respectability for the force as a whole. Professionalization for efficiency, in contrast, is tied to the administration and its handling of social control operations. Are there mechanisms in place to keep one branch in balance with another? Are there watchdogs on site to minimize waste and expose corruptive practices? Is the social control force overall effective and efficient in terms of operational performance, managerial process, and taxpayer accountability? In Asia and the Pacific, there are closed states that sometimes spare no effort in putting a positive face on their social control force in the public eye, especially on the eve of a national event that is a spectacle to the outside world. There are also open societies where a control force is routinely scrutinized by different interest groups for its integrity or effectiveness, so much so that it wonders if it can afford to spend enough on any image-building campaign in public arenas.

Synthetic Integration

Professionalization of social control may begin with different dimensions. A country that already has a formal social control force in place benefits most when it fashions its professionalization in the direction of secularization, furthering substance, morality, operation, and efficiency to balance its routinized formality, technology, organization, and public image. In the United States and other developed economies, social control is integrated into the political system. There are law schools to prepare lawyers, prosecutors, and judges; police academies to train law enforcement agents; and other formal procedures to screen people for correctional staffs. Social control personnel move up or down along a civil service system or through a democratic mechanism. The social control force as a whole is organized, giving the populace a general image that it is up to the challenge of its task. Now the question is, how closely it connects to the people and their changing social life? Specifically, does it spend taxpayer's money wisely? Does it put people first in all its activities? Do all its members take to their heart the fundamental rights of people? Do social control personnel resonate with prevailing sentiments in their community?

In countries where social control remains immersed in civil vigilance, political manipulation, and economic domination, establishment of an independent police force is the first step toward professionalization. Members of an emerging force may not necessarily understand all the knowledge, skills, and procedures pertaining to their job. However, as long as they patrol the street in uniform, they create an impetus for progress, from moral disciplining to technological learning. As long as they function within organizational constraints, they build pressure for procedural clarification, structural improvement, and systemic advancement. In fact, only when they have moved enough in the direction of technological or physical professionalization can they determine how much secularity or community connectedness they want to keep in their professional outlook.

Japan, Singapore, Hong Kong, and a few other developed societies across Asia have each kept much of their fine tradition in social control, especially communal embedment and social connection, while making significant strides in technology, bureaucratization, and formalization. For both developed and developing societies, control systems in these societies serve as models in blending tradition with modernity, more generally, in achieving a genuine synthesis of various seemingly opposing developments in the sphere of social control professionalization.

On the international stage, social control systems in developed, democratic, and capitalist countries are generally high on professionalization, not only in terms of form, technology, organization, and public impression, but also in terms of content, morality, operation, and managerial efficiency. In developing, undemocratic, or socialist states, however, most social control forces still struggle to overcome their own technological simplicity, operational irregularity, and organizational inefficiency for a better professional image in the eyes of the public and greater independence from the dominant structure of power. In Asia and the Pacific, an encouraging development in closing the gap first arrived on the scene when China sent some of its would-be social control personnel to study law, technology, and professional protocols in the United States and other Western societies. Now as terrorism and organized crime emerge to become a common threat to international order, individual countries seem to be more and more willing to look to each other for insightful ideas and effective measures in social control. Only through mutual learning can true professionalization take place, as well as a synthesis of control systems for the world as a whole.

Modernization of Control Systems

At the system level, social control faces a general challenge of modernization, above and beyond change of ideology, transfer of technology, professionalization, or any combination thereof.

Historical Background

As part of the social control system, law enforcement has pursued its own modernization on many different fronts. Externally, it first sought to become independent from politics. With regard to the community, police officers and police departments initially emphasized fighting crime and enforcing the law as their basic duties. However, when they realized that crime fighting and law enforcement functions had alienated them from the community, they experimented with various innovative methods to change their public image. Internally, efforts were made from time to time to improve procedures for recruitment, training, performance, evaluation, and disciplining. With regard to organization, attempts to streamline structural establishments, standardize procedural protocols, and improve managerial cost-effectiveness surfaced from place to place as goals on various police reform agendas. In the United States, following a long path of modernization, policing now revolves around law enforcement, order maintenance, and community service. The community service function engages many American local police forces in foot patrols, bicycle patrols, team policing, problem-oriented policing, and community policing, all of which help police departments overcome public distrust, defuse social tension, and build cooperative relations with the general populace (Walker, 1992; Peak, 2006; Melossi, 2008).

The court initially referred to the castles occupied by the king, the queen, and nobles. Since it was also the place where important business was conducted, the court was later equated with power and its massive apparatus. For example, the court of the King of England symbolized the authority he held over all of England and beyond. Justice, as part of power, was determined in the court. The guilt or innocence of a person accused of a crime was adjudicated through a trial procedure. The trial was a time for adversaries to confront each other in open court. The judge ensured that procedures were followed. He pronounced judgment when the trial was over. The British common law took root in the New World. Over the years, in its drive for modernization in the court system, the United States has made efforts to specify jurisdictional interfaces between state and federal courts; to clarify the roles of prosecutors, defense counsels, civilian jurists, and trial judges through criminal proceedings; and to standardize penal dispositions in the aftermath of a conviction. Guiding these efforts are four principles: due process, fundamental fairness, judicial impartiality, and sentencing comparability (Meador, 2000; Segal, Spaeth, & Benesh, 2005).

Corrections take place in the process that implements sentences imposed by the court. In the Old World, major penal inventions included the use of spectacular executions, experimentation with galley slavery, establishment of Bridewells, building of panopticons, and transportation of convicts to the colonies (Morris & Rothman, 1995). In the New World, the first systematic effort was to use the penitentiaries for separate confinement or congregate labor. A reformatory movement attempted to end the imposition of suffering on convicts and substitute it instead with moral regeneration and reformation. From World War I to World War II, a medical treatment model gained popularity when psychiatrists and psychologists became involved in the treatment of inmates and the reform of the penal system. As the medical model developed into a more general therapeutic and rehabilitative approach, community involvement rose to prominence. Probation, parole, halfway houses, work release, and other community diversion projects were used in later years. Beginning in the 1960s, a prisoner's rights movement started to build momentum. Through legal battles, the movement has eventually won for prisoners all the rights guaranteed by the Constitution. Now in the face of overcrowding and various court-sanctioned reforms, the American correctional system is more than ever in need of innovative ideas and practices, which may include such recent developments as probation with intensive supervision, home confinement, restitution, community service, shock incarceration programs, and systems of fines (Clear, Cole, & Reisig, 2005; Melossi, 2008).

Opposing Forces

Figuring first in the debate is system integration. Supporters hold that law enforcement, the court, and corrections must coordinate with each other to save taxpayers' money, minimize organizational friction, and serve the interest of social control. It is a waste of resources as well as a blow to social order when the police work to catch criminal suspects, many of whom were those former inmates corrections sought for early release. System integration helps fight abuse, contain corruption, and improve efficiency when the court intervenes to order reform for the prison. But to what degree does a court-imposed order become an unnecessary interference in a correctional system's independent functioning? Opponents thus maintain that law enforcement, the court, and corrections are separate entities, each of which has its own tradition to continue and its own mission to fulfill. Around Asia and the Pacific, individual social control components have yet to develop and differentiate in many undeveloped or developing societies. A premature push for integration can only cause harm to the much-needed growth of each component in an emerging social control system.

Another argument revolves around the role of politics in social control. People who call for independence from the political process argue that crime is a general social challenge. Fighting crime is to the benefit of all. A modernized social control system distinguishes itself by going beyond and staying above the interests of groups and social classes. It maintains social order for the common good of an entire society. People in favor of political integration, on the other hand, insist that crime is socially defined. Social control is part of the political establishment. A modernized social control system is clear on what interest it stands for, what social order it defends, and what group it protects. In fact, only when it aligns well with the political process can social control become purposeful and effective. The alignment explains why social order tends to be definite and routine in traditional or authoritarian societies where social control falls firmly in the hands of the ruling class. In free and democratic contexts, on the other hand, social order becomes diverse and changeable, often because social control agencies are out of alignment with political power.

Still another argument focuses on synchronization with the general public. Supporters point out that crime occurs among people. When citizens take actions to ensure their own safety, they can change the whole crime scene. Social control, similarly, is people's business. When social control professionals work with people in the community, they can function not only as a force of deterrence against crime, but also as a net of service for peace. The more a social control system is modernized, the better it will resonate with people in society. Opponents, in contrast, place faith in the neutrality of social control. To ensure its integrity, social control needs to be exercised at some distance from the community. Across the developing world, it is not uncommon that social control forces fail in popular votes of confidence because they are so mired in communal affairs. For the same reason, some social control forces even lose the trust of the government under which they are supposed to operate. In a sense, a modernized social control system is one that transcends specific communal interests so that it can relate professionally to the public as a whole.

The fourth point of debate surrounds the use of technology. The general consensus is that modernization goes hand-in-hand with technology. No social control system qualifies as modernized if it does not incorporate a sufficient amount of technology in its structure and operation. However, there are critical divisions. In developed societies, technology has penetrated so many aspects of social control that it creates a state of dependency. Social control succeeds when technology is advanced. Social control professionals become stranded when equipment fails. In developing countries, on the other hand, technology is so lacking that social control personnel either wonder what technology could do for them or fantasize about how technology might revolutionize their job functioning. Between developed and developing nations, there are sometimes struggles that involve the former's attempts to sell technology versus the latter's efforts to mobilize resources to acquire it, the former's desire to withhold sensitive high-tech patents versus the latter's willingness to duplicate common low-tech instruments, or the former's interest to maintain technological supremacy versus the latter's motive to foster its own ability to invent.

Finally, in the debate on discipline, some argue for discipline from outside, whereas others advocate discipline from within. Supporters of the former look beyond the control apparatus to find social mechanisms, such as mass media and civilian involvement, that keep social control agents and agencies in check regarding use of power and performance of duty. Supporters of the latter, in contrast, delve into the control system itself to identify institutional means—internal audit, periodic evaluation, reward, punishment—to make control personnel perform and control units operate within the bounds of efficiency and professionalism. As to the content of discipline, some emphasize competency and efficiency on the basis of knowledge, technology, and organization, whereas others stress loyalty and commitment with respect to ideology, political affiliation, and social integration. For example, to those who believe more in moral than technological input in self-discipline, a modernized social control system is one in which control professionals serve as role models for the citizenry and control organizations commit to the protection of the social establishment.

Synthetic Integration

Regardless of social context, a modernized control system must have a rational division of labor while allowing for mutual supervision and support among its individual parts. It must maintain sufficient autonomy while remaining current in political processes. It must also rise above group or class interests while resonating with general social sentiments. Technology is used to the extent that it is in line with institutional resources, personnel competency, and traditional means of social control. Discipline is maintained in the sense that due process, equity, and justice procedures are in place to reconcile institutional requirements with individual performance, technological proficiency with moral conscience, and social demands with organizational reality.

Within individual societies across Asia and the Pacific, people in developing contexts may put system integration on the backburner when they struggle to expand each social control component. To win support from the government as well as the populace, a growing social control system may not be as assertive as it would like on the issues of independence and impartiality. Use of technology can only be pursued in a piecemeal fashion as resources are lacking, staff personnel are ill prepared, and the infrastructure remains poor. Discipline may hinge more upon individual conscience than institutional safeguards, more ideological brainstorming than technological learning, or more external scrutiny than internal review. In developed countries, by comparison, greater system integration is in order since each social control component itself is established, and sometimes, entrenched. Better coordination with the political process is needed because claims for autonomy can push social control to a point where it serves more of its own interests than those of society. More synchronization with the general public rises to the forefront, as the interests of the community are often sacrificed to the needs for equipment and bureaucratization. Similarly, widespread use of technology can be compensated by focal application of commonsensical wisdom and communal heritages so that harmony is kept among people rather than brought from the outside, and order is maintained within a society rather than imposed from above. Finally, in an era when people count on external forces, such as technology and the media, to elicit desirable conducts, self-discipline and internal corrections can be particularly appealing forces that encourage positive behavior.

On a global scale, synthesis calls for dialogue between modernizing and anti-modernizing forces. Among forces of modernization, developed societies possess capital, manpower, and an infrastructure to produce and export consumer products, management protocols, and technology in every arena of life, including social control. Developing countries are pressured to give up tradition, import technology, and undertake reform as they open up to the outside for opportunities toward social prosperity. And criminal elements become organized to the extent that they are able to acquire technology and achieve operational effectiveness at a level comparable to or even higher than some formal social control agencies. The situation challenges authorities to pursue further modernization. Anti-modernizing forces, on the other hand, feature postmodernization in developed nations where work on specifics, harmonization with localities, and synchronization with temporalities make their way to fill blanks left by standardization in the modernization drive. Thus, community policing, diversion, and restorative justice gain popularity as alternatives to crime fighting, imprisonment, and retributive penology. Throughout the developing world, anti-modernizing forces often manifest in grassroots initiatives, patriotic fervor, citizen vigilance, or mass justice. On the part of criminal elements, there are still perpetrators who appeal to superstition, religion, and custom when they offend. The reality calls for more human-focused work rather than technology-centered intervention. For example, how much technology is needed to prevent and catch fortune-tellers, members of a religious cult, or miraculous healers who prey on local residents for money and sex?

As opposing forces confront each other in equilibrium, they create a collection of premodern, modern, and postmodern residues on the face of the earth. In social control, modern as well as postmodern residues may range from spy satellites in orbit, surveillance devices within organizations, high-speed boats over the water, all-wheel drive vehicles on mountain terrains, and antiterrorist equipment throughout transit systems, to weapons and protective gadgets carried by squad teams on public streets. Premodern, anti-modern, or postmodern residues, in contrast, may include both acts and artifacts. As for acts, police officers walk on foot from block to block in the downtown district, giving residents and tourists a sense of protection. Undercover law enforcement agents mingle with ordinary people in everyday routines, spotting suspicious activities by specific groups and individuals. Older, traditional means of social control outside the public system can include dogs raised by residents to scare off strangers around private homes, hidden traps installed by farmers to catch thieves in the crop field, and simple shooting devices made by villagers to deter transgressors in isolated lands. In synthesis, a modernized social control system will incorporate the residues of traditional systems—what worked well down the years—as well as newer technologies.

Overall, to bring about a full modernization of social control in Asia and the Pacific, developed societies need to break down technological barriers, share advanced knowledge and effective practices, offer financial aid, provide professional training, and foster a spirit of co-security, co-safety, and co-prosperity. They also need to learn from developing or undeveloped experiences and preserve the best of their own tradition. Developing countries, on the other hand, need to overcome their own sense of disadvantage, recognize the value of their existing system, and face the challenge of their changing social reality while being open enough to embrace new ideas, methods, and procedures in social control. A synthesis of modernization in social control throughout Asia and the Pacific and around the world will inevitably lie in the fusion of science with common sense, technology with instinct, modernity with tradition, and professional outlook with community connectedness in the cooperative interface between developed and developing societies.

References

Bakken, B. (2007). *Crime, punishment, and policing in China*. Lanham, MD: Rowman & Littlefield Publishers.

Barlow, H. D. (2000). *Criminal justice in America*. Upper Saddle River, NJ: Prentice Hall.

Bayley, D. H. (1991). *Forces of order: Policing modern Japan*. Berkeley, CA: University of California Press.
Benekos, P. J., & Merlo, A. V. (2006). *Crime control, politics and policy*. Cincinnati, OH: Anderson Publishing.
Berg, S. O. (1970). Sherlock Holmes: Father of scientific crime detection. *Journal of Criminal Law, Criminology, and Police Science, 61*(3), 446–452.
Black, D. (1984). *Toward a general theory of social control*. Orlando, FL: Academic Press.
Chan, W. C. (2007). *Support for victims of crime in Asia*. New York: Routledge.
Clear, T. R., Cole, G. F., & Reisig, M. D. (2005). *American corrections*. Belmont, CA: Wadsworth Publishing.
Clements, P. (2008). *Policing a diverse society*. New York: Oxford University Press.
Cohen, S., & Scull, A. (1983). *Social control and the state*. New York: St. Martin's Press.
Davis, D. E. (2006). Undermining of rule of law: Democratization and the dark side of police reform in Mexico. *Latin American Politics and Society, 48*(1), 55–86.
Davis, N. J., & Anderson, B. (1983). *Social control: The production of deviance in the modern state*. New York: Irvington.
Deflem, M. (2006). Global rule of law or global rule of law enforcement? International police cooperation and counterterrorism. *The Annals of the American Academy of Political and Social Science, 603*(1), 240–251.
Du Guerny, J., & Hsu, L. N. (2002). *Toward borderless strategies against HIV/AIDS*. Bangkok: UNDP South East Asia HIV and Development Program.
Gibbs, J. P. (1981). *Norms, deviance, and social control*. New York: Elsevier.
Goldsmith, A., & Dinnen, S. (2007). Transnational police building: Critical lessons from Timor-Leste and Solomon Islands. *Third World Quarterly, 28*(6), 1091–1109.
Hirschi, T. (1969). *Causes of delinquency*. Los Angeles: University of California Press.
Horwitz, A. V. (1990). *The logic of social control*. New York: Plenum.
Huntington, S. P. (1993). The clash of civilization? *Foreign Affairs, 72*(3), 22–49.
Inglehart, R., & Baker, W. E. (2000). Modernization, cultural change, and the persistence of traditional values. *American Sociological Review, 65*(1), 19–51.
Inman, K., & Rudin, N. (2000). *Principles and practice of criminalistics: The profession of forensic science*. Boca Raton, FL: CRC Press.
Janowitz, M. (1975). Sociological theory and social control. *American Journal of Sociology, 81*(1), 82–108.
King, M. (2009). *Comparative policing: Contemporary issues in policing change*. Devon, UK: Willan Publishing.
Liu, J. H., Zhang, L. N., & Messner, S. F. (2001). *Crime and social control in a changing China*. Westport, CT: Greenwood Publishing Group.
MacMichael, P. (2003). *Development and social change: A global perspective*. Thousand Oaks, CA: Pine Forge Press.
Marx, G. T. (1997). Social control across borders. In W. McDonald (Ed.), *Crime and law enforcement in the global village* (pp. 23–39). Cincinnati, OH: Anderson Publishing.
Matza, D. (1964). *Delinquency and drift*. New York: Wiley.
Meador, D. J. (2000). *American courts*. Eagan, MN: West Publishing Company.
Melossi, D. (2008). *Controlling crime, controlling society: Thinking about crime in Europe and America*. Cambridge, UK: Polity.
Morris, N., & Rothman, D. J. (1995). *The Oxford history of the prison: The practice of punishment in Western society*. New York: Oxford University Press.

Nagel, S. (2003). *Policymaking and peace: A multinational anthology.* Lanham, MD: Lexington Books.

Newman, G. (1999). *Global report on crime and criminal justice.* New York: Oxford University Press.

Pawar, M. S., & Goyal, R. M. (1994). Computer crime in Bombay: Efforts to alert this problem. *International Journal of Offender Therapy and Comparative Criminology, 38*(3), 241–246.

Peak, K. J. (2006). *Justice administration: Police, courts, and corrections management.* Upper Saddle River: NJ: Prentice Hall.

Reckless, W. C. (1961). A new theory of delinquency and crime. *Federal Probation, 25,* 42–46.

Reiss, A. J. (1951). Delinquency as the failure of personal and social controls. *American Sociological Review, 16,* 206.

Ross, E. A. (1901). *Social control: A survey of the foundations of order.* New York: Macmillan.

Roucek, J. S. (1978). *Social control for the 1980s: A handbook for order in a democratic society.* Westport, CT: Greenwood Press.

Segal, J. A., Spaeth, H. J., & Benesh, S. C. (2005). *The Supreme Court in the American legal system.* New York: Cambridge University Press.

Shaw, V. N. (1996). *Social control in China: A study of Chinese work units.* Westport, CT: Greenwood Publishing Group.

Shaw, V. N. (1998). Productive labor and thought reform: A historical and comparative analysis. *The Prison Journal, 78*(2), 186–211.

Shaw, V. N. (2002). *Substance use and abuse: Sociological perspectives.* Westport, CT: Greenwood Publishing Group.

Sung, H. E. (2006). Democracy and criminal justice in cross-national perspectives: From crime control to due process. *The Annals of the American Academy of Political and Social Science, 605*(1), 311–337.

Sykes, G., & Matza, D. (1957). Techniques of neutralization: A theory of delinquency. *American Sociological Review, 22,* 664–670.

Terrill, R. J. (2007). *World criminal justice systems: A survey.* Cincinnati, OH: Anderson Publishing.

Theoharis, A. G. (2004). *The FBI and American democracy: A brief critical history.* Lawrence, KS: University Press of Kansas.

Thorwald, J. (1967). *Crime and science.* New York: Harcourt, Brace & World.

Toby, J. (1957). Social disorganization and stake in conformity: Complementary factors in the predatory behavior of hoodlums. *Journal of Criminal Law, Criminology, and Police Science, 48,* 12–17.

Walker, S. (1992). *The police in America.* New York: McGraw-Hill.

Welsh, W. N., & Harris, P. W. (2004). *Criminal justice policy and planning.* Cincinnati, OH: Anderson Publishing.

Wong, K. C. (2007). Studying policing in China: Some personal reflections. *International Journal of the Sociology of Law, 35* (3), 111–126.

Xu, X. Y. (1995). The impact of Western forms of social control on China: A preliminary evaluation. *Crime, Law and Social Change, 23,* 67–87.

Growth and Development of Women Police in India

4

ADKI SURENDER

Contents

> You can tell the condition of a nation by looking at the status of its women. The Progress of a country can be judged by seeing the status of its women.
>
> **—Jawaharlal Nehru**

Introduction

The advancement in science and technology has brought changes in the socioeconomic and political perspective that exaggerated gender discrimination in the developed and developing countries in the world. India is one of the countries that provides equal justice to women by phasing out the disparities of gender. It is interesting to note that Indian women held an equal status with that of men during the Vedic period of 4000 bc, in fact, a superior position to men.* India is the original home of the Mother Goddess. The ancient history of India has many examples of women scholars and women rulers. Stories from mythology and folklore are recounted to prove that women in India have always been honored and respected. It is a matter of pride to note that India is one of the first countries in the

* Report (2006) on "Status of Women's Act in Empowering Women in Thanjavur District Tamil Nadu," submitted by Periyar Maniammai, College of Technology for Women, Thanjavur, T.N. India.

world to give women the right to vote and contest elections.[*] Thirty-three percent of seats are reserved for women in local government.[†] The Indian Constitution is one of the most progressive fundamental laws in the world, which guarantees equal rights for men and women.[‡] All this is cited as evidence to support the contention that Indian women are free and equal members of society.

The above discussion emphasizes the fact that in the transformation of society women are empowering themselves to achieve the status of equality on par with men and are able to exhibit their talents even in so-called male-dominated areas like the Army and the Police, both of which provide national security and maintenance of law and order. The development of any nation mostly depends on the maintenance of law and order, which is the primary objective of the public administration of the State. Of late, to achieve this objective, the State has recognized the need for women in the Police Force. This transition in the gender composition at the workplace has brought forth several issues such as discrimination, equality of opportunity, harassment, and so on.

An attempt is made in this study to analyze various dimensions such as the problems in regard to the induction of women in the Police Force; crime against women and involvement of women in crime; the role of the women police in discharging the functions of the Police Department such as maintaining law and order effectively; and the steady growth of the women police to ensure gender pride. This study, having contemplated all such issues, draws a few ways and means that would be helpful to improve the administration of the Police Department in enriching its objectives of serving the people more effectively with the effective role of the women police.

The assumption is that the government can provide security and criminal justice to women more effectively if the women in the police organization

[*] Smt. Pratibha Patil, the first Indian woman elected as President of India in 2007, which is the largely ceremonial post.

[†] 73rd and 74th Amendment Act of the Indian Constitution provides 33 percent of reservation for women in all elected Representations of the Local Bodies.

[‡] The Indian Constitution provides some provisions to ensure gender Justice, such as:

Article 14: Equality before Law.

Article 15/1: No discrimination by the State on the grounds only of Religion, race, caste, sex, place of birth and any of these.

Article 15/3: Special Provision to be made by the State in favour of Women and Children.

Article 16: Equal opportunity for all citizens in matters relating to employment or appointment to any office under the State.

Article 39/a: State policy to be directed to securing for men and women equally, the right to an adequate means of livelihood.

Article 39/b: Equal pay for equal work for both men and women.

(No discrimination by the State on the grounds only of religion, sex, place of birth or any of these.)

play an effective role in the implementation of laws. The emphasis is placed on utilization of the existing data, although a few attempts are made to generate primary data. Few interviews were conducted to get the opinion of the women police personnel in this regard.

Police in India

India is one of the oldest civilizations in the world. It has achieved multifaceted socioeconomic progress during the last 60 years of its independence. India is known as a subcontinent with a large area of 3,287,782 square kilometers and with a population of 1.02 billion accounting for 17% of the world population. The male population is 532 million and the female population is almost half of the total population, i.e., 496 million. The sex ratio is 933 per thousand men. It is a union of 28 States and 7 Union Territories. The total Police population of India as of January 1, 2007, is 1.51 million. The ratio of police, population, and area shows that every Police Constable covers 701 people and 2 square kilometers of geographical area in the country. The police system in India is one of the largest and oldest in the world.

The history of modern Indian Police can be traced back to 1861 when the Indian Police Act was passed. The Police is an important arm of the government. Article 246 in VI Schedule of the Indian Constitution designates the Police as a State Subject. Each State and Union Territory of India has its own separate Police Force, for which the respective State Governments frame the rules and regulations, which are contained in the police manuals. The organizational structure and working of the State Police Forces are governed by the Police Act of 1861, which is applicable to most parts of the country, or by the State Police Acts modeled mostly on the 1861 legislation including Andhra Pradesh.

The head of the police force in each state is the Director General of Police (DGP), who is responsible to the state government for the administration of the police force in the state. He gives advice to the government on police matters. The hierarchical structure of the police in India follows a vertical alignment consisting of senior officers drawn, by and large, from the Indian Police Service (IPS), who do the supervisory work. The "upper subordinates" (Inspectors, Sub-Inspectors, and Asst. Sub-Inspectors) work generally at the police station level, and the police Constabulary are delegated the patrolling, surveillance, guard duties, and law and order work. The Constabulary accounts for almost 88% of total police strength.

Though the Constitution of India has mandated "Police and Public Order" to be State subjects, there are certain provisions in the Constitution that empower the Central Government to intervene in some situations and perform special functions in police matters. It is the duty of the Central Government to protect the State against internal disturbances and to ensure that the governance of every State is carried on in accordance with the provisions of the Constitution (Article 355). To perform these functions, the Central Government maintains and deploys seven Para-Military Forces to assist the civil police, which are Assam Rifles, Border Security Force, Central Industrial Security Force (CISF), Central Reserve Police Force (RPF), Indo-Tibetan Border Police (ITBP), and National Security Guard (NSG). Apart from the above forces, other organizations include the Bureau of Police Research and Development (BPRD), Central Bureau of Investigation (CBI), Directorate of Coordination of Police Wireless (DCPW), Intelligence Bureau (IB), National Crime Record Bureau (NCRB), National Institute of Criminology and Forensic Science (NICFS), and the National Police Academy (NPA). It has been found that except for CRPF and CISF, no other groups have women police forces.

Policing is one of the world's most masculinized occupations. However, there is a glaring difference between the role of police in developed societies like the United Kingdom and the United States and developing societies like India. Many advanced countries have accepted a "citizen's police," whereas in India the police are still considered as a semi-military force. Traditionally, law enforcement has been viewed as a field exercise involving substantial use of physical prowess and, therefore, has tended to remain a mostly masculine job. Most police forces continue today as semi-military, strictly hierarchical organizations with deeply sexist views about women, and are deeply resistant to change.

The possibility of women functioning as full members of the police force and playing a role in achieving its objective was not well perceived in the early years of evolution of the police system. However, changes in the social situation, with increased association of women in performing field duties in several branches of administration, and the problems arising from increased juvenile delinquency and involvement of women in crimes, either as victims or accused, progressively necessitated the employment of women police officers as such in a variety of police tasks. Women police have now become an integral part of police forces in almost all countries of the world.* The employment of women in police establishments reflects not only socio-economic advancement, but also changes in the attitude toward the role of women in society.

Evolution of Women Police in India

Participation of women in the Indian police force is of recent origin when compared to other advanced countries. The United States was perhaps the

* Fifth Report (1977) of National Police Commission, Ministry of Home Affairs, Govt. of India.

first country in the world that recognized the need for women in the police force. Women had been involved in police work since 1845, when they were assigned as matrons in the New York City Police Department; it was not until 1893 that a woman was actually given the rank of "policeman"* with the powers of arrest. Subsequently, Canada inducted women in the police force in 1896, followed by Germany (1903), Australia (1915), Britain (1933), France (1935), Japan (1946), Singapore (1949), Italy (1959), and Israel (1960).

According to various studies, the origin of women police in India may be traced back to Kautilya's Arthashastra of the 4th century bc. Women were employed mainly as spies and armed women who guarded the harems of kings of ancient India. There are references also to Mauryan Kings who were guarded by Amazon women trained in the use of swords and archery. It is also said that trained tribal women resisted invaders alongside their men folk in the northern parts of India. The National Police Commission Report (1977)† shows that, in the past, as required under the law, the services of women as private individuals had been utilized casually as and when required for searching female persons in custody, but such women were not employed in the police force on a regular basis.

There is no record about the induction of women on a regular basis in the modern Indian police organization until the 20th century. The historical sources mention the use of women by police in India during the British rule to aid the suppression of brothels in 1919. However, the need for women police was first felt during the labor strike in Kanpur in the year 1938. In this strike, women laborers also participated actively by lying down at the entrance of the mill and obstructing the entryway. The police, called in by the management, had to face a very delicate situation of physically lifting the women workers. To meet any eventuality in the future, policewomen were appointed in Kanpur in 1938. The erstwhile princely state of Travancore also experimented with the appointment of women as Special Police Constables in the year 1939. In 1942, all these constables were absorbed into the regular police force. It is also reported that a few women were appointed in the port cities of Mumbai, Calcutta, and Chennai for frisking duty. Women were also inducted in the police force in greater Mumbai in the year 1939, and subsequently in the districts of Sholapur, Kolhapur, and Pune in 1950. However, women police were appointed in the police force on a regular basis in various states only after the independence of the country.

* Reports (2006) of International Association of Women Police.

† Fifth Report (1977), National Police Commission, Chapter XLII, Govt. of India, Ministry of Home Affairs. New Delhi.

Reasons for Induction of Women in Police

The realization of the need to have women in the police force can be attributed to the following conditions, which emerged during the pre- and post-Independence periods:

- The partition of India in 1947 in its wake brought endless misery, squalor, and moral degradation. The worst in man came out in full force. The honor and security of women became a problem. There were large-scale kidnappings, abductions, and sexual offenses. Relief Camps were started for unattached women, girls, and children. Policemen were needed to check Muslim women in *purdah* at border check posts. These circumstances necessitated the induction of women in the police force. Therefore, Delhi and Punjab police forces came forward to recruit women on a regular basis in 1948.
- Moreover, the partition of the country resulted in a large-scale influx of refugees from Pakistan to India, who suffered heavily due to communal frenzy. There was a rush of grief-stricken and distressed women who were approaching the government daily. To aid the grief-stricken females, women had to be inducted in the police force, which until then had consisted of men only.
- To provide security to Mrs. Indira Gandhi, the then Prime Minister of India, against intruders, the Delhi Police appointed women to the regular police force. Further, the Ministry of Relief and Rehabilitation also needed women police for the recovery of abducted women.
- The newly acquired independence, large-scale movements of the population in search of shelter and work, and rapidly changing socioeconomic conditions created a new dimension of policing in India. In several states political agitations, *bundhs* (closure of streets), strikes, and linguistic and communal riots were becoming the order of the day. The participation of women in the agitations was increasing every day. This created a new dimension for the law-enforcing agency, particularly in view of the delicacy of the problem of handling women agitators.
- Further, socioeconomic conditions also forced changes in the attitude and perception of Indian women and they started to demand equal justice and rights. These situations further added problems for policemen.

Due to the above changes the traditional law enforcement agency was confronted with the problem of bringing drastic change in the attitudes, behavioral pattern, and methods of functioning of their personnel. In the post-Independence years the Government of India enacted a number of social laws, such as the Hindu Marriage Act 1955, Immoral Traffic (Prevention) Act 1956, Dowry Prohibition Act 1961, Family Courts Acts 1984, Indecent Representation of Women (Prohibition) Act 1986, Commission of Sati Act 1987, Commission of Sati (Prevention) Rules 1988, and had taken various other measures for the protection of women and children.

The concept of equality in the Constitution of India, expansion of education among women, new avenues of employment, and the rapid growth in urbanization and industrialization were some of the socioeconomic factors that helped women in their struggle for liberation. The challenges of the new situations, particularly to deal with women and children, led to a growing realization among the police administrators of the necessity to have women in the force.

Crime Against Women

Apart from the socioeconomic and political developments that necessitated the induction of women in the police force, another important reason for the induction of women in policing was an alarming increase in the number of women and children as criminals, suspects, witnesses, and victims of crime. Although women may be victims of many of the general crimes such as murder, robbery, cheating, etc., only the crimes that are directed specifically against women are characterized as "crimes against women." Various new legislations have been brought and amendments have been made to existing laws with a view to handle these crimes effectively. These are broadly classified under two categories: (1) The crimes under the Indian Penal Code (IPC) and (2) the crimes under the Special and Local Laws (SLL). The following table shows the IPC & SLL crimes and crimes committed against women.

Crime against women is increasing faster in most countries including India, although it constitutes only a small portion of the total number of recorded crimes. Table 4.1 reveals that a total of more than 164,765 incidents of crime against women were registered in the country during the year 2006 as compared to 155,553 cases during 2005, indicating a marginal increase of 5.9%. The State of Andhra Pradesh has the highest number of cases registered, i.e., 13.4% of total incidents of crime against women in the country by a reported 20,819 cases. Torture cases registered highest in India followed by molestations, rape, and kidnapping. It has been observed that every 60 minutes almost seven torture cases and two rape cases were registered during 2006; overall, every day 451 cases were registered involving women. The proportion of crime against women under IPC is shown in Table 4.2.

Table 4.1 Classes of Incidents of Crime against Women during 2001–2005

Sl. No.	Crime Head	Year 2001	2002	2003	2004	2005	2006
1	Rape (sec. 376IPC)	16,075	16,373	15,847	18,233	18,359	19,348
2	Kidnapping (363 to 373)	14,647	14,506	13,296	15,578	15,750	17,414
3	Dowry (302 & 304B)[a]	6,851	6,822	6,208	7,026	6,787	7,618
4	Torture (498A)	49,170	49,237	50,703	58,121	58,319	63,128
5	Molestation (354)	34,124	33,943	32,939	34,567	34,175	36,617
6	Sexual harassment (509)	9,746	10,155	12,325	10,001	9,984	9,966
7	Importation of girls (366B)	114	76	46	89	149	67
8	Sati Prevention Act 1987[a]	0	0	0	0	1	—
9	Immoral Traffic (P) Act 1956[a]	8,796	6,598	5,510	5,748	5,908	6,124
10	Indecent Rep. Women (P) Act 1986[a]	1,052	2,508	1,043	1,378	2,917	3,014
11	Dowry Prohibition Act 1996[a]	3,222	2,816	2,684	3,592	3,204	1,469
	Total	**143,795**	**143,034**	**140,601**	**154,333**	**155,553**	**164,765**

Sources: National Bureau of Police Research and Development Reports, 2006, and National Crime Record Bureau.

[a] Special and Local Laws case.

Table 4.2 Proportion of Crimes against Women (IPC) to Total IPC Crimes

Sl. No.	Year	Total IPC Crimes	Crime against Women (IPC Cases)	Percentage of Total IPC Crimes
1	2001	1,769,308	130,725	7.4
2	2002	1,780,330	131,112	7.4
3	2003	1,716,120	131,364	7.6
4	2004	1,832,015	143,615	7.8
5	2005	1,822,602	143,523	7.9
6	2006	1,878,293	164,765	8.77

Source: National Bureau of Police Research Reports, 2006.

Table 4.2 shows the rapid increase of IPC cases against women from year to year. The proportion of IPC crimes committed against women to total IPC crimes has increased continually in six years from 7.4% in 2001 to 8.77% during 2006. The IPC component of crimes against women has accounted for 92% of total crimes and the rest (8%) were SLL crimes against women.

It has been observed that the number of cases registered against women has not crossed 9% of the total IPC cases. The discussions with the police officers, members of women commissions, and NGOs highlighted the fact that on the one hand women are not willing to register their cases due to various social reasons, and on the other the majority of the reported cases are not registered by police officers.

In the above circumstances, the men police find it very difficult to deal with women criminals in the detection of crime, at almost all the stages of arrest, search, and interrogation. The problem becomes too delicate when the woman is not the criminal but the victim of crime. By nature, Indian women are homely, shy, and not bold enough to talk freely about personal problems before policemen. Moreover, there might be many delicate matters that cannot be disclosed before the policemen, particularly in cases where the modesty of women has been outraged or in cases of kidnap or runaway girls. Even in other cases where exact information is to be extracted from women, the policemen find the job very difficult to get the true picture. Further, Section 51(2) of the Code of Criminal Procedure* also stipulates that whenever it is necessary for a female to be searched, the search shall be done by another woman with strict regard to decency. For this purpose, the absence of women police made the police officers hire women.

All kinds of violence against women outside and inside the domain of their home are essentially administrative, police, and legal matters. Voluntary organizations/civil society organizations have a small role to play in this, except for mounting pressure on the official machinery to act in a non-partisan manner. Lower level officials who deal with such cases are often lured by the enticements of the perpetrators of crime and work in such a manner that is against the spirit of criminal justice. In such cases the organizations mount pressure on the officials by reporting the matter to the higher officials, or to various bodies constituted for women like National and State Commissions for Women.

In view of the above problems, of late the government has come out with a separate police force with women and women police stations, called *Mahila Thanas*. These police stations were established in major cities and district headquarters of the States of the country. In 1973, the State Government of Kerala did a novel experiment by establishing a first-ever all women police station with one sub-inspector, two head constables and ten constables. Perhaps this women police station was the first of its kind in the country and the second in the world (the first being in Uruguay where a women police station was established in 1931). At present there are 326 women police stations in the country, which constitute 3.11% out of 12,702 total police stations

* Ghosh, S. K. and Rustamji, K. F. (1994), *Encyclopaedia of Police in India*, Vol. II, Part A, New Delhi.

Table 4.3 Strength of Women Police Forces during 2001–2006

Year	Total Strength	Women Police Strength	Percentage of Total Strength	Women Police and Crime Ratio
2001	14,79,024	24,413	1.65	5.89
2002	14,49,761	26,018	1.79	5.49
2003	14,33,217	41,939	2.93	3.35
2004	14,44,706	40,737	2.81	3.78
2005	15,30,389	39,954	2.61	3.89
2006	15,79,697	45,886	2.90	3.59

Source: National Resource Center for Women, New Delhi, 2006.

(see Table 4.3). An overwhelming majority of these, i.e., 60%, are in the State of Tamil Nadu alone with a total of 196 women police stations, followed by Andhra Pradesh with 26, Jharkhand with 22, Rajasthan with 14, Uttar Pradesh with 12, and Karnataka with 10 women police stations. The remaining states have fewer than 10 police stations. All of these women police stations are established at district headquarters and cities. However, there were 14 States and Union Territories where there were fewer than 10 police stations as of January 1, 2007.

The author would like to highlight the fact that after discussions with the female police officers these woman police stations have inherent problems. Their jurisdiction is the entire district; they are ill equipped in terms of communication and mobility; and their human resources are drawn from other police stations of the districts concerned. Moreover, the women cops are not tuned to the kind of work they are expected to do. On the one hand, women cops are trained to act firmly with criminals, and on the other they are supposed to act with sensitivity with women while working in the women police stations. Lastly, they have to engage themselves in normal policing duties with long working hours. Under these circumstances, it becomes quite difficult for them to discharge the role at the woman police station.

Growth of Women in Policing

The growing importance attached to women police has led to a large number of women being recruited into the police force. Almost all the States of the country have recognized the importance of women police and appointed a separate police force with women. Table 4.4 gives a detailed analysis about women police forces in the states of India.

The statement in Table 4.4 elucidates that by 1977 almost all the states in India appointed women police on a regular basis as they realized the need and importance of women in police. The approximate initial strength of women police was 473 by 1977, which has increased to 45,886 by 2006, almost more

Table 4.4 Details of Women Police in the States/Union Territories as of 2006

Sl. No.	Name of State	Year of First Women Appointment	Initial Strength of Women Police	Women Police Strength in 2006	Increase over Initial Strength	Total Police Strength in the Country	No. of Women Police Stations 2006–2007
1	Andhra Pradesh	1959	39	1,484	1,445	91,082	26
2	Arunachal Pradesh	—	—	65	—	5,718	—
3	Assam	1967	15	535	320	54,562	1
4	Bihar	1952	30	884	854	71,497	—
5	Chatisgarah		—	589	—	30,406	3
6	Goa		—	232	—	4,472	1
7	Gujarat	1948/1949	10	2,331	2,321	63,911	7
8	Haryana	1966	29	892	863	47,584	1
9	Himachal Pradesh	1966	42	152	150	14,700	—
10	Jammu and Kashmir	1965	33	1,541	1508	62,032	3
11	Jharkhand		—	1,934	—	47,427	22
12	Karnataka	1960	142	3,127	2,985	89,227	10
13	Kerala	1939	13	2,766	2,753	39,707	3
14	Madhya Pradesh	1961	NA	1,371	—	74,311	9
15	Maharashtra	1939	NA	6,850	—	177,737	—
16	Manipur	1961	07	251	244	16,475	1
17	Meghalaya	1973	08	84	76	10,234	—
18	Mizoram		—	156	—	7,874	—
19	Nagaland	1968	NA	259	—	19,960	—
20	Orissa	1961	27	342	315	38,989	6
21	Punjab	1949	49	1,515	1,466	71,907	4

(continued)

Table 4.4 Details of Women Police in the States/Union Territories as of 2006 (Continued)

Sl. No.	Name of State	Year of First Women Appointment	Initial Strength of Women Police	Women Police Strength in 2006	Increase over Initial Strength	Total Police Strength in the Country	No. of Women Police Stations 2006–2007
22	Rajasthan	1955	14	940	926	71,327	14
23	Sikkim		—	180	—	4,019	—
24	Tamil Nadu	1973	22	10,184	10,162	98,683	196
25	Tripura	1961	NA	777	—	23,681	1
26	Uttar Pradesh	1967	42	1,919	1,917	172,265	12
27	Uttaranchal		—	677	—	16,154	2
28	West Bengal	1949	NA	1,016	—	82,287	—
29	Andaman Nicobar		—	156	—	2,901	1
30	Chandigarh	1977	10	265	255	4,628	—
31	Dadra and Nagar Haveli		—	22	—	199	—
32	Delhi	1948	21	2,265	2,244	59,900	—
33	Daman and Diu		—	28	—	246	—
34	Lakshadweep		—	17	—	349	—
35	Pondicherry		—	80	—	3,246	3
	Total		**473**	**45,886**	**45,413**	**1,579,697**	**396**

Sources: Ghosh S. K. (1981), *Women in Policing*, New Delhi: Life and Light Publishers; and BPRD Reports, MHA, New Delhi.

than 96% added to existing strength. However, the total percentage of women police has not crossed 3%. Delhi was the first city to introduce regular women representation in the police force in the year of 1948, followed by Gujarat and Punjab in 1949. Chandigarh was the last Union Territory to induct women police in 1977. In Andhra Pradesh, women were inducted in the police force in 1959, three years after the formation of the State in 1956, by merging of Hyderabad and Andhra States (in the erstwhile State of Hyderabad women police were inducted in 1952) with the initial force of one sub-inspector, six head constables, and 32 police constables. The present strength is 1484, which consists of only 1.62% of the total police force of the State.

Further, as is evident from Table 4.4, appreciable progress in the strength of women police has been made especially in the southern States like Tamil Nadu, Karnataka, Kerala, and Andhra Pradesh, and in the west in Maharashtra and Gujarat, and among the northern States, Madhya Pradesh, Uttar Pradesh, and Delhi have shown special interest to increase the women police. In other parts of the country, like the northeastern States and some States like Jharkhand, Chatisgarah, Uttaranchal, which are newly formed states, have made special pains to build up a strong force of women police. Tamil Nadu from the south has the largest number of women police (10,184) and the Lakshadweep Union Territory has the lowest number (17). The growth of women police in the country during the last six years, from 2001 to 2006, is shown in the following Table 4.3.

Table 4.3 shows that during the year 2001 the strength of women police in the total police force was only 1.65%, which increased to 2.90% by 2006, indicating an increase of around 1.25% during the period. Regarding the strength of women police and crime ratio, during the year 2001 the women police and crime ratio was 5.89, which decreased to 3.59 by 2006, indicating an increase in the women force. Although there has been a steady growth in the number of women entering police service, the strength of the women force is far from adequate. In the years to come, it will be essential for the police to enlist and involve more and more women in their strength and tasks. The percentage of women police in the police forces of several other countries is much higher than India, for instance, in the United States it is 15%, in the United Kingdom it is 14%, and in Australia it is 15%.

To sum up, the representation of women in the security and police forces is very low, even to implement some rules of the Indian Penal Code, including the arrest and search of women offenders. The presence of women in the security forces will sensitize men toward "the fair sex." The Ministry of Women and Child Development feels that only economic empowerment can set women free and asked the Home Ministry to raise women's strength in the central security and police forces to 30%. The Ministry of Home Affairs,* government of India, has agreed to increase the representation of women in the police forces to 10% against the demand for 30%.

The study found after discussions with the women officials that there are a number of factors that are responsible for the slow growth of women police in India. First, the police service as a whole had a very poor image. It was known for its brutality, abusive language, indecent behavior, and corruption. The very idea of women from respectable families joining police services was unthinkable. Added to this was the male resistance for different reasons. Second, in many States women were appointed against the existing vacancies of policemen, which was bound to be resisted by them. Finally, it is also seen from the available sources that women police were employed in maximum numbers in the lowest subordinate ranks, in keeping with the general universal trend of the police organization. Table 4.5 highlights the strength of women in various ranks of police forces in the country.

The table explains the role of the women police in the Indian police force. It shows that until 2005 no woman police officer had become the director general of police (DGP) and nor reached additional DGP rank posts. In fact, since first entry of a woman in the Indian Police Service occurred in 1972† until 2006, no woman had matured to occupy the highest rank in the police force.‡ The table further elucidates that the women police strength was only 2.90% of the total police force during 2006 in the country. Of this, more than 89% of women personnel belong to the lower subordinates like head constables and constables. At the executive and policy-making levels of policing, very limited representation of women has been found. Top echelons of the uniformed ranks of IPS cadre posts, like superintendent of police to director general of police ranks, consist of only 2.71% women; the lower supervisory ranks, which are state cadre posts like assistant sub-inspectors to deputy superintendent of police rank, consist of 2.40%; and subordinate posts like head constabulary and below rank posts consist of 2.97% of women in the total police force.

To sum up, the above analysis shows that since Independence no action has been taken by the government to improve the strength of women police.

* Patil, Shivraj, Minister of Home Affairs, Govt., of India reported to Smt. Renuka Chowdhary, Minister for women and Child Development, Govt. of India on 8th June 2007.

† Dr. Kiran Bedi, was the first Indian Police Officer of India; she took voluntary retirement from the services in December 2007. The reason for her voluntary retirement was that she was never considered for the post of the Police Chief of Delhi.

‡ During 2005–2006 Smt. Kanchan Choudhry Battacharya was the first woman Director General of Police occupy the State Police Chief position in Uttaranchal State, and Ms. Latika Saran was appointed as the Commissioner of Police for a Metropolitan city of Chennai in 2006.

Table 4.5 Rank-Wise Strength of Women Police in Total Force as of 2006

Rank	Total Strength in States/UT	Women Police in 2006	% in Total Force 2006	% in Women Force
		Top-Level Officers		
Director General of Police	68	—	—	
Addl. DGPs	240	4	1.66	0.008
Inspector General of Police	477	9	1.88	0.018
Deputy IGs	575	10	1.73	0.021
Asst. IGP/Senior Superintendent of Police	2,772	89	3.21	0.19
Total	**4,132**	**112**	**2.71**	**0.24**
		Middle Supervisory Level		
Deputy SPs	9,989	215	2.15	0.47
Inspectors	24,014	513	2.13	1.11
Sub-Inspectors	85,628	2,937	3.42	6.40
Asst. Sub-Inspectors	85,279	1,270	1.48	2.76
Total	**204,910**	4,935	**2.40**	**10.76**
		Lower Subordinate Level		
Head Constables	248,385	4,087	1.64	8.90
Constables	1,122,270	36,752	3.27	80.9
Total	**1,370,655**	40,839	**2.97**	**89**
TOTAL	**1,579,697**	45,886	2.90	100

Source: Data on Police Organisation Reports, 2006.

It is also seen from the available sources that women police were employed in maximum numbers in the lowest subordinate ranks, in keeping with the general universal trend of the police organization. The need for women police increased with the rise in number of women accused, criminals, and victims of crimes such as rape, kidnapping, sexual harassment, dowry deaths, etc. It is surprising to note that apart from the various organizations like National Conferences of Women Police, the Ministry of Women and Child Welfare demanded for 33% of women in the total police force. But the Ministry of Home Affairs recently announced plans to improve up to 10% of women police.

Functions of Women Police

There is a serious confrontation regarding the distribution of duties to women police personnel all over the world. Women police officers are generally employed to carry out all police duties, but in many countries, including India, the women police have not been assigned all duties of the police jobs that could be assigned to women police. Particularly, it is seen that only male police officers perform motorcycle patrol duties and search-and-rescue duty.

A survey of the working of police women around the world shows that in the majority of countries, duties in connection with arresting, questioning, searching, and fingerprinting of women and juvenile suspects in crime investigation, and investigation of cases involving vices and sexual offenses such as rape or trafficking in women and girls are earmarked for performance exclusively by women police. In some countries, guarding of female prisoners in police lock-ups and escorting them to court are also assigned. In Pakistan, women police are assigned duties to register and investigate women cases only. Israel's women police comprise 90% of the excellent traffic police force. In Japan, a large number of women police are deployed on traffic duties. The use of women police on patrol and in crowd control duties has been growing steadily in the United Kingdom and the United States.* The experiences of the other foreign countries have proved that the induction of women in the police force can not only help to create a better image of the police, but can also bring down the crime rate. For instance, in demonstrations women police have a greater calming effect on aggressive behavior and elicit less violence and abuse than male officers.

There is no uniformity in the functions that are being performed by women police all over India. A number of Police Commissions at the State and National level have recommended a number of functions to be performed by women that are confined to women and children only. The Delhi Police Commission entrusted a few more duties like traffic control.

Based on several surveys and reports, it has been shown that in the performance of general functions in India, 80% of women police are utilized mostly in performing specialized tasks of dealing with women and children. The remaining 20% are utilized for traffic regulations, communication, and law and order. In this context, the National Police Commission (1977) has stated that women police have not been given an equal share in various areas of police work and recommended that they be more actively and directly involved in the police.† Further, the National Conferences of Women Police (NCWP; 2002, 2005), also emphasized that equal opportunities may be assigned to women police in allotting functions on par with male police. The government considered the recommendations of

* Ghosh, S. K. (1993), *Encyclopedia of Police in India*, Ashish Publishing House, New Delhi.

† Police Organisation in India (2001), Commonwealth Human Rights Initiatives, New Delhi, India.

the NCWP, which would pave a way to empower the women police to join the mainstream.

In Andhra Pradesh, women police perform functions mainly relating to women and child offenses, although traffic duties are also entrusted to them, especially in the district areas. In this connection, it is surprising to note that in Hyderabad, the capital city of Andhra Pradesh and fifth largest and fastest growing city of India, the women police have no role in traffic enforcement and regulations. The discussions with the police officers reveals that the Traffic Branch enforcement personnel are facing difficulties without women police in maintaining regulations and enforcing the traffic rules as more than 30% of vehicle drivers are women and their crime rate is not less than that of men.

Further, the discussion with the various ranks of women police personnel reveals that the main duties expected by women in the regular police force are the following:

1. Attending to complaints as duty officers in the reporting rooms of police stations
2. Escorting females accused or under trial to the courts or to lock-ups
3. Interrogating women victims in cases of rape, unnatural deaths of women, family disputes, etc.
4. Performing law and order duties
5. Recording first information reports (FIRs)
6. Communicating with women victims
7. Traffic regulations
8. Security jobs
9. Supervision
10. Controlling and working with juvenile delinquents
11. Controlling and supervising women demonstrators
12. Counseling women victims
13. Mediating in family disputes and solving family problems related to dowry, etc.
14. Performing miscellaneous jobs

Though women are expected to work with men on equal terms, in a country like India, people's perception of their role goes beyond the regular routine job of police personnel. Women police can play a major role in social change. It is felt that they need not copy the behavior pattern of their male counterparts, as women police can, in addition, help in sensitizing the police force toward the problems of women in society and family. Women police can help in upholding values, which can change the public's perception of police as a whole.

Perception of Women Police

The principles of new public management advocate clientele satisfaction as one of the important parameters to evaluate public organizations. Police across the world are no exception to this phenomenon. Efforts have been made by the police administration to create a positive situation in which their organization is perceived as an organization with good governance.

The Indian police are very much concerned to develop a positive perception of women police. The focus of this study was to secure police satisfaction in general and female policing satisfaction in particular (see Table 4.6). Efforts have been made to see whether police have succeeded in securing a positive image for themselves. In other words, an effort has been made by the researcher through the survey method to evaluate the reputation enjoyed by women police.

It may be necessary to outline the characteristics of the sample. The sample comprises 46 women police, which consist of 8 IPS cadre officers, 10 middle-level officers from sub-inspector rank personnel to assistant commissioner of police rank officers, and finally, 28 lower-level personnel consisting of assistant sub-inspector rank to constable rank personnel. This survey was confined to the Andhra Pradesh State only.

Regarding job satisfaction, a general feeling of the women police is that they are satisfied with their job. This opinion was expressed by 67.39% of respondents. However, intensity of the perception varies from category to category. This opinion was shared by 75% of the top-level officers who are

Table 4.6 Satisfaction of Women Police in the Organization

	No. of Women Police Officers			
Question/ Response	Top Level	Middle Level	Lower Level	Total
		Job Satisfaction		
Satisfied	6 (75%)	7 (70%)	18 (64.28%)	31 (67.39)
Not satisfied	2 (25%)	3 (30%)	10 (35.72%)	13 (32.61)
Total	**8 (100)**	**10 (100)**	**28 (100)**	**46 (100)**
		Attitude of Superiors		
Satisfied	7 (87.5)	8 (80)	20 (71.42)	35 (76.09)
Not satisfied	1 (12.5)	2 (20)	8 (38.58)	11 (23.91)
Total	**8 (100)**	**10 (100)**	**28 (100)**	**46 (100)**
		Social Recognition		
Satisfied	8 (100%)	8 (80%)	21 (75%)	37 (80.43)
Not satisfied	0 (nil)	2 (20%)	7 (25%)	9 (19.57)
Total	**8 (100)**	**10 (100)**	**28 (100)**	**46 (100)**

in a decision-making position. However, in the middle and lower category levels the satisfaction percentage decreased to 70% and 64.28%, respectively. In other words, a sizable number of women police (32.61%) expressed their unhappiness in the duties. It is interesting to note that the lower-level officers like sub-inspectors, head constables, and constabulary (35.72%) have a comprehensively negative opinion. An interesting feature of this finding is that sizable numbers of those who are at middle and top levels have expressed a positive opinion on job satisfaction.

Regarding women's satisfaction with the attitude of men police, the study showed a surprising result. More than 76% of women police expressed their satisfaction. In fact, top-level personnel had a higher percent of satisfaction whereas lower-level personnel expressed a lower percentage. More than 38% of respondents expressed their dissatisfaction with the attitude of men police. The reason is that lower-level personnel have been facing serious problems with odd duties, and a lack of transportation facilities and other facilities at the workplace.

Further, the survey found that regarding social recognition more than 80% of women police expressed their satisfaction. It is interesting to note that at the higher level 100% personnel have this opinion. But, at the lower level only 75% personnel have shown their happiness. At the middle level and lower level, 20% and 25% of personnel, respectively, are not satisfied with their social recognition. During the survey, the women police personnel expressed their desire to have women hired, evaluated, and promoted on their own merit and not as tokens to satisfy some statistical requirements of the government or some political needs. On the positive side, the women who were interviewed believe that women police bring special qualities and attributes to police work such as compassion, communication skills, and maturity.

To sum up, the women in the police force are satisfied with their job, social recognition, and relations with the men police. But, it has been found that at the lower level women personnel are not satisfied in all levels—top, middle, and lower. Taking this into account, the author feels that there is a need to take necessary steps to bring confidence to lower-level personnel and a need to provide safety and security at the workplace. The survey construes that women police may be treated equally and on par with men in all levels, and they should be provided special facilities at the workplace. At the same time they demand an increase in the strength as per the population ratio.

Conclusion

In any tradition-bound society, changes challenging the social structure are not accepted easily. The fact that it had taken a long time for women to stabilize themselves in the police department is testimony to this. With the commitment of the Government of India to bring about a socioeconomic change in the society and uplift the status of women, women's involvement in policing in increasing numbers is very essential. The study observes that in spite of the many steps that have been taken by the government to improve the role of women in police organizations, it still fails to achieve maintaining equality on par with men in all aspects. At the same time women are also facing injustice in their representation in policy making roles as well as in supervisory levels of police organizations. It is hoped that this study has provided reasonable evidence in support of the hypothesis formulated for the purpose of the study. Today the police force cannot perform its function effectively without the help of women police. Further, to improve the situation the study would like to make a few suggestions.

Suggestions

- In spite of many steps that have been taken by the government to improve the strength of women in policing, they are not able to reach even 3% in total strength. Many women organizations including Women and Child Ministry and National Women Police Conferences strongly feel that they can only do justice when the strength is improved. In view of the above feelings the study suggests increasing the strength of the women police force to 33% in total strength. To increase the representation of women in the police from the present national average of less than 3%, a phase-wise increase in the strength of women in police in all ranks through recruitment would be appropriate.
- The study suggests that women police should be made an integral part of the police force. They should be trained and employed to handle all job roles on par with men police and be entrusted more with mainstream duties of crime prevention and investigation.
- To expect a police woman to be not only a professional, but also a manager of her household, we have to ensure that she is given adequate wherewithal and opportunities to take care of both. It is suggested that the accommodation be provided on priority basis and ensure that her home is close to her workplace.
- Due to the odd times of the work the women police may be provided transportation facilities. Apart from this other welfare measures like a rest room, day care centers, and crèche facilities may be provided at the workplace.
- Due to the increasing crime rate of women and involvement of women in crime, necessary steps may be taken by the government to

establish All Women Police Stations (AWPS) in all States and reduce the jurisdiction to divisional levels instead of the existing jurisdiction of District areas. Further, in view of the increase in domestic violence the study suggests that in all States Women Counseling Cells/Women Protection Cells may be established to avoid filing cases and instead settle issues at the primary level.

- The study also suggests that for efficient and effective enforcement of police laws, necessary steps may be taken by the government to ensure that a sufficient number of women police should be appointed at all police stations; such steps may not only solve the women's problems but also bring drastic changes in the attitude of male police personnel.

References

1. Aleem, Shameem (1983), "Emerging Role of Women in Law Enforcement—A Study of Women Police with Special Reference to Andhra Pradesh", *Indian Journal of Public Administration*, Vol. XXIX, No.1. Jan-March.
2. Bouze, V. (1975), "Women in Policing", *FBI*, Vol. 44, September.
3. Ghosh, S. K. (1981), *Women in Policing*, New Delhi: Life & Light Publishers.
4. Ghosh, S. K. (1981), *Encyclopedia of Police in India*, New Delhi: Ashish Publishing House.
5. Lokamudra (1981), "Growing Importance of Women Police," *Social Welfare*, Vol. 28, December.
6. Jones, Sandra (1986), *Police Women and Equality—Formal Policy v/s Informal Practices*, London: Macmillan Press Ltd.
7. Indian Police Act of 1861, Ministry of Home Affairs, Government of India, New Delhi.
8. Criminal Procedural Code of India Act 1974. Government of India.
9. Fifth Report of National Police Commission (1980), Ministry of Home Government of India.
10. Basic Data on Police Organization of India (2006), Bureau of Police Research and Development, Ministry of Home Affairs, Government of India, New Delhi.

On Police and Policing in Slovenia
Obstacles and Challenges

5

GORAZD MEŠKO AND DARKO MAVER

Contents

Introduction

This chapter discusses some questions related to police-based research in Slovenia and its impact on police since the mid-1970s, when the first research into, and reflections upon, policing matters were publicized in Slovenian criminological literature. It is an overview of the most important research projects regarding policing in Slovenia between the 1970s and the present day. The focus is on significant developments and obstacles to police professionalism in Slovenia. In addition, problems related to police and policing in general and indications of individual and organizational disregard of human rights, the rule of law, and human dignity are discussed. If such obstacles are overcome, then we are convinced that the Slovene police will start to perform democratic policing in its broadest sense.

Efforts to develop a more professional police service are common to all societies. However, achieving such a goal requires substantial changes to be made to the professional culture of the police. This is especially true in post-socialist countries where the police are facing even greater degrees of change than any Western police force. A changing society also requires changes to the police and to their practices. Currently, one of the more popular policing philosophies is that of community policing, which has been incorporated into the mission and vision of many police forces worldwide. Community policing, as performed in the United States and the United Kingdom, has been tested in post-communist countries. The results of research (Beck, 2004; Meško and Lobnikar, 2005) have indicated numerous obstacles and dilemmas in its implementation. The main problem is still the transposing of foreign models of community policing without carefully adapting and changing them to fit the local (legal and cultural) conditions (Beck, 2004; Meško and Lobnikar, 2005). Contemporary policing is not only limited to community policing but also consists of the activities of other law enforcement policing agencies such as CID and other specialized police units. In order to better understand the present state of policing in Slovenia we will outline the origins of Slovenian policing, from a historical point of view, as well highlighting the contemporary priorities of the senior management of the Slovenian police.

The beginnings of the development of the Slovene police reach as far back to the Austro-Hungarian monarchy, to the year 1849, when the Gendarmerie Corps was founded. A century and a half is a substantial period and the police have, since then, taken increasingly self-confident steps toward being a modern police force that respects human rights and freedoms and which is aware that the rights of one person are limited by the rights of another (Kolenc, 2003).

Before 1991, the Slovenian police were part of the Yugoslavian police. Initially it was a centralized police force, although the Yugoslav police had gradually become more decentralized and transferred a lot of responsibilities to the individual republics within the Socialist Federative Republic of Yugoslavia. In that time, policing was a matter for the "milica" (militia) that was located in the Secretariat of the Interior, which was renamed the Ministry of the Interior in 1991 when Slovenia became an independent country. Slovenian policing since 1991 has been characterized by several attempts at police reform in order to move closer to a Western style of policing. Despite organizational and professional cultural obstacles, some changes have been achieved. The first reform project was initially called "Public Security" and was later renamed "The Police on the Local Level." The main goal of the project was to ensure that the Slovenian police would be comparable to modern European police forces. In addition, two further goals of the project were to achieve a higher level of professionalism and depoliticization within the police. One of the project group's results was the adoption of the new Police Act (1998). The most important innovation introduced in the Police Act was the changed status of the police. The new Police Act transformed the police into an independent agency under the auspices of the Ministry of the Interior. This new status of the police dramatically changed the relationship between the police and the Ministry of the Interior. While previously the Minister of the Interior was the highest person in the police chain of command, directly supervising its operations, the Minister of the Interior was now replaced in this position by a newly formed post of Director General of the Police, who was appointed by the government of the Republic of Slovenia. The Director General is, at least in theory, therefore a professional and not a political position. The person in this position should not automatically be replaced due to a change of government or Minister of the Interior. The police perform their tasks on three levels: state, regional, and local. Organizationally, it is composed of the General Police Directorate (state level), Police Directorates (regional level), and police stations (local level) (Pagon, 2005a).

The present orientation of the Slovene police is very close to the slogans of "protect and serve" used in Western European and American police forces. In addition to traditional policing, a type of community policing seems to be another central focus of the Slovene police. The Slovene police (Kolenc, 2003) have published a book on the role of the police in Slovenian society in which it is stated that the police are one of the guardians of national security who ensure that a high degree of internal security exists for all the citizens of the Republic of Slovenia by protecting the constitutional system, the democratic political system, human rights and fundamental freedoms, and other constitutional legal values. The work of the police is based on respect for and the enforcement of legal order, and the respect of European conventions and recommendations regarding ethnicity, professionalism, human rights, and fundamental freedoms. In modern, communication-oriented societies open-mindedness and effective communication skills are increasingly important for the achievement of high quality police work.

The directives laid down in the European Code of Police Ethics (Council of Europe, the Internet) with reference to transparency are adhered to when it comes to the education and training of the police. This is evidenced by the fact that, in addition to their internal education and training, police are required to take part in other forms of education offered by external institutions. The Slovene police also hope to accomplish transparency in their work by encouraging and supporting research into their activities by both the police themselves and by external institutions. In this respect, universities play a special role. Through research and cooperation with external institutions the police can scrutinize ethical issues in more detail. Such a requirement is defined by the principles of applicative realization of the imperatives of the police profession, the values of police work, and the virtues of the police, but also included in the establishment of standards of professional and ethical behavior. The Slovene police therefore have a number of strategic aims and directions. However, their basic aim is short and concise—to ensure the internal security of the Republic of Slovenia and to play a part in ensuring global security. A security system, which will enable high quality work and preserve public safety as one of the recognizable characteristics of Slovenia, can only be created in partnership with citizens who feel safe and secure, who can enjoy their life and thereby contribute to the development of society. "We are the security partners of the citizens" is the motto of the Slovene Police and this includes the mission and their aims (Kolenc, 2003; The Slovene Police, Internet).

The aspirations of the Slovene police are commendable, but in reality there exist many obstacles to achieving the stated goals of contemporary Slovene policing. What follows is a discussion of the problems that have been researched in Slovenia since the mid-1970s when the first scientific research projects on policing were conducted at the Institute of Criminology at the Faculty of Law, University of Ljubljana (Pečar and Skalar 1973; Skalar 1976). Prior to that date only a few publications exist and these were more related to theoretical commentaries surrounding police professionalism and efficiency rather than focused upon actual practical problems. Since 1990 the main research attention to police and policing problems came from the College of Police and Security Studies, an affiliated member of the University of Ljubljana, and formerly a department of the Ministry of the Interior's Educational Centre. The College of Police and Security Studies has subsequently developed into an academic institution, which now covers the entire scope of criminal justice and security studies and, in 2003, became the Faculty of Criminal Justice and Security at the University of Maribor.

Research on Policing before 1991

Pečar and Skalar (1973) discuss police–public relations. They state that police officers should know how to behave professionally, respect legal norms as citizens, and enforce laws as professionals. Furthermore, it is also important to know how to perform efficiently when on duty and serve citizens in order to create good police–public relations. The implication of their reflection is that police professionalism and accountability are the most important factors that contribute to positive police–citizen relations. The authors also suggest that the learning of basic communication skills and a code of conduct for police officers should follow principles of human communication, with an emphasis on respect for human dignity and individuality. They also discuss the importance of polite behavior among police officers during police procedures. In fact, they require more than that, namely, professional attitudes and skilled professionals who are proficient in legal matters regardless of whatever group of people they are dealing with.

In the former Yugoslavia, a police cadet educational system was the most commended system of training police officers. Before it was abolished, at the end of the 1990s, police cadet training was the prevailing form of police training. In addition to the police cadet training, short police training for adults who wanted to join the police force was also offered. Police cadets started police training after finishing primary school (at the age of 14 or 15), whereas courses for adult recruits were appropriate for individuals who had previously finished high school education and wanted to join the police force. Skalar (1976) conducted an extensive study on the selection, training, and professional success of the former police cadets who constituted the Police Cadet School's first seven cohorts. Skalar's study covered, for example, the socio-demographic characteristics of the police officers, their success in police training, adaptability to work conditions, psychological characteristics, and other work-related issues such as a superior's satisfaction with a police officer's performance, discipline, obedience, and motivation for police work. The study shows positive and negative aspects of police cadet training and professional socialization into the police culture.

The results of this study are presented because of the high quality of the research, and the intriguing findings of this very critical piece of research that was conducted during the socialist era when Slovenia was part of the Socialist Republic of Yugoslavia.

Skalar's first principal finding was related to a positive correlation between the physical ability of police officers and their efficiency at work. The more physically able police officers were, the more their superiors valued their performance. In addition to physical ability, personality characteristics, such as reliability, psychological stability, and absence of physical and mental anomalies, were appreciated the most in police officers (Skalar, 1976). The social origin of the police officers was quite typical, with the majority of the police in the study belonging to the working class and hailing from rural areas (Skalar, 1976). The adaptability of the police to their social and professional role was also related to the police officer's partner's educational level (which was generally quite low in the study) and the social networks of police officers in places of both work and residence (the more socially inclined police officers were more successful and less deviant).

The motivation for joining the police force was an issue of special interest to Skalar. Joining the police force was related to the following factors: prestige and social power, feelings of inferiority, a romantic view of policing and material and social expectations about the police profession, family tradition, and parental motivation (for example, it was not uncommon for officers to have experienced parental pressure to join the police, so as to become more disciplined).

Skalar's study showed that 50% of the officers were very satisfied with their job. Police chiefs' assessment of police officers' performance was based upon their perception of police officers' attitude toward their uniform, their willingness to take orders, and how seriously they took their job. Conformity to the rules of police conduct was the key criterion used by police chiefs when considering the professionalism of officers. A low level of discipline was associated with those officers who exhibited poor attitudes toward their uniform and superiors. A police chief's perception of a police officer's professionalism was also found to be related to an officer's years of police service. Skalar (1976) stated that increased years of service bring a higher quality of policing but at the expense of an increase in skills to cover up minor mistakes and faults, and police chiefs and senior police officers were found to be more critical toward junior police officers. This finding implies the existence of professional socialization where junior police officers have to internalize the values and norms of the professional (sub) culture as well as the legal and general moral issues that pertain to policing.

Another interesting finding of Skalar's was related to the success of individual police officers undertaking basic training. The higher the marks scored by an officer in the final exam in the Police Cadet School, the better the police chief's assessment was of that officer's performance. Police chiefs were satisfied with 54.7% of their subordinates and would trust them in any police operation.

Skalar (1976) also dealt with police deviance and some elements of anomie. He stated that the following problems were worth special attention: alcohol and drug abuse (especially taking tranquilizers and amphetamines), neuroticism, bitterness, cynicism, suicidal behavior, and socializing with "problem people." Social inclusion of police officers is also found to be a significant characteristic of the studies on police officers. The more socially included and sociable police officers were, the fewer conflicts they had with citizens while on duty.

Besides the two studies detailed above, prior to 1991 there was no empirical research addressing police professionalism and other legitimacy issues. Other papers were generally focused upon legal or philosophical issues and failed to draw on empirical evidence to explore the extent and nature of the problem being discussed (see Meško, 2004a). One can draw the conclusion that Pečar and Skalar are, in fact, the pioneers of police research in Slovenia since they have conducted the majority of significant work in this field. Skalar later turned to social educational studies of prisons and educational institutions, while Pečar remained in the field of criminology and, in particular, focused on social control theory. Pečar and Skalar trained the younger generation of researchers (Dvoršek, Maver, Lobnikar, Meško, and Pagon), who subsequently researched policing and other criminological issues, at either undergraduate or postgraduate level.

Pre-1991 studies focused on police and public relations (Pečar and Skalar, 1973), key issues of police work, and the characteristics of police officers, with an emphasis upon the psychological dimensions of police officers' characteristics (Skalar, 1976). Nevertheless, Pečar and Skalar's research was of an enviable quality and comparable to Western research carried out during the same period. These studies were, after 1991, complemented by further research informed by approaches including sociology and social psychology. Post-1991 research on policing in Slovenia will be presented in the next section of this chapter.

Post-1991 Research on Policing

Intensive empirical research on police professionalism, legitimacy, ethics, deviance and human rights was initiated with Pagon's (1993) paper on police cynicism. This paper significantly contributed to the development of research into democratic policing and reminded professionals of the significance of democratic policing. The Slovenian government, in comparison to other criminological issues, neglected to initiate research into policing issues. Priorities are still being given to other criminological research, such as criminological theory, juvenile delinquency, juvenile justice, penology, crime reduction policy, victimology, criminal investigation, and specific issues of social control (Meško, 2004a). Even when the Ministry of the Interior or the police force were interested in researching policing issues, projects tended to be low budget and short term. Nevertheless, the College of Police and Security Studies (now the Faculty of Criminal Justice and Security, University of Maribor) has conducted a number of research projects on policing, criminological issues related to policing, and security matters (Meško, 2002), especially in cooperation with partners from foreign universities. Since 1996 the Faculty of Criminal Justice and Security has organized five international conferences on policing. The papers presented at these conferences have been very well publicized and published in a conference publication. The conferences have not only focused on policing in a Central and Eastern European context but also encompassed a wider and international dimension with participants coming from all five continents. The problems discussed have largely been about comparing contemporary Western and Eastern knowledge and research on policing (Pagon, 1996), managerial and human resource issues in police (Pagon, 1998), ethics, integrity and human rights (Pagon, 2000), deviance, violence and victimization (Pagon, 2002) and dilemmas of contemporary criminal justice (Meško, Pagon, and Dobovšek, 2004). In addition to the conferences on policing, a national conference on criminal justice organized by the Faculty of Criminal Justice and Security has been held annually since 2000, which acts as a forum for the discussion of problems of policing in Slovenia. Further efforts of the Faculty of Criminal Justice and Security have been directed toward the development of productive relationships between practitioners and academics.

Meško (2002) states that in 1996 a (re)birth of police-oriented research occurred in Slovenia. Associates of the Faculty of Criminal Justice and Security have published extensively on many policing-related topics, both in Slovene and other languages. The conferences on policing have made it possible for many Slovenian and other Central and Eastern European criminologists to publish their research results and reflections in English. Publishing in English is becoming increasingly important as "the world of criminology" does not exist, to any great extent, outside of the main international languages. Consequently, writing in "exotic" Slavic languages does not get the attention of Western criminologists. Accordingly, the biennial conference on policing in Central and Eastern Europe has built a bridge between Eastern and Central Europe and the rest of the world.

Slovenian criminological and criminal justice research entered a period of intense activity during the mid-1990s. Previously, however, Slovenian "research" had reflected De Nike's (1995) depiction of an academic endeavor that consisted of either a literature review followed by reflection without any empirical exploration, or, alternatively, the transposition of foreign research models onto an Eastern European context. Police-related research has continually been challenged by new and international developments and, in particular, through international cooperation.

Meško (2002) identified four groups of research conducted at the College of Police and Security Studies in Ljubljana. The groups of research are as follows: general issues on policing, security issues, criminological issues, and criminal investigation issues. The following focus will be on the first category of policing and give attention to the issues of (1) training, (2) police professionalism, (3) legitimacy and ethics, and (4) integrity and police deviance. Papers and research projects focusing solely on empirical Slovenian policing research are presented.

Basic and On-the-Job Training

Djurić and Meško (1996) implemented a study of on-the-job police training in Slovenia. They surveyed police officers, instructors, planners, and organizers of such training. The research findings showed that the police need to tailor police training according to their practical professional needs. The most intriguing finding in respect to community policing is related to the fact that the police training center trained local community policing officers but not their superiors (police station commanders and regional community policing inspectors). This can cause all kinds of obstacles because of the nature of hierarchical police organization. They suggest the following improvements regarding preparation, organization, and implementation of future forms of police training.

Professionalism and Ethics in Policing

Policing is getting increasingly professionalized, a change long advocated by police scholars. Police aspirations to professionalization either create, or at least re-emphasize, several requirements such as the need for a wide-ranging discretion, higher educational requirements, higher standards of professional conduct, and self-regulation.

There are several reasons for this, the major ones being the paramilitary philosophy of policing (from the communist era) and a misunderstanding of the need for police ethics (Pagon, 2000). First, within the paramilitary philosophy of policing, police officers are assigned the role of executors of orders from their supervisors. They are not supposed to question those orders, so there is not much need for moral deliberations. The basic virtue of police officers within this framework is one of absolute obedience. Police leadership, on the other hand, is either not considered accountable to any particular person or body (since they are setting their own goals and can always tailor the statistics to fit their needs) or they are accountable only to the political party in power, with whom they have a symbiotic relationship. It is not surprising then that police ethics do not thrive in such a context. Second, quite a few police officers are misled by a belief that, so long as police officers perform their work strictly according to the law, there is no need for a debate on police ethics. Proponents of this view also deny police officers the right of discretion. Unfortunately, when one is faced with a moral or ethical dilemma, the laws often prove themselves to be of little use.

With the rise in new philosophies of policing (such as community policing and problem-oriented policing) and with the acceptance of police discretion as a necessary part of police work, the importance of police ethics is becoming increasingly appreciated. Nowadays it is hard to find a curriculum at a police academy or a program in police studies at a university that does not include a module on police ethics. At the same time, the number of police agencies with a department, task force, or committee on police ethics is rapidly increasing, and the majority of police agencies have also adopted codes of police ethics, in a variety of forms. But, as Pagon (2000) indicates, police ethics are still at an early stage of development. A number of courses on "police ethics" mainly deal with philosophical ethics, while the word "police" in the name simply means that police officers or students of police studies are the target group of the course. Following the postulates of applied ethics, the described development should be achieved by the joint efforts of police scholars (theoreticians) and police practitioners. According to Pagon (2000) this development should take place in three interrelated directions: (a) applying the principles of applied ethics to the police profession; (b) establishing standards of ethical conduct in policing; and (c) defining the means and content of education and training in police ethics. This development, of course, has to parallel other efforts for implementing both contemporary philosophy and other forms of policing in police professionalization (Pagon, 2000). From our perspective, Pagon's reflection implies new challenges for the police, especially in terms of the application of ethics in relation to marginalized groups, against the background of a shifting society.

Meško, Houston, Umek, and Ziembo-Vogl (2000) conducted a cross-cultural study on the moral values of Slovenian and American criminal justice students, police officers, and prison officers. The study indicated that Slovenian attitudes vary consistently from those found in West Michigan and tended toward greater leniency and tolerance. Unlike the West Michigan respondents who view morally debatable variables in strict black-and-white terms, the Slovenian sample views these same variables with a greater tolerance for the "grey" aspects of human behavior. The reasons for these more liberal attitudes may be complex. However, they may find explanation in the history of the past decade when Slovenes enjoyed the intense experience of political autonomy and personal freedom. Thus, the feeling may be that absolutes are few and far between and, correspondingly, an attitude based on the principles of laissez faire may have been adopted for situations where group cohesion remains unthreatened. This may be especially so in a country that, though small, has long been known for its strong sense of national identity and its fiercely maintained sense of independence, in spite of a history of political oppression.

Dvoršek, Meško and Viltužnik (1998) discuss some organizational aspects of policing and the values of police officers in Slovenia during a time of huge change to the police organization. Some models offered for organizational changes have, due to lack of interest and funding, been promoted though coercion. The results of their survey show that police chiefs who work at regional and state levels shared too many characteristics (such as setting priorities in solving local problems, perception of local public safety and crime problems, and understanding of a local police officer's duties and the necessary tools/skills for performing everyday policing) with local police chiefs. This indication can, on one hand, be considered as a positive since it implies that regional- and state-level police chiefs are aware of local police problems while, on the other hand, such local mentalities maintained at regional and state levels imply a lack of strategic management and decision-making skills. The authors also emphasize problems such as the motivation for work and career, trust between police officers, lack of specialisms, tendencies to undermine workplace behavior and a lack of "sound competition," organization of work at all three levels of police organization, and a low level of professional ethics. The study emphasizes a need for a serious reconsideration of both the values of the police as an organization and the role of the police in Slovenian society. The study also implies that police chiefs should receive extra training in strategic management for taking over positions at a regional and state level.

Lobnikar, Gorenak, and Prša (1999) investigated the reasons explaining the early retirement of 504 Ministry of the Interior employees, the majority of whom were police officers. The main rationale for deciding to retire early were bad relationships between employees and employers, feelings of uselessness, and a concern over changes in the Slovenian retirement system.

Recent studies of community policing in Slovenia (Meško, 2001; Meško and Lobnikar, 2005) show that there are still many obstacles on the path to the implementation of a coherent community policing model. The problems are largely related to a lack of flexibility in solving problems in complex situations and a rigid and legalistic mentality among the majority of police officers. It has become evident (Pagon, 2004a; Meško and Klemencic, 2007; Meško and Lobnikar, 2005) that under the "old" (socialist) system, the Slovenian police organization was quite decentralized at the local level. Before 1991, all police stations in the country were considered community-level units and the commanders at these stations were appointed by local governments, after such appointments were approved by the Secretary of the Interior. Under the current system, all police stations are state-level units, which operate solely at the local level. The local government has no say in their operation or in the appointment of their commanders. At the same time, however, the police want to practice community policing, by appointing certain police officers as "community level" police officers with no reactive duties, but only preventative ones. No wonder, then, that community policing is perceived by Slovenian police as just another technique within the framework of traditional policing, rather than a completely new and organization-wide philosophy of policing. Similar problems were identified in other Eastern European countries (Beck, 2004). Meško and Lobnikar (2005) present the results of a study on partnership in local crime prevention and local partnership-based provision of safety. In addition to the idea of working together with citizens, local safety councils are meant to be a place where communities, police, and other agency representatives meet and try to find common solutions for the reduction of local safety and security problems. The results suggest that local communities in Slovenia tend to perceive violence as the predominant safety problem, followed by other kinds of disorder and crime. Violence (including domestic violence, violence in public, violence at school/violence by youths, often in combination with bullying and vandalism) is the most urgent and serious safety problem, followed by the use of drugs (including alcohol), traffic safety, property crimes, public disorder, economic crime, corruption, and criminal gangs. Responsibility for solving these safety and security problems is allocated to the police who, the respondents indicate, should cooperate with other institutions, civil society, and local government. The analysis of local safety problems is still performed mainly by the police. It is also the police who are supposed to reassure citizens and reduce fear of crime through their presence in local communities. In this sense we have a paradoxical situation—the majority of the most appropriate crime prevention activities are of the so-called "social crime prevention" variety. The attribution of responsibility to perform these activities lies with the police, who are seen to be the universal solution to societal and social problems. A ranking of responsibility for resolving local safety/security and crime problems emerged from this study. This ranking is as follows: the police, social care institutions, the prosecutor's office, the courts, other law enforcement agencies, NGOs, and educational institutions. In solving the problems related to youth, at least one representative of the youth community should take part in the process whereby decisions are made about any actions to be taken. The results of the study show that a low level of responsibility and a lack of coordination, training, and knowledge are the main obstacles to developing unified efforts in local community safety and crime prevention projects. Suggestions made by the police for better policing of their communities are related to increasing the numbers of police officers on the beat in local communities, greater visibility and approachability of police officers, better cooperation and communication between the police and local people, adequate police training in communication skills, and respect for social and cultural diversity. In the view of the respondents, in order to promote "community policing" it is first necessary to pay more attention to professionalizing policing, the acquiring of problem-solving skills, and the development of a sense of community cohesion.

Furthermore, these research results indicated that the most significant obstacles to local safety projects are as follows:

- Unclear roles of institutions and representatives of civil society in such activities
- Diverse understanding/conceptualization of safety problems
- Diverse understanding of partnership
- Vertical relations among partners
- Lack of executive powers
- Lack of political will and departmentalism
- Police officers' questionable willingness to listen to those who do not share the same perception of the problem
- Perceptions of councils as an extension of the police (in all cases the police initiated the establishment of such councils)
- Ignorance and apathy of local citizens (crime prevention is not an attractive and "profitable" activity)
- Centralized arrangements and localized problem solving (no firm legal background)
- "Informal for the purpose of formal"—cooperation was only based on the good will of the representatives of state/local institutions,

local administration, and civil society without any responsibility or firm legal framework

In contrast, the advantages of such councils were outlined:

- Democratization of formal social control
- Cooperation of (responsible) citizens and established relationships
- Facilitation of "safety consciousness," discussion of local problems, and a "communities that care" mentality (Meško and Lobnikar, 2005)

Issues on Legitimacy and Ethics

Maver (2000) in his study undertaken among police investigators in Slovenia states that actions taken by police officers or investigators during a criminal investigation (as well as their attitude toward suspects, victims, and witnesses) depend on the level of sophistication of a police officer's or investigator's conception of what is ethically right or wrong. The nature of the investigative process can be subject to ethical conflicts. Even though the principle of "equality of arms" is not completely valid during the investigative procedure, investigators are bound to face many obstacles and difficulties, which are not imposed on offenders. This occurs despite the fact that investigators often find themselves caught between ethical principles and the requirements of efficiency, necessitating a walk along the sharp edge between the legal and the illegal, and between criticism and sanctions. Investigators have to respect human rights in general, as well as more specific ethical principles. The more frequently that the situations faced by police officers during investigations are studied and analyzed, as well as the reasons for and the manner of their reactions under such conditions, the more one will be able to suppress inappropriate or unethical decisions and actions, or—at least—one will be able to understand and evaluate such temptations.

Over the last few years several research projects in Slovenia revealed the possibility of negative encounters between the police and victims of crime (Dobovšek, Meško and Umek, 2000; Gorenak, Dvoršek, Lobnikar, Maver, Meško, Pagon, and Umek, 2002). The above studies focus on victims of property crime and their satisfaction with police work. Importantly, they can serve for the improvement of police practice in dealing with victims of property crimes, which are the most frequently reported crime to the police. Both of the above studies are examples of victimology in practice, and led to an initiative whereby a group of psychologists were employed by the police to prepare a booklet for both the police and victims of crime about emotional responses of victimized people and victims' rights in police procedures.

Dvoršek (2000) discusses the ethical dilemmas associated with the investigation of organized crime in Slovenia. He addressed undercover investigative methods, which are indispensable in the successful suppression of organized crime and pose new challenges to criminal investigators. These methods are largely performed out of the public eye and, similarly, there is often limited scope for such investigations to be directed by police chiefs and prosecutors. Moreover, the pressure on investigators to be both successful and effective is very high. Criminals try to entice organized crime investigators into criminal activities in various ways. Organized criminals try to reveal criminal investigators' identities by means of new defense strategies such as presenting themselves as instigators of the criminal activity. Their own mistakes can cost criminal investigators their life or the life of a colleague. Their contribution to a successfully concluded investigation remains hidden, and if they cross the thin line between legal and illegal conduct, they cannot avoid public condemnation. With limited funds criminal investigators have, as effectively as possible, to protect the witnesses who incriminate the offenders. The above circumstances cause various ethical dilemmas for undercover investigators. An adequate security mechanism can only be established by highly professional ethical standards. Besides undercover agents, prosecutors and judges are also often faced with ethical dilemmas. They have few opportunities to acquaint themselves with the findings of criminal investigation methods, which are necessary for a correct evaluation of the facts and evidence pertaining to a particular case. Contrary to ethical principles, it is a fact that criminal proceedings are conducted by jurists with insufficient knowledge of criminal investigation. The author supports the idea that criminal investigation, as a subject, should get a more prominent role in the curricula of law schools since it is often the case that criminal investigators who finish police training or training at the Faculty of Criminal Justice have a more detailed knowledge of the criminal investigation of sophisticated forms of crime than state prosecutors.

Police Integrity

Pagon (2000) conducted a study on police integrity. Integrity in policing means that police officers genuinely accept the values and moral standards of policing and possess the virtues of their profession, and that they consistently act, of their own will, in accordance with those values, standards, and virtues, even in the face of external pressures. Why do some people lack integrity? Why is it so hard to achieve? Pagon agrees with Becker (1998) who offers the three most common reasons. First, not everyone is rational. Integrity requires the discipline of purpose and a long-range course of action, selecting corresponding goals and pursuing them fervently, carefully choosing the means to one's ends and making full use of one's knowledge. Second, a person may lack integrity because of desires that are inconsistent with moral values. If a person, when under temptation, fails to call upon his or her rational mind, acting instead upon the whim of the moment, he or she will lack integrity. The same is true when an irrational fear drives behavior. Similarly, an individual's integrity will be called into question if he or she does not put rational principles into practice purely through indifference. Third, and probably most commonly, a person may lack integrity if he or she succumbs to social pressure. Social pressure may come from numerous sources (e.g., co-workers, bosses, or clients) and take many forms (e.g., physical intimidation or verbal and nonverbal disapproval). A person with high integrity will not allow popularity to take priority over rational convictions (Pagon, 2000).

Police Deviance

The first paper on police deviance published by Meško (1994) in the Slovenian *Journal of Criminal Investigation and Criminology* triggered angry criticism by police managers because it revealed a taboo theme. Papers and articles on "dark sides" (police misconduct and police deviance) of policing have become a part of the critical criminological analysis of Slovene policing. Meško (1998) discusses police personality characteristics and police officers' attitudes toward marginal social groups. He states that the following factors are typical for police officers' personality and attitudes: real-self (emotional instability, anxiety, neuroticism, and femininity), pro-social orientation (extraversion and sociability), professional self (toughness, rigidity, physical power, and self-control), attitudes toward deviants (feelings of inability, "respecting" criminals and a belief that crime pays, inefficient criminal justice system, and too few police powers), and cynicism (bitterness, spontaneous aggressiveness, distrust of police chiefs, and a "them and us" mentality). The most intriguing finding is related to the positive attitudes displayed by police officers toward criminals and the negative ones presented to victims of crime. These findings call for the reconsideration of police professionalism and the policing role in society. The avoidance strategies of police officers in cases of conflict, on the one hand, and potential aggressiveness, on the other, were also significant results emanating from this study. Attitudes toward marginal groups were found to be quite positive, but attitudes toward victims of crime were much more negative than those toward criminals. These findings indicate questionable police professionalism in Slovenia. In addition to negative attitudes toward victims of crime (attribution of one's own contribution to his/her victimization, being difficult with police officers while reporting crimes, and an inability to learn from previous victimization), Meško (2000) found that police officers believe that suspects and public disorder offenders come from specific social groups and, therefore, can be easily recognized because of their appearance and language (non-Slovenes). Officers perceived that victims contributed to the criminal offense through their own carelessness and ignorance. Findings of this research demonstrate the prejudiced behavior of police officers in their dealings with social groups (Reiner, 1992) from specific social classes.

Umek, Meško, and Abutovič (2000) conducted an extensive study of police officers' attitudes toward different social groups and the attitudes held by police officers in respect of their colleagues, based on their ethnic origin. The results of this study reflect many other similar studies on police prejudice (Ainsworth and Pease, 1987) that reveal the negative attitudes and prejudice of police officers toward ethnic minorities and socially marginalized groups. It is important to stress that police officers are not more prejudiced than the majority of the population in the area where they live and work. It simply means that police officers reflect the attitudes and prejudices characteristic of their environments. The Slovene public opinion polls on national conscience and ethnic relations imply two main findings: (1) the Slovene national and ethnical conscience is strongly expressed, and (2) it is evident that phenomena such as xenophobia and ethnocentrism are increasing (Toš, 1994). The Slovenes also express a high level of social distance toward such socially marginalized groups as drug users, alcoholics, homosexuals, and AIDS victims. The Slovene population also expresses extremely negative attitudes toward Muslims, Jews, and Gypsies/Roma.

Perhaps the employment of more police officers from the social groups that attract the attention of the police would be worthy of reconsideration. As in some Western countries, police officers from minority groups could deal with the problems of their specific community. This approach has two advantages and at least one disadvantage. First, such police officers understand the problems and needs of such communities and deviant individuals. Second, they influence and diminish the negative attitudes and prejudices of their police colleagues. Third, this can be a problematic approach because of the marginalization of the excluded groups. Therefore, the authors recommended the teaching of respect for diversity among all officers (regardless of their ethnic background) rather than to further exacerbate the schism between groups by hiring an officer of a particular ethnic grouping to deal with the citizens of another ethnicity. Working together (the mixing of ethnic groups) is a potential solution.

Another issue is the control of the quality of police service. Police chiefs are supposed to ensure the good conduct of police officers according to the laws and the Code of Police Ethics that requires police officers to be fair, polite, professional, thorough, and impartial. Police officers are also obliged to respect human rights and the dignity of members of the public without regard to ethnicity, gender, race, language, religion, education, and social status (Umek et al., 2000).

Pagon (2002), in his study on sexual harassment in the Slovenian police force, records that deviant behavior does not only occur against police clientele. It also exists within a professional group of police officers and is manifested through, for example, indecent talk, verbal harassment, sexual relationships, physical harassment, and demands for sexual favors.

Police Cynicism—A Key Obstacle on the Path to Police Professionalism?

Organizational cynicism is directed against the methods of managing law enforcement organizations, and against the procedures, rules, and regulations used by their leadership. This workplace cynicism is exhibited as a contemptuous distrust toward law enforcement and the services provided to the communities where officers work. It can be described as the loss of respect and pride for the police profession (Pagon, 1993). Four dimensions of police cynicism are discussed and reflected upon: (a) cynicism toward the leadership of the police, (b) cynicism toward norms and laws governing the behavior of officers during their work, (c) cynicism toward the legal system that restricts police activities, and (d) cynicism concerning the respect of the public for officers. Similar dimensions of police cynicism are also revealed: cynical attitudes toward the public, cynical attitudes toward the organization; cynicism is reflected also by officers' attitudes toward their work, toward relations with the community, and by a cynical attitude toward the role of education and training within the police profession (Pagon, 1993).

Meško (1998) reveals the cynicism of police officers toward members of the public and of police chiefs toward police officers. Meško (1998, 2004) discusses the following types of police behavior which can be attributed to specific work conditions: authoritarianism, suspiciousness, cynicism, rejection of representatives of other cultures, isolation/solidarity, conservativism, macho behavior, pragmatism, bigotry, and violence. Meško (1998) reveals a typical career development in Slovene police officers: idealism (in the beginning of a career—high aspiration/unskilled, pro-social orientation), realism (experiences—high aspiration/skilled, pro-social orientation), cynicism (high level of aspiration—obstacles—low level of aspiration/rebellion, antisocial orientation), and resignation (low level of aspiration—ignorance—retreat to individualism).

Cynicism was the most significant characteristic because it appeared in police officers at very different times (in terms of length of police service) after having joined the police force. In some police officers a cynical view of the world and their work conditions occurred very soon after joining the police, while in others it occurred after some years of service. The truth is that every police officer has to deal with the onset of his or her cynicism sooner or later. In Meško's 1998 study, cynicism was understood as a rebellion within the context of Merton's terms of anomie (Merton, 2003).

Lobnikar and Pagon (2004) state that their results parallel the findings of other researchers that police cynicism is a multidimensional concept. Similar to the results of other studies, Pagon and Lobnikar's (2004) research reveals four dimensions of police cynicism:

- Cynicism toward the police supervisors
- Cynicism toward the community where the officers perform their duties
- Cynicism toward the working rules and procedures that the officers have to observe
- Cynicism toward the rules and the regulations governing police work

The fact that police cynicism is closely related to a host of personal, interpersonal, and organizational factors emphasizes the importance of studying and understanding this phenomenon in police settings. It has been shown, as so many times before, that interpersonal relationships within the police organization are a determining factor of the officers' well-being and the organization's proper functioning.

In this study, it turned out that social undermining as well as violent and aggressive behavior in the workplace were positively correlated with police cynicism, while the correlation between social support and cynicism was also a positive one. This corresponds with the findings of previous research (Ganster, Pagon, and Duffy, 1998; Lobnikar and Pagon, 2004). Therefore, it is in the area of management, leadership, and people skills that the cure for police cynicism should be sought.

Concluding Remarks and Challenges for the Future

Pagon (2005) states that the main impediments to professional policing in Central Europe are as follows:

- Police subculture
- Paramilitary structure and philosophy of policing
- Political pressures and political criteria in selection (chiefs of police)
- Poor management
- Leadership and people skills
- Lack of standards and best practices in European policing
- Large diversity in police education and training
- Lack of research and critical distance

However, he sees opportunities for the development of policing by means of a European code of police ethics, the further development of police studies and research, the broadening of European and international support, and increased public pressure.

Currently, political pressure still exists and politically influenced appointments to senior police positions still take place in Slovenia. At the same time, there has been a lowering of the selection criteria for police recruits who wish to join the police force. This is due to the provision of the Slovenian quota of police officers needed to protect the Schengen border (southeastern border of the European Union). In the last decade several problems related to the police training and education system have led to significant challenges. There have been complaints against the police (including lawsuits) because of the non-professional treatment of people by the police and a poor knowledge of police powers among police officers. In addition, and with regard to police training, the social structure of police officers has changed from the traditional police cadet route into the profession to a more open selection procedure, which selects police recruits from all parts of Slovene society.

To determine the causes of such a presumably low level of police professionalism, a group of researchers, at the bequest of the Slovenian Ministry of the Interior in 2004, started a research project that focused on the accountability of state and local law enforcement authorities in performing public powers. Preliminary findings suggested that police officers lacked a sufficient level of skills to perform their duties and, in particular, a lack of training for performing specific tasks, especially communication skills and problem resolution skills (Rejc and Kečanović, 2005).

Causes of the present state of an increased number of complaints against the police and the presumably low quality of police service may be attributed to occupational stress, a lack of supervision and support at work, concerns over the well-being of police officers and organizational commitment, job-related self-efficacy, supervisors' behavior toward police officers, and cynicism. The latter deserves the special attention of researchers, policy makers, and police practitioners. The attainment of high goals (Kolenc, 2003) in a police organization full of cynical individuals appears to be a particularly challenging commitment (Meško, 2004a).

Possible ways to diminish the influence of negative factors upon both the police organization and individual police officer's performance lie in increasing employees' organizational commitment, well-being, and self-efficacy through empowerment and encouragement (Pagon, 2005).

In conclusion, this chapter refers to Villiers (2003) who states that

- Every police officer is a leader.
- A "military" style of leadership still exists.
- Leadership by example has been neglected.
- There is the need for a new style leadership.
- There is a growth of the blame culture.

- There is a culture of generalized cynicism.
- There is distrust of charisma.
- There is a masculine culture.
- There is a culture of anti-leadership.
- There is a need for the recognition of doctrine.

It is also our belief that progressive leadership in the police force is a crucial factor in "problem" reduction and in increasing the professionalism of police officers. This concerns the values and the visions of police leaders. More important than charisma, bearing, or interpersonal skills is the secret ingredient of leadership, namely, the ability to convey a sense of vision and mission in such a way that it transforms and enhances the follower's sense of the possible. Leaders motivate their followers to transcend self-interest for the sake of organizational goals and values. Moreover, this raises their need level from security and safety to self-esteem or autonomy. It also leads them to share with the leaders a common vision of the importance of the leader's goals or values to the future well-being, effectiveness, and professionalization of the police organization. In the process, leaders motivate followers to achieve more than they thought possible, strengthen their commitment to the organization, and induce feelings of trust, admiration, loyalty, and mutual respect. Police respect of "communities" starts with a mutual respect of police officers within the police organization. Another issue, in addition to training and education, which is a particular challenge for the Slovenian police organization, is that of lifelong learning and the individual police officer's need for additional knowledge and information to develop both personally and professionally. In addition to the above, it should be perpetually emphasized that police officers have to serve the public as well as possible while following the rule of law and respecting human rights and people's dignity. It is time to start implementing "the police service."

References

Ainsworth, P. B., Pease K. (1987). *Police Work*. London: The British Psychological Society, Methuen.

Beck, A. (2004). Understanding the Criticality of Context in Developing Community Policing: A Post Soviet Case Study. In Meško, G., Pagon, M., Dobovšek, B. (eds.), *Policing in Central and Eastern Europe—Dilemmas of Contemporary Criminal Justice*. Ljubljana: Faculty of Criminal Justice, 49–65.

Becker, T. E. (1998). Integrity in Organizations: Beyond Honesty and Conscientiousnews. *Academy of Management Review, 23* (1), 154–161.

Code of Police Ethics, from http://www.coe.int/t/e/legal_affairs/legal_co-operation/police_and_internal_security/Docurnents/Docurnents.asp, Accessed February 4, 2010.

De Nike, H. J. (1995). Riding the Learning Curve or How Read These Essays. In De Nike, H. J., Ewald, U., Nowlin, C. J. (eds.). *Crime in East Europe—Recent Reflections From the Eastern Academy*. Bonn: Forum Verlag Godesberg, 15–18.

Djurić, M., Meško, G. (1996). How to Modernize Police Training in Slovenia: Results of Research. In Pagon, M. (ed.), *Policing in Central and Eastern Europe—Comparing Firsthand Knowledge with Experience from the West*. Ljubljana: College of Police and Security Studies, 605–614.

Dobovšek, B., Meško, G., Umek, P. (2000). Victims of Property Crime on the Work of Police Officers and Criminal Investigators. In Breur, C. M., Kommer, M. M., Nijboer, J. F., Reintjes, J. M. (eds.), *New Trends in Criminal Investigation and Evidence, Volume 2*. Oxford: Intersentia, 185–196.

Dvoršek, A. (2000). Ethics in Criminal Investigation of Organised Crime. In Pagon, M. (ed.). *Policing in Central and Eastern Europe—Ethics, Integrity, and Human Rights*. Ljubljana: College of Police and Security Studies, 323–329.

Dvoršek, A., Meško, G., Viltužnik, R. (1998). New Police Organisation: The Way to Success? In Pagon, M. (ed.), *Policing in Central and Eastern Europe—Organizational, Managerial and Human Resource Aspects*. Ljubljana: College of Police and Security Studies, 245–252.

Ganster, Daniel C., Pagon, Milan, Duffy, Michelle. Organizational and interpersonal sources of stress in the Slovenian police force. V: Pagon, Milan (ur.). Policing in Central and Eastern Europe : comparing firsthand knowledge with experience from the West. Ljubljana: College of Police and Security Studies, 1996, str. 425–433. [COBISS.S1-1D 1226003<http://cobiss.izum.si/scripts/cobis, command=DISPLAY&base=COBIB&RID=1226003>]

Gorenak, V., Dvoršek, A., Lobnikar, B., Maver, D., Meško, G., Pagon, M., Umek, P. (2002). Stališča oškodovancev premoženjskih kaznivih dejanj do dela policistov. Ljubljana: Visoka policijsko-varnostna šola. [Property Crime Victim Opinion on Police Service, a Research Report].

Kolenc, T. (2003). *The Slovene Police*. Ljubljana: Ministry of the Interior.

Lobnikar, B., Gorenak, V., Prša, J. (1999). Vzroki predčasnega upokojevanja delavcev ministrstva za notranje zadeve in policije. *Varstvoslovje*, 2, 9–17. [Reasons for Early Retirement among the Employees of the Ministry of the Interior and the Police]

Lobnikar, B., Pagon, M. (2004). The Prevalence and the Nature of Police Cynicism in Slovenia. In Meško, G., Pagon, M., Dobovšek, B. (eds.), *Policing in Central and Eastern Europe—Dilemmas of Contemporary Criminal Justice*. Ljubljana: Faculty of Criminal Justice, 103–111.

Maver, D. (2000). Ethics in criminal investigation. In Pagon, M. (ed). *Policing in Central and Eastern Europe, Ethics, Integrity and Human Rights*. Ljubljana: College of Police and Security Studies, 109–120.

Merton, R.K. (2003). Social Structure and Anomie. In Bean P. (ed.), *Crime: Critical Concepts in Sociology*. London: Routledge.

Meško, G. (1994). Policijska subkultura. *Revija za kriminalistiko in kriminologijo*, 2, 143–149. [Police Subculture]

Meško, G. (1998). Strukturalna analiza stališč med policisti in nepolicisti. Ljubljana: Univerza v Ljubljani (doctoral dissertation). [Police Officers's Personality Characteristics and their Attitudes toward Marginal Social Groups]

Meško, G. (2001). Gorazd. V skupnost usmerjeno policijsko delo izziv za slovensko policijo. Teorija in praksa, Mar./Apr. Vol 38, 2, 272–289.

Meško, G. (2002). *Research at the College of Police and Security Studies 1996–2001*. Ljubljana: College of Police and Security Studies.

Meško, G. (2004a). Oblike vedenjskega prilagajanja policistov na specifit'ne zahteve in obremenitve pri opravljanju policijskega dela. In Seligkar Toš M. (ed.), Odgovornost drzave, lokalnih skupnosti in drugih nosilcev javnih pooblastil za ravnanje svojih organov in uslu 2 bencev. Ljubljana: Pravna fakulteta, 105–143.

Meško, G., Houston, J., Umek, P., Ziembo-Vogl, J. (2000). Comparing Moral Values of Slovenian and American Criminal Justice Students, Police Officers and Jail Officers. In Pagon, M. (ed.), *Policing in Central and Eastern Europe—Ethics, Integrity and Human Rights*. Ljubljana: College of Police and Security Studies, 371–382.

Meško, G., Klemencic, G. (2007). Rebuilding legitimacy and police professionalism in an emerging democracy: the Slovenian experience. In: Tyler T.R. (ed.) Legitimacy and Criminal Justice: International Perspectives. New York: Russell Sage Foundation, 84–114.

Meško, G., Lobnikar, B. (2005). The Contribution of Local Safety Councils to Local Responsibility in Crime Prevention and Provision of Safety. *Policing: An International Journal of Police Strategies and Management*. (28), 2, 353–373.

Meško, G., Pagon, M., Dobovšek, B. (2004). Some Dilemmas of Contemporary Criminal Justice. In Meško, G., Pagon, M., Dobovšek, B. (eds.), *Policing in Central and Eastern Europe—Dilemmas of Contemporary Criminal Justice*. Ljubljana: Faculty of Criminal Justice, 17–37.

Pagon, M. (1993). Policijski cinizem: vzroki, značilnosti in posledice. [Police Cynicism: the Causes, Characteristics and Consequences.] *Revija Policija*, 4–5, 389–403.

Pagon, M. (ed.) (1996). *Policing in Central and Eastern Europe: Comparing Firsthand Knowledge with Experience from the West*. Ljubljana: College of Police and Security Studies.

Pagon, M. (ed.) (1998). *Policing in Central and Eastern Europe: Organizational, Managerial, and Human Resource Aspects*. Ljubljana: College of Police and Security Forces.

Pagon, M. (2000). Police Ethics and Integrity. In Pagon, M. (ed.), *Policing in Central and Eastern Europe—Ethics, Integrity and Human Rights*. Ljubljana: College of Police and Security Studies, 3–14.

Pagon, M. (2002). Deviance, Violence and Victimization: Are the Police a Part of the Problem or a Part of the Solution. In Pagon, M. (ed.), *Policing in Central and Eastern Europe—Deviance, Violence and Victimization*. Ljubljana: College of Police and Security Studies, 3–13.

Pagon, M. (2005). Opportunities and Impediments to Police reform in Eastern Europe. In Uildriks, N. (ed.), *Police Reform and Human Rights: Opportunities and Impediments in Post-Communist Societies*. Oxford: Intersentia, 43–48.

Pagon, M., Lobnikar, B. (2004). Comparing Supervisor and Line Officer Opinions about the Code of Silence: The Case of Slovenia. In Pagon, M. (ed.), *Policing in Central and Eastern Europe—Ethics, Integrity and Human Rights*. Ljubljana: College of Police and Security Studies, 197–210.

Pečar, J., Skalar, V. (1973). Milicionarski odnosi sa javnošću. Beograd: Stručna biblioteka službe javne bezbednosti, Savezni sekretariat za unutrašnje poslove. [Police-Public Relations]

Reiner, R. (1992). *The Politics of the Police. Second edition.* London: Harvester Whetsheaf.Resource Aspects. Ljubljana: College of Police and Security Studies.

Rejc, A., Kečanović, B. (2005). Modeli strateške kontrole vzrokov za odškodninske zahtevke. In Seliškar, Toš M. (ed.), *Odgovornost države, lokalnih skupnosti in drugih nosilcev javnih pooblastil za ravnanje svojih organov in uslužbencev.* Ljubljana: Pravna Fakulteta, 73–86.

Skalar, V. (1976). *Izbor, usposabljanje in delovna uspešnost miličnikov kadetov.* Ljubljana: Univerza v Lj., Inštitut za kriminologijo pri Pravni fakulteti. [Selection, Training and Work Efficiency of Police Officers Who Finished the Police Cadet School].

The Slovene Police. www.policija.si (Accessed, April 15, 2005).

Toš, N. (1994). 0 nacionalni identiteti in etnonacionalizmih. Slovensko javno rnnenje 1992–1993. Ljubljana: FDV.

Umek, P., Meško, G., Abutovič, R. (2000). All Different All Equal—A Fairy Tale about Police Impartiality. In Pagon, M. (ed.), *Policing in Central and Eastern Europe—Ethics, Integrity and Human Rights.* Ljubljana: College of Police and Security Studies, 397–406.

Villiers, P. (2003). Philosophy, Doctrine and Leadership: Some Core Beliefs. In Adlam, R. and Viliers, P. (eds.). *Police Leadership in the Twenty-First Century.* Winchester: Waterside Press, 15–33.

The Study of Policing in China

6

KAM C. WONG

Contents

Introduction

Chinese policing is a much-neglected field of study. Our knowledge about policing in China is sketchy, spotty, and superficial. The dearth of scholarship resulted from a lack of research interest, resources, facility, and access. As recently as the 1960s, research in China was handicapped by the unavailability of sources,[1] inaccessibility to places/people,[2] and scarcity of bi-lingual and bi-cultural researchers.[3] It was not until 1972 that China opened its door to foreign visitors and scholars.[4] Chinese research in non-Western countries (e.g., Japan, Vietnam) confronted similar problems and experienced other unique difficulties.[5]

In the field of Chinese studies there have long existed two parallel scholarly worlds: Chinese and Western. They are separated by distinctive intellect traditions, different academic interests, and dissimilar research methodologies. The two intellectual domains diverge because as Kang observed,[6] there is no shared conceptual understanding of "jingcha" (police), an imported idea and practice. More specifically, the Western notion of police fails to capture the broad coverage of the term in China, e.g., from political to social to moral ordering. It also fails to give vent to the multifarious methods of social control, e.g., from self-cultivation[7] to moral education[8] to family discipline[9] to clan rule[10] to social surveillance[11] to communal self-help[12] to government administration.[13]

Existing (occidental) literature shows that we know a lot about imperial China's social control system—its historical roots, philosophical foundation, structural elements, and functional process. However, there is currently very little research and still less raw data on how Chinese police worked in the past[14] or how PRC public security functioned.[15]

This chapter introduces readers to the study of policing in China—problems and issues, approaches and methods. It discusses problems with the study of Chinese policing in the West, using Dutton's seminal work as a convenient example and "ideal case."[16] The section about Policing with Chinese Characteristics: Another Approach, argues for studying Chinese policing from the inside out and the bottom up, with indigenous perspectives and empirical evidence.[17] The next section provides a brief overview of how to conduct police research in China: sources to consult and issues to think about. Section 11.4 concludes that the study of policing in China, as with other cross-cultural ventures, must be conducted with an intimate understanding of local history, deep appreciation of indigenous culture, and broad knowledge of people's ways and means.

Problems With the Study of Chinese Policing in the West

Western studies of Chinese law enforcement and policing have been afflicted with ethnocentrism and cultural ignorance.

In law, a generation of Western legal scholars has adopted the view that China has no (functional) legal system when there is ample evidence suggesting otherwise, e.g., the Qing dynasty had a sophisticated legal code and effective justice administration system.[18]

Michael R. Dutton wrote the seminal book[19] on Chinese policing.[20] The book addresses the question, how does traditional technology of policing fuse with the present social control framework?[21]

Dutton began with the observation that the PRC's household registration system is a reproduction and sublimation of past practices, rather than a new invention. Specifically, China's present control method is a "remnant" of past feudal practices, conveniently borrowed to serve new governance needs.[22]

In terms of method, Dutton employed Foucault's "genealogical method" to (re)construct "histories of the present." In the main, Dutton relied mainly on secondary English materials to complete his study.

In terms of theory, Dutton adopted Foucault's theoretical insight[23] to analyze China's household registration regime, observing that Chinese state control has moved away from inflicting pain on the body to marking the files of the person. As evidence, Dutton pointed to Chinese uses of statistical records to effectively track and keep people in place.

In terms of thesis, Dutton postulated that in imperial China the state controlled a person's behavior by anchoring the person within an intricate web of relationships starting with the family. Individuals were kept in place by critical self-introspection, stern family discipline, and ubiquitous community surveillance. In contemporary China, the state replaces communal supervision with state administration, in the guise of a comprehensive household registration system: "[W]e may now see a regime which centers on work and production rather than on family and Confucian ethics, but the form of its policing, the modes of its regulation and the way it constitutes its disciplinary subjects all have resonance in the past."[24]

As a critique,[25] Dutton's book tells us more about social control than law enforcement, more about administrative regulation than police supervision. In superimposing Foucault on China, Dutton tells us what the West *thinks* of China as an administrative state more than what Chinese people *experience* about state governance.

Radcliffe-Brown has cautioned against such Western cultural imposition, sold as sociological imagination[26]: "In the primitive societies that are studied by social anthropology there are no historical records. ... Anthropologists, thinking of their study as a kind of historical study, fall back on conjecture and imagination, and invent 'pseudo-historical' or 'pseudo-casual' explanations."[27]

In essence, where Dutton discovered clear and convincing archeological evidence of historical continuity in a disciplinary state, Chinese people found coincidental confluences of people, events, and circumstances vying for influence over the individual. Where Dutton discovered a grand design in explaining state governance, the Chinese people settled upon human nature ("renxin")[28] and heavenly providence ("tianming")[29] to explain personal discipline and justify collective obedience. Dutton seeks to make sense of China from above and afar, temporally and culturally. Chinese people experience China, intimately and intuitively. Thus observed, Dutton's "theory of policing" is irrelevant to Chinese's understanding of their personal conditions and collective fate.

The existence of two views of China shifts the intellectual discourse from what counts as a sound theory (i.e., validity issues) and accepts as good evidence (i.e., reliability problems), to who counts (i.e., political consideration) to what matters (i.e., policy concerns). The shift in discourse further implicates paradigmatic issues of positivism versus postmodernism.

On a still larger intellectual compass, Westerners, the likes of Dutton, go about (re)constructing China out of whole cloth and in accordance with a grand scheme (vision) of things, while Chinese people continue to weave their life course stitch by stitch corresponding with the dynamic "way" ("dao") of the universe.

This line of critique finds empirical support in Chinese law and society research. Theoretically, it has been observed that law in action is mediated by powerful social actors as driven by a convergence of social and cultural forces. In "The Practice of Law as an Obstacle to Justice: Chinese Lawyers at Work,"[30] Ethan Michelson found that legal justice in China was subjected to and subverted by the lawyers who acted as gatekeepers to law and justice. Accessibility to the legal system was dictated by professional interests (i.e., who can pay) and circumscribed by cultural values (i.e., who is deserving of help). Empirically, he found in "Why Do They Not Comply with the Law? Illegality and Semi-Legality among Rural-Urban Migrant Entrepreneurs in Beijing,"[31] that in practice the "hukou" system did not comport with the administrators' design or people's expectations. Ultimately, the "hukou" system did not serve to "discipline" the migrants (as intimated by Dutton) but was negotiated by all those who were affected by it (police, migrants, business) to serve their respective institutional or personal interests.

If we find Dutton's approach to studying policing in Chinese studies wanting—sterile and irrelevant—how might we improve? To this central issue we now turn.

Policing With Chinese Characteristics: Another Approach

The study of Chinese policing suffers from cultural (pre-)dispositions, as driven by self-evident political ideology (e.g., democratic governance)[32] and fortified with embraced ignorance (e.g., lack of language skills).[33]

Harry Harding once observed that the misperception of Chinese reform has more to do with observers' disposition toward China than reflecting true conditions in China. Sentiments toward China ran from unrestrained romanticism over Mao's egalitarian and utopian quest, circa 1970s, to bitter resentment resulting from abject disappointment over China's oppressive policy and repressive practices, circa 1980[34] (p. 396). The reassessment resulted in part from "Changing Intellectual Assumptions" (p. 942): (1) The prevailing assumptions in the 1970s were that we have no right (at least not being fair) to judge China by Western standards or values, such as freedom and human rights issues (p. 943). (2) Economically, Chinese people are less developed and thus care more about economic survival than liberty. Culturally, Chinese people have no history and tradition of democracy, privacy, and individualism. As such these rights mean very little in China. (3). In the 1970s we often judged China by the lofty goals espoused by the leaders and not their actual implementation or eventual success or failure at the grassroots level (p. 944). By far the most established assumption shared by many who engaged in State and society research in China is the idea that there is a connection between economic development and demands for political liberation. See Elizabeth J. Perry, "Trends in the Study of Chinese Politics: State-Society Relations," *CQ* No. 139: 704–713 (1994).[38]

Taking this admonition to heart, we find that few if any existing social or police theories, mostly developed in the West, can be easily made to fit China's particularistic cultural pattern, multifaceted social conditions, and complex political circumstances without suffering from various minor inaccuracies[35] and/or gross distortions.[36] More significantly, there is not enough valid and reliable empirical data[37] to support any theory building.[39]

Reflecting on my own experience, I can make three observations to improve upon Chinese police studies.

First, China is made up of many distinctive parties to an ill-fitting whole. There is a tendency to lump PRC police together as a monolithic entity and treat policing as uniform activities. This tendency is caused by a misconception that China is (has been) laboring under a uniform Confucius culture and dictated by a unifying communist ideology.[40] Or more simply put, Chinese people (including or particularly with police) think and act alike.[41] Nothing can be further from the truth.[42] The public reception of and reaction to government policy in China varies, depending on locale,[43] contingent on issues[44] and change with people.[45] In like manner and for these reasons, police in China police differently.

China is a big country with diverse conditions, in geography, ethnicity, and culture. Inasmuch as policing is a grass roots activity and public order is a local concern, we can expect that national priorities are not equally shared locally.[46] Similarly, social problems and political dynamics affect different communities differently.[47] When devising legislative solutions, national law must be made to fit local conditions. Local governments must be afforded the flexibility to creatively apply national law and boldly experiment with local regulations,[48] starting with the police.[49]

As one might expect, what is required by the Communist Party of China or instructed by the Ministry of Public Security (MPS), might be differently applied in local context. For example, when national police leadership called for police reform in 2001, provincial police bureaus chiefs reported different focus and varieties of achievements in 2002:

1. Shanghai municipality reported focusing on modernization of the police department, i.e., systemization (*zhiduhua*), regularization (*guifan hua*), and legalization (*fazhi hua*).

2. Henan Public Security Bureau reported focusing on improving political ideology and professional accountability of the police when engaging in "strike hard" (*yanda*) campaigns. The major focus was on ridding the police of corruption and abuse, e.g., the existence of "protective umbrella" (*baohu san*).
3. Anhui Public Security Bureau reported focusing on eradicating organized gangs and secret societies (*heshehui*). The other focus was in reforming the police work style with the conduct of three education campaigns. Four police reform projects were at hand: establish and perfect the education and training system (*jiaoyu peixun*); management and appraisal process (*guanli kaohe*); command and control structure (*jiandu zhiyue*); protection for police work (*jingwu baozhang*).
4. Jingsu Public Security Bureau reported focusing on improving upon the service quality of the police officers through enhancing police law enforcement standards and introducing police management review and technology upgrade, i.e., "Golden Shield" ("Jindun") project.
5. Sichuan reported focusing on speeding up the police reform process in making police work more transparent and accountable to the public. The police reformed the household registration system in order to make it more rationalized and efficient. It also tried to address recurring and persistent police service problems and public complaints, e.g., impolite and unresponsive police attitude.
6. Xianxi Public Security Bureau reported focusing on "yanda" over serious crimes. The major focus was on building a comprehensive public security prevention and control system (*zhian fangkong xitung*). The police reform process should be further strengthened to lay a foundation for the future economic development of the west. In this way, the police subscribed to the "three years" reform plan as directed by the MPS and espoused by Jia Chunwang.
7. The Helungjian Public Security reported focusing on "break through" in six reform areas: (1) maintaining public order; (2) "striking hard" at criminal offenders; (3) promoting social order; (4) serving the nation's open door and economic reform needs; (5) using technology to enhance police performance (*kexue qiangjing*); (6) facilitating police troop construction (*duiwu jaingshe*).
8. The Guangzhou Public Security reported focusing on six objectives. The police reform work revolved around improving public security and social order within two years and making arrangements to deal with public order problems associated with World Trade Organization (WTO). Particularly, the police focused on liberating ideas, pledge to work for economic reform, step up with public

> security and social order campaign, speed up public security reform, and enhance public security quality and standards.[50]

The implication of this observation for Chinese police scholars is as stark as it is clear: any attempt to theorize about conditions in China in universal and essentialist terms, without grounded research, is likely to fail.[51]

Second, we need more reliable data than critical opinions. Most, if not all, China-bound police researchers relied heavily on government data. Information supplied by the Chinese government (official statistics, policy papers, legislative documents, court cases, journal articles, media accounts) deserves careful reading, paying attention to possible incompleteness, omission, distortion,[52] misrepresentation, bias,[53] lack of uniformity, and/or sheer incompetence.[54] Data and analysis provided by elites are more likely to be driven by theory than practice, ideology than facts. Both information sources are unlikely to have been informed by grass roots experience and bottom-up perspective. All this is to remind China-bound researchers that it is difficult to ascertain the truth about the state of policing in China once we get away from official pronouncements and expert analysis. It is appropriate to end this observation with the often quoted statement: "Everyone is entitled to his own opinions but not his own facts."

The implications for Chinese research are clear—we need to look at China from the inside out[55] and the bottom up.

Third, China must be understood on her own terms—in the context of Chinese history and culture, more recently ideology and personalities. If we were to make an effort to understand Chinese policing in Chinese terms, we should start by investigating local communal, familial, and self-control. That is to say we should take a bottom-up more so than a top-down approach, seeking/explicating rich empirical observations more than imposing/expounding essentialistic theoretical postulates.

If we should look at China from the bottom up and empirically, we will find that "policing" as a function starts with self and ends with the family/community, i.e., self-governance.[56] The Kongfu (Confucius) household in imperial China is an ideal type[57] of self-governance and informal social control.[58] In China, the Kongfu was considered first among equals in ethical matters.[59] In order to honor Confucius and set an example for the people to emulate, Confucius' (Kongzi) descendants were conferred the honorary title (*Cifeng*) of "Yansheng gong" by emperor Song Renzon (960–1279) in the second year of Zhihuo.[60] The title was affirmed by the Emperor's decree on the eleventh day of the eighth month of the Dai Ming Yuanwu yuannian.[61] The memorial to the throne ("zoushu") "Pingding shandong sier ce" ("Ten strategies to pacify Shandong") provided in item 7 to "Chong shengxue" (Revere the sage learning) as follows:

> The historical sage ("xiangsheng") Kongzi is the ancestor of eternal Confucius orthodoxy ("wanshi daotong"). In the beginning of our dynasty, all our cardinal guides and constant virtues ("gangchang" or more specifically "sangan wuchang")[62] were developed from this. *Li* required officials to revere sacrifices, reinstating the titles ("feng") of Yangshenggong and sishi xuebao.[63]

From early history, the Kongfu occupied a unique position in Chinese history. Generations of emperors deferred to it for moral authority. Local officials were guided by its ethical principles. People followed its exemplary way of life. Kongfu's household was given special authority, e.g., the head of Kongfu's household could nominate local officials without being objected to. Kongfu's household was given special rights, e.g., it enjoyed exemption from certain taxes and requirements.

More significant for our illustration purpose, the Kongfu household enjoyed delegated rights of self-government and autonomous powers of social control. Kongfu enjoyed hereditary nobility. Kongfu was given property to manage. Kongfu has a right to appoint officials, to levy tax, and to select local magistrates. The head of Kongfu has a right to govern its household members exclusively and discipline its charges summarily. Kongful household has full authority to establish conduct norms within its household and over the disposition of its property in the community. It could discipline and punish its household members, charges, and intruders, summarily and without recourse. Kongfu has a right to make enforceable rules to protect its communal welfare and seek the help of the officials to promote its collective interests. At all times, Kongfu mediated between its members and the outside world. Officials could only approach, communicate, and deal with Kongfu members with the special permission of the emperor, by and through the head of Kongfu household.[64]

The conclusion from this brief excursion is as unmistakable as it is revealing: the Kongzi household played a significant role in social control matters in imperial China through independent moral leadership and by virtue of delegated governmental social control powers from the emperor. As a result it shared in social control responsibilities with local officials, as co-equals. It was a "private government" unto itself.

The delegation of social control powers and sharing of social control responsibilities affected Kongfu materially in the following ways: The Kongfu possessed more legal rights and privileges than the commoners.[65] The Kongfu enjoyed exemption from legal prosecution by the officials.[66] The relationship of the Kongfu to the Chinese emperors resembles closely (if not even duplicates) that between the kings and lords in medieval Europe:

> In Western Europe ... they (lords) were no longer ordinary subjects, but possessed economic and legal privileges, granted or accepted by the sovereign ... They were considered outside the general subordination of subjects ... by the very terms of investiture. They owed fealty, counsel and aid, but in return were exempted from all obligations and impositions. They represented and personified both the population of their territories in their relationships with the sovereign, and public authority within their territories.[67]

For all intent and purpose, the Kongfu acted as a form of delegated government in disciplining family members at home and securing the Kongfu household against transgressors from without.

Thus to observe that China has no institution of formal police might be technically correct. But to imply that there was no informal policing in China before 1898 is a gross misunderstanding as a result of the focus on and pre-occupation with the West's idea of "police."[68] The idea of police as we know it today is beholden to the Western conception ideology (democratic[69]), organization (centralized, bureaucratic, specialized, professionalized[70]), style (legalistic[71]), and means (coercion[72]).

In summary, the way forward in Chinese police studies is to take a different approach, one that is informed by indigenous perspective and driven by empirical data, or simply a more context-anchored, bottom-up, and facts-driven approach.

The remainder of this chapter details difficulties of and ways to go about conducting research into PRC policing practices—what sources to consult, which journals to read, and what Chinese and English language literature exists.

Researching PRC Policing

Research Difficulties

Before we start, a brief discussion on problems and methods with research into PRC police and policing is in order.[73] Researching on public security and policing in China is a difficult task. Cohen's observation about the difficulties of researching in China, while dated, remains relevant.[74] The communists are not given to open government. The PRC police are not keen on sharing state secrets, private information, criminal intelligence, and operational details with outsiders, much less foreigners.[75] There is no right to public information in China.[76] Publicly available data are often "sanitized" to serve the State's propaganda, education, and socialization needs.[77] Field survey research is officially prohibited. Document 598 circulated by the State Education Commission in December of 1990, "Notice of Issues Relating to Cooperation with Foreigners: Doing Social Investigation in our Country," prohibits "all higher education institutions from conducting sociological survey in the form of public opinion poll or written questionnaire with foreign academic institutions and research institutes. This includes cooperative research based on questionnaire."

On a more optimistic note, researching in the PRC is getting easier. Consistent with PRC overall policy to open up government agencies, including the police,[78] for citizens' inspection and public scrutiny, more and more information is made available to the people, e.g., books, journals, and papers designated for internal circulation are increasingly being placed in public circulation and for private subscription. For example, *Gongan Yanjiu* (Public Security Research) is now freely circulated and *Renmin Gongan Bao* (Public Security Press) is made available on the Web (Zhongguo gongan baike quanshu editorial committee, 1989:22). While the PRC government still does not welcome outside scholars to study the PRC police system and process, PRC scholars have been allowed to conduct research and publish their findings, much more so than before.

Emergence of Police Studies in China

Until very recently, there was no formal police studies program or independent research enterprises on police and policing in China. Police role and functions were accepted as an act of faith and based on ideological dogma, i.e., police as with law is an instrumentality of the ruling class to exercise domination and impose control on class enemies. Policing methods and practices are never questioned, as shown by history, as informed by experience, and as instructed by culture.

Police research in order to gain wide audience and publication in official journals must accept political correctness editing in terms of topic, theme, and content. As a PRC police scholar made clear with reference to quality control in official public security journals:

> Political nature of topic choice (*suan ti de zhengzhi sheng*). Public security journal periodicals are in the service of public security troop construction (*jian she*), education (*jia xu*) and research (*ke yan*). Its political nature cannot be challenged. Thus the articles published cannot be against party direction and policy, against Marx' viewpoint and perspective, nor against the nation's basic state policy.[79]

These and other problems with police studies and research in China are best stated in the General Administrative Office of Ministry of Public Security's "The Notice about Enhancing Research Work into Public Security Theories and on Improving further Public Security Studies" Gongban (2000) 82 Hao:

> However, it must be noted that currently public security research, in particular theoretical development, is a little inadequate, it is specifically reflected in: some theoretic research has been stylized (cheng shi hua); certain questions involving the totality of public security work lack in-depth general theoretical support; many (discussion of) public security controversial issues and (analysis of) difficult problems lack insightful (jiandi) and focused research; many fresh experiences from local level public organs await theoretical treatment and improvement. (Gongan Yanjiu, 2000:8)

There are encouraging signs. Police studies and research are increasingly being recognized. In 1993, the Minster of Education first approved the study of public security–related subjects in universities as first degrees, including criminal investigation, public security, police administration, risk management, and police physical education. In July of 1998, the Ministry of Education recognized public security studies (*Gongan Xueke*) as a subdiscipline to Jurisprudence (*Faxue*) in the "Putong gaodeng yuanxiao benke zhuanye mulu" (general higher education school undergraduate course professional catalogue). The newly mined discipline has eleven primary study fields (*kexue menlei*) and 72 sub-fields (*erdang lei*). Primary subjects of study include police theory (*lilun gongan xue*), police history (*lishi gongan xue*), and public security studies (*gongigan xue*), etc. Secondary fields include public security studies (*zhian xue)* and investigative studies (*zhencha xue*). This means that police studies have now developed to a stage of maturity with theories, concepts, research methods, and findings. The first master's degree program in criminal procedure was approved in December of 1993. By 2002, there were nine master's programs in the nation: five at PSU and four at Criminal Investigation College.[80]

Notwithstanding the gradual gain in maturity and stature of police studies as a discipline in China, substantial issues remain as to the discipline's mission, boundary, method, focus, and contribution. In essence there was little consensus and many contentions as to what the discipline is all about and where it is going.[81] For example, a majority of the scholars feel that it is an independent discipline, since it professes to have well-defined subject matter, a student body, education objectives, and course content. However, there is a sizable minority who argued that police studies is a multiple discipline field, integrating theory and practice, natural science and social science, arts and humanities. There was much disagreement over the research focus. Some scholars were of the opinion that police studies should be devoted to the study of police origin, development, and regulations, in search of patterns and theory. This school argued against pairing researchers with actual police work, e.g., criminal investigation or police administration. Others insisted on a broad approach to police studies as a scientific field. According to this vision, scholars should apply scientific methods to the study of police work in theory and practice. Still others thought that the investigation of police in China should be linked to police theory and research development in other parts of the world.

Police theoretical research is necessary to improve upon applied police work.[82] The solution to improve upon public security research in China is with more scientific studies and empirical researches. This requires the dedication of resources and training of people to conduct police research.[83]

Not only police studies and research are pursued for their own sake. There is an overall tendency to ignore the importance and usefulness of research in daily police work. There is now a common saying within police circles that "police studies and theory sound important when proposed, appear to be necessary when applied, not used when in urgency." This is to observe that, as with other police officers from around the world, Chinese police officers at the operational level do not think that police theory, research, and findings are useful in their day-to-day work, i.e., not applicable in the real world. More to the point, police theories have been relegated to a secondary position in daily police work (*Gongan Yanjiu*, 2000a:77–79).

Police reformers and enlightened administrators, however, consider police theoretical research to be most necessary to improve upon existing police work (*Gongan Yanjiu*, 2000b:6–7). The solution is to improve upon public security research to provide more relevant and useful scientific researches and empirical findings. This calls for the dedication of more resources to research and training of more researchers (*Gongan Yanjiu*, 2000b:8).

There are three ways to jump start police research: (1) provide an incentive structure for people to conduct research, (2) speed up the processing and distribution research finding, and (3) develop police scholars by inviting outside researchers to share insights and viewpoints (*Gongan Yanjiu*, 2000a:8).

How to Conduct Police Research in China

In terms of research materials, there are original data in the form of legislation and regulation, National People's Congress (NPC) reports and communications, crime statistics, and police documents. There is an abundance of Chinese published materials, mostly by scholars and teachers associated with public security universities or higher education.[84]

Legislation

Commonly confronted research materials are the legislative and regulatory materials.

Constitutionally, there is one national law uniformly enforced in China. "The Legislation Law of the People's Republic of China"[85] (hereinafter "LL") makes provisions for how national, local, and administrative laws and regulations are made and interpreted.

The highest authority to make and interpret law in China is vested with the National People's Congress (hereinafter "NPC"). Article 7 of LL provides, "the National People's Congress and Standing Committee thereof shall exercise state legislative power," and Article 42 of LL provides, "the power to interpret a national law shall vest in the Standing Committee of National People's Congress."

The other nation rule-making authority is the State Council. Article 56 of LL provides, "the State Council enacts administrative regulations in accordance with the Constitution and national law," i.e., MPS can promulgate regulations as empowered by NPC.

Finally, local legislators—province, autonomous region, municipality directly under the central government—are allowed to make law *subject to national laws* and central administrative regulations. Article 63 of LL provides, "in light of the specific situations and actual needs of the jurisdiction, the People's Congress of a province, autonomous region, municipality directly under the central government and the Standing Committee thereof may enact local decrees provided that they shall not contravene any provision of the Constitution, national law and administrative regulations."

As an illustration of how the police legislation—national, administrative, local—work to control police conduct, we address common police research questions. On the issue of arrest by police, are warrants or summonses always issued by the Public Security Bureau (PSB)? Are there instances in which they are not issued, and if so, under what circumstances or conditions?

We start with the observation that when processing crimes and handling criminals, PRC police officials are governed by Criminal Procedure Law of the People's Republic of China (<<Zhonghuarenmingongheguo xingshi susong fa>>) (hereinafter CPL) and People's Police Law of the People's Republic of China (<<Zhonghuarenmin gongheguo jingcha fa>>) (hereinafter JCF),[86] both of them national laws, as implemented by "Procedure regulations of Public Security organs in handling criminal cases" (<<Gongan jiguan banli xingshi anjian chengxu guiding>>) (hereinafter PSR),[87] an administrative regulation.

Specifically, the issuance of warrants or summonses[88] is provided for in "Article VI Compulsory Measures" of CPL (Articles 50 to 78) and PSR (Articles 61 to 154), and "Article II Functions and Powers of JCF" (Articles 7 to 9).

Article 50 of CPL provides that "the People's Courts, the People's Procuratorates and the public security organs *may*, according to the circumstances of a case, issue a warrant to compel the appearance of the criminal suspect or defendant, order him to obtain a guarantor pending trial or subject him to residential surveillance" (emphasis provided), suggesting that the Courts or Procuratorates have the authority, but are not required, to issue a warrant on application of the police.[89]

Article 59 of CPL provides that "arrests of criminal suspects or defendants *shall be subject to approval* by a People's Procuratorate or decision by a People's Court and shall be executed by a public security organ" (emphasis provided), suggesting the police must apply for a warrant before an arrest.

Police are allowed to make arrests without warrant in very limited and clearly defined circumstances.

Article 61 of CPL provides that public security organs may initially detain an active criminal or a major suspect under any of the following conditions:

1. If he is preparing to commit a crime, is in the process of committing a crime or is discovered immediately after committing a crime
2. If he is identified as having committed a crime by a victim or an eyewitness
3. If criminal evidence is found on his body or at his residence
4. If he attempts to commit suicide or escape after committing a crime, or he is a fugitive
5. If there is likelihood of his destroying or falsifying evidence or tallying confessions
6. If he does not tell his true name and address and his identity is unknown
7. If he is strongly suspected of committing crimes from one place to another repeatedly or in a gang[90]

Article 62 provides: that the persons listed below may be seized outright by any citizen and delivered to a public security organ, a People's Procuratorate or a People's Court for handling:

1. Any person who is committing a crime or is discovered immediately after committing a crime
2. Any person who is wanted for arrest
3. Any person who has escaped from prison
4. Any person who is being pursued for arrest

In both instances, the police must follow up with a detention warrant. Article 64 of CPL provides: "When detaining a person, a public security organ *must* produce a detention warrant."

There is little doubt, from this brief legislative law and administrative regulation analysis, that arrest or detention without a warrant is not allowed, as Article 71 of CPL makes clear: "When making an arrest, a public security organ must produce an arrest warrant."[91]

The research into the legislative–regulatory framework for police arrest powers only begins the research exercise. The next issue is how such laws and regulations are interpreted and applied across the nation and in different locales. Thus, the second question: Do arrest procedures in practice vary from locale to locale in China, or are they uniformly implemented across the country?

In this we learn that the implementation of CPL has always been a major concern.[92] While the PRC government has taken drastic and increasingly effective steps to make sure that police follow CPL,[93] it has not always been successful.

In principle, CPL and police JCR covering arrests are supposed to be uniformly interpreted and enforced nationwide. Violation of CPL or JCR is subject to party discipline, organization sanction, administrative appeal, legal challenges, media supervision, and legislative (NPC) oversight.[94]

However, in terms of actual practice, arrest procedures differ from locale to locale, having to conform to local customs as reflecting indigenous circumstances.[95]

More pertinently, under the current command and control structure, police in China are subject to dual rule. Professionally and administratively, local police are commanded by the central government through province police bureaus and county police offices. Financially and operationally, police at the county, township, and village levels are provided for and directed by local Party and government institutions and philosophy.

The above dual command and control structure resulted in big disparities and wide variation in police operational practices. In reality, central command and control of police existed in name only.

There are a number of reasons accounting for such local disparities. First, the public security leadership, particularly those at the rural, village, and township level, are ignorant as to the legal responsibility and authority of the police. They overemphasized the necessity to coordinate local police work with central Party policy directives, at the expense of national laws and administrative regulations.[96] Second, the public security officials at the local areas routinely fail to follow established laws and regulations. Consistently, they are not able to resist illegal orders from local Party leaderships who have a say over their appointment, employment, or promotion. They are also afraid of spoiling the "good" or "established" relationship with the local village and township leadership, thereby making their work difficult.[97] Third, there is a lack of a checks and balances system guarding against abuses of police authority.[98] Fourth, public security suffers from inadequate and uncertain financing. Normally, public security is funded by local governments, e.g., of villages and townships. According to historical data, the county and township are only able to fund one-fifth or three-fifths of public security expenditure. The public security officials are expected to raise their own operational funding, e.g., by way of fines. In some cases, the village and township leadership even goes as far as requiring them to provide sufficient funds to finance police operations or risk having their salaries deducted. In other cases, the county and township pay only for salaries, leaving daily expenses, e.g., office rent, room and board, phone, water, and electric, to the village or township government. In such cases, the local police must obey the instructions and follow the directions of the local village or township officials or risk having their office closed or electricity or water turned off.[99] Oftentimes, this means abuse of laws and neglect of procedures, which means central control gives way to local misconduct.

In conclusion, arrest procedure is governed by national law and central procedures in theory but is subject to different interpretations and divergent application in practice by local Party and government officials. The Ministry of Public Security is keenly aware of the problem and has taken big steps to remedy the situation, e.g., by rationalizing the budget process, such that the local police managers do not need to look toward the local Party and government officials for financial support.

The lesson we learn from this research exercise into Chinese police law is that we must not only look at national laws and police regulations but also seek to understand how such laws and regulations are interpreted and applied.

MPS Administrative Documents

Public security scholars defined *gongan* "xingzheng gongwen" as "documents compiled during the administrative process that are with legal and prescriptive effect ("falu xiaoli de guifan ti weshu").[100] The State Council further elaborated upon the purposes and functions of such documents as:

> Administrative agency documents ("xingzheng jiguan gongwen" … are an important tool for the communication and implementation of the Party and State's principles, policy, promulgated administrative rules and regulations, execution of administrative measures, request for instructions and answer to questions, giving directions, planning and discussion of work, reporting, exchanging of views.[101]

All public security administrative documents have the following intrinsic and defining functional characteristics: political ("shengzhi sheng"), legal ("fa dings sheng"), authoritative ("quanwei sheng"), and restrictive ("guifeng sheng").[102] In terms of classification, official documents are of three kinds:

1. Directive document ("zhiling sheng gongwen"), i.e., order or instruction from the Party, State, government officials above to subordinates below, such as "mingling," "jueding," "pifu," "yijian";

2. Informative document ("zhaohui sheng gongwen"), communication between public security organs, e.g., "tongzi," "tongbao," "tonggao," "hanjian," "huyi jilu";
3. Reporting (for approval) document ("baoqing sheng gongwen"), i.e.,

The State Council has provided for methods in dealing with a variety of administrative documents.[103] There are 12 kinds of administrative documents a researcher might likely encounter. The following four illustrate such a diverse administrative framework:

1. "Mingling"[104] or "ling" (order or instruction).[105] This can be used to issue administrative rules and regulations; disciplinary measures; or void government actions.[106]
2. "Yian"[107] (proposal or motion).[108] "Yian" are legislative proposals submitted by government units at various levels to People's Congress or its Standing Committee at the corresponding level, as required or permitted by law.[109]
3. "Jueding"[110] (resolution or decision).[111] "Jueding" are major legal, policy, operations, or personnel decisions.[112]
4. "Zhishi"[113] (direct or instruct). These are directives to subordinate agencies for uniform actions.

These documents, to the extent they are available,[114] are indispensable for conducting police research. Such documents, if properly analyzed, tell us what is going on inside the public security by providing context,[115] revealing mindset,[116] describing problems,[117] registering concerns,[118] interpreting laws, analyzing issues, articulating policy, outlining strategies, explaining methods, and documenting results. The limitations of using such documents are many, e.g., many of the documents are not made available and those that are available hide more than they reveal. Finally, there is always the concern of politics, e.g., to what extent reports reflect reality and administrative utility or political correctness.

Books

To obtain an overview of public security work in China, consult *Dangdai Zhongguo gongan gongzhuo* (Contemporary public security work in China) (1992). To understand the characteristics of PRC policing in the 1990s—socialist policing with Chinese characteristics—one is well advised to consult *Zhongguo teshe gongan zhi yanjiu* (Research into public security with distinctive Chinese characteristics) (Chinese Police Studies Association, 1996). To trace PRC legal development from 1949–1988, consult *Xin Zhongguo fazhi jianshe Shisi nian yao lan: 1949–1988* (New China

Legal System Construction: Forty Years of Overview of Significant Events, 1949–1988) (1990). To learn about the techniques, skills, and procedures of PRC police investigation, consult *Zhonghua renmin gongheguo jiancha yewu quanshu* (Comprehensive manual for PRC investigation work) (1990). To read about laws, rules, and regulations affecting public security work, consult *Gongan fagui huibian (1950–1979)* (Compilation of public security rules and regulations) (1980) and *Gongan fagui huibian (1980–1986)* (1987). If one is interested in finding out official interpretations and notices pertaining to laws, rules, and regulations affecting public security work, consult *Zhonghua renmin gongheguo falu guifanxing jueshi jicheng* (A Compilation of PRC law and regulatory explanations) (1990). More recently, scholars interested in police laws, regulations, policies, and interpretations should consult the *Zhonghua renmin gongheguo gongan falu quanshu* (Compendium of PRC Public Security Laws) (1995). There are many books written by serving officers or academics on various aspects of PRC police and policing, e.g., Xian Dang's *Police work implicating foreign concerns* (Zhongguo shewai jingwu) (1991) tells you everything you want to know about how PRC police deal with crime implicating foreign persons and interests, and Yan Li's comprehensive working manual for working in the police posts should provide an inside look at the business of grass roots policing, *Gongan paichusuo yewu quanshu* (A comprehensive manual for public security post) (1994).

Finally, there are two source books that are necessary companions to every China-bound police researcher. The *Zhongguo gongan baike quanshu* (Chinese Public Security Encyclopedia) (Zhongguo gongan baike quanshu editorial committee, 1989) is a handy reference to everything you want to know about PRC policing. It is especially useful in defining terms and finding (summary) important documents. The problem is that it is dated—a big problem in a fast-changing field. The other is an annual series—the *Law Yearbook of China* contains data on law activities in China, more pertinent for our purposes, on police strengths, crime statistics, and important events affecting PRC police.

Journals

To keep professionally current and conduct scholarly research into specific issues on PRC policing, one cannot do away with reading public security journals. These are journals sponsored by the Ministry of Security but managed editorially by the respective public security universities.[119] It is commonly recognized in the PRC and by China-bound police scholars that public security higher education journals in China suffer from a lack of scholarship, starting from less than competent and scholarly editors to less than demanding standards. The editors are neither specialists (*zhuan men*) nor scholarly (*xuezhe*) (Jia 1999:101-103).

The journals also suffer from having to be politically correct in abiding by Marxist principles and following Party lines. Articles published must also be of practical value (*you shiyong jiazhi*) and of a suitable subject (*shiyong*). This means that articles published must deal with concrete and relevant issues of the day.[120] They are not allowed to be critical of the PRC political authority or police administration.

The three most prominent and often consulted public security journals of "official" standing are:

Gongan Yanjiu (Public Security Studies) is the official journal of the Chinese Police Studies Association (Zhongguo Jingcha Xuehui). It is managed and edited by the Ministry of Public Security, Public Security Research Bureau. The journal is a bi-monthly scholarly publication devoted to police theoretical studies (*jingcha liun yanjiu*). It is designated as an international journal, freely subscribed to by police scholars and practitioners all over the world. Being an official publication, it insists on political correctness. At a recent editorial board meeting (October 25–27, 2000),[121] the board made this observation: "Yanjiu wu jinzu, xuanquan you jilu" (There is no forbidden zone to research, but there should be discipline in promotion (of ideas). For example, confidential data should not be published.[122] The journal has been published monthly since 2001.

Gongan Daxue Xuebao (Journal of Chinese People Public Security University) is the official publication of the PRC Public Security University. The journal is a bi-monthly professional publication devoted to applied police studies, mostly reports of police experience from field officers all over the nation. It is managed and edited by the Public Security University (*zhuban*). The Ministry of Public Security is the Competent Authority (*zhuguan*). It is considered one of the most authoritative, prestigious, and influential journals in the PRC policing community in China. This journal is one of the "core" (*hexin*) police journals. The journal, now in its 15th year, was first available (in 1988) as internal printed materials (*nei bu kanwu*). Beginning in 1996, the internal circulation restriction was lifted. In 1998, according to "Zhongyang guanyu jiaqiang xinwen chunban guangbo dianshi ye guangli de tongzhi" (Notice regarding strengthening the management of news, publication, broadcast, and television), a number of high-quality internally circulated public security journals were publicly released.[123] Since 2000, police university journals are free to spread police research and science products in order to strengthen police operations and services through exchange of ideas and findings by way of research and publication.[120] The journal retains its format throughout, though the substance and quality of the articles have improved through the years in terms of rigorousness of research and sophistication of arguments. To date, it is a much more academic and less ideological journal but it still promotes "ideological zealousness" and "political correctness" in uncommon candor, if one were to read between the lines. Public security higher education journals are required to adhere to "dangxin yuanzhe" ("Principle of Party spirit") (Yang 1999:103-107). This means that articles selected for publication should be informed by Marxist basic principles and follow the Party line (*dang luxian*), guiding principles (*fangzhen*) and policies. Articles are grouped under different headings for ease of reference, e.g., public security management (*zhian guanli*), public security management research (*gongan guanli yanjiu*), jurisprudence research (*faxue yanjiue*), and crime research (*fanzui yanjiu*). Such headings change from issue to issue, but remain basically the same thematically.

Gongan Lilun Yu Sijian (Theory and Practice of Public Security). The journal is published under the auspices of Shanghai Public Security Bureau and edited by Shanghai Public Security Academy (Shanghai Gongan Gaodeng Zhuanke Xuexiao), reported here as an example of one of the more famous regional/local journals. The journal was first published in 1987, originally as a quarterly. Beginning with the first issue of 1999 (Issue Vol. 9[1]), the journal was also published under the joint title of Shanghai Gongan Gaodeng Zhuanke Xuexiao Xuebao and in English as the Journal of Shanghai Public Security Academic. From this date, the journal became available for public circulation by subscription, domestically as well as abroad. This is a deliberate and concerted move to make the journal more academic, professional, and relevant.

Newspapers

Currently, the most accessible data for China policing comes mainly from the *Renmin gongan bao* and related public security publications, e.g., *Gongon Juanjiu*. It is an official newspaper published by the PRC Ministry of Public Security. It was first published in October of 1984 and was at first restricted to internal circulation. The paper provides public security officers with up-to-date information and education. The content of the paper includes guidelines, policies, and directives of the administration; legal and public security information and crime reports; and police stories and related articles. On July 1, 1988, the paper was released for public and foreign distribution.[124]

The most common strategy to uncover and discern what is happening with the PRC police is to follow four steps. The first is to analyze the public pronouncements of PRC public security officials reported as "zhongyao yanlun" ("important opinions")[126] in public security media. Such policy initiatives often surfaced when national political leaders or public security executives made speeches at important events. The second is through investigating the policy debate and disseminating initiatives during national or provincial public security meetings. The third is by examining the application of such policy initiatives at the grass roots and operational levels. This is best done by reading articles about how such policy initiatives transformed actual operational measures and practices and by reading on how local police managers seek to realize national policy initiatives in concrete terms and material ways. Real case studies of successful implementation of such policy initiatives are most illuminating, as are annual reports of success of the initiatives. The fourth and last step is to read how the police discuss among themselves the relative merits and/or problems of various policies and practices.

Some Personal Reflections: A New Research Agenda

The above discussion suggests that there is a dire need to study police and policing in China with an open mind, particularly, to trace, analyze, and discuss recent developments—ideology, philosophy, organization, law, operations—in China policing within a broader context of Chinese history of social control and PRC political reform since 1979. This kind of study will help to discern historical legacy, emerging patterns, and speculate upon future trends. The hope is that this kind of scholarship can contribute to our growing, albeit very superficial and tentative, understanding of PRC police as an evolving entity and pragmatic enterprise[127] caught between past dreams and future hope, traditionalism and liberalism,[128] ideological dogma,[129] and practical necessities,[130] all the while struggling to maintain a semblance of continuity and order amid fast paced, propitious, and precipitous political, economical, social, and cultural changes and disjuncture that *is* a reformed and reforming China.

The study of Chinese policing should consider five issues. First, police institutions—organization, process, and practices—are not the same everywhere.[131] Police agencies differ in institutional mandate, e.g., political versus social policing, organization structure (e.g., bureaucratic versus communal control), and operational process (e.g., rule of law or rule by law), as determined by historical legacy, structured by current needs, and driven by a future vision. They also share much commonality in terms of goals, i.e., maintenance of order, and means, e.g., use of force, as reflecting more universal human nature and enduring communal needs. In order to study police cross-culturally,[132] we need to understand similarities and discern differences of policing between nations and across cultures.[133] This requires building a database of police organizations and practices in many countries as a first step, one country at a time.

Second, in order to improve upon policing in China, it is necessary to gather empirical data about the performances of police reform programs, process and outcome, for analysis and assessment purposes.[134]

Third, in order to build up a Chinese policing study field outside of China,[135] domestic literature, indigenous perspectives, local data, and inside-out, bottom-up views must be recorded.[136] One proposal is to encourage bi-cultural researchers who are at ease in two cultures.[137] It is observed that intimate knowledge of a culture and a good facility with the language allow a researcher to reach back into forgotten historical memory, dig deep into obscured cultural meaning, and access latent emotional feelings to provide a more complete and holistic picture of matters under investigation and materials to be interpreted.[138] While Huang made clear that his preference for bi-cultural researchers is not meant to exclude "foreign" researchers, it is also clear that Huang thought that researchers locally born and bred have a natural advantage over and above those who just learned about China by education and through immersion.[139]

Fourth, there is a dire need to supplement the foreign view of China reform in general and police reform in particular,[140] counter-balancing such views with internal perspectives, domestic voices and grass root understanding.[141]

Finally, such a study contributes to our growing understanding of PRC police as an evolving institution caught between past legacy and future vision while struggling to maintain a semblance of continuity amid fast-paced political, economic, social, and cultural change that *is* China in the last 38 years.[142]

China must be studied and engaged on its own terms with a mixture of domestic and domesticated viewpoints[143] to gain a better—fuller, deeper, richer, diverse, nuanced—understanding of a yet to be explored policing system in PRC.[144]

Endnotes

1. The American Consulate in Hong Kong was translating and archiving Chinese newspaper items and Berkley, Hoover, and Harvard Universities were collecting primary documents for depositories.
2. Field research involved exit interviews of refugees conducted in Hong Kong.
3. Howard L. Boorman, "The Study of Contemporary Chinese Politics: Some Remarks on Retarded Development," *World Politics* Vol. 12 (4): 585–599 (1960).
4. John Gittings, "The Years of Great Debate," *CQ* No. 143: 685–688 (1995).

5. Mark Sidel, "The Re-Emergence of China Studies in Vietnam," *CQ* No. 142: 521–540 (1995); Ryosei Kokubun, "The Current State of Contemporary Chinese Studies in Japan," *CQ* No. 107: 505–518 (1986).
6. Kang Daimin, *Discourse on Broad Concept of Public Security* (Beijing: Qunzhong chubanshe, 2001).
7. Donald J. Munro, *The Concept of Man in Early China* (Stanford: Stanford University Press, 1969).
8. T'ung-Tsu Chu, *Law and Society in Traditional China* (Paris: Mouton & Co., 1965).
9. FEI, Chengkang, *The Family and Clan Rules in China* (Shanghai: Shanghai shehui kexue chubanshe, 1998).
10. Hsien Chin Hu, *The Common Descent Group in China and Its Functions* (New York: Johnson, 1964).
11. Michael R. Dutton, *Policing and Punishment in China: From Patriarchy to "The People"* (New York: Cambridge University Press, 1992). Y. Y. Hsu, *The Pao-Chia System in China*, Far Eastern Survey Vol. 12 (24): 236–238 (1943).
12. Men Juntian, *China Bao Jia System* (Shanghai: Commercial Press, 1936).
13. B. E. McKnight, *Law and Order in Sung* (Cambridge University Press, 1992).
14. Jia Yuying, *Zhongguo gudai jiancha zhidu fazhang shi* (A developmental history of traditional China supervision system) (Beijing: Renmin chubanshe, 2004), p. 3.
15. A corpus of PRC policing literature is emerging: Ralph L. Powell and Chong-Kun Yoon, "Public Security and the PLA," *AS* Vol. 12 (2) 1082–1100 (1972); Elmer H. Johnson, "Neighborhood Police in the People's Republic of China," *Police Studies*. Vol. 6 (4): 8 (1983); Fu Hualing, "Police Accountability: The Case of the People's Republic of China," *Police Studies*. Vol. 14 (3): 140 (1991) and "Patrol Police: A Recent Development in the People's Republic of China," *Police Studies*. Vol. 13 (3): 111 (1991); Du Jinfeng and Sarah Biddulph, "Review of police powers of administrative detention in the People's Republic of China," *Crime and Delinquency*. Vol. 39 (3): 337–355 (1993); Sheng, Dai Yi, Zu-Yuan Huang, "Organization and Functions of Public Security Agencies of the People's Republic of China," *Eurocriminology*. Vol. 5 (6): 137 (1993); Fu Hualing, "A Case For Abolishing Shelter For Examination: Judicial Review and Police Powers in China," *Police Studies*. Vol. 17 (4): 41 (1994); "Police-public relations—A Chinese view," *Australian & New Zealand Journal of Criminology*, Vol. 30 (1): 87 (1997); Yu, Olivia, Zhang, Lening, "The under-recording of crime by police in China: a case study," *Policing*. Vol. 22 (3): 252–264 (1999); Liqun Cao, Charles Hou., "A comparison of confidence in the police in China and in the United States," *Journal of Criminal Justice*. Vol. 29 (2): 8 (2001); Michael Dutton, "The end of the (mass) line? Chinese policing in the era of the contract (1)," *Social Justice* Vol. 27 (2): 61–106 (2000); Yue Ma, "The powers of the police and the rights of suspects under the amended Criminal Procedure Law of China," *Policing*. Vol. 26 (3) 490–512 (2003); Lening Zhang, Jianhong Liu, "Official status and the swiftness of criminal arrest: A Chinese case of the impact of social position on criminal justice," *Policing*. Vol. 27 (1): 82 (2004). Fu Hualing, "Zhou Yongkang and the Recent Police Reform in China," *Australian & New Zealand Journal of Criminology*. Vol. 38 (2): 241 (2005); Kam C Wong, "Govern police by law (Yifa Zhijing) in China," *Australian & New Zealand Journal of Criminology*. Vol. 37

(Special): 90 (2004) and "Law of assembly in China: People's Republic of China vs. Republic of China," *International Journal of the Sociology of Law*, Vol. 33 (4): 215 (2005).

16. Marx Weber, "Definition of Sociology" (1897). http://www.marxists.org/reference/subject/philosophy/works/ge/weber.htm
17. See Sherman, "Evidence Based Policing," Police Foundation (July 1, 1998). http://www.policefoundation.org/pdf/Sherman.pdf. Whereas Sherman wants to subject police work—theory and practice—to stringent field tests, to find out "what works" or discover "best practice," as a way to professionalize the police, I insist on gathering empirical evidence as a research strategy to give voices to people who matter most in any research process, here domestic scholars and grassroots officers, as a means to keep outside observers in check and foreign researchers at bay.
18. William P. Alford, "Law, Law, What Law?: Why Western Scholars of Chinese History and Society Have Not Had More to Say about Its Law," *MC* Vol. 23 (4): 398–419 (1997).
19. Frederic, Jr. Wakeman's seminal book *Policing Shanghai, 1927–1937* (University of California Press; reprint edition (November 6, 1996) covers only a short 10 years of China history.
20. Michael R. Dutton, *Policing and Punishment in China: From Patriarchy to 'the People'* (Cambridge University Press, 1992).
21. *Id.* pp. 5–6.
22. *Id.* p. 6.
23. *Discipline and Punishment: The Birth of Prison* (Harmondsworth: Peregrine Books, 1979).
24. *Id.* p. 5.
25. For other critical reviews, see "Reviewer *Borge Bakken*: Policing and Punishment in China: From Patriarchy to 'The People' by Michael R. Dutton," *The Australian Journal of Chinese Affairs* No. 31: 121–123 (1994). "Reviewer Arif Dirlik: Policing and Punishment in China: From Patriarchy to "the People." by Michael R. Dutton," *The American Journal of Sociology* Vol. 99 (4): 1145–1147 (1994).
26. Mills, C. Wright, *The Sociological Imagination*. (New York: Oxford University Press, 1959 [1976]). (Sociological imagination allows us to see mundane and random social facts in revealing and patterned ways.)
27. A. R. Radcliffe-Brown, *Structure and Function in Primitive Society: Essays and Addresses*. London: Cohen and West. (Radcliffe-Brown 1952), p. 3.
28. Homer H. Dubs, "'Nature' in the Teaching of Confucius," *Journal of the American Oriental Society* Vol. 50: 233–237 (1930).
29. Tao-Wei Hu, "The Chinese Version of the Law of Nature," *International Journal of Ethics*, Vol. 38 (1): 27–43 (1927).
30. "The Practice of Law as an Obstacle to Justice: Chinese Lawyers at Work" 40 *Law & Society Review* 1 (2006).
31. "Why Do They Not Comply with the Law? Illegality and Semi-Legality among Rural-Urban Migrant Entrepreneurs in Beijing," *Law & Society Review* Vol. 39 (3): 527–562 (2005).
32. For a trenchant critique of postmodernist scholarship in rescuing the Chinese scholars from the pitfall of liberal critique of China, see Joseph W. Esherick, "Cherishing Sources from Afar," MC Vol. 24 (2): 135–161 (1998) (*Symposium:*

Theory and Practice in Modern Chinese History Research. Paradigmatic Issues in Chinese Studies, Part V). McCartney Hervin's *Cherishing Men from Afar* (1995) provided a revisionist reading of China. His observations of China were based on mistranslation of primary sources and misinterpretation of secondary historical data, all the time being.

33. Generations of Chinese legal scholars have adopted the view that China has no or non-functioning legal systems when there was ample evidence suggesting otherwise, i.e., the Qing dynasty had a sophisticated legal code and effective justice administration system. William P. Alford, "Law, Law, What Law?: Why Western Scholars of Chinese History and Society Have Not Had More to Say about Its Law," *MC* Vol. 23 (4): 398–419 (1997).
34. "Harry Harding Review: The Study of Chinese Politics: Toward a Third Generation of Scholarship," *World Politics*, Vol. 36 (2): 84–307, 289 (1984).
35. Lucian W. Pye, "Review: Social Science Theories in Search of Chinese Realities," *CQ* No. 132: 1161–1170 (1992). (Career-minded young Asian scholars wanting to establish themselves or seeking to secure tenure tried to force ill-fitting Western theories in their respective disciplines to explain the complex and complicated world of China.)
36. See "3. Jingcha xue xueke yanjiu ben tu hua de wenti." In Zhu Xudong, "Regarding certain issues regarding research on police studies" ("Guanyu jingcha xuexi yanjiu zhong jige wenti de tantao") *PSUJ* Vol. 101: 149–155 (2002). ("Ben tu hua" or "domestication" of foreign ideas and practices, privileged Western ideas over domestic ones. This resulted from an uncritical acceptance of positive science in the academic community in the 19th century, as championed by England, France, Germany, Italy, and the United States. With the decline of European and United States' influence in world affairs and the emergence of postmodernism and multiculturalism, the positive scientific model's "objective" view of the world is increasingly being challenged by culturalists and ridiculed by the postmodernists. Since policing research is a local knowledge ("di fang sheng zhishi") (C. Geerz), foreign and imported police ideas and practices must be subjected to local adaptation before used. Specifically, police studies must reflect and be informed by Chinese historical, social, and cultural characteristics. Police research must focus on China problems and issues. Police research must be an independent exercise and be critical of status quo. Police research must make independent contributions to China policing and purge foreign influences, entirely. (pp. 153–154).
37. In other areas of research, archives are opening up for inquisitive scholars, Philip C. C. Huang, "County Archives and the Study of Local Social History: Report on a Year's Research in China," *MC* Vol. 8: (1)133–143 (1982).
38. Elizabeth J. Perry, "Trends in the Study of Chinese Politics: State-Society Relations," *CQ* No. 139: 704–713 (1994).
39. Philip C. C. Huang, "Theory and the Study of Modern Chinese History: Four Traps and a Question," *MC* Vol. 24(2): 183–208 (1998) (*Symposium: Theory and Practice in Modern Chinese History Research Paradigmatic Issues in Chinese Studies, Part V*). (Empirical historical research is better than theoretically driven research in understanding China. Theory might be too simplistic, ideological, or ethnocentric to obscure in capturing true conditions in China.)

40. Lucian W. Pye, "On Chinese Pragmatism in the 1980s," *CQ* No. 106: 207–234 (1986). (The ideological furor of Maoism in the 1950s has given way to economic utilitarianism, technocratic managers, and pragmatic socialism in the 1980s.)
41. Randle Peerenboom, "Human Rights, China and Cross-Cultural Inquiry: Philosophy, History and Power Politics," *Philosophy East & West*, Vol. 55 (2005). (Critiquing "Human Rights and Chinese Thought: A Cross-Cultural Inquiry" by Stephen Angle, Peerenboom observed that there is no one concept of human rights but many discourses of human rights in China.)
42. James Q. Wilson, *Varieties of Police Behavior* (Boston, Mass: Harvard University Press, 1968). (Style of policing contingent on community make up.)
43. Linda Chelan Li, "The 'Rule of Law' Policy in Guangdong" *CQ* No 161: 199–220 (2000).
44. Julia Kwong, "The 1986 Student Demonstrations in China: A Democratic Movement?" *AS* Vol. 28 (9), No. 9: 970–985 (1988). (Students from various universities who took to the street under the banner of democracy were agitated by different things and wanted different recourses from the government.)
45. Jie Chen, "Comparing Mass and Elite Subjective Orientations in Urban China," *The Public Opinion Quarterly* Vol. 63(2) 193–219 (1999). (Mass and elite held different views on regime legitimacy, reform assessment, and democratic principles.)
46. Linda Chelan Li, "The 'Rule of Law' Policy in Guangdong: Continuity or Departure? Meaning, Significance and Processes," *CQ* No. 161: 199–220 (2000).
47. Kevin J. O'Brien and Lianjiang Li, "Accommodating 'Democracy' in a One-Party State: Introducing Village Elections in China," *CQ* No. 162 Special Issue: Elections and Democracy in Greater China: 465–489 (2000).
48. Peter Howard Corne, "Creation and Application of Law in the PRC," 50 *Am. J. Comp. L.* 369 (2002). (Flexibility in national law, manifested as general rules and vague provisions, is deemed necessary to accommodate local needs for adjustment, experimentation, and change [pp. 375–376].)
49. *Id.* The Ministry of Public Security amended Article 39 of the "Regulations of the PRC on Administrative Penalties for Public Security" with Article 3 of the "Explanation of Various Problems of the Public Security Bureau's Implementation of the Regulations of the PRC on Administrative Penalties for Public Security which interpreted Article 39 of the Regulations of the PRC on Administrative Penalties for Public Security" (adopted by the NPC Standing Committee on September 5, 1986) to shorten the period for application for relief from 5 days (Article 39) to 2 days (Article 3). This was rejected by the Xingyang District Intermediate Court.
50. "All areas resolutely implement the spirit of National Public Security Bureau Chiefs Meetings" ("Gedi guanche luoshi quanguo gongan-ting-ju zhang huiyi jingshen") *China Police Daily* Online. Jan. 11, 2002.
51. Gary G. Hamilton, "Patriarchalism in Imperial China and Western Europe: A Revision of Weber's Sociology of Domination," *Theory and Society*. Vol. 13 (3): 393–425 (1984). ("I suggest that western typology of traditional, charismatic, and legal domination needs revisions if it is to help and not hinder understanding of non-Western societies."(p. 405)

52. Li Jianhe, "Thinking about 'A Topic of General Interest' in Comparative Police Discipline," *PSUJ* Vol. 101: 43–48 (2002). (China criminal rates cannot be meaningfully compared with those from the West because there are a lot of "dark figures" of crime resulting from the following: (1) PRC Criminal Law have fewer kinds of crime. (2) PRC official crime rate—"Criminal Case Recording Rate"—("Xingshi anjian fa an shu") only reports/records cases from public security, not other branches of law enforcement, e.g., custom, court, procuratorates. (3) China reports minor public order cases ("zhian guanli chufa tiaoli") while Western countries do not count misdemeanors as crimes. (4) Western countries record all property crime. China only records crime when minimum "li an biaozhun" is met. (5) In the US about 35% of crimes happened in supermarkets. In China most businesses do not report such crimes, preferring to taking care of them in house. (6) Urbanization has a direct relationship with crime rates. In the US 80%–90% of the country is urbanized. In China only 30% is.)
53. Media scholars and communication experts have long pointed out that in the public domain there is no reality but "socially constructed" ones. The media is a prime institution in the construction of news—setting agenda, providing for interpretation framework, evoking emotions. See Ray Surette, *Media, Crime, and Criminal Justice: Images and Realities*, Second Edition (Wadsworth 1998), especially Article 1: "Media and the Construction of Crime and Criminal Justice", pp. 1–23. In the context of China, Public Security Legal News has been relied upon by many police researchers, inside and outside China, to provide empirical data for research or use case studies as illustration. But such media reporting has no guarantee of validity and reliability. Zhang Jing, "Getting out of problems areas in Public Security Legal News reporting" ("Jiuchu Gongan fazhi baodao de wuqu") *PSUJ* Vol. 54: 79–81 (1995). (The quality and reliability of "Public Security Legal News" is put into question. The reporting has been pandering to the public, i.e., violence and sex, reporting on crime details and investigation process. The reporting is driven by the market, compromised by irresponsible reporters with little supervision and still less accountability.) For the political role and function of the mass media in reformed China, see also Daniel C. Lynch, *After the Propaganda State: Media, Politics and "Thought Work" in Reformed China* (Stanford University Press, 1999).
54. Police and legal documents might not have been carefully written with proper use of terms and terminologies. This caused confusion and misunderstanding. First, officers who are not familiar with the legal terminologies have a tendency to substitute common social usage of terms instead of specific legal ones required by law: (1) "yingwei fanzui" (not "consider" as crime) was used in lieu of "bukou cheng fanzui" (not "constituting" a crime) (p. 75R); (2) "airen" (love ones—spouse) was used in lieu of "fufu" (husband and wife); (3) "zhengdang fanwei guodang" ("improper use of justifiable defense") was written as "zhengdang fanwei *guodang*" ("justifiable defense in the excess") (p. 75L). Second, officers might choose to use non-recognized police terms, either in terms of abusive use or inappropriate application. For example: (1) "beigao" (accused) is not to be confused with those arrested or detained. They might or might not be the accused (p. 76R); (2) "xingxiong sharen" ("murder" PYECD p. 773R) does not distinguish between "guyi sharen" (intentional murder) or "guoshi saren" (negligent homicide) (p. 76L). Third, officials might be using vague and confusing

terminologies. For example: (1) "duoci suo an" (commit many crimes) is not as clear as a given number (p. 76R); (2) "quzhong" (people) is not as clear a description of the kinds of people by name or type (p. 76R). Tian Rushua and Zheng Baitong, "Avoding Five Misused of Terms in Police and Justice Documents," *PSUJ* Vol. 54: 75–79 (1995).

55. It should be pointed out that "inside out" research, i.e., seeing things from inside or with an indigenous perspective, is not the same as engaging in "insider" research. While a person from the inside is likely to share a local view and indigenous perspective, it need not be so, e.g., whereas the "yu shi" (censorial officials) in imperial China as with the *New York Times*' reporters in the Iraq war were embedded within the officials' ranks, they do not necessarily share the "insider's" perspective to things. "Insider's" research might also raise thorny methodological issues, i.e., myopic view and partiality of judgment. What is gained by intimacy of knowledge and uniqueness of perspective might in turn causes narrowness of vision and bias of opinion, leading to invalid and unsound findings.
56. "The Philosophy of Community Policing in China," *Police Quarterly* Vol. 4(2): 186–214 (2001).
57. "An ideal type is formed by the one-sided accentuation of one or more points of view and by the synthesis of a great many diffuse, discrete, more or less present and occasionally absent concrete individual phenomena, which are arranged according to those one-sidedly emphasized viewpoints into a unified analytical construct." (Weber) Marx Weber, *The Methodology of the Social Sciences*. Translated and edited by Edward A. Shills and Henry Finch. (New York: The Free Press, 1949), p. 90.
58. One should be careful in using parsimonious "ideal type" to capture rich national history and nuance human experience; see Robert M. Marsh, "Weber's Misunderstanding of Traditional Chinese Law," *The American Journal of Sociology* Vol. 106, No. 2 281–302 (Sep., 2000). (Marx misconceived China's legal system as irrational when ample historical evidence showed that China has a predictable legal system as supported by meticulous rules and controlling cases.) The problem rested with the fact that Weber did not speak or read Chinese and relied on selective and supportive secondary data, rather than comprehensive and contradicting primary sources for his assessment; a caveat that should be taken to heart when conducting comparative research, especially in China.
59. Confucius or Kong Fuzhi was born in 551 b.c. in the feudal state of Lu in modern Shantung, China. Originally an official of the Zhou dynasty (1100 to 475 b.c.), he was later much disenchanted with the breakdown of political, social, and moral order during the Warring State (475 to 221 bc) He attributed the disintegration of the society to a breakdown of the moral order and rite system. In response he established the school of thought called Confucianism, which called for the practice of *ren* (humanity) and the following of *li* (rites). Confucianism has since been adopted as a state-sponsored philosophy. For a discussion of Confucius' contribution to Chinese culture, see generally, Yu Yingshi, *Shi yu zhongguo wenhua* (The Intellectuals and Chinese Culture) (Shanghai renmin chubanshe, 1984).

60. *Kongfu dangan xuanpian* (Collection of Confucius household records) (Zhonghua shuju, 1982), 2 Vol. CS1169 K84 1982. Kongdang (*Confucius Records*) 1114.
61. *Confucius Records*, p. 2.
62. The feudal Confucius ethics code consisted of three cardinal guides (ruler guides subject, father guides son, and husband guides wife) and the five constant virtues (benevolence, righteousness, propriety, wisdom, and fidelity).
63. *Confucius Records*, p. 2.
64. For discussion of powers and prerogatives of Kongfu, see Article One of *Confucius Records*.
65. For a discussion of how the Kongfu exploited its powers and prerogatives to the disadvantage of the commoners, see *Confucius Records*, Article 3: The rent exploitation of Kongfu; Article 4: Other exploitation of Kongfu; and Article 6: The impact of farmers on the Kongfu and Kongfu's farm households rent protest and struggle against officials.
66. See the case of Liu Shangqi opening up waste land (*kaihuang*) vs. Kongfu claim to ceremonial plot (*jitian*) in the 31st year of Qianlong in *Confucius Records*, pp. 107–126. (A conversation analysis [O'Barr, 1994] of the trial record shows that the Kongfu enjoyed favorable treatment by the hearing official. Particularly, the Kongfu was talked to, reasoned with, and persuaded to do things.) For anecdotal accounts of how Kongfu was favorably treated by emperors and officials, see generally the oral history of Kong Demao, *Kongzi neizhai yishi* (Anecdote at the Confucian household) (Tianjin renmin chubanshe, 1981).
67. See Antonio Marongiu, *Medieval Parliaments* (London: Eyre & Spottiswoode, 1968), p. 24.
68. Kang Daimin, *Discourse on broad concept of public security* (Beijing: Qunzhong chubanshe, 2001).
69. Charles Reith, *Police Idea, its History and Evolution in England in the Eighteenth Century and After* (1938).
70. Albert J. Reiss, Jr., "Police Organization in the Twentieth Century," *Crime and Justice* Vol. 15, Modern Policing (1992), pp. 51–97.
71. James Q. Wilson, *Varieties of Police Behavior* (Boston, Mass: Harvard University Press, 1968).
72. Carl B. Klockars, *The Idea of Police* (Sage Publications, 1985).
73. For a research note on sources and methods, see M. Taylor Fravel, "Online and on China: Research Sources in the Information Age," *CQ* No. 163: 821–842 (2000). (Pre-1960s data on China is all but inaccessible, as with knowledgeable China researchers. In the early 1960s, most of the research was based on translated materials—mostly newspapers and government documents, by the U.S. Consulate in Hong Kong. In the mid- to late 1960s, this was supplemented by exit interviews in Hong Kong. In the 1970s, many more illegally obtained documents that bear on the cultural revolution were available. Since 1979, mainland libraries and national archives were made available. Discreet visits and personal interactions provided the bulk of the research materials. Finally, since the 1980s, researchers from China were allowed to study outside of China. They brought with them valuable data sets, personal experience, and family connections. In the 1990s, the Internet provided armchair researchers with direct access to many of the library sources or local materials that could only be had by having

personal access or physical visits. For a research source note into Chinese law, see Wei Luo and Joan Liu, "A Complete Research Guide to the Laws of the People's Republic of China (PRC)." http://www.llrx.com/features/prc.htm, and Joan Liu, "Update to Beyond the Border: The Chinese Legal Information System in Cyberspace." http://www.llrx.com/features/china2.htm

74. Jerome Alan Cohen, "New Developments in the Study of Chinese Law: Introduction," *The Journal of Asian Studies* Vol. 27 (3): 475–483 (1968). (Chinese law research suffered from a lack of language skills and poverty in cultural perspective. The tendency of Western lawyers, particularly those from the U.S., is to view China from its own cultural lens and to understand China legal terms by referring to its own development [pp. 479–483]). Howard L. Boorman, "The Study of Contemporary Chinese Politics: Some Remarks on Retarded Development," *World Politics* Vol. 12 (4): 585–599 (1960). (Prior to WWII, American study of China was limited to a handful of experts trained in the French sinology tradition, which stressed a linguistic, biographic, and philosophical preparation and approach. China scholars have always suffered from linguistic and social barriers, and after the establishment of PRC, political obstacles were added as problems [pp. 588–589]. In the 1960s, China was virtually inaccessible.) Kenneth Lieberthal, "China and Political Science, " *PS* Vol. 19 (1): 70–78 (1986). (The study of China politics is hampered by a number of facts: First, study in and of China requires substantial investment of time and effort to submerge oneself in the mastering of a difficult language, familiarization with a long history, and sensitivity to rich culture [p. 71R]. Second, while the field of political science was moving toward quantitative analysis in the 1960s and 1970s, statistical data is not available from China before and well into the reform era [p. 72L]. Third, political development in the U.S.—most noticeably McCarthyism in the early 1950s—all but deterred students from entering the field [p. 72R]. After 1979, serious investigation into China was made possible by a sea change of attitude on the part of Chinese political leadership and the corresponding scholarly community. Political leaders wanted to gather useful scientific [p. 74R] data for reform purposes, while the scholarly community looked toward the West to jump start a long neglect educational system [p. 74R])
75. Ministry of Public Security ("Gongan bu"), "Notice regarding prohibiting foreign journalists from illegal reporting activities ("Guanyu jizhi weiguo jizhe feifa caifang hudong de tongzhi") (April 22, 1994). *Compendium of PS Law* pp. 1296–1297. (Foreign reporters have been found to report on sensitive areas and subjects. Foreign reporters are forbidden to liaison with dissenters or report on major disasters without first asking for permission and having video/sound recordings examined.)
76. This is not the same as saying that there is not systematic and comprehensive data gathering in China. In fact, political doctrine in China from Marx to Mao to Deng calls for finding ideas in matters (Marx), integrating theory with practice (Mao), and seeking truth from facts (Deng). George Braybrooke, "Recent Developments in Chinese Social Science, 1977–79," *CQ* No. 79: 593–607 (1979). (China political leadership and policy makers have long been interested in social research and ethnographic studies as a way to inform policy and design strategy. The premier scientific and policy research agency is of course the CASS—

Chinese Academy of Social Science.) But inasmuch as such research data and findings are driven by political ideology and administrative needs, such data and findings might be contaminated.

77. Ole Bruun, Soren Poulsen, Hatla Thelle, *MC Research Danish Experience* (University of Copenhagen, 1991) Center for East and Southeast Asian Studies, U. of C., Stokhusgade 5, DK-1317 Copenhagen K, Denmark. (The book is a collection of papers from a seminar held November 1–2, 1990, at U. of Copenhagen on Problems and Methods in MC Research. The seminar was convened by four major China research institutions in Denmark: the Center for East and Southeast Asian Studies at U. of Copenhagen; East Asian Institute at U. of C.; the Nordic Institute of Asian Studies, Copenhagen; and the East Adian Institute, U. of Aarhus. The seminar provided a reflection on China research experience since 1978: "What methods are suitable for understanding the mechanisms of the Chinese society? What problems confront the researcher? What are the ethical questions involved, and what are reasonable considerations for our informants?" (p. 4). The recurring problems of research in China are evasive answers, unkept promises, classified material, and regions 'out of bounds' for foreigners" (p. 5). The major issue is cross cultural communication.) Ole Odgaard, "Data Collection and Use of Local Statistics—Some Experiences from Field Studies in Sichuan" (pp. 18–29). In China "even non-controversial statistics can be difficult to collect during field studies, and the reliability of local statistics is often questionable" (p. 18). The accessibility problem is due to lack of connections (*guanxi*) and lack of openness. The reliability issue is a result of manipulation for self-serving reasons (Ibid). For example, tax figures may be deliberately underreported if the local authorities hope to retain a larger portion of taxes collected. In a survey of 38 private enterprises it was found that their taxes and levies were substantially higher than recorded by the county tax bureau (p. 19–20). There is always a disparity between the *Statistical Yearbook* and local data. The differences of rural income may be due to sample differences or percentage to calculate cost and expenses, a figure that is arbitrarily arrived at or politically determined and never economically decided (p. 22).
78. Zhang Chao "Discussion of framework of opening of police work" ("Lun jongwu gongkai zhidu goujian") *PSUJ* Vol. 99: 97–105 (2002).
79. Ma Li, "On Improving the Quality of Police Journal," *PSUJ* Vol. 67: 107–109 (1997).
80. Zhou Zhaoping and Zhang Xiaolin, "A Summary of Symposium of Reconstruction of Police Disciplines in China," *PSUJ* Vol. 95: 106–111 (2002). (Between November 16 and 18, 2001, the PSU organized the "National Police [Public Security] Scientific Discipline Construction Seminar" to discuss the status, achievements, focus, and future of police science as a study discipline and education field. The conference was well attended by scholars, experts, policy makers, and political leaders from MPS, Ministry of Education, public security universities nationwide.)
81. The consensus is that the target of police studies is the police. The objective is to apply science to the study of police and policing in search of patterns and theory. *Id*. p. 107.

82. The Editorial Office, "To Enhance the Research of Public Security Theories and Guide the Practice of Public Security Work," *Gongan Yanjiu* Issue 72 (2000), pp. 6–7.
83. *Gongan Yanjiu* Issue 78 (2000), p. 8.
84. Public security literature includes books, journals, newspaper, meeting records, scientific-technical reports, government publications, student dissertations, public security files, and press releases. In terms of academic journals, every one of the 24 public security colleges and universities publishes one or more law or police journals. According to the public security integrated index, a typical public security college library carries about 341 foreign police journals/magazines and 228 domestic ones. Since 1998, libraries collected about 1,800 public security and law types of books, increasing about 300 per year. Public security literature is being used for three purposes: policy making, operational direction, and teaching and research. Zheng Ling "A brief discussion of development and use of public security literature" ("Qiantan Gongan wexian de gai liyong,") *PSUJ* Vol. 55: 78–81 (1995), p. 39.
85. Adopted by the 3rd Session of the Ninth National People's Congress on March 15, 2000.
86. Adopted at the 12th Meeting of the Standing Committee of the Eight National People's Congress on February 28, 1995, promulgated by Order 40 of the President of the People's Republic of China, and effective as of the date of promulgation.
87. Promulgated on May 14, 1998, by the Ministry of Public Security (MPS) as "MPS Order 35" [Gonganbu di 35 hao ling]
88. I have provided a legal brief to the Immigration and Refugee Board on the issue of summonses in June of 2004. The subject of summonses will not be further discussed.
89. Arrests made by procuratorates are governed by other regulations, besides relevant provisions in CPL Article II, Compulsory Measures. See generally *Procuratorate handbook* ("Jiangcha guan shouce") (Shanxi renmin chubanshe, 1995), pp. 297–309.
90. See identical provision in PSR Article 225.
91. See PSR 123: "In making arrest, the arrestee must be shown arrest warrant" ("dibu zheng").
92. "Top Legislator on Implementation of Criminal Procedure Law," *People's Daily*, Monday, November 20, 2000 (Li Peng, chairman of the Standing Committee of National People's Congress [NPC], observed frequent police violation of PRC Criminal Procedure Law and called for vigilant compliance). See Kam C. Wong, "Police Powers and Control in the People's Republic of China: A case study of shouron shencha," *Columbia Journal of Asian Law* Vol. 10 (3): 367–390 (1996).
93. See Kam C. Wong, "Govern police by law," *Australian New Zealand Journal of Criminology* (2005) Vol. 37(4): 90–106.
94. "Police Legitimacy Crisis and Police Law Reform in China II," *International Journal of Police Science and Management* Vol. 7(3) (2005) Vol. 7(1): 1–13.
95. "Sheltering for Examination: Law, Policy, and Practice," in *Occasional Papers/ Reprints Series in Contemporary Asian Studies*, University of Maryland, School of Law (9/1997), p. 53.

96. Wan Shenzi, Li Zhenyu, Zhang Caigui & Zhang Lincun, "The issue about police participating-non-policing activities" ("Guanyu gongan minjing canyu fei jingwu huodong de tiaocha") *Public Security Studies* Vol. 69, Issue 1: 21–24 (2000), p. 22R.
97. *Id.* p. 22R.
98. *Id.* p. 23L.
99. *Id.* p. 23L.
100. Ding Shijie and Fung Liping, *Public security applied writings* ("Gongan Yingyong Xiezuo") (Beijing: Zhongguo renmin Gongan daxu chubanse, 2002), Article 1: Public security official documents ("Gongan jiguan xingzheng gongwen").
101. "Methods of dealing with documents of state administrative agencies" ("Guo jia zingzheng jiguan gongwen chuli banfa"). (Promulgated by State Council on February 18, 1987. Amended on November 21, 1993, and August 24, 2001. Effective January 1, 2001.) See also "Methods of dealing with documents with Chinese communist agency" ("Zhongguo gongchangdang jiguan gongwen chuli tiaoli").
102. *Id.* pp. 30–39.
103. "Methods of dealing with documents of state administrative agencies" ("Guo jia zingzheng jiguan gongwen chuli banfa"). (Promulgated by State Council on February 18, 1987. Amended on November 21, 1993, and August 24, 2001. Effective January 1, 2001.) See also "Methods of dealing with documents with Chinese communist agency" ("Zhongguo gongchangdang jiguan gongwen chuli tiaoli").
104. *PYCED*, p. 477R.
105. Administrative records, Article 9 (1) (1993).
106. See discussion and examples in "Article 1", *Public security applied writings*, pp. 49–50.
107. *PYCED*, p. 822L.
108. Administrative records, Article 9 (2) (1993).
109. *Id.*
110. *PYCED*, p. 373R.
111. Administrative records, Article 9 (3) (1993).
112. *Security applied writings*, pp. 52–53.
113. *PYCED*, p. 902L
114. See for example *Compendium of People's Republic of China Public Security Laws* (*Compendium of PS Law*) "Zhonghua renmin gonghe guo Gongan falu quanshu" (Jilin: Jilin Chubanshe, 1995). [Organized by public security functions: "xianfa bian" (Article on Constitution) (pp. 3–24), "xingfa bian" (Article on Criminal Law) (pp. 29–155), "xingshi suxong fa bian" (Article on Criminal Procedure Law) (pp. 159–359); "zhian bian" (Article on Public order) (pp. 363–679); "huji bian" (Article on Household Registration) (pp. 683–741); "jiaotung bian" (Article on Traffic) (pp. 745–1026); "xiaofang bian" (Article on Fire prevention) (pp. 1031–1223); "churu jing bian" (Article on Border Exit and Entry) (pp. 1227–1316); "laodong jiaoyang bian" (Article on Reform through Labor) (pp. 1321–1382); "xingzheng susong yu guojia peichang bian" (Article on Administrative Appeal and State Compensation) (pp. 1387–1425); "jingchafa bian" (Article on Police Law) (pp. 1431–1599); "xiong guan fa bian" (Article on Related Laws) (pp. 1603–1791).]

115. Party central social order comprehensive management committee ("Zhong yang shehui hian zhonghe zhi weiyuan hui"), Ministry of Public Security ("Gongan bu"), Ministry of Civil Affairs ("Minzheng bu"), Ministry of Agriculture ("Nonye bu"), "Comments regarding strengthening village public security committee work" ("Guan yu jiaqiang non cun zhibao hui gongzuo de yijian") (November 21, 1994). *Compendium of PS Law*, pp. 459–461. (The "yijoian" described in great detail problems with the withering away of village public security committees: lack of leadership, aging membership, decline of interests. This provides a context to discuss the need to provide ways of rehabilitating the public security committee, e.g., recruit young people and provide for incentives.)
116. *Id.*
117. Ministry of Public Security ("Gongan bu"), "Notice regarding stern execution of inspection of vehicle registration" ("Guanyu yange jixing hefa cheliang paizheng guiding deng wenti tongzhi"). *Compendium of PS Law*, p. 939. (MPS discovered the problems with local public security organs issuing illegal official vehicle registration plates.)
118. *Id.*
119. Ji Wei Wei, "Analysis on Calculation of Quotation in Journal of Jiansu Police Officer College," *Journal of Jiansu Police Officer College*, No. 89: 181–188 (2003).
120. This means that articles must help with policy choice (relevancy); proposed ideas supported by facts (empirical); and point out patterns and regularities of police work (theoretical).
121. Jia Yongsheng, "My Opinion on Improving Police Higher Education Journal," *JCPPSU* Issue 77: 101–103 (1999).
122. Wu Yiqing, "Summary of the 12th Meeting of the Special Invited Senior Editors of "Police Studies" *Policing Studies* Vol. 97: 88–91 (2002).
123. Yang Hongping, "The Role of Publishing Articles by Academic Magazines by Police Colleges," *JCPPSU* Issue 77: 103—106 (1999).
124. Yan Zhifen, "The Development Sense of the Newly Publicly Issued Academic Journals," *JCPPSU* Issue 77: 106–107 (1999).
125. Zhongguo gongan baike quanshu editorial committee, Zhongguo gongan baike quanshu (China police encyclopedia) (Jilin: Jilin Cjubanshe, 1989), 22.
126. The People China's Daily Online has published "zhongyao yanlun" since its inception: http://www.cpd.com.cn/flmen.asp?menulb=109%D6%D8%D2%AA%D1%D4%C2%DB&menujb=3 On June 6, 2002, there were a total of 18 columns reported, i.e., (1) "Women gaixian Xiao Yuquan xuexi shenme" (What can we learn from Xiao Yuquan" (May 28, 2002); (2) "Silun jiaqiang he gaijing gongan jiguan zuofeng jianshe" (Fourth discussion on measures to strengthen and improve public security organs work style) (May 21, 2002); (3) "Yongtiao zhongdan zhongcehng weidang" (Eager to carry the heavy burden, being true to the Party) (May 5, 2002); (4) "Guanjian zai 'yiba shou'—sanlun jiaqiang he gaige he gaijing gongan jiguan zuofeng jainshe" (Third discussion on measures to strengthen and improve public security organs work style) (April 25, 2002); (5) "Erlun jiaqiang he gaijing gongan jiguan zuofeng jainshe" (Second discussion on measures to strengthen and improve public security organs work style) (April 2, 2002); (6) "Yi quanju he zhanlue gaodu chuji jiaqiang he gaige paichusuo gongzuo" (Use comprehensive and strategic measures to launch attacks

on strengthening and reforming police post work) (March 20, 2002); (7) "Yixin zuofeng qude cheng xiao: Yilun jiaqiang he gaijing gongan jiguan zuofeng jainshe" (Use work style to achieve effects: First discussion on measures to strengthen and improve public security organs work style) (February 27, 2002); (8) "Laoji zeren zai chuang huiwang: 2002 nian xinnian xianqi" (Keep firmly in mind in order to achieve new glory: New year speech of 2002) (December 31, 2002); (9) "Shiying xin xingshi yingjie xing tiaozhan" (Adjust to new situations, embrace new challenges) (December 22, 2001); (10) "Jiaqiang xunlian tigao jinang" (Strengthen training promote competence) (December 3, 2002); (11) "Quanmian jiaqiang neibu jiandu jiaqiang jifa shiping" (Strengthen overall internal supervision, improve upon law enforcement standards) (October 17, 2001); (12) "Xuexi "Mukang jingshen" shijian "sandaibiao" (Learn about "Mugang spirit" realize "three represents") (September 19, 2001); (13) "Zhidu guanli yifa zhijing" (Systemize control, legalize regulation of officers) (July 6, 2001); (14) "Zai dalao xixiang shang henxia gongfu" (Work hard to improve and focus on the foundation of ideology) (July 6, 2002); (15) "Xiun zaohao "sanxiang jiaoyu" (Tenth discussion improving "Three kinds of education" (July 5, 2001); (16) "Hang yang kuangrong, jiang ding lixiang xinlian" (Achieve the tradition of grand glory, holds firmly to ideal) (June 26, 2002); (17) "Fang Guanxi gongan ting jingzhen zong duichang Liang Hongwei" (Interview with Guanxi public security department, economic crime investigator chief, Liang Hong wei) (n.d); (18) "Yilun zhengdun he guifan shjichang jingji zhixu, yanli daji jingji fanzui" (First discussion on recognizing and structuring economic order, strike harsh at economic crime) (n.d.).

127. As a street-level bureaucracy, police cannot help but be pragmatic in their outlook and practical in their approach while doing the people's business. Kevin J. O'Brien and Lianjiang Li, "Selective Policy Implementation in Rural China," *Comparative Politics* Vol. 31 (2): 167–186 (1999). (As street-level bureaucrats, local cadres at village level have multiple responsibilities and competing demands. They have to be flexible in negotiating their duties and dispensing their responsibilities.)

128. The ideological war between neo-conservative (in the guise of traditionalism and nationalism) and radical democratic forces (over rule of law and human rights) is far from over, particularly when the latter suffered declining influence after June 4. The conservatives are more emboldened than ever by increasing signs of reform failures, such as huge unemployment, gross inequality, and exploding criminality. The cultural implications, social impact, and, in the end, political fallout of such a war of words and ideas over reform direction and process have yet to be fully played out. In the meantime China forged ahead with the reform program under Deng's last words calling for pragmatism ("It does not matter if the cat is white or black. If it can catch a mouse, it is a good cat") and experimentalism ("Crossing the River by Feeling Each Stone"). *Feng Chen*, "Order and Stability in Social Transition: Neoconservative Political Thought in Post-1989 China," *CQ* No. 151: 593–613 (1997).

129. PRC Constitution (adopted at the Fifth Session of the Fifth National People's Congress and Promulgated for Implementation by the Proclamation of the National People's Congress on December 4, 1982): "The basic task of the nation in the years to come is to concentrate its effort on socialist modernization. Under

the leadership of the Communist Party of China and the guidance of Marxism-Leninism and Mao Zedong Thought, the Chinese people of all nationalities will continue to adhere to the people's democratic dictatorship and follow the socialist road, steadily improve socialist institutions, develop socialist democracy, improve the socialist legal system and work hard and self-reliantly to modernize industry, agriculture, national defense and science and technology step by step to turn China into a socialist country with a high level of culture and democracy. "Chen Yun (陈云) (*June 13, 1905–April 10, 1995*), a participant of Long March (1934–1935) and a long-time member of the Politburo Standing Committee of the Communist Party of China (中国共产党中央政治局常务委员会) is one of the most conservative, ideologically. Chen Yun: "one must note that opening to the world will inevitably be accompanied by capitalistic ideology and life style, both of which are detrimental to our socialist cause." He wanted the reform limited with his now famous "bird-cage economy" analogy.

130. Lucian W. Pye, "On Chinese Pragmatism in the 1980s," *CQ* No. 106: 207–234 (1986). (Pragmatism becomes the official ideology of the reform period under Deng. This is reinforced by Chinese people's ingrained national character of nationalism and social practice of guanxi and loyalty.)
131. Deflem, Mathieu. 1997. "Policing International Society: Views from the United States." Review essay on 'Cops Across Borders,' by Ethan A. Nadelmann and 'Crime and Law Enforcement in the Global Village,' edited by William F. McDonald. *Police Forum* 7(3): 6–8; Deflem, Mathieu, and Amanda J. Swygart. 2001. "Comparative Criminal Justice." Pp. 51–68 in *Handbook of Criminal Justice Administration*, edited by Toni DuPont-Morales, Michael Hooper, and Judy Schmidt. New York: Marcel Dekker Publishers.
132. I take to heart my mentor Professor Bayley's constant and emphatic admonition that "comparative" policing between countries is a misnomer. First, comparison is what we do as students and scholars. It is our stock of trade. It is through comparing of ideas and contrasting of practices that we come to discern similarities and differences, and learning and understanding the things under examination in the process. "Comparative policing" is a species of comparative exercise, not a unique field of study. Second, when one engages in "comparing" police from two societies, we are not just looking for formalistic similarities and superficial differences. In actuality, we are really engaging in a study of culture to find out why police behave differently in two diverse cultural systems, separated by time and/or place. Thus, it is more appropriate to call "comparative policing" the "cross-cultural" study of policing.

    True cross-cultural policing research and study is rare and is being marginalized. J. I. Ross, "The current status of comparative policing in the curriculum," *Journal of Criminal Justice Education* Vol. 7: 263–273 (1996); J.P. Brodeur (Ed.), (1995), Comparisons in policing: An international perspective (Aldershot, England: Avebury, 1996). Annmarie Cordner, Harry Dammer, Frank Horvath, "A national survey of comparative criminal justice courses in universities in the United States," *Journal of Criminal Justice Education* Vol. 11 (2): 211–225 (2000) ("58 (34%) of the sample schools included at least one course in their curriculum").

133. Many of the current comparative criminal justice researches are not true comparative studies but country studies, placed side by side, e.g., E. Fairchild, *Comparative Criminal Justice Systems*. (Belmont, CA: Wadsworth Publishing Co., 1993).
134. David H Bayley spearheaded such an effort in *Patterns of policing: a comparative international analysis* (New Brunswick, N.J.: Rutgers University Press, 1985).
135. Chinese police studies with Chinese characteristics.
136. William P. Alford, "Law, Law, What Law?: Why Western Scholars of Chinese History and Society Have Not Had More to Say about Its Law," *MC* Vol. 23 (4): 398–419 (1997).
137. Philip C. C. Huang, "Biculturality in Modern China and in Chinese Studies," *MC* Vol. 26 (1): 3–31 (2000).
138. For a rejoinder, see Prasenjit Duara, "Response to Philip Huang's 'Biculturality in Modern China and in Chinese Studies'" *MC* Vol. 26 (1): 32–37 (2001) [Bi-cultural approach provides no escape from globalization of knowledge, universalization of culture, and commodization of ideas, especially when the underlying indigenous culture (China) (willingly or by force of circumstances, consciously or unconsciously) increasingly takes on a modernized look and feel.] In response to Duara, my sense is that the transformation of indigenous culture, while a distinct possibility, does not mean that local knowledge and indigenous understanding are no longer necessary for researcher. First, cultural transformation is an incremental, interactive, and intergenerational project. Japan today still enjoys a village-like culture, in many respects. David Bayley, Forces of Order (University of California Press, 1991). Second, local memory is cumulative and becomes part of a bi-cultural person's persona, once assimilated. All understanding of a culture will relate back to his/her exposure to a culture, especially when one is being brought up in a certain cultural milieu in time and place. The culture will change, but one's cultural identity and memory stays, and keeps renewing and reinventing itself. This cultural exposure become one's life experience and provides the context, and facility, for one to make sense of what one sees and hears in later life. Berman, Harold J., "The Historical Foundation of Law" Emory Law Journal Vol. 54 (2005). Learning a language and culture is thus learning how to negotiate in a given social milieu; what things mean and potent. Thus to understand a language is also to understand life as experienced in a group. Michael W. Nicholson, "Abusing Wittgenstein: The Misuse of the Concept of Language Games in Contemporary Theology," Journal of the Evangelical Theological Society Vol. 39(4): 617–630 (1996).
139. Huang's bi-culturalism debate recalls and reinvigorates the debate in criminal justice over whether "insider" vs. "outsider" is better able to study a criminal justice system in action. The "insiders" (those who has been through the system) is supposed to have better access to secret information and possess unique insights not (easily?) available to the "outsiders." For example, convict criminologists conduct correctional research as informed by a convict's personal experiences and from a critical perspective. They argued that scholarship in general and convict criminology in particular is intimately and irrevocably linked with one's personal identity, experiences, sensitivity, perspective, and ideology, as an integrated whole. J.I. Ross and S. Richards, "What is The New School of Convict Criminology?" *The Blanket* (August 2003). Opponents to "insider scholarship,"

including this author, claim that it suffered from conceptual, theoretical, empirical, methodological, and philosophical problems. *Conceptually*, who is considered an "insider"? Does insider include researchers married to an insider? *Theoretically*, "insider" researchers might not have much to offer to the readers. If all that an "insider" can offer is secretive, hidden, or contextual information, there are other ways to obtain such information, e.g., participatory observer (the term in vogue is "embedding") or having insider informants [the case in point is "deep throat," see O'Connor, J. "I'm the Guy They Called Deep Throat," *Vanity Fair* May 30 (2005)]. However, if "insider" researchers' voices are treasured, not for their substantive knowledge, but for their unique perspective and radical insights arising from their identity [see V.K. Kanuha, "'Being' Native versus 'Going' Native: Conducting Social Work Research as an Insider," *Social Work* Vol. 45 (5): 439–447 (2000)], deriving from their experience [see M. Polanyi, *The Tacit Dimension* (Garden City, NY: Anchor Books, 1967)] and emulating from their emotional resonance, i.e., how Chinese police officers think and feels about (aspects of) policing are very much driven by their pride in PRC and their profession, there are other unique perspectives and insights that are as worthy of reporting as a special brand of scholarship, e.g., police spouse's perspective, police parents' insights, and police siblings' reflection [see R. Adlam, "Developing Ethics Education for Police Leaders and Managers: action research and critical reflection for curriculum and personal development," *Educational Action Research* Vol. 6 (1) (1998)]. *Methodologically*, "insider" research in the first person with an agenda to pursue, ideology to promote, and interest to advance contributes to bias observation and partisan analysis. Instead of being a disinterested reporter of social conditions, "insiders" become committed advocates for change (see H. Garza, "Objectivity, Scholarship, and Advocacy: The Chicano/Latino Scholar in America," Julian Samora Research Institute, Occasional Paper No. 58, March 1999). *Empirically*, "insiders" might not know as much as "outsiders." "Insiders" also might include people who are not in the know, i.e., past insiders, such as retired police officers who are out of touch, or current police officers who are promoted/transferred from a knowledge depository site [see J. Chan, *Changing Police Culture: Policing in a Multicultural Society* (Cambridge: Cambridge University Press, 1997)]. More damningly, "insider" as an all-embracing term—once a "Chinese" cop always a "Chinese" cop—fails to sufficiently discriminate between police practitioners who know something about the area of inquest and those who do not. Chinese police is a complex institution, no "insider" is capable of knowing it all (W. St. John, "Professor with a past" *New York Times*, August 9, 2003). *Philosophically*, treating "practitioner scholarship" differently also sends the wrong (at least mixed) signals to the research community, i.e., it is who you are not what you know or have to say that matters in the academic world.

140. With an abiding faith in U.S. ideological exceptionalism (democracy, equality, rule of law) and an equally strong conviction in scientific universalism (rationality, objectivity, generalizability), American scholars have a tendency to examine societies everywhere under a microscope, in order to validate the absolute superiority of American theories or downplay the possible contribution of non-American paradigms. Lucian W. Pye, "Asia Studies and the Discipline,"

PS: Political Science and Politics Vol. 34(4): 805–807 (2001). ["But does anyone believe that American practice can be treated as the norm for everyone? Or even for any other particular country?" (p. 805).]

141. In 1999, the author started with other interested Asian police scholars from Taiwan, PRC, Hong Kong, and Korea the Asian Association of Policing to bring indigenous voices to the study of Asian policing. "Closing Remark" (AAPS Presidency Inauguration Speech) AAPS Third Annual Conference: Asian Policing in the 21st Century, Open University, July 29, 2002. Co-sponsored by Center for Criminology, Hong Kong University, Open University, Chinese University of Hong Kong. Kam C. Wong, Asian Policing in the 21st Century (Proceedings) (Hong Kong: AAPS, 2002) (There is a need to study policing from a local perspective and with indigenous data, looking at policing from inside out and bottom up. Comparative policing should be taught with local content and within local context.) Many of the recent Chinese political science and police studies research and writing are by first and second generation Chinese scholars who are educated in the West, e.g., Wu Guoguan, a Princeton political scientist from Victoria University, was within the inner circle of PRC Premier Zhao Zhiyang before his demise, and Fu Hualing, who single handedly plowed the field of Chinese police studies in Hong Kong University in the 1990s, was educated at the University of Toronto and was a PRC police instructor in the 1980s. David Shambaugh, "Keeping Pace with a Changing China: *CQ* at 35," *CQ* No. 143: 669–676 (1995). [The *China Quarterly* now has outstanding contributions from mainland Chinese emigrants who bring with them personal experience and nebu (internal) documents, connections within China, and contacts inside institutions.]
142. Chen Yuanxiao, "Ponder over the Sustained Development and Improvement of Policing," *Public Security Studies* Vol. 78: 22–26 (2001). [The current police system, process, and methods are not keeping pace with radical economic reform and catching up on rapid social changes. Specifically, there are three kinds of "bottlenecks." First, the police administration bottleneck, i.e., there is no central administration of police resources and coordination of operations (p. 22L). Currently, public security officers are funded and directed by local government and Party officials, but have to report to the MPS chain of command. Second, police quality and capacity bottleneck (p. 22R). Police are lacking in critical skills, e.g., computing, financial, business skills. Currently, police colleges and universities are only teaching general academic and abstract theoretical knowledge. They are not providing new officers with functional skills and in-service officers with specialized and professional knowledge. Third, complex bureaucratic and tall hierarchy command structure bottleneck. Currently, the command and control structure of the police is at the municipal and county level. There is a long chain of command. Some cases require senior officers to be on scene, but this cannot be done in a timely manner. The reporting process and command practice slows down operations (p. 23R). Fourth, adherence to traditional ideas bottleneck. Currently, criminal investigation is based on "on scene inspection, personal investigation, and surprise interrogation." There is no attempt to adopt more modernized technology and progressive techniques of investigation. In terms of police operations, they are based on mass campaign and collective actions, one after another. There is no attempt to target special

problems for focused treatment. In terms of order maintenance, there is a reliance on legal prohibition and physical punishment. There is no attempt to ameliorate disorderly conduct or forestall risky activities. In terms of policy decision making, the reliance is on seniority and experience, not systematic investigation of problems or broad consultation with the people (p. 23R).]

143. An issue is raised as to whether domesticated foreign ideas take on local roots and indigenous characteristics, which require a local person (or bicultural) person to investigate, meaningfully. This issue should not detain us for long. "Foreign" or "alien" ideas once transplanted take on local content and characteristics, and must be understood in local terms and within local context. A trip to McDonald's in China has different cultural meaning and social significance than in the United States. In the United States it is a fast food trip to fill the stomach for a busy blue collar worker. In China it is an expensive date for two newly met romancing young people.

144. Philip C. C. Huang, "The Paradigmatic Crisis in Chinese Studies: Paradoxes in Social and Economic History," *MC* Vol. 17(3): 299–341 (1991). (The way to neutralize ill-conceived theories, East or West, is to engage in micro-social empirical research, or simply let the facts of specific cases speak for themselves, when found to be in contradiction with macro-general theory.)

7 Development of Guidance Activities by Police for Prevention of Juvenile Delinquency in Japan

MINORU YOKOYAMA

Contents

Introduction

In this chapter, the development of guidance activities by police until the present era of police without borders is discussed. A modern society, which becomes more complicated and sophisticated, will suffer great damage if someone commits a crime or causes an accident by negligence. Therefore, the police are inclined to invest more resources for the prevention of crime and juvenile delinquency. The preventive activities for juvenile delinquency have been carried out in the local community. However, in Japan the activities are generally directed by the National Police Agency. From a historical viewpoint, I would like to analyze the development of the guidance activities by the Japanese police since the end of World War II in 1945.

Poor Guidance Activities by Police Immediately After World War II

Before World War II we had the centralized national police, which oppressed human rights during the war. After the defeat in World War II, in August of 1945 it was disbanded for democratization by the General Headquarters of the Allied Powers (GHQ) in which officials coming from the United States took the initiative (Yokoyama, 2001a:190). By the direction of GHQ we adopted the local autonomous police following the U.S. model. In addition, GHQ ordered the purge of police leaders who had contributed to oppressing people, above all, political criminals during the war. In such a situation the police did not have enough power to maintain security and order well. They had few resources to guide juveniles to prevent their delinquency. Therefore, they failed to catch many juvenile offenders.

In 1946 the total number of juvenile Penal Code offenders caught by the police amounted to 111,790. Their rate per 1,000 population between 10 and 19 years of age was only 6.7 (Research and Training Institute of the Ministry of Justice, *White Paper on Crime in 1999* [written in Japanese]:496). Behind the above-mentioned total number of juvenile Penal Code offenders there was a great dark number. At that time the highest number of juveniles committed offenses in our history (Yokoyama, 2001:175).

At the end of the war we suffered from the shortage of goods, above all, food. People living in a city had to get their necessary goods at a black market, which gangsters controlled with poor regulation by the police. In such a chaotic situation we saw many youngsters, especially orphans, commit property crimes such as theft and robbery because of their hunger.

During the later period of World War II, many boys and girls were taken from their cities to rural areas to escape bombing by U.S. fighting planes.

Table 7.1 Juvenile Vagrants Reported by Protection Section at Children Bureau's of Welfare Ministry after World War II

	Male	Female	Total
Fiscal 1946	9,209	1,944	11,153
Fiscal 1947	11,532	2,477	14,009

Their parents and protectors were killed by large-sized bombs. Therefore, we saw many homeless orphans in big cities after the war. They made their livelihood by behavior such as robbing, picking up cigarette ends, helping at the black market, shining shoes, begging, selling newspapers, selling cigarettes, prostituting themselves, working as physical laborers, pick-pocketing, loitering in rural areas, taking charge of children, taking seats for people to ride trains, helping at farmhouses, and selling candy.

To protect juvenile vagrants, officers in charge of child welfare began to guide them. The officers sent them to a facility for child welfare.* Table 7.1 shows the total number of juvenile vagrants found by officers in charge of child welfare. However, it was the tip of the iceberg of juvenile vagrants. By the way, the total number of juvenile vagrants increased from 11,153 in 1946 to 14,009 in 1947. This phenomenon was caused by more earnestly protective activities rather than by a true increase in juvenile vagrants.

By the guidance of GHQ we began to respect child welfare, because we regarded children as the rising generation for democracy. At that time officers in charge of child welfare worked earnestly for protecting poor juveniles who committed deviant behavior and crimes. Under the Child Welfare Law enacted on December 12 in 1947, all Japanese are obliged to birth a baby healthily and to rear a child soundly. Under this law the protective measures for juveniles including those for juvenile delinquents confined to Kyogo-in (a reformatory home) were improved.

After the Child Welfare Law was enforced on April 1 in 1948, the Child Consultation Center was the main organization to aid children who had needs for protection and education. In 1948 the Child Consultation Center gave consultation to 73,615 children, of whom 26,320, or 35.8%, were given educative measures (Table 7.2). Many vagrant juveniles who committed delinquency were sent to Kyogo-in. Kyogo-in had several small-sized dormitories in which a teacher and his wife took care of the children like their parents.On the other hand, the police, especially those in big cities, also began to improve

* We saw the news film, by which we were informed that many vagrant juveniles slept on underground pathways at Ueno Railway Station. One day, officers in charge of child welfare and the police officers caught them. DDT was sprinkled on their hair to kill lice. Then the children were sent by truck to a facility for welfare. They were given poor accommodations at the overcrowded facility.

Table 7.2 Activities of Child Consultation Center in 1948*

	Number Aided	Percentage
Total of children aided	26,320	(100.0)
Sent to facility for protection	9,485	(36.0)
Appointed guide	6,813	(25.9)
Warning given	4,397	(16.7)
Sent to reformatory school	2,913	(11.1)
Sent to home for orphans	950	(3.6)
Sent to nursing home	651	(2.5)
Sent to facility for mental disorders	631	(2.4)
Sent to foster parent(s)	480	(1.8)

* Total of 73,615 children consulted.

Table 7.3 Runaway Juveniles in Fiscal 1948 Based on Records of Tokyo Metropolitan Police Headquarters

	Male	Female	Total
Fiscal 1948	3,370	1,979	5,349

their activities to guide juvenile delinquents. For example, in December of 1945 the Tokyo Metropolitan Police Headquarters established two task forces in charge of juvenile delinquents* (Hattori and Sasaki, 2000:645-646). Tokyo Metropolitan Police Headquarters began to guide runaway juveniles earnestly. In fiscal 1948 the police officers at Tokyo Metropolitan Police Headquarters found 5,349 runaway juveniles, of which 3,370 or 63.0% were male (Table 7.3).

Establishment of the System of Juvenile Police Before Second Peak of Juvenile Delinquency in 1964

On September 30 in 1946 a director of the Bureau on Police and Security in the Ministry of Home Affairs issued a memorandum on the improvement of a system to prevent juvenile delinquency, which was addressed to all prefectural governors. By this memorandum several large prefectures such as Tokyo and Kyoto founded sections for juveniles, while other small prefectures created task forces for juveniles.

* Tokyo Metropolitan Police Headquarters founded the Second Task Force on juvenile crimes and the disposition of the crimes at Police Section 1 in the Criminal Division, and the Second Task Force on prevention of juvenile delinquency and guidance at the Prevention Section in the same division.

Our new Juvenile Law was proclaimed in July of 1948, and was enforced at the beginning of 1949. By this law "juveniles" are defined as those under the age of 20, raised from 18 years of age in the old law (Yokoyama, 2002:325). The police and the public prosecutors lost their discretion power to screen juvenile cases. Therefore, all cases are sent to the family court where a probation officer works as a case worker. The family court has jurisdiction over three kinds of juveniles: juvenile offenders between the ages of 14 and 19; law-breaking children under the age of 14; and pre-offense juveniles under the age of 20 who are prone to commit some criminal offense.

Under Article 41 of our Penal Code, children under 14 years of age should not be criminally punished for their behavior. Therefore, they are not regarded as juvenile offenders, and are defined as law-breaking children. On the other hand, the protection of pre-offense juveniles is justified by the idea of "parens patriae." By Paragraph 1 of Article 3 of the Juvenile Law, pre-offense juveniles are defined as those who are pone to commit some crime or some law-breaking in the future judging from their character and environment when they have committed one of the following five kinds of behavior: habitual disobedience to supervision by their protector; no approach to their home without any due reason; association with a person having criminal tendencies or an immoral person; entry to an indecent place; or a tendency to commit behavior to harm their own virtue or some virtue of another person. From the viewpoint of the respect of due process this category is defined more minutely than that in the old Juvenile Law of 1922.

After the enactment of the new Juvenile Law we witnessed an upsurge of volunteers' activity to prevent juvenile delinquency. On November 14 in 1949 the first nationwide program for rearing and protecting juveniles was carried out. The first movement for brightening society was held in July of 1951, following the event by the Ginza Merchants Association in Tokyo in the previous year* (Yokoyama, 2000:304). This movement has continued by the initiative of the Ministry of Justice, and the main human resources are volunteer probation and parole officers. In response to the enforcement of Juvenile Law, in December of 1949 a vice director of the National Community Police Headquarters issued a memorandum on the strengthening of juvenile police.† The police began to guide juveniles with problems, whom the Juvenile

* The Offenders Rehabilitation Law was enacted in 1949. To celebrate the enactment and to campaign for the prevention of crime and juvenile delinquency, the Ginza Merchants Association held a special week-long fair in July. Following this event, volunteers, of which the core was composed of volunteer probation and parole officers, have carried out the movement for "brighter society." The main organization to support the movement is the Ministry of Justice, although the police participate in the movement.

† By the Police Law enacted in 1947 the public safety commission and the community police were introduced. The National Community Police Headquarters was founded as the office to serve for the National Public Safety Commission.

Table 7.4 Juveniles with Problems Guided by Police

	Number[a]	Rate per Population[b]
1949	106,345	5.1
1950	155,122	7.3
1951	381,007	17.7
1952	268,666	12.4
1953	352,162	16.3
1954	430,459	20.1
1955	404,735	18.4
1956	456,474	20.2
1957	637,689	27.3
1958	720,606	30.2
1959	790,104	32.5
1960	843,168	34.9
1961	798,118	32.9
1962	932,188	39.1
1963	993,082	41.9
1964	1,323,981	55.8

[a] Includes pre-offense juveniles.
[b] Rate of pre-offense juveniles per 1,000 population between 14 and 19 years old.

Law did not define as juvenile delinquents. They guided 106,345 juveniles in 1949 (Table 7.4). Most of the juveniles were only given a warning or advice by a police officer, while only a small number of those were referred to family court as pre-offense juveniles.*

In 1950 the Ordinance on Guidance for Juveniles with Some Problem was issued. Under this ordinance the police were activated to guide juveniles to prevent their delinquency. In 1951 the total number of juveniles with problems guided by the police amounted to 381,007. We saw the first peak of juvenile Penal Code offenders in 1951, when the rate per 1,000 population reached 9.5 percent.

To organize the citizens' movement for the prevention of juvenile delinquency the municipal government in Kyoto and Osaka founded a juvenile guidance center in 1952. Most of the juvenile guidance center is managed by the Education Board or the Division of Child Welfare in a municipal government with or without the cooperation by the police. However, in Tokyo the Metropolitan Police Headquarters has managed the center from the start. By the way, some case workers work in the juvenile guidance center to give

* The total number of juveniles protected in practice under the Correction Bureau of Judicial Ministry amounted to 49,657 in 1948, of which 696 or 1.4% were pre-offense juveniles (Tani, 1950:28-29).

counseling to juveniles with problems as their protectors. In addition, they organize volunteer patrols in the amusement area to warn juveniles who might commit delinquency, and to improve the moral environment for rearing juveniles soundly.

On June 8 of 1954 the new Police Law was enacted in the opposition movement by the left wing.* Under this law all community police were absorbed by a prefectural police. The National Community Police Headquarters was reorganized as the National Police Headquarters. One reason for this change was that the community governments did not want to maintain their police because of their poor budget. Another reason was that the national government wanted to strengthen the police power to prevent the prevalence of communism and cope with the Cold War between Western countries and the communist countries. We saw the shift from local, small-sized police agencies to the prefectural police under the control of the National Police Agency mainly through the budget and personnel management (Yokoyama, 2001a:192).

The National Police Agency does not have its own police forces, and the prefectural police maintain forces in order to perform such functions as enforcing laws, maintaining security and order, and providing people living in the community with services. The agency is responsible for the following tasks: planning laws concerning policing, and standardizing police activities and various police systems; supporting activities in the prefectural police with both "hard-ware" and "soft-ware"; and coordinating the activities of the prefectural police.

On October 5 of 1954 the Deputy Commissioner-General of the National Police Agency issued a memorandum on the management of juvenile police, which was addressed to all prefectural forces. As the activities by the juvenile police were standardized, more juveniles were guided for the prevention of their delinquency. The total number of juveniles with some problem increased to 430,459 in 1954 (Table 7.5). In 1955 the police began to employ female guidance officers for the prevention of juvenile delinquency.†

In February of 1955 the National Police Agency made out the plan for the prevention of delinquency in the community for the first time.‡ On July 11 of 1957 the National Public Safety Commission issued the Rule on Norms of Criminal Investigation. By this rule police officers are obliged to work in the spirit of contributing to rearing a juvenile soundly when they investigate a case.

* The left wing opposed this law, because they worried about the restoration to the centralized authoritative police system.

† At that time the police was a male-dominated organization, in which no female officers worked.

‡ To realize the plan of the National Police Agency, the police in some selected communities embarked on a pilot practice and were given a special budget. If the pilot practice is successful, the practice would be adopted all over the country by the direction of the National Police Agency and the practice in the juvenile police is improved.

Table 7.5 Juveniles Guided by Police in 1952 and 1960 Classified by Age

	1952		1960	
	Guided Juveniles	Rate of Population	Guided Juveniles	Rate of Population
Under 14 years of age	53,891 (20.1)	4.8	160,056 (19.0)	11.9
Between 14 and 17 years of age	136,867 (50.9)	19.4	411,799 (48.8)	59.5
Between 18 and 19 years of age	77,908 (29.0)	22.8	271.313 (32.2)	70.6
Total	268,666 (100.0)	12.4	843,168 (100.0)	34.9

Source: Research and Training Institute of the Ministry of Justice, *White Paper on Crime* [written in Japanese], 1962, p. 101. Tokyo: Printing Bureau of the Ministry of Justice.

Juvenile Police in the Early 1960s

On March 18 of 1960 the Deputy Commissioner General of the National Police Agency issued a memorandum on activities of the juvenile police, in which the guidance activities for juveniles was formally defined for the first time.* In this memorandum guidance activities were regarded as the activities of all officers for the prevention of juvenile delinquency and the promotion of child welfare. The memorandum authorized such police activity as finding a juvenile delinquent, giving a warning and advice to him/her, investigating him/her, and referring him/her to another organization in the juvenile justice system or to child welfare.

To improve the juvenile police system, in July 1960 each prefectural police headquarters hired a juvenile guidance officer to be responsible for all juvenile guidance activities in the prefecture. At the beginning of April 1961 the Section for Prevention in the National Police Agency was renamed the Section for Prevention and Juveniles.

The police did not have enough officers to prevent juvenile delinquency. Therefore, at many police stations in big cities officers organized community leaders as volunteers for guidance to prevent juvenile delinquency. By the memorandum issued in June of 1962 the system of volunteers for guiding juveniles became nationwide.

Soon after World War II the left wing opposed the strengthening and widening of police power. Therefore, the police used the term "a juvenile with

* The left wing regarded the guidance activities by the police as an invasion of juveniles' privacy. Therefore, the police could not authorize the guidance activities under the law enacted in the Diet.

some problems," so they would not be blamed for expanding their guidance activity, which was not authorized by the law enacted at the Diet. However, in the early 1960s they began to use the term "a pre-delinquent," which was the main target of their guidance activity.

The police succeeded in establishing their system to prevent juvenile delinquency around the first peak of juvenile delinquency in 1964. A section titled "Juvenile Police" appeared for the first time in the *White Paper on Crime in 1964*. It provided the following definition of the juvenile police:

> The juvenile police stand in the forefront of such activity as arresting and guiding juvenile delinquents. The juvenile police are the whole police system specialized for the prevention of juvenile delinquency. Each prefectural police headquarters and each police station has a section for juveniles, at which specialized police officers cope with juvenile delinquency. In cooperation with the specialized officers ordinary police officers investigate a juvenile offender, and participate with the prevention of delinquency. The most important task for the juvenile police is to find a juvenile delinquency earlier, to screen the case after the research on his/her proneness toward delinquency and to notify or send to other facility. In a case of a juvenile with some problem the police give such measures as a warning, an advice, the contact with his/her family, school and work place to prevent his/her future delinquency, by which they contribute to activities for rearing juveniles soundly. (pp. 302-303)

Activities of Juvenile Police Around Second Peak of Juvenile Delinquency in 1964

In the early 1960s the baby boomers became teenagers.* At that time we drew attention to juveniles' violence. In 1964 we saw the second peak of juvenile delinquency after World War II, when the rate of juvenile Penal Code offenders per 1,000 population was 11.9%. The total number of juvenile Penal Code offenders amounted to 238,830, of which 56.9% committed theft. On the other hand, the percentage of such violent offenses as injury, extortion, and assault amounted to 7.0%, 6.4%, and 5.8%, respectively. The police became more serious about catching juveniles who committed some minor violence, as such serious offenses as robbery decreased.†

In 1964 the total number of juveniles caught for violating some special criminal law amounted to 17,155, of which 56.2% were charged with an offense

* Soon after the end of World War II many youngsters got married after they returned from the war field. Therefore, at that time we saw the baby boom.

† Robbery committed by juveniles decreased drastically from 2,903 in 1946 to 1,987 in 1964.

of the Firearms and Swords Control Law. The police activated the regulation of a juvenile holding a firearm or a sword to prevent violent behavior.

To cope with a group of juvenile gangsters, on July 23 of 1963 the director of the Security Bureau of the National Police Agency issued a memorandum on the measures. On October 10 of 1963, together with the director of the Bureau for Elementary and Middle Education in the Ministry of Education, the director issued another memorandum on the strengthening of liaisons between the police and schools for the prevention of juvenile delinquency. After this issuance the school–police conference was established in the community for the prevention of juvenile delinquency, especially violence in school.*

With industrialization and urbanization many youngsters moved from their native place to large cities after they graduated from junior high school. They lived in a dormitory or in their employer's house. If they lived in an alienated situation, they left their work place to seek fun. Such alienated juveniles sometimes committed delinquency, or became members of Boryokudan, the gangsters' group. To prevent them from committing delinquency, the work place–police conference was organized. At the conference the police gave information about juvenile delinquency in the community to employers and managers. The police asked them to appoint an officer in charge of taking care of young employees, especially those living in dormitories.

In the early 1960s many poor youngsters, especially those coming from rural areas after their graduation from junior high school, admired Boryokudan members for their luxurious lives. In addition, the Boryokudan functioned as a refuge, in which youngsters dropping out from school and the work place could be emotionally satisfied through the face-to-face human relations (Yokoyama, 2000:4). Therefore, we saw the highest total number of Boryokudan members. We blamed the Boryokudan for their violent behaviors. In the upsurge of the anti-violence movement in 1964 the National Police Agency carried out a strategy against the Boryokudan by mobilizing all prefectural police forces (Yokoyama, 1999:148) and drawing attention to violence committed by youngsters.

Activation of Guidance Activities in the Early 1960s

As the increase in juvenile offenses was regarded as a serious social problem, the police activated their guidance activities to prevent delinquency. The

* After World War II the teachers' union was organized. Teachers affiliated with the union opposed the cooperation with the police for the prevention of juvenile delinquency. However, as juvenile delinquency and, above all, violence in schools drew people's attention, they failed to oppose the establishment of the school–police conference. The number of teachers affiliated with the union decreased drastically after 1990.

total number of juveniles with some problem guided by the police increased to 1,323,981 in 1963 (Table 7.4). In this process the police began to use the category of "a pre-delinquent" in the place of "a juvenile with some problem." In 1960 the police explained that their guidance activity focused on juveniles with problems including those having needs for protection (*White Paper on Crime in 1960:298*). Two years later we saw the explanation that the police guided pre-offense juveniles in the wide definition, in which so-called pre-delinquents were included (White Paper on Crime in 1962:102).

Soon after World War II the police did not have sufficient human resources to catch juveniles for minor offenses and deviant behavior. However, with the help of many volunteers the police guided more juveniles with problems (Table 7.4). Until 1960 juveniles with problems under 14 years old amounted to about 20% (Table 7.5). However, as the baby boomers became older, this decreased to about 10% in 1964 (Table 7.8).

Around 1963 police officers and guidance volunteers guided mainly law-breaking children under 14 years old for truancy and juvenile offenders between 14 and 17 years old for smoking cigarettes, immoral association with the opposite sex, drinking liquor, and association with a delinquent (*White Paper on Crime in 1963:289*).

Table 7.6 shows the status of juveniles with some problem guided by the police. The others, most of whom were youngsters with or without a job after graduation from junior high school, amounted to about 50% until 1960. This percentage shows that it was important to prevent young laborers, especially those living in loneliness in a big city, from committing a crime.

The total number of juveniles with problems increased from 430,459 in 1954 to 1,323,981 in 1964 despite guidance activities (Table 7.7). Around 1964 we drew our attention to violence by youngsters. If youngsters committed a violent act, they were usually arrested for such an offense such as extortion,

Table 7.6 Juveniles with Problems Guided by Police in 1956 and 1960 Classified by Educational Status

	1956		1960	
Educational Level	Total Number	%	Total Number	%
Total	456,474	100.0	843,168	100.0
Elementary school	61,113	13.4	93,772	11.1
Junior high school	95,654	21.0	163,723	19.4
Senior high school	66,823	14.6	128,812	15.3
College or university	4,471	1.0	6,040	0.7
Others	228,413	50.0	450,821	53.5

Source: Research and Training Institute of the Ministry of Justice, *White Paper on Crime* [written in Japanese], 1962, p. 102. Tokyo: Printing Bureau of the Ministry of Justice.

Table 7.7 Juveniles with Problems Guided by Police in 1954 and 1964 Classified by Behavior

	1954		1964	
	Number	%	Number	%
Total	430,459	100.0	1,323,981	100.0
Violent behavior	2,022	0.5	8,661	0.7
Fighting	5,444	1.3	17,139	1.2
Extortion	805	0.2	2,346	0.2
Holding a weapon	1,367	0.3	4,531	0.3
Smoking a cigarette	99,472	23.1	535,484	40.4
Drinking liquor	16,114	3.7	58,604	4.4
Truancy	59,714	13.9	95,079	7.2
Leaving the work place			30,206	2.3
Running away	23,811	5.5	43,947	3.3
Removing something from their homes	7,777	1.8	6,165	0.5
Wasting money	9,957	2.3	9,420	0.7
Tempting a female and committing indecency	2,470	0.6	4,742	0.4
Immoral association with the opposite sex	12,932	3.0	36,117	2.7
Association with a delinquent	8,432	2.0	55,415	4.2
Joining gangsters' group	439	0.1	1,261	0.1
Involvement in unsound leisure	28,256	6.6	108,848	8.2
Loitering at amusement quarters	39,518	9.2	59,296	4.5
Outdoor pleasure-seeking at night	—	—	100,785	7.6
Others	111,929	26.0	145,935	11.0

or assault. As previously mentioned, the total number of juveniles caught for such violent offenses increased around 1964. However, until 1964 the police handled juveniles having committed minor violence, even extortion and fighting, by giving them only a warning.

We saw a similar phenomenon concerning juveniles with weapons. If they held a weapon such as a firearm or a sword, they were arrested for an offense of the Firearm and Sword Control Law. However, juveniles holding a less dangerous weapon such as a knife or an imitation gun were only guided as juveniles with some problem.

Police officers in charge of guidance activities often patrolled the amusement quarters with the guidance volunteers. If they found a juvenile committing some deviant behavior they gave a warning to him/her. In Japan juveniles under 20 years of age are prohibited from smoking cigarettes and drinking liquor. Therefore, a juvenile smoking cigarettes and drinking liquor, is guided by the police. The total number of juveniles guided for smoking cigarettes increased drastically from 99,472 in 1954 to 535,484 in 1964.

Youngsters playing truant and those leaving the work place without their employer's permission were usually found loitering at the amusement quarters. They were prone to committing crimes or being victimized, especially a Boryokudan member. To prevent their crime or victimization the police officers and the guidance volunteers patrol.

Around 1964 many youngsters living in rural areas admired the bright life in a big city. Such youngsters sometimes ran away to seek excitement. Students in junior high school ran away soon after the spring and summer vacations, especially. Therefore, in April and in September the police carried out the special patrol at the amusement quarters, especially around the main railway station, to find runaway juveniles.

Many poor youngsters did not have a lot of pocket money. To supplement it, they sometimes carried items from their houses. With the high economic growth in the 1960s youngsters' economic status was also improved. Therefore, juveniles guided for carrying something out of their house decreased after 1954. In addition, juveniles caught for wasting money also decreased. With the increase in income, people might have tolerated juveniles' waste of money.

With liberalization after World War II more juveniles enjoyed their association with the opposite sex. However, around 1964 juveniles' immoral association was regarded as deviant behavior to be guided by the police. As the total number of both juvenile males and females was similar, most of them were guided as pairs. The police also guided male youngsters for tempting females and committing indecency.

Around the second peak of juvenile delinquency we began to cope with a group of juvenile gangsters, as previously mentioned. Therefore, the total numbers of juveniles guided for association with a delinquent and for joining a gangsters' group increased to 55,415 and 1,261 in 1964, respectively.

With economic development more juveniles, especially those living in cities, enjoyed loitering until midnight for pleasure seeking and involvement in unsound leisure. Of all guided juveniles, the percentage guided for such deviant behavior amounted to 20.3% in 1964.

Concerning the age of juveniles guided by the police in 1964, we saw a peak in 17-year-olds (Table 7.8). The percentage of 19-year-olds amounted to only 10.9%. As previously mentioned, juveniles were guided for such deviant behavior as smoking cigarettes and loitering until midnight. If juveniles of 19 years of age committed such behavior, they were usually treated like an adult. Therefore, it was more infrequent for police officers and guidance volunteers to guide them as juveniles with some problem.

Concerning the sex of juveniles guided in 1964, 92.7% were male and 7.3% were female. At that time female juveniles were more protected in their homes. For example, they were prohibited from going out alone after midnight. Therefore, the percentage of female juveniles guided by the police was

Table 7.8 Juveniles with Some Problem Guided by Police in 1964 Classified by Age and Sex

	Total		Male		Female	
Age (Years)	Number	%	Number	%	Number	%
Total	1,323,981	100.0	1,226,716	100.0	97,265	100.0
Under 14	136,841	10.3	125,904	10.3	10,937	11.2
14	95,008	7.2	84,593	6.9	10,415	10.7
15	146,887	11.1	131,064	10.7	15,823	16.3
16	236,020	17.8	214,185	17.5	21,835	22.4
17	297,605	22.5	277,800	22.6	19,805	20.4
18	267,909	20.2	255,540	20.8	12,369	12.7
19	143,711	10.9	137,630	11.2	6,081	6.3

Source: Research and Training Institute of the Ministry of Justice, *White Paper on Crime in 1966* [written in Japanese], 1966, p. 216. Tokyo: Printing Bureau of the Ministry of Justice.

small. Females mature earlier than males. Therefore, it is difficult for police officers and guidance volunteers to guide females 18 and 19 years of age as juveniles with some problem. The percentage of guided female juveniles amounted to only 6.3%.

In the early 1960s many juveniles moved from rural areas to big cities for jobs after they graduated from junior high school. Police officers and guidance officers guided such juveniles earnestly to prevent their delinquency. Therefore, the juveniles having jobs among all guided juveniles amounted to 45.0%, although the rate of females was 30.0% (Table 7.9).

We saw the difference in deviant behaviors between males and females guided by the police. Concerning violence, more male juveniles were guided for violent behavior, fighting, and extortion (Table 7.10) and more boys were caught for holding weapons.

Table 7.9 Juveniles with Some Problem Guided by Police in 1964 Classified by Status and Sex

	Total		Male		Female	
	Number	%	Number	%	Number	%
Total	1,323,981	100.0	1,226,716	100.0	97,265	100.0
Pupils and students	610,265	46.1	558,465	45.5	51,800	53.3
Juveniles with jobs	596.252	45.0	567,040	46.2	29,212	30.0
Juveniles without jobs	117,464	8.9	101,211	8.3	16,253	16.7

Source: Research and Training Institute of the Ministry of Justice, *White Paper on Crime in 1966* [written in Japanese], 1966, p. 217. Tokyo: Printing Bureau of the Ministry of Justice.

Table 7.10 Juveniles with Some Problem Guided by Police in 1964 Classified by Deviant Behavior and Sex

	Total		Male		Female	
	Number	%	Number	%	Number	%
Total	1,323,981	100.0	1,226,716	100.0	97,265	100.0
Violent behavior	8,661	0.7	8,465	0.7	196	0.2
Fighting	17,139	1.2	16,544	1.3	595	0.6
Extortion	2,346	0.2	2,282	0.2	64	0.1
Holding a weapon	4,531	0.3	4,516	0.4	15	0.0
Smoking a cigarette	535,484	40.4	527,263	42.8	8,221	8.5
Drinking liquor	58,604	4.4	56,467	4.6	2,137	2.2
Truancy	95,079	7.2	84,857	6.9	10,222	10.5
Leaving the work place	30,206	2.3	27,827	2.3	2,379	2.5
Runaway	43,947	3.3	30,344	2.5	13,598	14.0
Carrying something out of their house	6,165	0.5	5,777	0.5	388	0.4
Wasting money	9,420	0.7	8,501	0.7	919	0.9
Tempting a female and committing indecency	4,742	0.4	4,729	0.4	13	0.0
Immoral association with the opposite sex	36,117	2.7	18,025	1.5	18,092	18.6
Association with a delinquent	55,415	4.2	44,213	3.6	11,202	11.5
Joining gangsters' group	1,261	0.1	1,227	0.1	34	0.0
Involvement in unsound leisure	108,848	8.2	104,920	8.6	3,928	4.0
Loitering at amusement quarters	59,296	4.5	52,284	4.3	7,012	7.2
Outdoor pleasure-seeking at night	100,785	7.6	91,314	7.4	9,471	9.7
Others	145,935	11.0	137,156	11.2	8,779	9.0

Sources: Research and Training Institute of the Ministry of Justice, *White Paper on Crime* [published in Japanese in 1960], and p. 214 in *White Paper on Crime in 1966* [published in Japanese in 1966].

Police officers and guidance volunteers most frequently guided juveniles for smoking cigarettes. For this reason 42.8% of males were caught, and the rate was 8.6% for females. The rate of males caught for drinking liquor was double that of females.

Fourteen percent and 10.5% of juvenile females were guided for running away and truancy, respectively. Usually, girls running away and playing truant went to the amusement area in a big city, where they might be easily victimized. For example, if they met a Boryokudan member there, they might be raped and urged to prostitute themselves under his supervision. To prevent such a tragedy, police officers and guidance volunteers patrolled more frequently to find runaway and truant girls from the viewpoint of protection from rather than prevention of a crime.

The highest rate of female juveniles, 18.6%, was seen in those guided for immoral association with the opposite sex. Therefore, 18,025 boys and 18,092 girls were guided for their immoral association as juveniles with some problem.

We saw a higher rate in the case of males guided for tempting females and committing indecency, for joining a gangsters' group, and for involvement in unsound leisure, while a higher rate of females was guided for waste of money, association with a delinquent, loitering at amusement quarters, and outdoor pleasure-seeking at night. From the viewpoint of protection a higher rate of females seemed to be guided for association with a delinquent and loitering at amusement quarters.

Under the Juvenile Law enacted in 1948 the police and the public prosecutor lost the discretion power to screen juvenile cases. All cases of juvenile offenders and a pre-offense juveniles had to be referred to family court. In 1962 the police sent almost all juvenile offenders via the public prosecutor or directly to family court* (Table 7.11).

By Paragraph 2 of Article 3 of the Juvenile Law, the family court has jurisdiction over a case of a law-breaking child, if the case is referred from the Child Consultation Center. Therefore, the police notify the Center of cases of a law-breaking child or dismiss him/her immediately after the guidance. Of all law-breaking children guided by the police in 1962, 57.7% were notified by the Child Consultation Center.

The police guided many juveniles as juveniles with some problem, of which 98.7% were dismissed immediately after receiving an informal warning or advice by a police officer or a guidance volunteer. The police regarded only 1.3% of juveniles with some problem as pre-offense juveniles, who could be referred to the Child Consultation Center or to family court. In the case of law-breaking children under 14 years of age, the police can notify the Child Consultation Center of these cases. For those between 14 and 17 years of age, the police have alternatives, that is, notification to the Center or referral to family court. In the case of those of 18 and 19 years of age the police should

* The Supreme Court, the Supreme Public Prosecutors' Office, and the National Police Agency had a meeting to improve the referral system to family court in juvenile cases. After this meeting the summary referral system was introduced on June 7 in 1950. By this system the police sent 499 juvenile offenders having committed a minor offense directly to family court. In 1969 the system was improved, by which the police refer juvenile offenders at the end of every month to family court.

Table 7.11 Disposition of Juvenile Delinquents by Police in 1962

	Juvenile Offenders against Penal Code		Law-Breaking Children		Juveniles with Some Problems	
	Number	%	Number	%	Number	%
Total	162,773	100.0	60,498	100.0	932,188	100.0
Referral to public prosecutors' office	162,187	99.6	0	0.0	0	0.0
Referral to family court	499	0.3	0	0.0	5,467	0.6
Notification to the Child Consultation Center	0	0.0	38,898	57.7	6,197	0.7
Diversion by police	0	0.0	25,600	42.3	920,524	98.7
Others	87	0.1	0	0.0	0	0.0

Source: Research and Training Institute of the Ministry of Justice, *White Paper on Crime in 1964* [written in Japanese], 1964, p. 303. Tokyo: Printing Bureau of the Ministry of Justice.

refer all cases to family court, because the Child Welfare Law is limited only to those under 18 years old.

Activation of Guidance Activities in Third Peak of Juvenile Delinquency Around 1983

To stop the increase in juvenile delinquency around 1964, our national government supported activities to prevent delinquency in the community. In April of 1964 the Ordinance on the Management of Guidance Centers was issued, by which the government began to give subsidiaries to the centers. In such a situation many middle-sized cities established a juvenile guidance center as the base to prevent juvenile delinquency and to rear juveniles soundly in the community.

In September of 1965 the Central Council on Juvenile Problems published the opinion about the measures for the prevention of juvenile delinquency. In November of 1965 the government advocated a nationwide movement for rearing juveniles soundly. As the organization in charge of this movement, the Juvenile Bureau was founded in the Prime Minister's Office. On the same day the Council on Juvenile Problems was established. To promote the movement for rearing juveniles soundly by the Ministry of General Affairs, the National Conference to Rear Juveniles was founded in May of 1966.

Activities for Juveniles After Second Peak of Juvenile Delinquency

To stop the increase in juvenile delinquency around 1964, our national government supported the activities to prevent delinquency in the community and the movement to rear juveniles soundly.

In April of 1964 the Rule on the Management of Guidance Centers was issued, by which the government began to subsidize the centers.

Expansion of the Volunteer System by the Police

On May 30 in 1967 the Ordinance on Management on the System of Guidance Volunteer for Juveniles was issued.

In April of 1982 the Police Cooperator for Juveniles started under a memorandum issued by the National Police Agency.

The main task of this volunteer is to disperse the groups of juvenile delinquents.

Guidance Activities Around 1983. Third Peak of Juvenile Delinquency in 1983

1. The third peak occurred in 1983, when the rate of juvenile Penal Code offenders climbed up to 17.1 per 1,000 population, the highest rate in our history. Although many second baby boomers were caught by the police, the majority of them committed only minor offenses such as shoplifting of some trifle or riding a bicycle without the owner's permission. The highest rate of juvenile delinquency was caused by net widening of the guidance activities by the police.
2. Pre-delinquents Guided by Police in 1983. In 1983 the police guided 1,429,898 pre-delinquents. The rates for each reason are as follows:

Smoking a cigarette	41.9%
Midnight loitering	24.8%
Driving a vehicle violently and noisily	7.6%
Association with a delinquent	6.3%
Drinking liquor	2.7%
Others	16.7%

3. Disposition of pre-offense juveniles at Family Court in 1983. In 1983 the family court disposed of 3,418 pre-offense juveniles. The rates for each reason why they were disposed of as pre-offense juveniles were as follows:

Runaway	43.7%

Association with a delinquent	13.1%
Immoral association with the opposite sex	11.8%
Truancy	5.5%
Involvement in unsound leisure	2.5%
Outdoor pleasure-seeking at night	2.5%
Others	20.8%

Activation of Guidance Activities After 1983

Introduction of the System of Instruction for Juveniles

In 1985 the Law on Regulation of Business Affecting Public Morals was enacted, in which the system of instruction for juveniles was introduced. At last the police succeeded in authorizing their volunteer system by a law enacted in the Diet.

1. The main task of an instructor for juveniles is to protect juveniles from an unsound environment.
2. Juvenile Delinquency after 1983. In the late 1980s the second baby boomers became adults. We saw the lowest level of juvenile delinquency in 1995. After 1995 we saw the prevalence of conservatism, in which our Juvenile Law was criticized as a law to spoil juvenile delinquents. In addition, in response to feedback by crime victims the police have strengthened the arrest and guidance of juvenile delinquents. The rate of juvenile Penal Code offenders increased until 2004.
3. Guidance Activities in 1983 and in 1995. The total number of pre-delinquents guided by the police decreased from 1,429,898 in 1983 to 673,345 in 1995. The change from 1983 to 1995 in the rate for each reason why they were guided is as follows:

Smoking a cigarette	41.9% up to 47.3% (1995)
Midnight loitering	24.8% up to 30.4% (1995)
Driving a vehicle violently and noisily	7.6% down to 6.0% (1995)
Association with a delinquent	6.3% down to 3.9 (1995)
Drinking liquor	2.7% up to 3.7% (1995)
Others	16.7% down to 8.6% (1995)

Guidance Activities in 1995 and in 2006

The total number of pre-delinquents guided by the police increased from 673,345 in 1995 to 1,427,928 in 2006 (Table 7.12). The change from 1995 to 2006 in the rate for each reason why they were guided is as follows:

Smoking a cigarette	47.3% down to 39.0% (2006)
Midnight loitering	30.4% up to 50.4% (2006)
Others	22.3% down to 10.6% (2006)

Many juveniles enjoy spending time outdoors until midnight. Therefore, they become a main target of guidance activities by the police.

The total number of pre-offense juveniles disposed of at family court decreased from 3,418 in 1983 to 770 in 1995 and to 698 in 2006.

The change in the rate for each reason why they were disposed of as pre-offense juveniles is as follows:

Runaway	43.7% down to 18.3%
Association with a delinquent	13.1% down to 3.7%
Immoral association with the opposite sex	11.8% down to 5.9%
Truancy	5.5% down to 1.9%
Involvement in unsound leisure	2.5% down to 0.3%
Outdoor pleasure-seeking at night	2.5% down to 1.7%
Others	20.8% up to 68.2%

Table 7.12 Pre-delinquents Guided by Police in 1983, 1995, and 2006 Classified by Deviant Behavior

	1983		1995		2006	
	Number	%	Number	%	Number	%
Total	1,429,898	100.0	673,345	100.0	1,427,928	100.0
Midnight loitering	353,973	24.8	204,722	30.4	719,732	50.4
Smoking a cigarette	599,774	41.9	318,637	47.3	557,079	39.0
Driving a vehicle violently and noisily	108,177	7.6	40,527	6.0	—	—
Drinking liquor	39,246	2.7	24,929	3.7	—	—
Association with a delinquent	89,301	6.3	26,386	3.9	—	—
Others	239,427	16.7	58,144	8.6	151,117	10.6

Sources: National Police Agency, *White Paper on Police in 1984* [published in Japanese in 1984], p. 107 in *White Paper on Police in 1996* [published in Japanese in 1996] and p. 116 in *White Paper on Police in 2007* [published in Japanese in 2007].

Disposition of Pre-offense Juveniles at Family Court in 1983 and in 2006

The total number of pre-offense juveniles disposed of at family court decreased from 3,418 in 1983 to 770 in 1995 and to 698 in 2006 (Tables 7.13 and 7.14). The change in the rate for each reason is as follows:

Runaway	43.7% down to 18.3%
Association with a delinquent	13.1% down to 3.7%
Immoral association with the opposite sex	11.8% down to 5.9%
Truancy	5.5% down to 1.9%
Involvement in unsound leisure	2.5% down to 0.3%
Outdoor pleasure-seeking at night	2.5% down to 1.7%
Others	20.8% up to 68.2%

Recent Net-Widening of Activities of the Juvenile Police

In the conservative atmosphere and in the response to feedback by crime victims the police arrest more juvenile offenders on charges of more serious offenses. For example, the police began to arrest juveniles for robbery causing injury in cases where they injured someone when they shoplifted or stole.

Table 7.13 Pre-offense Juveniles Disposed of at Family Court in 1983, 1995, and 2006 Classified by Deviant Behavior

	1983		1995		2006	
	Number	%	Number	%	Number	%
Total	3,418	100.0	770	100.0	698	100.0
Runaway	1,493	43.7	337	43.7	128	18.3
Association with a delinquent	449	13.1	126	16.4	26	3.7
Immoral association with the opposite sex	405	11.8	109	14.2	41	5.9
Truancy	188	5.5	45	5.8	13	1.9
Involvement in unsound leisure	87	2.5	9	1.2	2	0.3
Outdoor pleasure seeking at night	85	2.5	25	3.2	12	1.7
Others	711	20.8	119	15.5	476	68.2

Sources: Research and Training Institute of the Ministry of Justice, *White Paper on Crime in 1985* [published in Japanese in 1985] and pp. 44-45 in Supreme Court, *Annual Report of Judicial Statistics for 2006, Vol. 4 Juvenile Cases* [published in Japanese in 2007].

Table 7.14 Pre-offense Juveniles Disposed of at Family Court in 2006 by Their Sex and Deviant Behavior

	Total		Male		Female	
	Number	%	Number	%	Number	%
Total	698	100.0	317	100.0	381	100.0
Runaway	128	18.3	39	12,3	89	23.4
Association with a delinquent	26	3.7	15	4.7	11	2.9
Immoral association with the opposite sex	41	5.9	2	0.6	39	10.2
Truancy	13	1.9	10	3.2	3	0.8
Involvement in unsound leisure	2	0.3	1	0.3	1	0.3
Outdoor pleasure-seeking at night	12	1.7	3	0.9	9	2.4
Others	476	68.2	247	78.0	229	60.0

Source: This table was made by the use of pp. 44-45 in Supreme Court, *Annual Report of Judicial Statistics for 2006, Vol. 4 Juvenile Cases* [published in Japanese in 2007].

The more arrests by the police cause great impact to other facilities in juvenile justice. For example, we see over-crowding in juvenile training schools.

Issuance of a Rule on Activities of the Juvenile Police

In 2002 the National Public Safety Commission issued a rule on activities of the juvenile police. Under this rule the police decide to establish juvenile support centers all over the country.

In April of 2004 there were 181 centers, of which 55 were located outside a police facility. At the centers, there are about 100 specialist officers for juvenile counseling and about 1,000 officers for juvenile guidance work (Tables 7.15 to 7.17).

Decline of Guidance Activities at Juvenile Guidance Centers

In an aging society the local governments do not have enough budget to provide resources at juvenile guidance centers to promote the activities for rearing juveniles soundly.

The police do not have the jurisdiction over the activities for rearing juveniles soundly.

However, they participate with these activities through the National Association of Volunteers for Juvenile Police Activities, with which about

Table 7.15 Clients Given Consultation by Police in 1983, 1995, and 2005

	1983		1995		2005	
Kind of Client	Number	%	Number	%	Number	%
Total	119,733	100.0	89,460	100.0	90,283	100.0
Juvenile	40,579	33.9	23,087	25.8	21,443	23.8
Juvenile's protector	79,154	66.1	66,373	74.2	68,840	76.2

Sources: This table was made by the use of p. 34 in National Police Agency, *White Paper on Police in 1984* [published in Japanese in 1984], p. 117 in *White Paper on Police in 1996* [published in Japanese in 1996], and p. 142 in *White Paper on Police in 2006* [published in Japanese in 2006].

Table 7.16 Content of Consultations Given to Juveniles by Police in 1983, 1995, and 2005

	1983		1995		2005	
	Number	%	Number	%	Number	%
Total	40,579	100.0	23,087	100.0	21,443	100.0
Delinquency	3,902	9.6	2,192	9.5	1,974	9.2
Problem in family	2,621	6.5	1,429	6.2	1,922	9.0
Problem at school	6,300	15.5	4,439	19.2	3,218	15.0
Problem with association	13,889	34.2	4,676	20.3	3,526	16.5
Problem with sex and health	10,546	26.0	5,296	22.9	1,871	8.7
Crime victim	—	—	857	3.7	2,695	12.6
Runaway	—	—	—	—	438	2.0
Others	3,321	8.2	4.198	18.2	5,799	27.0

Sources: This table was made by the use of p. 35 in National Police Agency, *White Paper on Police in 1984* [published in Japanese in 1984], p. 117 in *White Paper on Police in 1996* [published in Japanese in 1996], and p. 142 in *White Paper on Police in 2006* [published in Japanese in 2006].

60,000 police volunteers are affiliated. Most directors of the association are former high-ranking police officials.

Revised Juvenile Law in 2007 Granting the Police the Power to Investigate a Law-Breaking Child

In July of 2003 a 12-year old student of a junior high school kidnapped a 4-year old boy, and thrust him to his death from the roof of a building. In June of 2004 an 11-year old girl stabbed her female classmate to death in a classroom. In the two cases the police could not research the causes of their heinous behavior. Therefore, they appealed to be given the power to investigate a law-breaking child.

Table 7.17 Content of Consultations Given to Juveniles' Protectors by Police in 1983, 1995 and 2005

	1983		1995		2005	
	Number	%	Number	%	Number	%
Total	80,101	100.0	66,373	100.0	68,840	100.0
Delinquency	30,090	37.6	16,475	24.8	17,944	26.1
Problem in family	29,320	36.6	8,598	13.0	11,213	16.3
Problem at school	5,807	7.2	8,030	12.1	8,809	12.8
Problem with association	8,839	11.0	7,090	10.7	4,476	6.5
Problem with sex and health	2,720	3.4	2,555	3.8	4,145	6.0
Crime victim	—	—	2,958	4.5	4,881	7.1
Runaway	—	—	11,632	17.5	6,508	9.5
Others	3,325	4.2	9,035	13.6	10,864	15.8

Sources: National Police Agency, *White Paper on Police in 1984* [published in Japanese in 1984], p. 117 in *White Paper on Police in 1996* [published in Japanese in 1996], and p. 142 in *White Paper on Police in 2006* [published in Japanese in 2006].

Under the revised Juvenile Law in 2007 they were given this power, although they failed to get the power to research a pre-offense juvenile.

Issues to Consider in Juvenile Delinquency Prevention

With transformation into a society without borders, juveniles have changed their lifestyle. For example, they enjoy spending time until midnight at the amusement quarters, which are located far from their own community. How should the local police guide them in cooperation with the city police to prevent their delinquency? With motorization more juveniles can cross the borders of their communities easily by riding motorcycles. How should the local police regulate juveniles who drive motorcycles recklessly and noisily across the border?

The local police have an advantage of giving service in response to residents living in their community. However, they cannot cope sufficiently with crimes across the borders of their community. The national police can cope with trans-border crimes more efficiently than local police.

In Japan we have the system of prefectural polices under the control of the National Police Agency. Should we strengthen this control to cope with wide-range crimes or international terrorism more efficiently?

Should We Establish International Police in the Age of Globalization?

At present each country has its own police power. With globalization such police cannot cope with trans-national crimes sufficiently. Should we establish international police beyond such an organization as ICPO (International Criminal Police Organization)? If so, how shall we do so?

References

All Japan Labor Union of Workers at Court (2000a). Activities for Prevention of Juvenile Delinquency in Community in Japan. In Tauber Istvan (ed.), *Tanulmanyok Vigh Jozsef 70. Szuletesnapjara*. Budapest: ELTE Allam-es Jogtudomanyi Kar: 292–307.

Research and Training Institute of the Ministry of Justice (1961), *White Paper on Crime*, Tokyo: Printing Bureau of the Ministry of Justice.

Research and Training Institute of the Ministry of Justice (1962), *White Paper on Crime*, Tokyo: Printing Bureau of the Ministry of Justice.

Research and Training Institute of the Ministry of Justice (1963), *White Paper on Crime*, Tokyo: Printing Bureau of the Ministry of Justice.

Yokoyama, Minoru (2000). Change in Japanese Organized Crime and Enforcement of the Law to Cope with Boryokudan in 1992. *Kokugakuin Journal of Law and Politics*, 38(3): 1–33.

______ (2001). Analysis of Japanese Police from the Viewpoint of Democracy. In Stanley Einstein & Menachem Amir (eds.), *Policing Security and Democracy: Theory and Practice*. Huntsville, Texas: The Office of International Criminal Justice, Inc.: 187–209.

______ (2001b). Tendency in Juvenile Delinquency and Criminalization in Japan [written in Japanese]. *Kokugakuin Journal of Law and Politics*, 38(4): 171–205.

______ (2002). Juvenile Justice and Juvenile Crime: An Overview of Japan. In Winterdyk, John (ed.), *Juvenile Justice Systems—International Perspectives* (2nd ed.). Toronto: Canadian Scholars' Press, Inc.: 321–352.

______ (2003). The Fifth Report of the Results of Research on Practice under Revised Juvenile Law. http://www.zenshiho.net/syotai20030926.html [written in Japanese] (accessed on April 22, 2007).

______ (2004). The Seventh Report of the Results of Research on Practice under Revised Juvenile Law. http://www.zenshiho.net/syotai20041118.html [written in Japanese] (accessed on April 22, 2007).

Yokoyama, Minoru (1999). Trends of Organized Crime by Boryokudan in Japan. In Stanley Einstein & Menachem Amir (eds.), *Organized Crime: Uncertainties and Dilemmas*. Chicago: The Office of International Criminal Justice, The University of Illinois at Chicago: 135–154.

An Innovative Police Project to Tackle Youth Crime Problems in Hong Kong

Operation Breakthrough

8

JESSICA LI CHI-MEI

Contents

Community Policing

Community policing is a popular term worldwide that has drawn the intensive attention of academics in the United Kingdom (Bennett, 1994; Friedmann, 1992; Schaffer, 1980), Canada (Leighton, 1994; Hornick, 1993; Murphy & Muir, 1985), the United States (Bayley & Sheering, 1997; Das, 1987; Goldstein, 1990; Kelling, 1988; Greene, 1989; Rosenbaum, 1994; Skogan, 1990; Skogan, 2000; Skogan & Hartnett, 1997; Trojanowicz & Bucqueroux, 1994), and even in Asian cities such as Singapore (Quah & Quah, 1987) and Hong Kong (Lau, 2004; Lo & Cheuk, 2003).

Not surprisingly, community policing suffers from many problems, for example, an inability to fit the local context of a society (Lau, 2004), inadequate skills training for police officers, and a lack of support from local governmental agencies and the public (Eck, 2004). However, there are also examples of success, such as the "Koban" in Japan, which serves as a form of community policing.

Community policing is a philosophy, rather than a set of practical strategies. Under the philosophy of community policing, police officers appear to be more personally involved, committed to community empowerment, willing to help people with special needs, supportive of all citizens, and proactive about crime control (Trojanowicz & Bucqueroux, 1994).

Additionally, collaboration with the public is the cornerstone of community policing. Bennett (1994) elaborates on the concept of community policing, as follows:

> The main elements of a community policing philosophy might be summarized in a single sentence as a belief or intention held by the police that they should consult with and take account of the wishes of the public in determining and evaluating operational policing and that they should collaborate with the public in identifying and solving local problems. (p. 229)

There is no standardized strategy for community policing. Instead, its strategies should be responsive to the local contexts of each society. Skogan (2000) explains:

> Community policing is not something that is easy to pin down. However, it is evident to this author that it involves reforming decision-making processes and creating new cultures within police departments; it is not a packet of specific tactical plans. It is an organizational strategy that redefines the goals of policing, but leaves the means of achieving them to practitioners in the field. (p. 160)

In short, according to the philosophy of community policing, a police officer is required to have close contact with the general public to achieve the objective of crime prevention. The contact may encompass many different activities that suit the characteristics of a particular societal context. In this connection, the type of community policing strategy that best suits Hong Kong's society is worthy of discussion and is the focus of this chapter.

Community Policing in Hong Kong

Hong Kong was a British-ruled colonial territory until it became a special administrative region (SAR) of the People's Republic of China in July 1997. The Hong Kong Police Force was formally established in 1844, following the territory's colonization in 1841. Under colonial rule, the police commissioner was directly responsible to the governor. Police officers were mainly European or Indian, but rarely local Chinese. A top-down approach to the management and operation of the force was adopted, and the main policing objectives were the suppression of violent crimes and mass outbreaks of disturbance (Gaylord & Traver, 1995). It is without doubt that police relations with the public were strained. However, a turning point came following the youth riot of 1967, when Hong Kong's government recognized the need to bridge the gap between itself and the general citizenry. The Royal Hong Kong Police were no exception. In the 1970s, the force began to make an effort to become closer to the public, and improvements in the police-public relationship were soon evident. Cases of complaints against the police have continued to drop over the past two decades, from 4,000 in 1984 to slightly more than 3,000 in 1999 and 2,500 in 2006 (Hong Kong Police Review, 2006).

The Hong Kong Police have not formally admitted to the adoption of community policing. Instead, some of the police initiatives designed to foster community relations over the past few decades appear to fulfill the philosophy of community policing. For instance, in 1974, the Police Public Relations Branch (PPRB) was established as a centralized unit to promote public relations, keep the public abreast of crime trends, and appeal through television programs such as the *Police Magazine* for information that could help in crime investigations. The PPRB has collaborated intensively with local broadcasting enterprises in these efforts.

At the district level, a Police Community Relations Officer (PCRO) was established at the Chief Inspector rank and is directly accountable to the District Commander for liaising with the community and improving relations between the police and the public. The PCRO is in charge of the Junior Police Call (JPC) and School Liaison Officer (SLO) schemes. The former serves as a youth club open to all youths between the ages of 9 and 16. It was launched in 1973 with the objective

> … to develop our members to work in partnership with the community and other agencies to fight against crime. We are committed to train our members

and to equip them with necessary abilities as future leaders in serving our community. We promote positive peer influence in tackling juvenile delinquency (Hong Kong Police, 2006).

In essence, JPC members serve as the eyes and ears of the police to assist in crime detection and prevention. The JPC membership has grown from 9,000 in 1974 to 134,809 (as of January 31, 2008, Hong Kong Police). In terms of the increasing size of the membership, it appears to be quite successful. However, the members of this scheme are mainly ordinary school children. High-risk youths who are unlikely to be absorbed into contemporary social activities are unlikely to benefit from it.

The SLO program is another initiative headed by the PCRO to promote good relations between the police and school children. There are currently 25 SLOs and 33 Secondary School Liaison Officers (SSLOs) serving 686 primary schools and 550 secondary schools in Hong Kong (Hong Kong Police, 2008). The designated role of the SSLO is to prevent youth crimes in secondary schools, for example, to crack down on school bullying and youth gang problems through a multiple-agency approach. In general, however, the SLO scheme has not been well received by some schools because they fear being labeled as crime ridden.

In addition to these initiatives operated by the Hong Kong Police Force, there are a number of other platforms through which the police can communicate with the public on issues of crime prevention. For example, in 1973 the government set up the Fight Violent Crime Committee, which subsequently became a policy-steering group called the Fight Crime Committee (FCC).* Today, the FCC is composed of 16 members, eight of whom are heads of the relevant government bureaus and departments, and the other eight of whom are members of the public appointed by the Chief Secretary for Administration. District Fight Crime Committees† (DFCCs) were formed in 1976, with members appointed by the government to monitor local anti-crime

* The objectives of the FCC include (a) to draw up plans for a co-coordinated effort to reduce crime; (b) to coordinate the work of the departments and agencies concerned in the implementation of such plans; (c) to receive and to assess reports from the departments and agencies concerned on the extent to which they have been able to implement the plans and on the results; (d) to determine ways in which the public can be stimulated to contribute to the reduction of crime; (e) to receive and process suggestions from any source on how crime might be reduced; (f) to recommend any legislative and administrative measures that the Committee considers necessary towards reducing crime; and (g) to report on progress to the Chief Executive once yearly (Fight Crime Committee, 2007).

† The objectives of the DFCCs include (a) monitoring the state of crime and law enforcement in the district; (b) co-coordinating district campaign activities; (c) promoting good relationships between the Police and members of the public; and (d) advising the FCC on administrative and community involvement measures to combat crimes (Fight Crime Committee, 2007).

campaigns in the 18 districts of Hong Kong (Fight Crime Committee, 2007). The author, a member of a DFCC from 1999 to 2001, observed that most of the members with political backgrounds looked only to campaigns that could forward their political objectives, such as gaining publicity and opportunities for intensive contacts with citizens. Thus, the crime prevention projects they proposed primarily comprised mass propaganda and recreational programs. In most cases, these programs were not responsive to the root causes of crime in society.

The Neighbourhood Watch scheme was transplanted from Britain in 1985 with the objectives of drawing the attention of residents to the importance of natural surveillance and reporting criminal activities to the police. Under this scheme, the residents of a particular community take turns patrolling the area around their properties. In the 1980s, in the face of a soaring number of robberies and sex crimes against women, this scheme was well received by local residents. An average of 1,524 units were established, and 17,015 households participated each year between 1986 and 1992 (Lo & Cheuk, 2003). However, the public response later cooled off, and the scheme has been inactive since the 1990s. This can be attributed to decreasing community solidarity in Hong Kong and to a discrepancy in the perceived role of the police between the citizenry and the police. The latter perceive their role in the scheme to be minimal, whereas the general public demands that they take a more active role. Consequently, citizen grievances are unavoidable, and this may erode relations between the police and the public.

It is obvious that none of the aforementioned police crime prevention projects target high-risk youth. Bearing in mind Trojanowicz and Bucqueroux's (1994) comments, it is clear that community policing needs to empower the population with special needs. Thus, police-initiated projects must take the needs and circumstances of juveniles into greater consideration.

Youth Crime in Hong Kong

Young people's engagement in criminal activities has drawn public attention in Hong Kong. In 2006, 4,510 juveniles (aged under 16) were arrested for crimes. Most were arrested for shoplifting (1,116 persons, or 24.7%), miscellaneous theft (1,014 persons, or 22.5%), or wounding and serious assault (697 persons, or 15.5%) (Hong Kong Police, 2006). Apparently, the majority of juveniles were arrested for minor offenses. As a result, the general phenomenon of the past few decades has been that around 40% of juveniles arrested have been placed under the Police Superintendent's Discretion

Scheme,* rather than being dealt with through the courts (Fight Crime Committee, 2007). Needless to say, it is doubtful that a police caution alone will help to put troublesome youths back on the right track. To tackle the youth crime problem, therefore, support from the community is essential. Operation Breakthrough (OB) was just such a joint venture between police officers and social workers with the aim of reducing the likelihood of juvenile reoffending.

Program Features of Operation Breakthrough

OB was initiated in a police district (Tuen Mun) in Hong Kong in the summer of 1998 by a senior police officer who adopted the idea from a similar anti-juvenile crime initiative that was being run by the South Australian police force. On average, 22 police officers offered their help in the initiative. All of these officers volunteered to attend the camp, which was held during off-duty hours, on their own free time. In 2000, the scheme was extended from the aforementioned district to a number of other districts. The program was made up of the following "eight-Ps" critical features, which were fundamental to its success (see Figure 8.1).

Physical Training

Physical fitness is commonly regarded as a significant element of an individual's level of self-esteem. Therefore, the likelihood of youngsters offending would be much reduced if they developed a positive self-image due to improved physical conditioning. After having taken part in quite a strenuous physical training regimen, such as dumbbell sessions, boxing training, long runs, and night marches through mountains and country parks, many of the participating youths began to show a much greater interest in sports. This was certainly a good start, which gave them a clear example of the benefits of a healthy lifestyle and, in turn, helped to foster feelings of heightened self-esteem.

Personal Breakthrough

All of the participants had a chance to experience a personal "breakthrough" by accomplishing very demanding adventure training activities. In trying such

* Under the Police Superintendent's Discretion Scheme (PSDS), a police officer with the rank of superintendent or above may at his or her discretion administer a caution to a juvenile offender instead of initiating a criminal prosecution. With effect from September 1, 1995, the age ceiling of offenders eligible for the PSDS was 18 (Fight Crime Committee, 2007).

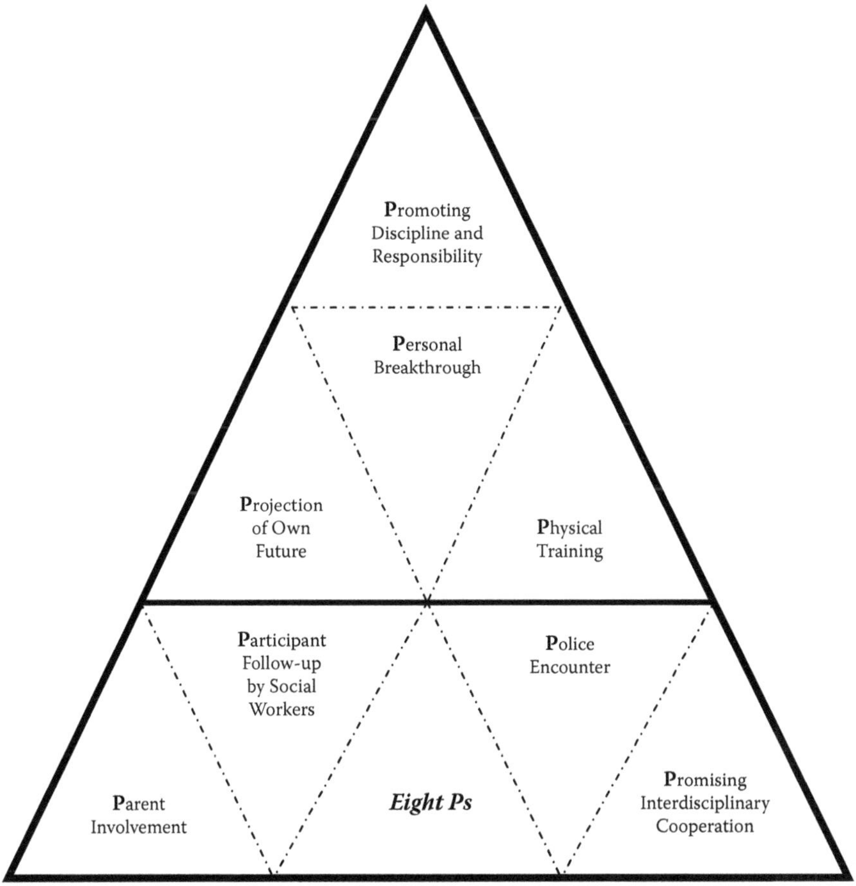

Figure 8.1 Critical features of Operation Breakthrough.

activities as abseiling, rock climbing, and long swims followed by a high water jump, they were able to overcome their own physical and psychological fears and limitations. Having successfully completed these activities, they not only experienced a strong sense of achievement, but also gained positive insights into their own abilities. They came to realize that seemingly insurmountable obstacles can be overcome with effort and a "never-give-up" attitude.

Promoting Discipline and Responsibility

OB placed strong emphasis on self-discipline, teamwork, and the importance of taking responsibility. This was partly accomplished through the appointment of a leader for each team who took charge of all of the team tasks. Foot drills and other camp activities were held to a tight schedule. It was hoped that participants would quickly see the value of discipline and teamwork and transfer the lessons learned in the three days of training to their daily lives, as well-disciplined patterns of life and better self-control can certainly help in preventing young people from getting into trouble again.

Projection of Own Future

The participating social workers conducted a workshop that focused on the negative consequences of criminal acts and the importance of having a plan for the future. The participants were invited to make up a realistic ending for an actual criminal incident that had occurred in Hong Kong. This helped them to form a clear idea of what they had to look forward to if they did not abandon their life of crime. In addition, they were asked to write down where they expected themselves to be in five years' time. In predicating their own futures, it was hoped that they would focus on setting personal goals and start looking forward and planning their own "destinations" in life.

Police Officer Encounter Session

OB also offered juvenile offenders a personal encounter with a selected police officer. This officer (usually from the Special Duties Unit [SDU]*) talked about his or her own background and work. The officer emphasized that with the right amount of ambition, determination, and effort, there was very little in life that could not be accomplished. This hard-hitting encounter session provided a suitable climax to a long, hard day of physical exercise, and it was usually here that we witnessed the turning point in the camp—the point at which the relationship between the police officers and the juveniles became friendlier and more relaxed and caring. In addition to the message of "self-empowerment" that was imparted, it was hoped that such sessions would help the juveniles to see the police as more humane, which could ensure that they cooperated better with them in the future.

Promising Interdisciplinary Cooperation

The success of a juvenile crime prevention initiative very often relies on smooth cooperation between the police and the social workers (Lam & Li, 2002). One of the main highlights of OB was the excellent level of cooperation between police officers and social workers and their complementary roles in planning, recruitment, and program implementation. Social workers located suitable target youths, encouraged them to take part in the program, and followed up with them once the camp was over. The police, most of whom had

* The Special Duties Unit is an elite counterterrorism team that was formally established in 1974. The police officers in this unit are perceived by the public as muscular and brave.

specialist professional training backgrounds (i.e., SDU and Airport Security Unit officers), took the youths through the physical and adventure training activities. The two sides maintained very close communication on the progress of the youngsters during the camp, which was useful for the social workers in continuing to help them during and after the program.

Parent Involvement

The program also called for the involvement of the participants' parents. The presence of parents at the final graduation ceremony provided great encouragement to the youngsters involved, and the parents got to see something they had seldom experienced, i.e., their children successfully completing a tough and demanding course. The barbeque afterwards served as a wonderful opportunity for parent-child interaction during which both parties could talk freely about their experiences. Although not all of the parents showed up, due to indifference or work engagements, this was an important part of the program and may have gone some way in healing the rift between the youths and their parents.

Participant Follow-Up by Social Workers

A number of the participants who took part in the camp's basic boxing training showed great interest in continuing with this activity. On average, between 20% and 30% of the participants in each OB camp volunteered to join the Boxing Club of their police region, which was organized by volunteer police officers. The club met twice a week in a Police Regional Headquarters. The trainees had to behave well and stay out of trouble to retain their membership. Nearly all of the participants continued to receive assistance from social workers, who helped them to deal with their problems in regard to family, schooling, and peer relationships.

Self-Perceived Changes in the Juvenile Offenders

OB catered to boys and 16 girls between the ages of 14 to 18 who were cautioned by police due to their commission of minor crimes, such as common assault or theft. After taking part in this project, all participants were invited to describe their perceived changes and impressions towards the police officers in their own words. In order to guarantee a high degree of accuracy and objectivity of the evaluation, all questionnaires were filled in anonymously and police officers were not present when the youngsters wrote down their answers. Quantitative and qualitative data were analyzed and compiled by a researcher who was independent of the police. The data were supplemented by personal observations of the researcher who participated throughout the initiative. These data indicated that the juveniles had benefited from the program not only in increased self-confidence, but also in positive changes in their values and attitudes.

Increased Self-Confidence

The juvenile participants were asked to rate themselves in the following areas after completing the program: (1) Have you developed more self-confidence? (2) Have you discovered more about your own abilities? and (3) Have you discovered more about your own inner strengths? An extremely high ratio of the participants, 185 out of 188, expressed increased self-confidence following the program. Similarly, 184 participants showed a better understanding of their own abilities during the course of the program. In terms of the discovery of inner strengths, the answers varied quite a lot between 1998 and 2001. Only 68% of boys in 1998 and 52% in 1999 could recognize inner strengths, whereas 84%, 96%, 73%, 78%, and 89% of boys in the last five OB programs, respectively, reported such strengths. Only 69% of girls in a particular year could identify their inner strengths. The program obviously brought about positive changes in self-perception among the participants. They were consistent in their descriptions of their impressions of the program. Some examples follow.

> I gained much more self-confidence and better self-discipline and became more organized. I realized that I loved challenging activities. My confidence towards police officers also increased. In my eyes, the police were a well-organized team. In fact, I gained many new and exciting experiences through participation in this program. (Case-199910)
>
> I found I was capable of accomplishing all of the activities. All of the activities were perfectly arranged by the police. The social workers did not show up frequently at the camp. However, some police officers kept us awake until very late, so we were too tired to take in the exercises on the following day. Most of the activities I had not tried before. I had great fun on the whole. (Case-199918)
>
> I have much more confidence and more understanding about myself after the three-day training camp. I am satisfied both with the police and the social workers. (Case-2000a11)
>
> I found myself smarter and more powerful than before. In fact, the police officers are nice guys. And I realize that those poor officers that I met are just a small number in a large bureaucracy. The program was exhausting. However, after finishing, I found it was not really as hard as expected. (Case-2000a13)
>
> After the three-day training camp, I learnt to be attentive and confident. I am impressed with the outstanding physical fitness of the police officers. They are nice guys and never look down on us for our lack of capability. Therefore, I feel more confident. Many thanks to the social worker who put me into this three-day training camp. (Case-2000a22)

Obviously, the participants treasured the unique experiences that they encountered in the three-day training program, during which they discovered their inner strengths. More importantly, they achieved a measure of success that they seldom had in the school system.

Improved Physical Condition

Of course, the juvenile participants benefited not only psychologically, but also physically. Having come through the harsh and demanding program, many of them found themselves in better physical condition. This type of positive change was very important for juveniles who generally pay a lot of attention to their appearance. Many of the participants mentioned this wonderful experience.

> My major limitation was in doing press-ups. They [the police officers] helped me overcome my constraints in area, but I was not strong enough to make it. The activities arranged were very interesting and exciting. It was exhausting, but was a good chance to improve my physical fitness. I hope I can take part in similar training again, and I am sure I will take part if I have the chance. (Case-2000a09)
>
> I became more muscular and thinner. The police officers were too strict at the beginning, but improved gradually. All of the social workers were very nice and brought along some fruit when visiting us in the camp. The activities were exciting, such as high jump, boxing, and night-walks. (Case-199904)
>
> I feel very satisfied with my physical fitness. I have done some activities, like jumping into the sea, rock-climbing, and mountain walking, that I have never tried before. Every police officer supported us despite the fact that we [my friends and I] had done something wrong in the past. If the program demanded more in physical training, the excitement could be greater. (Case-2000a01)
>
> I have become more muscular following the training camp! I have achieved many things that I never thought I could do. (Case-199904)
>
> Surprisingly, I found myself quite good at physical fitness. The police officers performed better than I expected. (Case-2001a23)

Gaining New Knowledge and Skills

The participants also reported that they had gained new knowledge and skills from the program, as can be seen from the following comments.

> I think in the programme, I can get more confidence and know how to communicate with each other. I learnt the communication skills. If we want to do well, we shall have work together, and then we will have a good result. At the same time, I feel that Hong Kong police is very kind; they can spend their free

> time to teach us. And the social worker is also very kind. (This questionnaire was written in English.) (Case-2002b05)
>
> I found that many things need cooperation. If nobody helps or supports each other, then it's impossible to complete [tasks]. I have greater confidence. I can do something that I usually think I can't as long as I give myself more confidence. (Case-2002a25)
>
> I think although the activities of this camp were harsh, I learned a lot in it. So it was worth the hard work. (Case-2002a10)

Change in Values and Attitudes

In addition to such benefits as increased self-confidence and improved physical fitness, the experiences of the program gave the participants insight. After taking part, they better understood the role and duties of police officers and had greater self-reflection ability. Some of the participants' answers follow.

> I became more confident when facing difficulty. The program was enjoyable and not really as difficult as expected. I found that something that seemed quite tough could be overcome by the end. (Case-2001a24)
>
> I hope there will be more activities which are diversified and can help teenagers. The police have contributed a lot to help us, to boost our confidence and endurance, especially in the fitness activities. I didn't know the fitness of the policemen was so good. This made us admire their team spirit in serving people and striving for improvement. (Case-2002a12)
>
> Having come through the three-day training program, I find myself not bad in nature. My major problem is that I seldom see things from different perspectives. Although the time spent with the police officers was short, I gained a thorough understanding of them, for example, of their families, their living environment, and many other aspects. They are no different from ordinary people when they are off-duty. For instance, they have their own families and daily life. In general, I was satisfied with the training program, and I found it meaningful. (Case-2002b10)

Change of Perceptions About Police Officers

All of the participants were asked if their level of trust in the police had increased upon completion of the project. A substantial number of them indicated a greatly increased level of trust (47% in 1998, 19% in 1999, 68% in 2000, 56% in 2001, and 85% in 2002). The participants were also invited to describe their impressions of the police officers. These descriptions were entirely positive. The youngsters appreciated the caring, helpful, and strict but friendly attitudes of the police. They also valued the officers' commitment to work and the strong sense of justice they exhibited. Some of their perceptions of police officers follow.

They were a little strict, but if they didn't force us, we wouldn't have done something we'd never done before. Besides, it was great of them to use their own time to help juveniles like us. (Case-2001b07)

I was very impressed with the police officers. They were strict with us because of their role. However, I surprisingly found that they were kind-hearted. (Case-2002b09)

In the first encounter, I did not have pleasant feelings about the police officers. However, I found them nice and easygoing as I stayed longer with them. (Case-2002b07)

They were so strict at the time of the training. But they were so kind, approachable, and enthusiastic during the free time. (Case-2002b04)

I found the police officers were, in fact, not rude to us, as I thought they would be. Instead they are human beings like every one of us. (Case-2002b05)

Some of them were rude, but some were pleasant. The others were not really consistent in their manner. (Case-2002b06)

Discussion

It can be concluded from the participants' feedback that OB achieved its objectives through the involvement and effort of different parties—police, social worker, parents, and young offenders. The following approaches and strategies of this program are worthy of our attention and appear to suit the local contexts of Hong Kong.

A Down-to-Earth, Proactive Approach

The ultimate goal of OB was to prevent high-risk youths from reoffending. It was a proactive way of cracking down on juvenile crime. Based on data from a wide variety of sources, the police developed and implemented a solution. In this case, the police officers integrated their understanding of juvenile crime with the ideas of social workers and probation officers about juvenile delinquency. It was believed that raising the self-confidence levels of young offenders and promoting a positive image of the police would be helpful in eliminating juvenile delinquency. Corresponding training activities were then tailored to high-risk youth. It seems to the author that this kind of training, which is aimed at youths with special needs, tends to be more tangible and down-to-earth than propaganda work in the community.

A Humane Approach

It can be seen in the written comments of the participants that having human contact with police officers was meaningful for juvenile offenders who had had negative encounters with police officers during arrest or detention. They mostly focused on the personal qualities of the police officers and their interactions with them. To gain the respect and trust of juveniles, it is essential that police officers are impartial and caring with a strong sense of discipline. It is probably true that if individuals are impressed with the police, then they are more likely to be law abiding and have respect for law-enforcement agents. It is definitely necessary that police officers undergo training that will facilitate their communication skills with juvenile delinquents and help them to understand the characteristics of juvenile delinquents.

A Cross-Professional Approach

Social workers also played a significant role in the OB project. Both they and the police had equal participation in identifying the underlying causes of juvenile crime, devising appropriate initiatives, sharing in program implementation, and having access to the evaluation at the end. The program indeed required the knowledge and expertise of different professions. Mutual respect and understanding are essential for smooth collaboration. To achieve it in this project, both professions had to have a preliminary understanding of each other's work culture in advance. It was also crucial that common ground was established with regard to the project's goal and strategy. Communication outside of formal meetings was indispensable.

Areas for Improvement

Although the program was well received by police officers, social workers, the participants, and their parents, there are areas for improvement. First, with respect to the operation of the program, it is possible that its impact would be longer lasting if the youngsters were provided with more debriefing afterwards. As there was a tight schedule for the training activities in the three-day period, there did not seem to be enough time to conduct in-depth debriefing. Also, over the course of the eight OB sessions, it became obvious that many of the parents were not very enthusiastic about the program, even though the social workers put a lot of effort into persuading them to come. In fact, the presence of those parents who did participate was a great encouragement to their children. If parents do not show up, then they can hardly expect to have a breakthrough in their impaired parent-child relationship. Finally, in terms of resources and manpower, it is quite demanding for police officers to have to undertake the program on their own time. If it can be shown that OB is helpful in preventing juvenile crime, then the police officers who assist in the training camp should be entitled to do so during working hours.

Conclusion

This chapter provides an encouraging example from the juvenile offender perspective of a community policing initiative that was implemented in Hong Kong. Undeniably, the Hong Kong Police Force has put a great deal of effort into nurturing its relationship with the public over the past three decades. The customer-oriented culture of the new millennium in Hong Kong has further facilitated police actions to become closer to the community. However, the community policing strategies that have been adopted are unlikely to be responsive to the needs and circumstances of high-risk populations. Operation Breakthrough, in contrast, can offer many insights into the implementation of crime-prevention strategies for young people.

References

Bayley, D., & Sheering, C.D. (1997). Future of policing. *Law and Society Review*, 30(3), 585–202.

Bennett, T. (1994) Community policing on the ground. In D. Rosenbaum (Ed.). *The challenge of community policing: Testing the promises* (pp. 224–248). London: Sage.

Das, D.K. (1987). *Understanding police human relations*. Metuchen, NJ: The Scarecrow Press, Inc.

Eck, J.E. (2004). Why don't problems get solved? In W.G. Skogan (Ed.). *Community policing: Can it work?* (pp. 185–206). Belmont, CA: Wadsworth/Thomson Learning.

Fight Crime Committee (2007). Fight crime committee report (No. 26 Report). Hong Kong: Author.

Friedmann, R.F. (1992). *Community policing*. Hertfordshire: Harvester Wheatsheaf.

Gaylord, M.S., & Traver, H. (1995). Colonial policing and the demise of British rule in Hong Kong. *International Journal of Sociology*, 23(1), 23–43.

Goldstein, H. (1990). *Problem-oriented policing*. New York: McGraw-Hill.

Greene, J.R. (1989). Police and community relations: Where have we been and where are we going? In Dunham, R.G. & G.P. Alpert (Eds.). *Critical issues in policing* (3rd ed.) (pp. 349–365). Prospect Heights, IL: Waveland Press.

Hong Kong Police (2006). Hong Kong police review 2006. Retrieved April 4, 2008, from http://www.police.gov.hk/review/2006/chart/chart_main.htm

Hornick, J.P. (1993). *Community policing in Edmonton*. Ottawa: Minister of Solicitor General of Canada.

Kelling, G.L. (1988). *Police and communities: The quiet revolution*. Perspectives on policing, no. 1. Washington, DC: National Institute of Justice, U.S. Department of Justice.

Lam, C.C., & Li, C.M.J. (2002). The police and social workers in juvenile crime prevention: Concepts and practice. *Journal of Youth Studies*, 5(1), 149–162

Lau, R.W.K. (2004). Community policing in Hong Kong. *Criminal Justice*, 4(1), 61–80.

Leighton, B.N. (1994). Community policing in Canada: An overview of experience and evaluation. In D.P. Rosenbaum (Ed.) *The challenge of community policing* (pp. 209–223). Thousand Oaks, CA: Sage.

Lo, C.W.H., & Cheuk, A.C.Y. (2003). Police-public projects in Hong Kong: An evaluation. *Asian Journal of Public Administration,* 25(2), 287–313.

Murphy, C., & Muir, G. (1985). *Community based policing: A review of the critical issues.* Ottawa: Solicitor General of Canada.

Quah, S., & Quah, J.S.T. (1987). *Friends in blue: The police and the public in Singapore.* Singapore: Oxford University Press.

Rosenbaum, D.F. (Ed.) (1994). *The challenge of community policing.* Thousand Oaks, CA: Sage.

Schaffer, E.B. (1980). *Community policing.* London: Croom Helm Ltd.

Skogan, W.G. (1990). *Disorder and decline: Crime and the spiral decay in American neighbourhoods.* Berkley: University of California Press.

Skogan, W.G. (2000). Community policing in Chicago. In G.P. Alpert & A.R. Piquero (Eds.). *Community policing: Contemporary reading* (2nd ed.) (pp. 159–174). Prospect Heights, IL: Waveland Press, Inc.

Skogan, W.G., & Hartnett, S.M. (1997). *Community policing, Chicago style.* New York: Oxford University Press.

Trojanowicz, R., & Bucqueroux, B. (1994). *Community policing: How to get started.* Cincinnati: Anderson Publishing Co.

"Non-Returnable" Arrest Warrants
A Form of Modern Banishment

9

RUBEN SORGE AND NAHANNI POLLARD

Contents

Introduction

For decades, fugitives with outstanding warrants for their arrest have come into repeated contact with police officers across Canada—often without consequence. Most offenders are aware of their outstanding warrants, and many have admitted to leaving those jurisdictions to avoid arrest.* Many of these fugitives go on to commit further crime, without ever having been brought to justice with respect to their previous offenses. This situation threatens the safety of the community, consumes police resources, and brings the administration of justice into disrepute. With tens of thousands of warrants issued each year in Canada, the problems posed by fugitives are present in every policing jurisdiction across the country.

Operational Definitions

The phrase "non-returnable warrant" is used to refer to an arrest warrant that was issued by another jurisdiction with a radius-of-return that does not extend to the jurisdiction in which the police contact is made with the offender (i.e., British Columbia). Thus, warrants become non-returnable when the subject moves outside the radius-of-return. By extension, the term "fugitive" is used to refer to subjects for whom a non-returnable warrant is outstanding. The term "contact" is used to refer to instances wherein a police officer meets and stops a fugitive in the course of duty.

Arrest Warrants: A Primer

In Canada, arrest warrants can be issued for various reasons, and at various points in time in the criminal justice process. Many arrest warrants are issued to assist with the apprehension of suspects. Other arrest warrants are issued when accused persons have been charged with a criminal offense but fail to appear in court for some aspect of the criminal justice process, such as "fingerprinting, interim hearing, preliminary trial, trial, [and/or] sentencing" (Rossmo, 1987:50). Similarly, warrants can also be issued when offenders breach some aspect of their probation or release conditions. In sum, the primary reason a warrant is issued is to bring offenders before the court.

* Data from the study indicate that on average, nearly 90% of offenders were aware of their arrest warrant, and 36% specifically left the jurisdiction issuing the warrant to avoid arrest.

Whenever an arrest warrant is issued in Canada, a record of that warrant is created on the Canada Police Information Centre (CPIC) database by the issuing jurisdiction. The Royal Canadian Mounted Police (RCMP) makes CPIC accessible to all police officers in the Canadian law enforcement community. Remarks can be added to CPIC warrant records, and as such, issuing jurisdictions use this opportunity to determine and communicate the warrant's radius-of-return. These radii are usually Canada-wide or province-wide, but in some provinces, they are as limited as city-wide. The radius-of-return serves to notify other jurisdictions that, if the fugitive is found outside of the radius, the issuing jurisdiction will not cover the cost of having a fugitive escorted back to the issuing jurisdiction to face charges. Therefore, such remarks are used by police officers to determine whether or not a fugitive is "arrestable" and "returnable." For example, if a CPIC warrant record shows the radius-of-return of a warrant issued by Toronto to be city-wide, then most police officers in Canada will conclude that the warrant is only executable within the city of Toronto. The practical effect of these kinds of administrative CPIC notes is taken by police officers to mean that the jurisdiction that issued the warrant will not cover the cost of transporting a fugitive.

These long-standing practices have contributed to the widely held belief among members of the Canadian law enforcement community that a warrant with a limited radius-of-return cannot be executed by a police officer who comes into contact with the fugitive outside of the radius-of-return. Ultimately, this commonly held understanding of the law is what has created the concept of non-returnable warrants, and in turn, an apparent arrest loophole in the Canadian criminal justice system.

Radius Warrants: A Closer Look

The Origins of Radius Warrants

In Canada, sections 91 and 92 of the Constitution Act (1867) set out the division of power between the federal and provincial governments. According to section 91, the federal government has legislative authority relating to criminal law. Indeed, the *Criminal Code of Canada* contains numerous provisions relating to the issuance and execution of arrest warrants. However, section 92 of the Constitution Act (1867) charges the provinces with the administration of justice. It is because of this provision that the provinces have been left to decide how to coordinate the execution of warrants and transportation of fugitives across Canada.

Section 703 of the *Criminal Code* specifically addresses the effective scope of arrest warrants in Canada. Specifically, section 703(1) states that a warrant issued by a superior court may be executed anywhere in Canada. In other words, warrants issued for indictable offenses have a Canada-wide radius-of-return. Similarly, section 703(2) states that a warrant issued by a provincial court may be executed in the province of issuing jurisdiction. In this light, the implementation of warrant radii is governed by legal statute. Within the context of section 703, it could be argued that all Canadian *Criminal Code* warrants should have only two possible radii: Canada-wide or province-wide.

Differential Warrant Radii Guidelines: Policies, Procedures, and Practices

Fugitive escorts can be expensive, as both the cost of transporting the arrested individual as well as the wage and transportation costs of the sheriffs and/or law enforcement officers escorting the individual must be covered. These costs are typically absorbed by the jurisdiction that issued the warrant in the first place. Many jurisdictions have developed their own warrant radii policies, arguably in response to the cost implications of return escorts. This practice has led to the creation of differential warrant radii guidelines among, and even within, provinces. In other words, one jurisdiction may recognize a *Criminal Code* offense to be serious enough to justify a Canada-wide radius, while another jurisdiction may issue a province-wide, or even city-wide radius warrant for the same offense. Such disparate warrant radii guidelines prevent the criminal justice system from dealing with offenders in a consistent way.

In 1995, British Columbia became the first province in Canada to develop standard warrant radii guidelines, through the collaborative efforts of Vancouver Crown Counsel and the Vancouver Police Department (VPD). The Criminal Justice Branch of British Columbia later developed a clear policy that identifies Crown Counsel as being responsible for determining the radii of return associated to warrants. In 1999, the warrant radii guidelines listed in the *British Columbia Crown Counsel Policy Manual* were revised to reflect the severity of the offense, as directed by section 703 of the *Criminal Code* (see Table 9.1).

In contrast, the warrant radii guidelines of other jurisdictions differ widely. In fact, some warrant radii guidelines are largely inconsistent with the direction set out by section 703 of the *Criminal Code*. For instance, some jurisdictions in Ontario issue warrants with city-wide radii for indictable offenses, while other jurisdictions follow the direction set out in the *Criminal Code* and issue Canada-wide or province-wide warrants for indictable or dual offenses. As a result, this disparity in practice does not lend itself to a uniform application of justice across Canada.

Table 9.1 Warrant Radii Guidelines for British Columbia

Offense	Warrant Radii-of-Return
Indictable offenses	Canada-wide
Hybrid offenses (proceeded by indictment)	Canada-wide
Hybrid offenses (proceeded by summary conviction)	Province-wide
Summary conviction offenses	Province-wide

Source: Adapted from Criminal Justice Branch. *Crown Counsel Policy Manual: Warrants—Radius of Return*, Ministry of Attorney General, Victoria, BC, 1999.

It should be noted that the warrant radii guidelines included in the *British Columbia Crown Counsel Policy Manual* also address instances wherein a person wanted in British Columbia is found in a jurisdiction beyond the warrant's radius-of-return. In this instance, Crown Counsel is instructed to (1) extend the radius of the warrant, (2) request a summons for the accused, or (3) enter a stay of proceedings on the charge when they are notified that one of their fugitives is in the custody of an officer from another jurisdiction. Arguably, whenever a Canadian police officer comes into contact with a fugitive who is wanted by another jurisdiction, the officer should contact the police agency or Crown Counsel office of the issuing jurisdiction to notify them of the offender's whereabouts, and determine whether they will have him/her transported back to face charges. If the Crown Counsel office of the issuing jurisdiction does not agree to extend the radius of the warrant, then that office should arrange for the warrant to be vacated and removed from the system (including CPIC) (Marion Paruk, Deputy Regional Crown Counsel, personal communication, October 25, 2005).

In practice, however, most police officers do not contact the jurisdiction that issued the warrant and advise that they have had contact with a wanted person or that the person is in their custody on a different offense. This is primarily because police officers assume they "know" that the issuing jurisdiction is not going to cover the cost of returning the fugitive to face charges (Appleby, 1990:A1). Even when police officers do advise Crown Counsel in such situations, many Crown Counsel do not extend the radius, request a summons, or enter a stay of proceedings on the charge. By failing to enforce these warrants, they remain on the CPIC system but have little practical effect from a law enforcement perspective.

When warrants are left on the CPIC system without a practical means of enforcement they nevertheless often come to act as a modern form of banishment. These warrants may reduce the costs associated with the processing of an individual for the issuing jurisdiction; however, this may not be a true cost savings, but rather a false economy. When viewed from a national perspective, one jurisdiction may save money by transferring the costs associated with dealing with a fugitive to another jurisdiction. However, this often occurs at the expense of the additional criminal activity that the offender may commit in the new jurisdiction, the costs of which include policing the fugitive for the new crime(s) (i.e., police contact, investigation, arrest, detention, prosecution, etc.) along with the monetary and emotional costs of the crime to the new victims (i.e., medical, insurance, security, social services, victim services, etc.). The costs are experienced on a national level, where they "simply encourage reciprocal policies, reduce police accountability and erode respect for the criminal justice system" (Rossmo, 1987:24-25). Interestingly, the guidelines for British Columbia explicitly state that radius warrants should not be used to banish individuals from an area. This important policy position should be emulated by all other jurisdictions.

The accumulation of numerous active warrants on the CPIC system means that many of these warrants are old, and that often no specific enforcement action related to these warrants has been taken. This is a concern because Canadian case law states that warrants must be executed in a timely fashion. In the case of *Askov* [1990], the Supreme Court of Canada clarified the meaning of "reasonable delay." This decision resulted in thousands of dropped charges. The Court revisited the issue and provided more flexible guidelines in *Morin* [1992] and introduced a test to assess unreasonable delay. This test calls for a review of the reasons for the delay, the actions of Crown Counsel, and institutional resources (or lack thereof). It is significant that the Court also recognized that delay will often work against Crown Counsel. Accordingly, the warrant radii guidelines of British Columbia note that negative implications may arise if Crown Counsel fails to execute a warrant in a timely manner.

If a jurisdiction decides not to cover the cost of transporting a fugitive back to face charges, the jurisdiction should enter a stay of proceedings for the charge. If a stay of proceedings is not entered, *Askov* [1990] and *Morin* [1992] may be cited to argue that the Crown Counsel had the opportunity to execute the warrant, but deliberately chose not to proceed. This may be fatal to the charge, as Crown Counsel, in failing to previously transport the accused, would be the direct source of the "unnecessary delay" associated with bringing the accused before a judge.

Police Response: A Brief History

The Vancouver Police Department has been urging the government to address the problems posed by non-returnable warrants for decades. Unfortunately, the issues of cost and cooperation have continually impeded efforts to find a solution. After an examination of the problem in the mid-1970s, British Columbia implemented a pilot program whereby all offenders were returned at the province's expense. However, the cost of airfare proved to be "astronomical" and the program was discontinued (Appleby, 1990:A2).

The second study into the problem was conducted by the Planning and Research Section of the VPD in 1982. In 1983, the BC Attorney General acknowledged that disparate warrant radii policies across Canada contribute to the unequal application of the law, and bring the administration of justice into disrepute. However, it was suggested that before the law is changed, the 1982 study should be replicated on a Canada-wide level (see Rossmo, 1987).

In 1984, the Assistant Deputy Minister of the Police Services Branch requested that all police forces in British Columbia conduct a study to determine the extent to which other jurisdictions come into contact with fugitives for whom non-returnable warrants have been issued. The Police Services Branch also wanted to determine whether other jurisdictions would support the recommendation that all warrant radii become Canada-wide (Rossmo, 1987). The findings of this initiative were as follows:

> On February 7, 1984 the Deputy Solicitor General of Canada advised the Deputy Attorney General of British Columbia that none of the other provinces [there were seven respondents to the survey] supported the recommendation of a Canada-wide policy on warrant radii, since it was felt that such a policy would reduce their existing discretion. They claimed not to have a problem of similar magnitude to British Columbia (although no studies were ever conducted), and were not interested in returning fugitives to their own jurisdictions (Rossmo, 1987:59).

The data collected by the VPD for the purpose of this 1984 study were used by Kim Rossmo to examine the relationship between fugitive migration patterns and disparate warrant radii policies across Canada (Rossmo, 1987). Rossmo's data-set consisted of information relating to 757 fugitives and a total of 1,167 police contacts. Only 12.3% of these fugitives were arrested and booked into the Vancouver City Jail at the time of the study. Rossmo showed that warrant radii guidelines were widely disparate across Canada, and that this disparity is related to fugitive migration patterns. Further, Rossmo and Routledge (1990:293) estimated the size of the criminal population to be about 1,700 in Vancouver in 1984. The examination of this problem as informed by environmental criminology, rational choice theory, and social control theory suggests that various other push and pull variables, such as climate and sentencing patterns, may contribute to the phenomenon of fugitive migration (Rossmo, 1987). Pointedly, Rossmo's research also showed that fugitives knew that their outstanding warrants were non-returnable, and that the fugitives fled the issuing jurisdiction to avoid arrest.

In 1990, British Columbia's Attorney General called for a national approach to address the problem. The VPD collected data from police departments across Canada to determine the extent to which they come into contact with arrestees who have non-returnable warrants, so as to encourage a national approach to the problem. The findings suggested that police agencies from British Columbia to Saskatchewan have the problem. It is unclear whether the eastern Canadian provinces participated in that study.

In 1993, the Union of British Columbia Municipalities crafted a resolution requesting that the Attorney General of British Columbia urge the Federal Attorney General's Office to establish national warrant radii guidelines, and to provide the support necessary to ensure that fugitives are returned to the jurisdictions that have issued warrants for their arrest (Union of British Columbia Municipalities, 1993). Further, in 1996, the Ottawa-Carleton Regional Police Services Board created a resolution that again called for the federal government to establish national guidelines with respect to warrant radii, and considered the existing system to be an insult to the administration of justice (Ottawa-Carleton Regional Police Services Board, 1996:8).

Many were hopeful that a solution to the problem would be attained through the assistance of the Criminal Justice Branch, which spearheaded the Fleeing Fugitive Agreement between provinces that came into effect on May 1, 1996. Unfortunately, the initiative did not apply to the majority of fugitives in British Columbia. The agreement was so complex and resource intensive that it had a minimal effect on addressing the problem.

In 1997 and 1998, the Canadian Association of Police Boards (CAPB) issued resolutions regarding the problem of non-returnable warrants. These CAPB resolutions on non-returnable warrants urged the federal government of Canada to address the problem through legislation (Canadian Association of Police Boards, 1997, 1998).

Bryon Wilfert of the Liberal Party eventually raised the issue of non-returnable warrants in Parliament in 1997 during an oral question period (Hansard, 1997). Mr. Wilfert asked the Solicitor General about the steps being taken to ensure that fugitives arrested in one jurisdiction are returned to the jurisdiction that issued the warrant for their arrest. The Solicitor General at the time, the Honorable Andy Scott, replied:

> ... under the *Criminal Code* you can exercise a warrant anywhere in the country. The final decision is left to the provinces. That is the reason why the federal government and the provinces have to work together (Hansard, 1997:1445).

Since then, the issue has not resurfaced in Canadian Parliament, nor has it been addressed through collaborative efforts by the federal and provincial governments.

The Vancouver Board of Trade (1997) *Report on Property Crime in Vancouver* showed that fugitives have been contributing to Vancouver's crime rate, and recommended that the federal government address the problem of non-returnable warrants through legislation and infrastructure. This recommendation was re-affirmed in the Board's 2003 *Report on Property Crime in Vancouver* (Vancouver Board of Trade, 2003).

In 1997, the provinces of Alberta, Saskatchewan, and Manitoba entered into protocol agreements with British Columbia regarding non-returnable warrants (Criminal Justice Branch, 1997). In these agreements, the provinces confirmed that a failure to execute the warrants of fugitives in a timely manner decreases respect for the criminal justice system. All four provinces agreed that a standardized approach was necessary, and that efforts to return prisoners would be in the interest of justice. These protocols also provided criteria for Crown Counsel to consider when contemplating the transfer of an individual, including (1) the seriousness of the crime; (2) the viability of the prosecution; (3) alternatives, such as the waiving of charges to the destination province for a guilty plea, conditional release, or interim release by remote appearance; and (4) whether the costs for return of the fugitive are in the public interest. While this step forward is commendable, it does not appear to have had the desired result, as a large population of individuals wanted on non-returnable warrants continue to reside in Vancouver.

Although the history related to the issue of non-returnable warrants reveals some minor success, it generally underscores the failure of the stakeholders in finding a viable resolution to the problem. This review also reveals the lack of literature and research on the subject. In an effort to effectively address the issues posed by non-returnable warrants, Chief Constable Jamie Graham of the VPD recognized that further examination of this problem was required. In 2005, the Chief Constable directed the Planning and Research Section of the VPD to conduct an in-depth analysis of this issue.

Research Question and Objectives

The situation posed by non-returnable warrants raises several questions, including (1) What factors contribute to this problem? (2) To what extent is this problem present across Canada? and (3) How can this problem be solved? Since the last major study into the problem of non-returnable warrants was conducted in 1984, the Executive of the VPD agreed that it would be advantageous to begin re-evaluating the problem by determining the extent to which it exists in Vancouver, British Columbia. Thus, the main question guiding the present study was identified as, *to what extent do members of the VPD come into contact with offenders who have non-returnable warrants for their arrest*? The primary objectives of this study were to (1) illustrate the extent of the non-returnable warrant problem in Vancouver, British Columbia, (2) develop a clearer understanding of the legal requirements related to this issue, and (3) bring the issue back into the public forum, so as to generate further discussion and debate with respect to possible solutions.

Research Method

Research Design

The present study set out to determine the extent to which members of the VPD come into contact with fugitives who have non-returnable warrants for their arrest, by way of a quantitative research method. Since the last major inquiry into this matter occurred in 1984, the present study was designed to be exploratory in nature.

Data Sources and Data Collection

Police officers working in several different Operational Units of the VPD, including the Patrol Teams, Traffic Unit, Emergency Response Section, and Youth Services Section, were directed to assist with the data collection portion of the study. Specifically, during the period between January 1, 2005, and March 31, 2005, inclusive, police officers were directed to note, on the copies of the data collection instrument provided to them, the name and date of birth of every subject with whom they came into contact, if that person had at least one outstanding non-returnable warrant. The officers were also instructed to note the date and location of each contact. This information was then sent to the Planning and Research Section of the VPD for further analysis, whereby information relating to the outstanding warrants, charges, and criminal histories of the subjects were retrieved from CPIC.

Sampling

The police officers were instructed to gather data every time they came into contact with a fugitive for whom a non-returnable warrant was outstanding. The objective was to capture data on the *entire population* of fugitives who come into contact with police in Vancouver. However, the true extent to which data was collected from this population is unknown, since some police officers may not have fully assisted with the data collection component of this study for various reasons (e.g., lack of copies of the data collection instrument on hand, etc.). Thus, the data represent the minimum number of contacts between fugitives and the police.

Findings

Fugitive Contacts

Analysis of the data revealed that a total of 726 subjects with outstanding non-returnable warrants came into contact with Vancouver police officers during the three-month study period. Indeed, a total of 2,183 police contacts were made with this group of 726 individuals, with a median of two contacts per person (e.g., one individual was checked 31 times). The average number of contacts per person was three. Most (87.2%) individuals came into contact with police between one and five times (see Table 9.2). The average age of the subjects was 35 years.

The City of Vancouver is divided into four districts for the purpose of operational policing. District 1 contains Vancouver's central business and entertainment districts. District 2 contains Vancouver's Downtown Eastside, which is known internationally as Canada's poorest neighborhood, juxtaposed against vibrant neighborhoods. District 3 is largely a residential area, while District 4 contains many of the affluent citizens of the city. Most police contacts (46.3%) with subjects for whom non-returnable warrants were outstanding occurred in District 2 (see Table 9.2).

Table 9.2 Descriptive Statistics—Subjects and Contacts

	f	*N*	%
	Age of Subject		
18 to 24 years old	96	726	13.2
25 to 34 years old	258	726	35.5
35 to 44 years old	263	726	36.2
45 to 54 years old	94	726	12.9
55 to 64 years old	15	726	2.1
	Police Contacts with Subjects		
Between 1 and 5	633	726	87.2
Between 6 and 10	75	726	10.3
11 or more	18	726	2.5

Table 9.3 Descriptive Statistics—Warrants, Issuing Provinces, Radii, and Warrant Charges

	f	*N*	%
	Outstanding Warrants Per Subject		
Between 1 and 5	694	726	95.6
6 or more	32	726	4.4
	Provinces "Wanting" the Subjects		
1 province	628	726	86.5
2 or more provinces	98	726	13.5
	Provinces of All Warrants		
Alberta	753	1,569	47.9
Ontario	462	1,569	29.4
Manitoba	164	1,569	10.5
Quebec	99	1,569	6.3
Saskatchewan	43	1,569	2.7
New Brunswick	18	1,569	1.1
Nova Scotia	15	1,569	—
Newfoundland	6	1,569	—
Yukon	4	1,569	—
Prince Edward Island	3	1,569	—
Northwest Territories	2	1,569	—
	Radii of All Warrants		
Less than province-wide	574	1,569	36.6
Province-wide	989	1,569	63.0
Unknown	6	1,569	—
	Warrant Charges		
Condition offenses	389	726	53.6
Property offenses	347	726	47.8
Violent offenses	167	726	23.0
Drug offenses	74	726	10.2
Other offenses	70	726	9.6
Driving offenses	57	726	7.9

Warrants

The 726 subjects had a total of 1,582 non-returnable warrants among them. However, the research team did not collect information on 14 of these warrants, because data were only collected on the first 10 warrants of each subject. Most (95.6%) of the subjects had between one and five non-returnable warrants outstanding, and most subjects were only wanted by one province (86.5%) (see Table 9.3). Notably, approximately half (47.9%) of the warrants examined in this study were issued by Alberta, and 29.4% were issued by

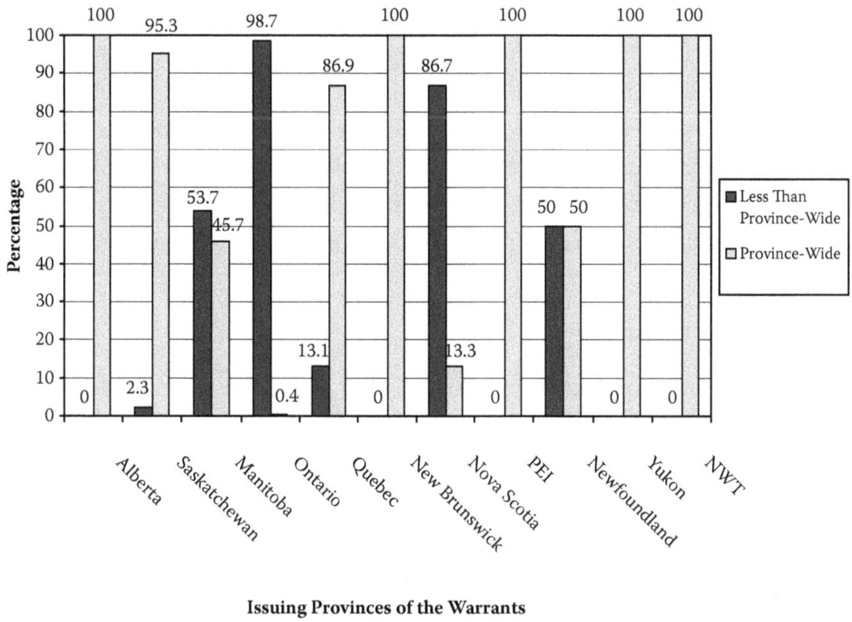

Figure 9.1 Issuing provinces by warrant radius.

Ontario. Further analysis of these data revealed that most of the subjects were wanted by the following jurisdictions: Edmonton (23.5%), Calgary (15.8%), Winnipeg (9.6%), and Toronto (9.8%). This is consistent with Rossmo's (1987) fugitive migration findings.

Most of the warrants (63%) had province-wide radii (see Table 9.3). However, a significant proportion (36.6%) contained less than province-wide radii. Surprisingly, 100% of Alberta's warrants were province-wide warrants, while 98.7% of Ontario's warrants were restricted to a specific city or jurisdiction (see Figure 9.1). These differential warrant radii policies effectively condone the issuance of warrants for the purpose of banishment, communicating to the offenders that they are free to go, as long as they do not return. Today, many offenders wanted on outstanding warrants completely avoid arrest and any judicial process; indeed, they could potentially do so for the rest of their lives. As this study illustrates, this occurs despite their repeated contact with the police. Clearly, there is an absence of less than province-wide warrants in the western provinces. This is arguably because Alberta, Saskatchewan, and Manitoba have each entered into an inter-provincial agreement with British Columbia that, among other things, identifies the issuance of warrants with a radii less than province-wide as an undesirable practice (see Criminal Justice Branch, 1997).

The charges on the subjects' warrants varied from drug-related offenses (10% of the subjects), to violent offenses including sex, weapons, and robbery offenses (23% of the subjects), to property-related offenses including fraud (47.8% of subjects), to breach of release type offenses (53.6% of the subjects) (see Table 9.3). The large number of warrants issued for the breach of release type offenses is not surprising, and may account for a general reluctance among agencies to cover the cost of a return escort. Nevertheless, the problems surrounding non-returnable warrants remain pressing, as many offenders who do not face justice for their original offenses continue to commit crime.

Outstanding Charges

Beyond these outstanding warrants, 43.7% of subjects generated additional criminal charges (see Table 9.4). About 29% of all the subjects had outstanding charges in the Greater Vancouver Regional District. In other words, about a third of this population entered Vancouver from other jurisdictions and continued committing offenses. Additionally, about 21% of all the subjects had outstanding charges originating from other jurisdictions.

The subjects' outstanding charges varied. Outstanding charges are those that are awaiting adjudication by the court. The top three types of outstanding charges were the same as those that accounted for the majority of warrant charges: 20.1% of the outstanding charges were property related, 15% were violence related, and 10.5% were related to breaches of a condition (see Table 9.4).

Criminal Convictions

Interestingly, most (88.7%) of the subjects with non-returnable warrants had at least one criminal record conviction (see Table 9.4). In fact, most (20.1%) subjects had between 1 and 10 criminal convictions, with the median being 12 convictions each. In particular, six individuals each had over 100 criminal offense convictions on their criminal records. The true extent of violence may be under-reported in this population because many potential incidents were not examined, such as when the offender had charges that were either not pursued or were later stayed. Property offenses characterized most of the subjects' criminal records (78%), followed by condition type offenses (71.6%) and violent offenses (60.1%). Violent offenses included attempted murder, sexual assault, robbery, and serious assault (e.g., aggravated assault, assault causing bodily harm, and assault with a weapon). While some of these offenses are strictly indictable, many are hybrid offenses, which means that Crown Counsel can choose to proceed by indictment or summary conviction. Only 21.8% of the population had active weapons prohibitions.

Table 9.4 Descriptive Statistics—Outstanding Charges and Convictions

	f	*N*	%
Total Number of Outstanding Charges Per Subject			
None	409	726	56.3
Between 1 and 5	296	726	40.8
6 or more	21	726	2.9
Outstanding Charges			
Property offenses	150	726	20.1
Violent offenses	109	726	15.0
Condition offenses	76	726	10.5
Drug offenses	61	726	8.4
Other offenses	24	726	3.3
Driving offenses	13	726	1.8
Total Number of Criminal Record Convictions			
None	82	726	11.3
Between 1 and 10	246	726	33.9
Between 11 and 20	150	726	21.0
Between 21 and 30	90	726	12.3
Between 31 and 40	58	726	8.0
Between 41 and 50	45	726	6.1
51 or more	55	726	7.6
Criminal Record Convictions			
Property offenses	568	726	78.0
Condition offenses	520	726	71.6
Violent offenses	436	726	60.1
Drug offenses	374	726	51.5
Other offenses	282	726	38.8
Driving offenses	241	726	33.2

Chronic Offenders

About 19% (n = 139 out of 726) of the subjects were identified as chronic offenders by the VPD's Chronic Offender Unit. This label is applied to offenders when the VPD's Records Management System reveals that the individual is named in at least five general occurrence reports as a "charged/accused" subject since 2001. As compared to the non-chronic offender population, the chronic offenders had more multiple (two or more) warrants outstanding than the non-chronic offenders. Indeed, 63% (n = 88 out of 139) of the chronic offenders had multiple non-returnable warrants outstanding, as compared to 57% (n = 336 out of 587) of the non-chronic offenders.

About 69% (n = 96 out of 139) had active outstanding charges, and 44.6% (n = 62 out of 139) had two or more such charges. In contrast, only 37.6% (n = 221 out of 587) of non-chronic offenders had active charges. Further, chronic offenders and non-chronic offenders were found to be relatively similar in the rate in which they breached conditions or failed to attend court proceedings.

The criminal records of the chronic offenders also proved interesting. Although the chronic offenders had an average of 35.8 convictions each, about 25% of this population had between 51 and 135 convictions. In fact, 85.6% of the chronic offender population had at least 11 convictions on their criminal records. When compared to the non–chronic offender population, the chronic offenders were seen to have significantly more convictions overall, accounting for the criminal records with over 101 convictions.

Reasons for Leaving

In Vancouver, data from the study indicated that on average, nearly 90% of offenders were aware of their arrest warrant, and 36% specifically left the jurisdiction issuing the warrant to avoid arrest (see Table 9.5). Overall, there was no overwhelming rationale for why these offenders chose Vancouver to migrate to. Just over one-quarter indicated they had family in the area, while another quarter indicated that job opportunities and weather conditions prompted their choice of location. However, a small percentage indicated that drug availability, lenient courts, and criminal opportunities were the precipitating factors in their decision.

Table 9.5 Reasons for Moving to Vancouver

	Yes (*f*)	*N*	Yes (%)
Knowledge of Warrant?	491	547	90
Leave to Avoid Arrest?	189	519	36
	Why Move to Vancouver?		
Family	130	476	27
Job opportunities	111	472	24
Treatment availability	18	471	4
Welfare accessibility	35	471	7
Weather	110	472	23
Drug availability	83	471	18
Lenient courts	65	472	14
Criminal opportunities	29	471	6

Discussion

Clearly, a large number of individuals with non-returnable warrants for various offenses continue to generate police contacts, engage in criminal activity, and build upon their already significant criminal histories. The public generally expects that a person for whom a warrant has been issued will be arrested by the police and brought before a court. Even most offenders have this expectation, which explains why a large number of them flee jurisdictions to avoid arrest. This is particularly troubling when some of them evade the law for serious violent incidents. From the perspective of a victim of an attempted murder, sexual assault, or robbery, the idea that a person can simply move away, and thereby avoid accountability for the crime, seems preposterous. The idea that the justice system would, in any way, be complicit in this circumstance is difficult to fathom. In their examination of police roles, Moore and Braga (2003:17) discuss the importance of bringing offenders to account. They state,

> It is worth keeping in mind ... that to many citizens, *justice* is as important as achieving the practical effect of controlling crime. To many, the idea of justice includes the idea that people ought to be held accountable for their crimes. It would be wrong for them to be excused, even if we could be assured that offenders would commit no future crimes.

Their emphasis is on accountability, and not incarceration. In other words, this issue does not directly involve sentencing. Rather, it is the idea that the offender should stand before a court of law to see that justice is done. When this does not occur, it is difficult to suggest that any justice has been achieved.

The court appropriately expects and requires compliance with its orders. This can be observed in numerous rulings that are related to environmental or public demonstrations and protests. Yet, while the court ensures that breaches of these orders are addressed and often sanctioned, this is not often the case for breaches of criminal justice system process. The case law is curiously silent with respect to an offender's repeated breaches of court-ordered conditions or court-required attendance. This contention seems to be supported by the findings of the present study, and by the BC Justice Review Task Force, which cites data from one survey that revealed that 22 offenders accounted for 70 breach charges, and 32 offenders accounted for 120 failures to appear (BC Justice Review Task Force, 2005:67).

The data clearly illustrate that many offenders wanted for serious offenses in other jurisdictions continue to engage in their activities, whether lawful or criminal, without any substantive likelihood of arrest. While this situation seems untenable, it continues to propagate unabated. Although many justice professionals are likely aware of this aspect of the Canadian criminal justice system, it remains, for the most part, hidden from the public. The reason for this may involve the confluence of a number of factors, including budget constraints, case law, *Criminal Code* requirements, the lack of standardization between jurisdictions, and a reluctance on the part of most of the police community to arrest an offender when the power to arrest exists.

Policy Implications

Arresting Offenders on Non-Returnable Warrants

Section 503 of the *Criminal Code* provides some remedy by enabling police officers to arrest offenders on so-called non-returnable warrants. Since police officers rarely have an arrest warrant in hand, almost all arrests are made without warrant. Accordingly, section 503(3) provides authority to a police officer to arrest an individual without warrant for an indictable offense allegedly committed in a jurisdiction other than where the arrest took place. As clearly stated in *R. v. Connors* [1998], the court affirms that indictable offenses include all hybrid offenses. When this occurs, a police officer must report the arrest to a Justice of the Peace (JP) in his/her jurisdiction. The JP must be satisfied on reasonable grounds that the person arrested is the one alleged in the warrant. If this cannot be proven, the arrested person is released. The JP has the authority to remand the accused person for a period not exceeding six days. During this time the police officer may use the process described in section 528 of the *Criminal Code* to have the inter-provincial warrant endorsed within the arresting jurisdiction. Alternatively, the police officer could contact the issuing jurisdiction and, with the assistance of that jurisdiction's police department and Crown Counsel, extend the radius of the warrant to be Canada-wide.

Sections 528(1) and 528(2) of the *Criminal Code* provide the procedure by which a police officer may execute a warrant issued by another jurisdiction. This section directs a police officer to contact the issuing agency's JP directly. The JP from the issuing jurisdiction may sign an affidavit to confirm the warrant and return it to the officer by fax (Ewaschuk, 2003:5-32). The requesting officer would then take the signed affidavit to a JP to endorse the inter-provincial warrant in the relevant jurisdiction. This allows the requesting officer and all officers within the requesting jurisdiction to execute the warrant and send the wanted party back to where the offense occurred (Ewaschuk, 2003:5-33). This option would likely be used to address wanted persons with extensive criminal records and/or warrants for serious, violent crimes.

This inter-provincial arrest process, as stated in sections 503 and 528 of the *Criminal Code*, is resource intensive and administratively complex. However, officers should consider and use this process when deemed appropriate. A failure by police officers to use this process prevents the jurisdiction that issued the warrant from having the opportunity to request that person's return. Moreover, the release of the accused person increases his/her opportunity to commit further offenses, all while an outstanding warrant remains executable.

Implications of Sections 503 and 528 on the Warrant Arrest Process

Section 703 of the *Criminal Code* specifically addresses the effective scope of arrest warrants in Canada. Specifically, section 703(1) states that a warrant issued by a superior court may be executed anywhere in Canada. In other words, warrants issued for indictable offenses have a Canada-wide radius-of-return. Similarly, section 703(2) states that a warrant issued by a provincial court may be executed in the province of issuing jurisdiction. In this light, the implementation of warrant radii is governed by legal statute. However, in some cases, warrant radii have become governed by provincial policy. Clearly then, information on CPIC regarding warrant radii are simply informal investigative notes to other police officers, informing them as to whether a jurisdiction will cover the cost to have a fugitive returned to that jurisdiction (Marion Paruk, Deputy Regional Crown Counsel, personal communication, October 25, 2005).

In other words, the *Criminal Code* does not provide for warrant radii that are less than province-wide. Rather, such restrictive warrant radii, particularly when related to cities or regions, are created at the behest of the originating agency, and seem to be extra-legal artifacts. Specifically, these kinds of warrant radii are based on agreements between provinces, jurisdictions, Crown Counsel, and police agencies, and have little to do with the law as set out in the *Criminal Code*. Indeed, within the context of section 703, it could be argued that all Canadian *Criminal Code* warrants should have only two possible radii: Canada-wide or province-wide. As discussed above, this is the case in British Columbia, and the *Crown Counsel Policy Manual* of British Columbia reflects this.

Cost as a Primary Impediment

Cost has likely been a major impediment to police officers who may have tried to use the outside jurisdiction arrest process set out in sections 503 and 528. When an accused is arrested on a non-returnable warrant and is then transported, the jurisdiction that issued the warrant must cover the cost of transporting the offender. In British Columbia, Crown Counsel covers this cost, while sheriffs usually handle the actual transportation. For this reason Crown Counsel in British Columbia have developed, with police input, a policy related to the radius of return of all warrants (Criminal Justice Branch, 1999).

In British Columbia, police officers in the field assess the willingness of Crown Counsel to transport an accused back to the jurisdiction that issued the warrant when they arrest fugitives. To the extent that officers believe that they might receive support from Crown Counsel for their efforts, they will proceed to request that an accused be transported to the jurisdiction. However, when officers believe that Crown Counsel will not support these requests, primarily due to an officer's own cost estimations, officers will not proceed with the arrest.

The degree to which officers believe that cost will overshadow other considerations may be related to an officer's use of the process set out by sections 503 and 528, even when those officers are fully aware of the process. Fundamentally, it may be that police officers consider it futile to approach Crown Counsel in other jurisdictions to transport individuals and, therefore, police officers generally do not engage in such activity. Further, Vancouver Police officers are particularly cognizant of the fact that many cities and police departments have little interest in having criminals returned to them. It is understandable that police agencies, as self-interested, rational entities, would prefer that these offenders remain outside of their jurisdictions. The economics are not complicated: if the set of people representing non-returnable warrants does not return to the jurisdiction in which the warrants are active, that jurisdiction will save the cost of policing, prosecuting, and imprisoning that individual. Therefore, given that return escorts are financed by the issuing jurisdictions, it is not in their best interest to approve these kinds of requests.

The reasons described here explain why officers may not arrest individuals who are wanted on non-returnable warrants. However, it is often an assumption by the police officer that a jurisdiction will not accept the return of an arrested individual. When officers fail to notify a jurisdiction about an offender wanted on their warrant, the jurisdiction is unable to review their case and determine whether or not to transport the offender. In so doing, police officers have effectively placed themselves in a position of making a decision that more legitimately falls under the auspices of that jurisdiction's police service or Crown Counsel. Further, police officers have taken on the responsibility for releasing an offender, when the decision to release should actually be made by the originating jurisdiction that issued the warrant.

In light of sections 503 and 528 of the *Criminal Code*, and the case law provided by *Askov* [1990] and *Morin* [1992], when an accused person is arrested on an outstanding non-returnable warrant and the issuing jurisdiction is notified, the issuing jurisdiction must make a choice concerning the warrant. If police or Crown Counsel of the issuing jurisdiction decide not to transport, then the jurisdiction should enter a stay of proceedings for the charge and arrange to have that warrant removed from CPIC. If a stay of proceedings is not entered, *Askov* [1990] and *Morin* [1992] provide compelling grounds for the accused to argue that Crown Counsel had the opportunity to execute the warrant, but deliberately did not. As discussed above, this may be fatal to the related charges, as Crown Counsel would then be the direct source of the unnecessary delay associated with failing to bring the accused before the court.

Policy Recommendations

The issues surrounding so-called non-returnable warrants must be addressed. The following measures are recommended to form a national standard. First, all provinces and territories should implement warrant radii in accordance with section 703 of the *Criminal Code*. This would eliminate limited radius warrants. Second, police officers should be informed of the inter-provincial warrant arrest process set out in sections 503 and 528 of the *Criminal Code*. This would allow officers to arrest individuals wanted for indictable offenses when they are found outside the jurisdiction that originally issued the warrant. Third, a national police policy should be developed and implemented to ensure that when officers come into contact with offenders with inter-provincial warrants, that officers notify Crown Counsel so that Crown Counsel may (1) extend the radius of the warrant, (2) request a summons for the accused, or (3) enter a stay of proceedings on the charge and arrange for the warrant to be cleared from the system. Fourth, a process should be developed to facilitate return-escort requests. Fifth, all provinces and territories should agree that the issuance of Canada-wide and province-wide warrants signifies an implicit agreement by the issuing jurisdiction to transport the offender. Finally, other key agencies, including Crown Counsel and the various Federal and Provincial Ministries, should be involved in the development of an effective and efficient process by which to facilitate the return of accused persons. The adoption of these policy options should address many of the problems associated with so-called non-returnable warrants, and ensure that a consistent process exists across Canada.

Future Directions

Although the foregoing has served to highlight this important justice issue, there continues to be many unexplored avenues. In particular, future studies should examine in greater detail the radii restrictions for various jurisdictions with respect to all warrants, and the offenses that these warrants are issued for. This should serve to highlight whether certain jurisdictions are truly applying differing standards of the "reach" of a warrant for indictable, hybrid, or summary convictions. It may also be advantageous to expand the scope of this study to assess exactly how many warrants are issued within a particular jurisdiction over a specified time frame, and conduct a follow-up of how many of those warrants become non-returnable by the offender fleeing the jurisdiction. This will better serve to establish a baseline of how prevalent this activity is, which will serve to strengthen the policy ramifications contained herein.

Conclusion

The present research provides a strong empirical foundation regarding the manner in which the police and the justice system presently fail to adequately deal with non-returnable warrants. Among other things, this initial analysis shows that Vancouver Police officers regularly contact individuals who have outstanding non-returnable warrants for their arrest. The *Criminal Code* clearly states that police officers can arrest offenders who have outstanding, so-called non-returnable warrants. What is much less clear is how the offender is to be dealt with after the arrest. At this time, no viable transportation network exists to transport offenders in an efficient and cost-effective manner. Any resolution to this issue will require the support and assistance of police agencies, Crown Counsel, the courts, and the provincial and federal governments. By working together, a practical and effective solution can be developed that will increase the safety of the public whom we serve.

References

Appleby, T. (1990). Costs make police ignore some arrest warrants. *The Globe and Mail*, April 17, 1990, A1–2.

BC Justice Review Task Force. (2005). *Beyond the revolving door: A new response to chronic offenders*. Report of the Street Crime Working Group to the Justice Review Task Force. Vancouver, British Columbia: Criminal Justice Reform Office, Ministry of Attorney General.

Canadian Association of Police Boards. (1997). *Resolution 97-6: Non-returnable warrants*. 1997 CAPB Conference. Retrieved on November 7, 2005 from http://www.capb.ca/services/conf_1997/conf3.shtml

Canadian Association of Police Boards. (1998). *Resolution 98-7: Non-returnable warrants*. 1998 CAPB Conference. Retrieved on November 7, 2005 from http://www.capb.ca/services/conf_1998/conf3.shtml

Criminal Justice Branch. (1997). *Protocol agreements: Fleeing fugitives*. Victoria, BC: Ministry of Attorney General.

Criminal Justice Branch. (1999). *Crown counsel policy manual: Warrants—Radius of return*. Victoria, BC: Ministry of Attorney General.

Ewaschuk, E. G. (2003). Chapter 5-2: Arrest, 5-32 to 5-33, in *Criminal Pleadings & Practice in Canada*. Aurora, Ontario: Canada Law Book Publishing.

Hansard. (1997). House of Commons Debates, Justice & Legal Affairs Standing Committee (2nd Session, 35th Parliament), Oral Questioning Period, December 8, 1997, 46:1440–5. Retrieved on November 7, 2005 from http://www.parl.gc.ca/36/1/parlbus/chambus/house/debates/046_1997-12-08/han046_1440-e.htm

Moore, M. H. and Braga, A. (2003). *The "bottom line" of policing: What citizens should value (and measure!) in police performance.* Washington, DC: Police Executive Research Forum.

Ottawa-Carleton Regional Police Services Board. (1996). Meeting minutes: March 25, 1996. Ottawa, Ontario. Retrieved on October 17, 2005 from http://ottawa.ca/calendar/ottawa/archives/rmoc/Police_Services_Board/22Apr96/PSM22APR.HTML

Rossmo, D. K. (1987). *Fugitive migration patterns.* Master's thesis. Burnaby, BC: Simon Fraser University.

Rossmo, D. K. and Routledge, R. (1990). Estimating the size of criminal populations. *Journal of Quantitative Criminology,* 6(3): 293–314.

Union of British Columbia Municipalities. (1993). UBCM resolutions and responses: Resolution B34 non-returnable warrants, Retrieved on November 7, 2005 from http://www.cserv.gov.bc.ca/lgd/pol_research/ubcm/1993/B34-non-returnable_warrants.html

Vancouver Board of Trade. (1997). *Report on property crime in Vancouver.* Retrieved on October 17, 2005 from http://boardoftrade.com/vbot_page.asp?pageid=161

Vancouver Board of Trade. (2003). *Report on property crime in Vancouver.* Retrieved on November 7, 2005 from ///www.boardoftrade.com/policy/PROPERTYCRIME-FINAL-OCT24-03-web.pdf

Cases Cited

R. v. Askov [1990], 2 S.C.R. 1199 (S.C.C.)

R. v. Connors [1998] 155 D.L.R. (4th) 391 (B.C.C.A.)

R. v. Morin [1992] 1 S.C.R. 771 (S.C.C.)

Spooking the Spooks Conducting Research into the UK's Integrated Special Branch

10

DAVID LOWE

Contents

Introduction

Spooks, spies, subterfuge, terrorism—these are all terms that have been a rich source of material for the spy genre of books, films, and television drama. That rich source of information has so far been pretty elusive to the academic world. As a result of restricted access there has, to date, never been any academic research that looks inside how agencies that police national security operate. That is, until now. One of the key roles of the UK's Integrated Special Branch (ISB) is to conduct surveillance, and arrest and interview suspects in counterterrorism investigations. In the UK, the ISB is a policing department that forms part of the overall policing of national security in the UK, and they work closely with the UK state agency MI5.

One unique aspect of the ISB is that the officers posted to the department come from the public police forces in the UK—they are not direct entrants into the department. Due to the secretive nature of their work, the ISB is one of the departments of the public police where very little research has been carried out, and to date there has certainly been no research where the researcher has had direct access to ISB officers and staff. When I was posted for the second time to the ISB as a detective sergeant in charge of a counterterrorism investigation team, I knew that I had a unique and potentially once-in-a-lifetime opportunity to conduct research into the inner workings of a department like the ISB. This allowed me to examine how they ran counterterrorism investigations. I commenced research into an ISB counterterrorist unit in a police force that comprised mainly an urban area but with a significant rural area at the beginning of 2001. My research was completed in 2004.

During the research period, in addition to running an investigation team I was also my ISB department's trainer, and I was still active with my force's Police Federation* branch board. The trainer responsibilities involved delivering short training inputs regarding changes of legislation as well as coordinating ISB officers' main national and regional training, examples of which include driver training, firearms training, or interview training. These three roles allowed me wide access to ISB managers, officers, and support staff from whom I could gather data for the research.

Unlike my first posting to the ISB as a detective constable where I was involved in counterterrorism investigations (mainly into the activities of the Provisional Irish Republican Army [PIRA]), having studied at university I had a more critical eye into ISB operations during my second posting. The nature of policing in England and Wales was changing with the British Home Secretary becoming increasingly influential in operational policing in England and Wales. An example of this is seen in the Home Secretary's powers through the Police and Magistrates Courts Act 1994 and Police Acts of 1996 and 1997 where the Home Office has direct control over every aspect of provincial policing (Oliver 1997; Jones 2003:607-611). I felt that I could make the most of the position I found myself in, and research how the ISB conducts its counterterrorism investigations.

Direct Home Office involvement (including involvement from the national security agency MI5) into ISB operations is not a new concept, as I noticed in both my first and second posting to the ISB the Home Secretary has a direct influence on the Branch's policing operations. Chief constables are literally figurehead leaders in relation to the ISB. In my second posting

* In the UK, police officers are not permitted to join a trade union. The Police Federation is the closest body the ranks of constable to chief inspector have to joining a trade union, as the Police Federation represents the interests of the lower ranks.

to the ISB, I noticed there had been changes in operational practice since my first posting. Apart from the changes in technological advances in the equipment used by ISB officers, the ISB had become increasingly involved in investigations where they cooperated with similar agencies in other states, especially with European Union (EU) member states. One significant change was in the UK law governing counterterrorist investigations that allows ISB officers to be more intrusive into the lives of UK citizens. Therefore, I took the opportunity to research the effects these legal changes had on the conduct of ISB counterterrorist investigations. This included examining how surveillance was authorized and carried out, the conduct of arrests, and how terrorist suspects were interviewed following arrest. The latter was of particular importance to see if the police interview techniques of suspected terrorists utilized in the 1970s and 1980s, especially on persons suspected of being members of PIRA, had changed.

This chapter discusses the method of research used to gather the data: covert participant observation. The discussion includes the physical difficulties of conducting covert participant observation without raising my colleagues' suspicion that academic research was being carried out. The analysis involved an examination of the activities used in data collection that on occasions had to be innovative, spontaneous, and resourceful. There is an ethical implication in using covert participant observation, and this is discussed. The main justification in carrying out covert participant observation is that the police as a whole and departments like the ISB are not vulnerable victims. The ISB is a powerful department in a powerful public institution that is robust enough to withstand the rigors of an academic study.

Method of Research Selected: Covert Participant Observation

I used covert rather than overt participant observation to collect the data on the ISB, as it is unlikely I would be allowed unfettered access to materials, personnel, or data due to the political sensitivity involved in counterterrorist investigations. In the wider operational field of policing, information on ISB investigations are withheld from police officers who are not in the ISB. This includes chief officer ranks (ACPO) unless there is a *need* for them to know that an investigation is running. Even where officers in an ACPO rank are informed that an investigation is running, they are not always allowed access to all of the information relating to the investigation. ACPO officers not posted to the ISB cannot order junior ranking ISB officers to inform them of all of the details of an investigation they are involved in. Based upon this premise it is virtually impossible for an academic researcher to have open access to the ISB and its operations.

One important factor related to accessing information on the ISB is that ISB work is subject to the UK's Official Secrets Act 1911. Even though the research was covert, it still placed limitations on what I could disclose regarding the running of the ISB. As a result, I did not disclose the type or details of technological apparatus used or how they were used. Neither did I discuss the ISB's use of informants (under the Regulation of Investigatory Powers Act 2000, informants are referred to as covert human intelligence sources [CHIS]). The reasons for this are twofold. First, there would be a potential breach of national security in relation to how equipment is used and informants are recruited and used in the operational field.

Most available ethnographic police research focuses on the role of uniformed police officers. Regarding research on uniformed officers, the researcher has requested and been granted access (even if limited by the police) leading to direct contact with operational uniformed officers. If I had made a formal request to conduct an overt piece of research into the ISB, I believe that the chief officer of the force I was working for would not only deny access, but also my posting would have been curtailed there and then. I had no choice but to collect the data covertly as I had unlimited access to operational ISB officers, ISB managers, and ISB files. Having noticed the changes in the running of the ISB and in the law that allowed the ISB to be more intrusive in citizens' lives, I had no choice but to use a covert method of research to collect my data. One of the risks I ran in using covert participant observation was in being caught by operational colleagues or the ISB management, where the penalty could have been severe (at the minimum end of the scale of punishment it would have meant a disciplinary hearing with a reduction in rank and/or a fine) due to the sensitivity of departments like the ISB to unauthorized exposure.

Jupp (1989) states why the police are very sensitive about opening their works to social researchers. This axiom is certainly applicable to the ISB and similar agencies involved in counterterrorism investigations, especially as they deal with sensitive and classified intelligence. Jupp states that the police use gatekeepers both formally and informally that allow the police to hide from view. He adds that these gatekeepers will erect barriers

> [To] insulate themselves from social researchers and others or by seeking to present a favourable image of their actions by mystifying and even falsifying the nature of police work. (1989:134)

Open access to policing agencies and departments involved in counterterrorism is extremely limited if not impossible to the academic researcher on two counts. First, is the fear of disclosure of the investigative methods and techniques used, and second, to prevent information from being inappropriately disclosed in relation to terrorist targets. Therefore, it would not be permitted for an outsider to come in and conduct an effective and meaningful piece of research into the ISB. To gain access to policing departments like the ISB, it is clear that covert participant observation is the most appropriate method of research.

The advantage of participant observation is that it provides a tangible way to collect data on how people create, transform, and give order and meaning to the working life of the subjects (Kane 2004:306). The main rationale behind the preponderance of police research is to uncover information that the subjects studied might wish to keep secret (Reiner 2000:218). Reiner states that the reason for this is that much of policing is dangerous, dirty work, as policing is about getting people to do what they do not want to do, or making them desist from doing what they want to do:

> The tactics used [by the police] for accomplishing this are almost inevitably going to be controversial even if they are legal, and they are frequently of dubious legality or clearly illegal. (2000:218)

Reiner makes this observation in the context of uniformed policework; however, his observation is still relevant to research on specialist police departments and agencies. Research into specialist CID departments like the ISB has not previously been conducted to examine whether Reiner's observation that tactics used are "dubious" or "clearly illegal." A problem with ethnographic research into the police is that it has decreased in the past 18 years and as a result the data has become dated (Marks 2004:866).

As this research examines how the ISB conduct the surveillance, arrest, and interview phases of counterterrorist investigations, researching how police officers interact naturally can be achieved only by covert participant observation. The observed behavior will be natural because the officers are not on notice that they are being observed for a piece of work that may find its way into the public domain. Jupp explains that participant observation is the most appropriate research method to obtain this type of data as it has its roots in ethnology, which examines how groups and individuals interact with one another. By having such an analytical ancestry, participant observation is an important research method in the examination of institutions, communities, and subcultural groups in modern industrial society because it provides data about culture, beliefs, values, meanings, and definitions in addition to the social interactions in which they are embedded (Jupp 1989:57). Ethnographic research provides a cultural knowledge, which is fundamental in understanding how the police go about doing their work and the choices they make, and police researchers should take heed of the fact that police culture is not monolithic (Marks 2004:869).

Both Jupp's and Mark's points are relevant to this research on two counts. First, as no ethnographic research has been conducted on the ISB, covert participant observation is more likely to produce natural behavior data into the culture, beliefs, and the interaction of the officers that previous police research has not had access to. Second, due to the organizational change in police management through New Public Management (NPM), deploying covert participant observation would provide a greater opportunity to assess if NPM has incurred a change in the operational police culture. Holdaway found that by using covert participant observation research, he, as a police officer with an academic background, had an opportunity to conduct observation on his fellow uniformed colleagues (1983:4), and it is a work that has become a classic police study. He says that the use of covert participant observation was the only effective research strategy that would "pierce" the police's "protective shield" (1983:5). Reiner and Newburn also recognize that in order to penetrate beneath the public face of the police, participant observation has been the main technique adopted by researchers wishing to analyze the practices and culture of policing (2008:354). Although not wanting to copy Holdaway's research, it was inspirational for me in deciding which was the most effective research method if I were to pierce the protective shield of the ISB.

The Strength of Covert Participant Observation: The Most Natural Data a Researcher Can Obtain?

Punch's study of the Amsterdam drug squad is a good example of the problems associated with participant observation (1979). He was given access to briefings, as well as accompanying officers conducting surveillance, arrests, and searches of premises, and interviews of suspects. He found the officers had a good working relationship, were fair in dealing with suspects, and there was no corruption. On completing the write-up of his research the media reported that the Amsterdam drug squad he researched was under suspicion for corruption and perverting the course of justice. Clearly, when Punch was in the company of those officers they were on their best behavior, as they knew he was watching them and recording his data, and those officers did not behave as they would in their normal operational culture. The data Punch obtained might have been different if his participant observation had been covert. On the theme of participant observation being an important method to observe behavior as natural as can be possible, Presdee says:

> [Ongoing] tradition acknowledges that what is important is the analysis of the way in which humankind makes sense of and, at times resist, existing and developing social structures. Such privileging of culture enables [researchers] to view behaviour as dynamic rather than determined and opens up the possibility of other ways of seeing transgressive and therefore criminal behaviour. (2004:267)

Clearly Punch did not view any dynamic behavior, which would have opened up the possibility of seeing transgressive or criminal behavior by the police. What Punch witnessed was determined behavior. Avoiding determined behavior was a key factor in my selecting covert participant observation, especially with ISB officers being involved in sensitive high policing activity involving covert surveillance and specialist investigation techniques. If the observation were overt, the observed behavior of the officers would not have displayed natural behavior. The only way to witness as natural behavior as possible is by using *covert* participant observation methods.

Jupp explains how, in effect, covert participant observation generates data that can cut through the image an institution wishes to portray. He says:

> One of the values of participant observation lies in the theoretical insights to be gained, insights which are made available by methodological commitments to naturalism, and explanation-by-understanding. *Another of its values lies in its commitment to overcoming the institutional constraints on research by the development of covert methods of collecting data.* It is ironic that adherence to such commitments generates parallel personal and ethical constraints upon the participant researcher himself, constraints which emanate from the dual role of being on the one hand participant and observer, and on the other police officer and sergeant [my emphasis]. (1989:62)

For Kane, covert participant observation is a useful method of research if we want to look beyond the quantitative data relating to effectiveness and performance of an institution. She says:

> [The] obsession with quantitative measures of significance in the wider field is in part a generalised attempt to compensate for and obscure logistical obstacles and the associated fears of weakening disciplinary authority. Such obsession has risen to the level of a dominant cultural force in mainstream criminology. (2004:304)

Quantitative data is relevant to policing agencies in measuring how they effectively deal with crime. The Home Office Website is a classic example of this because it covers a plethora of policing activity in its reports, containing a swathe of quantitative data with examples from the various 43 forces to support the point they make. What it does not tell you is how many times they failed, why they failed, or the methods used to achieve a success. That is why it is important to use covert participant observation to look at the operational and cultural context of policing from which the quantitative data is drawn.

When Holdaway carried out his research he was a uniformed sergeant in an operational section carrying out the role of patrol sergeant and custody officer (1983:6). In essence he, unbeknownst to his colleagues, was researching the operational culture of uniformed police officers. He had to furtively make notes when he could on comments said to him or of the conversations he had. The officers in his section knew he had an academic background, having completed his first degree in sociology under a scheme paid for by the police. In the late 1970s/early 1980s, there were very few graduate police officers, and of the officers who were graduates even fewer were graduates in social science (Reiner 2000:62). However, it appears that the influence his education had on his approach to policework resulted in his behavior standing out from the normal behavior displayed in the operational police culture of that time. This is seen in his view on the use of force, the manner in which evidence was gathered, how suspects was handled, and how he would tell his colleagues that his approach was a total variance to theirs (Holdaway, 1983:8).

I was a serving officer during the early 1980s, and I know that at that time for Holdaway to express such views was a brave thing to do if you did not want to be ostracized from your colleagues. It would not be difficult for police officers to know that he was conducting research on them. They knew Holdaway was one of the very few officers with a social science degree. This added to the fact that Holdaway let his colleagues know of his constant displeasure with their behavior to suspect that he was conducting research on them. This can be seen where his senior officers doubted his suitability for the police service (1983:8), his physical bravery on the streets being brought into question (1983:8), and being told by a constable to "switch the tape recorder off" (1983:10). At times it's difficult to believe if Holdaway's observations were covert due to the suspicion and mistrust of him by the officers he observed. Although the operational culture that existed during the period of Holdaway's research was macho, suffice it to say here that Holdaway's saintly behavior at that time would have put his colleagues on alert to watch their own behavior in front of him. Where covert participant observation is used as a research method to obtain data on the officers' natural behavior, it is important that you be accepted as one of them. This appears to be the case in all of Holdaway's observations. There are occasions where what he observed were deliberate exaggerations of police culture. An example of this was where a police officer directly approached him and said that he was going to "get a spade" and punched a fist into the palm of his hand (1983:12).

There are some similarities between Holdaway's research and mine. Both Holdaway and I were graduates. By 2000 the number of graduates in the police, including the lower ranks, had increased to such a level that it did not raise any suspicion among my colleagues that I would be conducting a piece of academic research. We had differences of opinion in approaches as to how to conduct operational policing; for example, my colleagues knew that I would not tolerate any form of discriminatory behavior displayed to either the public or colleagues. However, what differentiates my research from Holdaway's is in the acceptance of colleagues, where I was accepted as one of them and, as a result, what I observed was natural. There was no overt display of behavior for my benefit because I did not let it be known to my colleagues that I was that different from them. Among the factors that helped me be accepted as one of them was my reputation for arresting suspects. It is important among operational colleagues to have a reputation of being a good "thief taker." Another factor in my acceptance was my different view from Holdaway's regarding the use of force. It was known by my colleagues that I had used force on suspects during my early service, which may have been excessive on occasions, especially on suspects who had "touched the cloth." Touching the cloth relates to suspects who assault police officers. When policing violent parts of an urban area a show of force is needed rather than trying to pacify a situation through sociological discourse, as Holdaway espoused. My operational antecedents meant that operational colleagues trusted me. I was one of them.

Another factor that assisted in my colleagues accepting me was that I was a sergeant with more than 20 years of service, 10 as a sergeant. In their eyes I was an "old arse" sergeant, a view enhanced by the fact that even though I had passed the inspectors' examination in 1985, I had no desire to be promoted. Officers in my section regularly saw me question senior officers' actions. On the occasions when senior officers attended my team briefings and asked me to do something that I believed would put members of my team at risk, I would tell the senior officer. On occasions this would include a refusal on my part to carry out that senior officer's request. On one occasion, an ISB Detective Chief Inspector (DCI) ordered me to deploy members of my section in a certain way during the surveillance stage of an investigation. In front of the officers on my team, I replied saying that a risk assessment had to be completed first. His response was, "You will do as you're told" (DCI 2). My reply was, "I will enter this order into my notebook, state that no risk assessment had been carried out and that you are putting my officers in danger. That you are flagrantly breaching health and safety legislation and you will sign it. If you refuse I will also note that. These notes will be used in any subsequent court proceedings should anything go wrong." The DCI was clearly angry and simply replied, "You fucking smart arse, ok do a risk assessment." Standing up to the bosses and fighting for my colleagues' rights only enhanced my reputation as being one of them, adding to the trust the lower ranks had in me. If a key strength of participant observation is in its being a powerful method to evade the informal and formal institutional constraints placed upon social research (Jupp 1989:60), then it is logical to presume that covert participant observation is an even more powerful research method to examine police activity beneath the police public relations departments presentation. Hadfield raised this point when he was researching licensed premises. He says that he had to be a covert participant observer:

> … in order to avoid provoking actions by the researched that would have disrupted the *naturalism* of the setting. It was especially important for my purposes to prevent the possibility of compensatory behaviour that might have obscured more routine and deviant social practices [my emphasis]. (2008:479)

A major strength in deploying *covert* participant observation is that the data will be as natural as one can possibly obtain. This is important when researching the operational practices of an organization. As Reiner and Newburn point out, if the observation is overt there is the problem of determining whether the researcher has the trust of the research subjects and how their behavior may be modified by the presence of a researcher, adding that trust is unlikely to ever be complete (2008:354). That is why being covert and, as a result, being one of the people under observation allows the researcher to obtain the most natural data possible.

Other Methods of Research Considered for Data Collection

Consideration was given to using other methods of research to collect data during the research. When planning the research I did consider using semi-structured interviews on the occasions that I was in conversation with colleagues. I could not openly inform colleagues that I was conducting the research and that I wanted to discuss certain issues with them. The way I considered I could do this was by starting a conversation with colleagues on topics where I wanted their opinion. There was a problem in that there was no structure to the conversations, and I had no control of how a conversation would develop. It would be difficult to raise an unrelated topic during a conversation or to try and steer the conversation back to the theme I wanted to discuss without either raising suspicion or engendering a degree of bewilderment among my colleagues. If I had kept returning to a topic, telling my colleagues that they had not answered my questions, it is likely they would ask why I was so persistent in requiring an answer. This could have compromised the covert nature of my research. Most of the conversations with colleagues during the research (including those carried out during duty time) were on mundane everyday subjects ranging from football to holidays to cars. For example, during a conversation on whether the Chelsea Football Club has bought their recent success, to change the subject to ascertain colleagues' views on Muslims would literally be a conversation stopper. Before I could take a lead in the direction the conversation took, I would have to wait until another colleague introduced a relevant subject into the conversation. There were many occasions I could not control the direction of the conversation, especially where the company included three or more of us. There would be a tendency for over-talking to take place and, as usual, humor would be introduced, devaluing any genuine thoughts that were expressed. A typical example of how most conversations went was when three or more of us were in a static observation point. One of the officers raised the subject of the Muslim cleric Abu Hamsa, who was in the news that day. The conversation went as follows:

Officer A: "Did you hear about that Abu Hamsa, what a mad man. He should be kicked out of the country for preaching the hate he does." (D/C 3)

DL: "Don't you think he has a point considering how the West has treated the Arab people, especially Arab Muslims?"

Officer A: "I suppose so, especially Bush and how he winds them up, even how we treated them in the British Empire, look at Lawrence of Arabia."

Officer B: "Yes, it was a great film that, I like the bit where he goes into the officers' mess with the young Arab lad after going through the Sinai dessert dressed as a Arab and they would not serve him a drink." (D/C 5)

Officer A: "Yes, a great film, Peter O'Toole is really good in that, mind you he is a good actor."

The conversation then changed to films they enjoyed. For me to bring the conversation back to ascertaining their views on how Muslims are treated would either be a conversation stopper or result in some derisive comment being passed by my colleagues. In his study of conversational analysis and institutional talk, Heritage says that conversations are unpredictable as little of what we say, the actions we perform, or the order in which we do things are determined in advance (1998:165). Raising a topic in a conversation was just another technique used to collect data in covert participant observation, as conversations with colleagues about work-related matters as well as the mundane are part and parcel of the workplace. Raising a topic in a conversation is not a semi-structured interview because the interview needs a form of structure and typically uses checklists of topics to be covered (Jupp 1989:69).

The Ethical Implications of Covert Participant Observation: Can Powerful Organizations Be Vulnerable Victims?

An issue in using covert participation is the ethics of the research. One important issue centers upon trust between the researcher and the subjects of the research, which Holdaway refers to as the "calculated deception of trust" by the researcher (1983:13). As Holdaway's and my covert research was on the police, we were not dealing with vulnerable victims of crime where the betrayal of trust could have a detrimental effect on the subjects of the research. Holdaway says he conducted a covert strategy on the police, as they represent a powerful institution of our society which deals with the less powerful (1983:4). In justifying the use of covert participant observation on the police, Holdaway says:

> [It is] strengthened by the central and powerful situation of the police within our social structure. The police are said to be accountable to the rule of law, a constitutional constraint which restricts their right to privacy but which they can neutralise by maintaining a protective occupational culture. When such an institution is over-protective, its members restrict the right to privacy they possess. It is important that they be researched. (1983:5)

The difference between Holdaway's research and mine is that Holdaway researched a visible arm of policing, the uniformed branch, whereas I examined an invisible arm of policing. The ISB have greater legal powers than the uniformed branch in the performance of their duties. In my research, I have anonymized the police force and the individuals to prevent them from being identified. Perhaps the key issue regarding the ethical implications is the betrayal of trust, a point Reiner makes regarding researchers like myself. He says:

> A few researchers have been serving officers who systematically analyse their experiences as research material, having privately decided to leave and pursue academic careers. In effect they are covert participant observers, which clearly raises acute ethical issues about potential abuse of trust. (2000:221)

Betrayal of trust is an important implication in utilizing covert participant observation, and one seriously considered in this piece of research. As explained above, this research does not reveal any information regarding the equipment used during investigations; neither does it cover any information regarding informants (CHISs). What this research does reveal is how the ISB is run and how counterterrorist investigations are carried out with all of the police personnel involved being anonymized.

This is not a whistleblowing exercise where one has to consider whistleblowing ethics (Westmarland 2001:527-528). Even Holdaway makes this claim regarding his 1983 research. Holdaway states that his work was not that of a whistleblower that goes to the press releasing details of police activity for a sudden exposé; rather, his was a type of "public spiritedness" by revealing the inner workings of the uniformed section through empirically based academic work (1994:190). Likewise, this research is not whistleblowing. It resulted from a realization that there was a possible one-off opportunity to conduct research into the operational work carried out by police officers involved in counterterrorism investigations. From that opportunity a research strategy was planned from which the findings could be added to the wider academic field of police studies. Being covert, it can be argued that there was a breach of trust between the researcher and the subjects of the research, in particular the operational officers with whom I worked the closest. That breach of trust is not only in reporting my findings, but also in the fact that my former colleagues saw me as one of them, having no idea that I was observing them for the purposes of academic research. As Liebling and Stanko point out, "Ethical research is typically defined as that which safeguards the rights and feelings of those who are being researched" (2001:424). Liebling and Stanko are discussing dealing with victims of violent crime as subjects of research; clearly to abuse any trust between the researcher and the subject for such vulnerable victims is very clearly unethical. The issue for this research is whether the police officers are also vulnerable. This ethical issue would have had greater implications if I witnessed very serious breaches of police discipline or the law, as I would have been expected to deal with the incident in my role as a supervisor, not as a researcher. The vulnerability would not be in relation to the police officer that breached the law or the police discipline code, but the victim of the officer's behavior. As pointed out above, Holdaway states that the police are a powerful organization and that statement could be extended to include the individual officers.

Data Collection and Method of Analysis

The planning stage of the research involved ascertaining how the data would be collected, where the data could be collected, and who would be observed to obtain the most meaningful and representative data. Table 10.1 illustrates the data that was obtained, the method of analysis, and the main point of interest that data would reveal. From the outset, I knew that I would have at least three years to collect the data. This allowed me time to plan the most effective strategy I could achieve regarding how data could be collected. Another advantage was that I could be patient during the data collection period. This allowed me to gather data that was more natural and spontaneous rather

Table 10.1 Data and Analysis

Method of Collecting Data	Object	N	Method of Analysis	Main Point of Interest
D1: Participant observation on operational officer in the ISB	Obtain data on the ISB Team members' behavior, views, and their actions	12 investigations	Qualitative	ISB officers' attitudes and values towards targets during an investigation; also to gather data on the management of the ISB
D2: Participant observation	Weekly management meetings between team leaders (detective sergeants) involved in counterterrorism investigations and the ISB management (detective inspectors and detective chief inspectors)	72 meetings	Qualitative	Trigger factors regarding ownership of investigations Attitudes and values of team leaders and management towards targets and investigating officers
D3: Participant observation	ISB training events	8 half-day sessions on the law covering the Anti-terrorism, Crime and Security Act 2001 4 half-day sessions of the Human Rights Act 1998 6 half-day sessions on the law covering the Regulation of Investigatory Powers Act 2000 9 one-week investigative interviewing training events	Qualitative	Attitudes and values by officers attending the training events towards how counterterrorism investigations are conducted
D4: Participant observation	Liaison officers An Garda Siochana officers involved in counterterrorism, Budneskriminalamt (Germany), Dutch Police involved in counterterrorism and Europol	15	Qualitative	Comparative study on attitudes and values towards targets of investigations and on the conduct of investigations
D5: Participant observation	Crime pattern analysts	12 investigations	Qualitative	Classification factors in recording information obtained during an investigation

than contrived through questioning from me brought about by shorter time constraints in the field (see Table 10.1).

From the table one can see that I utilized my position in the ISB to observe as many activities as possible from which to collect relevant data.

D1: 12 Investigations

During the research period, I was able to collect data from the 12 investigations I was involved in. One key reason for having such a long data collection period is due to the nature of ISB investigations, some of which can last over six months. A 12-month period of data collection could only allow on average three investigations at the most. In those 12 investigations, I gathered data not only from my own team consisting of 10 officers, but also from officers in other teams within the same department and other forces when the investigation reached the cooperation stage. As a result I obtained data from a number of ISB departments in the UK as well as liaison officers from other states' policing agencies. From this, I was able to draw comparative data from other counterterrorism investigating teams as well as my own team. This allowed me to obtain the most representative data of the operational culture of the ISB as possible. The data did not come solely from the 10 officers in my team. The 12 investigations allowed me to obtain data from just over 60 officers in total. This figure does not include those officers I could monitor who were present at briefings, but also those officers who were carrying out other roles during the investigations, for example, specialist uniformed search or firearms officers. Any relevant comments from those officers were also recorded. In addition to the operational officers, the actions and behavior of the police officer managers were also recorded, where possible, during the investigation.

The scale of the difficulty in collecting the data during the investigations depended upon the situation or stage the investigation was in. If it was in a static observation point, I would act as the log keeper as it involved having to record what was occurring, highlighting and referencing what was being said by targets where covert listening devices were being used, for example. It was not uncommon for the log keeper to be writing and making notes while conversations were taking place between other officers. This allowed me to accurately record what was being said. There were occasions that I could order covert recording equipment for my team that was then attached to the officers involved in operations. I made use of this by using the equipment to record exactly what the officers said during the investigations where I was not the log keeper. The arrest and interview phase of an operation again allowed me to gather natural data of what the officers involved were saying. Most of the data in this phase of an investigation was gathered during the interview period, which was down to my role as an experienced interviewer.

In my role as senior interviewing officer, I had access to the working tapes of all the interviews that were conducted, as well as the ability to make notes in the interview team briefings held to discuss the progress of the investigation. One of my roles as the senior interviewing officer was to report back to the senior investigating officer (SIO), either to request further inquiries to be made due to what had been said during the interview, or to report on the progress of the interviews. During the interview phase of the investigation, it was common practice for the interviewing officers to make their own records of what was said in the briefing of a suspect's solicitor, which occurred prior to the suspect interview. Once again I had the opportunity to collect data in its natural situation without raising any suspicion that academic research was running in parallel to the investigation. Due to the covert nature of the ISB's operations, fellow operational officers as well as managers would regard any abnormal or irregular behavior as suspicious and they were encouraged to challenge such behavior. To avoid rousing any suspicion in my role as team leader, I was expected to put in the extra hours to complete operational reports, which involved preparing investigation updates that included photocopying. Also, being the ISB's trainer, it was not uncommon for me to be seen using reports to prepare realistic training materials. Again, I used this activity to the full to divert any suspicion.

D2: Weekly Management Meetings

The weekly meetings consisted of the team leaders, who are detective sergeants, the detective inspectors and detective chief inspector, and on occasion the detective superintendent. (During the last 12 months of the research, a detective chief superintendent became the head of department; this was due to the increase in personnel in the department that apparently facilitated the requirement for chief superintendent.) During these meetings the team leaders would give a situation report regarding the progress of the investigation they were involved in to the management. The management in turn would pass on information to team leaders regarding where the investigation sat within the national picture of operations as well as their opinion on performance of the respective teams. These meetings had to be minuted, and I would always volunteer. Out of the 72 meetings, I took the minutes for 63 of them because minute taker was not a popular role flooded with volunteers! The rationale for volunteering to be the minute taker was first, to gather as much data as I could, and second, recording what was said diverted any suspicion as to why I would be taking so many notes during a meeting. From those meetings there were two sets of minutes produced, one for the department, and a more detailed version to add to my own data collection.

D3: ISB Training Events

The main training events I obtained data from were in nine, week-long investigative interviewing courses I delivered with colleagues from other specialist CID departments. Also, I designed and delivered half-day training events to the ISB staff on the various legislation changes that occurred during my posting to the department. All of these events provided me with a rich source of data as, again, opinions of the police staff were expressed as well as assessing the officers' knowledge of the law. Regarding the recording of data in the training events, it is not uncommon for two trainers to run an event with the nonspeaking trainer making notes of what is being said. Again I took full advantage of this situation to record data.

D4: Liaison Officers

During the research period I was assigned as the ISB liaison officer with the Irish police, An Garda Siochana. This meant that I was a contact point for my Irish colleagues involved in counterterrorist investigations. This role involved my visiting Ireland not only for operational purposes, but also to attend conferences. In addition to this role, I met with liaison officers from Europol and other officers from EU member states' counterterrorist investigations. I managed to speak to 15 officers in total, from Ireland, Holland, Germany, and Italy. While the data was interesting, it could only be used as illustrative material, not as a central part of the data on which to base the analysis, because the sample size was too small.

D5: Crime Pattern Analysts

During the 12 investigations, I had access to the support staff crime pattern analysts. These personnel were not police officers. As a team leader, I fed them information/intelligence obtained during the investigations, and checked with the analysts any information/intelligence the ISB systems had on persons who came into our investigations. In addition to the constant dialogue I had with the analysts, on occasion they would brief my team on persons who came into the investigations. Here I had the opportunity to talk to them and gather data regarding their opinions on targets of investigations and how they recorded information/intelligence on the ISB systems.

Although detective sergeant is a junior rank, during the data collection period I found it to be a rank that allowed me to move more easily and naturally between operational officers and management. In addition to my operational role, being the department's trainer allowed me even greater access to the senior management of the department. Again, this gave me the opportunity to collect relevant data from the management.

Strengths and Weaknesses of the Data Obtained in Covert Participant Observation

A potential weakness in relation deploying covert participant observation is the reliability of the data, especially where there is the danger of the researcher "going native" (Jupp 1989:60). Going native can occur when the participant observation is overt as well as covert. Punch, in his study of the Amsterdam Police Drug Squad, stated:

> In my willingness to be accepted by the policemen I over-identified perhaps too readily and this doubtless endangered my research role. For the patrol group is a cohesive social unit and the policeman's world is full of seductive interest so that it is all easy to "go native." (1979:16)

Punch adds that the more he was accepted by the police officers, the more they expected him to act as a colleague, and he found himself involved in chasing suspects; searching people, cars, and houses; and even shouting at people who abused his new colleagues (1979:12). During the research I was a native as I was a police officer. Being native, the researcher can be vulnerable to the accusation that the data selected could skew the analysis to confirm the original hypothesis derived from the secondary research. This leads to the question of how far the participant observer should go, especially when covert, to obtain data that reveals the unpalatable as well as the palatable? Does the researcher join in unlawful activities, such as improperly obtaining evidence by using deception during interviews to get suspects to admit to the offenses for which they are being held in police detention?* Unlawful activity includes employment law issues such as discrimination in relation to colleagues; it could include discrimination relating to targets and suspects. Liebling and Stanko consider this issue in their discussion on researching violent crime. They consider the issues of allegiance and confidentiality of their research subjects. They state that if the law is continually trying to redefine criminality, so too are researchers, adding, "This is a moral as well as legal issue, as criminologists have so often argued in the past" (2001:425). Holdaway discusses this point, stating that there was a constant drift into taking things too much for granted, which stopped when he found that certain colleagues' behavior was what he considered distasteful. He says:

> I reacted badly to the conversation yesterday and want nothing to do with such sentiments. I remember saying to myself, "Underneath, these policemen

* In *R. v. Mason* [1987] 3 All ER 481 the police officer deceived M and his solicitor that M's fingerprint was on a bottle containing fluid used in an offense of arson. M and his solicitor were taken in and M admitted to the offense. The CA held that the admission was inadmissible under s.78 PACE.

> are ruthless and racist." I seem to have slipped into the mould easily during the last couple of weeks and wonder if I should have been so easy with my feelings. The balance of participant observation is one which can so easily be submerged and forgotten. Now it has been brought before me in glaring lights and all the old issues of ethics—*when to speak out, how involved one should get, whose perspectives one takes on*—loom large [my emphasis]. (1983:10)

The emphasized text above is crucial to the covert researcher when assessing how far to participate fully in certain situations or acquiesce to some colleagues' behavior. The dilemma for the covert participant observer is that the constant checking of unacceptable behavior with colleagues can have two effects: first, you can raise suspicion in colleagues that you are researching them, and second, their behavior would revert to that displayed to an overt participant observer as they watch how they behave in front of you. Checking a colleague's behavior when a blind eye is turned is an issue that the covert researcher has to judge carefully. This dilemma raises another issue regarding neutrality. One key rationale in employing covert participant observation is collecting the most natural data possible, but in doing so the issue also centers upon whether the data obtained is neutral and values-free.

Liebling considers this dilemma in discussing her research into prisons. She states that the dilemma is not about whether to take sides, but about whose side the researcher is on, adding, "It is impossible to be neutral. Personal and political sympathies contaminate … our research" (2001:472). This is an important consideration, especially when analyzing qualitative data. One result of taking nearly four years to conduct the research is that I worked with very closely and built up friendships with officers on my team. It is only natural that I do have sympathy for those officers. I accept that it has contaminated my research as most of the data collected on counterterrorism investigations is from their perspective. It was not only through the contacts/friendships developed during the research that it could be argued colored, to a degree, any neutrality. My previous experience and roles in dealing with police officer managers could also have impacted my neutrality. Certainly my involvement with the Police Federation had the potential to skew any objectivity I had toward the management. Liebling points out that ethnographic research has departed from its traditional striving for objectivity and distance in its faith in the transparency of reality, and has largely conceded to the values of involvement, perspective, and subjectivity. She adds:

> Ethnography "grounds" our thinking in the observable world in order to generate intellectual insight. Its approach accepts that world views are "situated" in meanings constructed by language, symbols, and practices; it aims to fill the gap between correlation and explanation, through meaningful

> understandings. It asks what and why, looking beneath official definitions of reality. (2001:475)

For Liebling there is a boundary between openness and the capacity to be sympathetic to a depth at which the research process operates. She points out that allegiances have implications for how the data is analyzed, but adds that "[a]llegiances developed during the research process make us wish to be sensitive and diplomatic through out the analysis and writing process as well as rigorous" (2001:475). This is an important point that has to be considered when using covert participant observation over such a long period where working relationships are developed during the data analysis and the writing up. While there are sympathies that can be demonstrated in the write-up, giving the reality and human touch to the work, the researcher still has to be true to required academic rigor and ensure that the data presented is as representative and honest as possible. This is perhaps the difference; it is more about openness and honesty than being values-free and neutral. To present your writing in such a manner is important, especially when the research is on an area or a group that has not been subject to prior research such as the ISB. There is an obligation on the researcher to present the data that leans more toward relevance than neutrality. As Liebling says, the relevance of research has possible cultural and moral implications that describe what "is" without always making what "ought to be" (which is neutrality). She adds, let "… the data speak for itself" (2001:474). To an extent, this is what I have tried to achieve in the write-up of my analysis. I have intended to show what actually exists and provide some analytical thought, but I have tried where possible to let the reader decide by letting my data speak for itself.

This leads to my final point in relation to covert participant observation: the reliability of data it generates. There are a couple of points for the covert participant researcher to be aware of and to defend. Questions surrounding how representational the data is and tests as to its validity are important. Holdaway found a similar experience in his covert research. He said:

> If the researcher is working alone, unable to hold research conferences with colleagues in the field, and is, so to speak, an apprentice, the problems of reliability and representativeness are considerable. (1983:11)

There is no other sociological barometer by which the data obtained can be verified and validated, thereby rendering it reliable. It is incumbent upon the researcher to ensure that, when the data is analyzed and produced in the write up, what is cited is a representative view of the majority. The problem with qualitative data is the responses are never identical. The researcher has to use judgment in categorizing the responses that are similar by using keywords, phrases, and sentiments expressed. This is what I did with the data collected in my research. Where it was an atypical response I indicated this in the text.

There has to be a degree of trust in the covert researcher since, upon publication, the researcher can face the wrath of the organization that was the subject of the research. Holdaway sums up this point succinctly, saying:

> Covert researchers … take risks when they publish their work: they risk the charges that they are simply engaging in a polemical expose of an easily accessible "whipping boy" and that their data is unreliable; they risk the possibility of action attempting to convey the truth about a powerful institution in British society; they risk the consequences of a calculated deception of trust. (1983:13)

By analyzing Holdaway's statement above we can ascertain what he means by taking risks. Liebling and Stanko (2004:473) discuss how they received "savage criticism" when their findings were sensitive and unwelcome. They say how researchers "… have to learn to handle media obsession and distortion." Baldwin provides a classic example that provides a warning for the covert participant observer in the work he carried out with Mike McConville into plea-bargaining by English lawyers prior to trial. During their fieldwork, Baldwin and McConville interviewed 121 defendants who, when awaiting trial, had their barristers discuss "out-of-court" deals with them. They ascertained that the barristers exerted pressure upon the defendants to persuade them to plead guilty (2008:388). Baldwin says it was an understatement to state that publication of their findings would have been "unwelcome." He says:

> It was considered bad form in many quarters even to raise the subject of plea negotiations, let alone discuss it in print. Months before publication, McConville and I found ourselves on the receiving end of a ferocious public attack, and we became extremely unpopular amongst senior members of the legal profession and the judiciary. (2000:389)

Research into a policing department like the ISB, especially where the data is collected covertly, could lead to such "savage criticism" by my former employers and associated government departments. I did not embark upon this research lightly—it was planned and calculated to ensure that the data obtained was as representative as it could be and that the analysis was a fair and balanced representation of that data. This was carried out in the knowledge that departments whose operations are covert would not take too kindly to any degree of revelation of their operations.

Conclusion

This article's focus centers primarily upon one method of data gathering: covert participant observation. This is simply due to the fact that it would be impossible to obtain any meaningful data, or in fact any data, on how the ISB conducts its investigations. As mentioned on a few occasions above, and it cannot be stressed enough, this is down to the nature of the ISB's role in policing national security. If an accurate analysis of how the ISB performs the surveillance, arrest, and suspect interview phases of a counterterrorist investigation is to be made, the data needs to be as natural as possible, not contrived by the subject of the research. For the purpose of this research, this can only be achieved through the use of covert participant observation, using the various means of data collection in the observation as outlined above, which ranges from minute taking to making notes as soon as you can to even covertly recording the officers as they carry out their duties.

An important issue surrounding the use of covert participant observation centers on the ethical issue of betrayal of trust, but as pointed out above, when researching the police you are not researching a vulnerable section of society; rather, it is the reverse—you are researching one of the most powerful groups in society. When deciding to use this method of research, you must consider whether you will damage the subject of your research, which is unlikely considering the number of public inquiries the police have endured and survived over the years.

In this chapter there is much comparison to Holdaway's work and this is because I could find no other research conducted on the police in the UK that used covert methods to examine the police. As far as I can ascertain there is only Holdaway's work. My research employed the same research methods on the police in the UK as Holdaway, because we both wanted to gather natural, uncontaminated data that revealed how the police carry out their duties. As Holdaway says at the end of his research methods chapter, "I will leave you to judge my work on the evidence presented and you will come to your own conclusions about the methods used to collect it" (Holdaway 1983:14).

References

Baldwin, J. (2000). "Research on the criminal courts" in King, R.D. and Wincup, E. (editors) *Doing Research on Crime and Justice* Oxford: Oxford University Press.

Hadfield, P. (2008). "Ethnographic research and the licensing courts" in King, R.D. and Wincup, E. (editors) *Doing Research on Crime and Justice* (2nd edition) Oxford: Oxford University Press.

Hertiage, J. (1998). "Conversation analysis and institutional talk" in Silverman, D. (editor) *Qualitative Research: Theory, Method and Practice* London: Sage.

Holdaway, S. (1983). *Inside the British Police* Oxford: Blackwell.

Holdaway, S. (1994). "Academic whistleblowing on the beat: The policeman's lot" in Vinten, G. (editor) *Whistleblowing, Subversion or Corporate Citizenship?* London: Paul Chapman.
Jones, T. (2003). "The governance and accountability of policing" in Newburn T (editor) *Handbook of Policing* Cullompton: Willan Publishing.
Jupp, V. (1989). *Methods of Criminological Research,* London: Unwin Hyman.
Kane, S.C. (2004). "The unconventional methods of cultural criminology" in *Theoretical Criminology* 8(3), 303–321 No. 3.
Liebling, A. (2001). "Whose side are we on? Theory and practice and allegiances in prison research" in *British Journal of Criminology 41*(3), 472–484.
Liebling, A. and Stanko, B. (2001). "Allegiance and ambivalence: Some dilemmas in researching disorder and violence" in *British Journal of Criminology 41*(3), 421–430.
Marks, M. (2004). "Researching police transformation" in *British Journal of Criminology 44*(6), 866–888.
Oliver, I. (1997). *Police, Government and Accountability* London: Macmillan.
Presdee, M. (2004). "Cultural criminology: The long and winding road" in *Theoretical Criminology* 8(3), 275–285.
Punch, M. (1979). *Policing the Inner City* London: Macmillan.
Reiner, R. (2000). "Police research" in King, R.D. and Wincup, E. (editors) *Doing Research on Crime and Justice* Oxford: Oxford University Press.
Reiner, R. and Newburn, T. (2008). "Police research" in King, R.D. and Wincup, E. (editors) *Doing Research on Crime and Research* (2nd edition) Oxford: Oxford University Press.
Westmarland, L. (2001). "Blowing the whistle on police violence" *British Journal of Criminology 41*(3), 532–535.

11

The Challenge of Transnational and Organized Crime in the Nordic Countries
The Case of Norway

VIVIANA ANDREESCU AND ODD BERNER MALME

Contents

Introduction

During the past decade, transnational organized crime has considerably increased its visibility, complexity, and impact. The globalization of criminal networks and advances in technology have significantly augmented threats made by international criminal organizations to most countries in the world. Transnational organized crime endangers border security; negatively affects public health through the trafficking of humans, illegal drugs, and counterfeit pharmaceuticals; and contributes to the corruption of public officials. While drug trafficking of the late twentieth century could be considered responsible for the internationalization of organized crime (see Albanese, 2003, 438–439), since then these criminal business enterprises have diversified, become more sophisticated, and identified new criminal opportunities. These novel criminal operations, which particularly target the United States and other wealthy nations, include the unlawful penetration of global energy and strategic material markets; provision of logistical and financial support to terrorists; the use of cyberspace to target persons and infrastructure; and the manipulation of securities markets and financial institutions. Fraud represents a worldwide problem and is increasingly used by criminal organized groups to generate money to finance drug trafficking, trafficking in human beings, identity fraud, counterfeiting, and terrorism. Fraud is significantly impacted by the rapid development of modern technology and law enforcement agencies in all countries are now facing a growing number of organized virtual crime groups (Europol, 2009).

As one scholar (Roth, 2010, 1), recently noted, contemporary organized crime groups "come in all shapes and sizes," (p.…). Today's groups, particularly nontraditional groups that do not confirm to the traditional Mafia paradigm are much more fluid, flexible, and pragmatic than past exemplars, with few regards to restricting membership by ethnicity and other related criteria." In addition, depending on geopolitics and changing markets, current organized crime groups shift from one activity to another with a chameleonic easiness (Roth, 2010, 3).

Although it is difficult to anticipate the future forms and targets of criminal business enterprise, there is no doubt that today organized crime is a global phenomenon and cannot be solved by one or more isolated agencies or jurisdictions. In an increasingly integrated world, actors, such as police, are no longer just representatives of nation states. Their role is much more complex and is shaped by new patterns of international cooperation. However, even if governments, law enforcement specialists, and experts agree that there is a stringent need for the coordination of organized crime policing, it is not yet clear whether this action is feasible and practical solutions to the problem still have to be found. In order to design appropriate responses and identify the best technical assistance interventions that would affect transnational organized crime, an essential prerequisite is to gather accurate information and reliable data regarding organized crime at state levels, which should also include overviews and impact evaluations of state attempts to counter criminal business enterprises.

Even though crime rates in Nordic countries are among the lowest in Europe, organized criminal activity exists here as well. This chapter will discuss challenges Nordic countries are facing when dealing with organized criminal activities and focus on Norway's experience and the country's efforts to establish international connections that parallel the national coordination of key agencies involved in combating serious crime. Recent improvements in Norwegian police activity and anticipated developments in the fight Norwegian police have waged against organized crime in Europe will be also discussed.

Crime Trends and Organized crime in Nordic Countries: The Case of Norway

Nordic Countries: Brief Overview

Nordic countries represent a region in Northern Europe which consists of five countries and three territories (Denmark and its territories—Greenland

and Faroe Islands; Finland and its territory—Aland; Iceland; Norway; and Sweden). Even though there are many interstate differences, Nordic countries are generally perceived by outsiders as a unique European block. These small centralized states are considered stable democracies, characterized by social cohesion and an egalitarian spirit. While at the beginning of the twentieth century Nordic countries were among the poorest in Europe, as a result of a fruitful combination of economic, social, and environmental policies judiciously coordinated by national governments, Nordic countries are today five of the most successful nations of the world (Kildal and Kuhnle, 2005).

The Kingdom of Norway occupies the western side of the Scandinavian Peninsula and also includes the volcanic island Jan Mayen and the Arctic archipelago Svalbard. During the first two decades following World War II, the country experienced rapid economic growth due to domestic industrialization and the significant development of the Norwegian merchant marine and shipping industry. The country's economic progress accelerated in the early 1970s and has continued as a result of the exploitation of important oil and natural gas deposits discovered in the North and Norwegian Seas. In monetary value, Norway, a nation with fewer than five million people but richly endowed with natural resources, is today considered the wealthiest country in the world. Based on macroeconomic data, the most recent World Economic Outlook (WEO) presented by the International Monetary Fund (IMF) indicated that in 2008, the GDP per capita (current prices) in Norway was the highest in the world ($95,062), approximately twice as high as the United States' GPD per capita, current prices ($46,859). The other Nordic countries ranked high as well, with GDPs per capita, current prices, varying from $52,789 in Sweden to $62,625 in Denmark (IMF, 2009).

Financial stability and economic power are not the only attributes of Norway. Since 1990, the Human Development Report has published the human development index (HDI). This composite measure includes three dimensions of human development (i.e., life expectancy, adult literacy and gross enrollment in education, and standard of living measured by the purchasing power parity income). Even if the HDI is not a comprehensive measure of human development, it offers a broader definition of general well-being and represents a solid indicator of the human progress. In the last published report, Norway had the highest HDI and was ranked the first among 182 countries with reliable data. Between 1980 and 2007, Norway's HDI rose by 0.28% annually and the country's HDI increased from 0.900 to 0.971. The other Nordic countries had equally high HDIs (e.g., Denmark – 0.955; Finland – 0.959; Iceland – 0.969; Sweden – 0.963), suggesting that the quality of life in this region of Europe is far superior to that found in other parts of the world (UNDP, 2009).

In addition, Nordic countries appear to be characterized by high levels of peacefulness and safety. Based on the 2009 Global Peace Index (GPI), which is calculated by experts from the Institute for Economics and Peace, Norway and Denmark ranked second with a score of 1.217. Among 144 independent states with reliable data, New Zealand is considered the most peaceful country in the world (GPI = 1.202), while Iraq (GPI = 3.341) appears to be the least peaceful nation. The index takes values from 1 (most peaceful) to 5 (least peaceful) and is composed of 23 qualitative and quantitative indicators, which combine internal and external factors (e.g., democracy and transparency; international openness; extent of regional integration; material well-being; culture and education; a nation's level of military expenditure; a nation's relations with neighboring countries; the level of respect for human rights; political instability; level of violent crimes; perceptions of criminality, etc.). The calculated GPIs for the other Nordic countries ranged from 1.225 for Iceland and 1.269 for Sweden to 1.322 for Finland. (Institute for Economics & Peace, 2009).

Crime and Criminal Justice Issues

A 2009 report on crime and criminal justice indicates that in Europe, total crime rates rose from 1999 to 2002, but have been falling consistently since then. However, national sources of information about crime in Europe reported 3% increase in violent crimes, 1% increase in drug trafficking and robbery, and 1% increase in prison population. The number of police officers in the EU states remained almost unchanged over the period 1998–2007 (see Tavares & Thomas, 2009). In Nordic countries, there are currently approximately two police officers per 1,000 residents. Table 11.1 presents selected crime statistics for Nordic countries.

From 1998 to 2007, nearly all Nordic countries registered a decrease in the total number of crimes recorded by police. In Sweden, however, the number of total crimes recorded by national police was about 10% higher in 2007 when compared to 1998. In 2007, Sweden also had the highest violent crime rate (11.76 per 1,000 population), approximately three times higher than Denmark and more than twice as high as in Norway. However, the highest 2005–2007 average homicide rate among Nordic countries was registered in Finland (2.23). This homicide rate was also higher than the average murder rate in Europe (1.4 per 100,000 pop.) for the period under observation. Among capital cities, Reykjavik, the capital of Iceland, had the lowest murder rate (0.77), while Copenhagen, the capital of Denmark, had the highest murder rate (2.13). In Oslo, Norway's capital city, the 2005–2007 average murder rate was 1.61 per 100,000 people.

It can be noticed that from 1998 to 2007, the number of drug-trafficking offenses increased in Denmark, Sweden, and Norway and decreased in

Table 11.1 Crime and Law Enforcement in Nordic Countries

	Denmark	Finland	Iceland	Norway	Sweden
Population 2008 (in millions)	5.50	5.31	0.32	4.77	9.22
Total Crime 1998	499,167	383,479	19,938	293,799	1,181,056
Total Crime 2007	445,271	343,820	13,038	271,712	1,306,324
Total crime rate per 1,000 pop. in 2007	80.96	64.75	40.74	56.75	141.68
Homicide 2005–2007 (annual rate per 100,000 pop.)	1.17	2.23	0.56	0.69	1.05
Homicide 2005–2007 (annual rate per 100,000 pop. in capital city)	2.13	1.96	0.77	1.61	n.d.
Violent crime 2007	20,673	41,664	n.d.	23,205	108,004
Violent crime rate per 1,000 pop. in 2007	3.76	7.85	–	4.86	11.71
Drug trafficking –1998	2,675	9,461	121	15,420	5,766
Drug trafficking – 2007	3,258	5,115	104	19,086	7,026
Drug trafficking rate per 1,000 pop. in 2007	0.59	0.96	0.33	4.00	0.76
Number of police officers in 2007	10,620	8,156	683	7,453	17,866
Number of police officers per 1,000 pop. in 2007	1.93	1.54	2.13	1.56	1.94

Source: Tavares & Thomas, 2009, pp. 2–8; World Bank, 2008. (The authors' calculations for crime rates and law enforcement rates.)

Finland and Iceland. In 2007, Norway had the highest rate of drug trafficking offenses (4.00 per 1,000 people) among Nordic countries. Norway had a comparable rate for drug trafficking offenses in 2002. During 2003–2005, the incidence of drug-related offenses decreased, but rose again in 2006. It should be noted that drug trafficking offenses recorded by national police and presented in the Eurostat report (see Tavares & Thomas, 2009) included illegal possession, cultivation, production, supplying, transportation, importing, exporting, and financing of drug operations not solely connected with personal use. In Europe, the 2006 rate for recorded drug trafficking offenses was 40 per 100,000 population and the 2006 rate for drug-related offenses was 170 per 100,000 population (UNODC, 2009, 289).

Organized Crime in Europe and the Nordic Countries: Current Concerns

The 2009 EU Organized Crime Threat Assessment (OCTA) produced by Europol offers an updated picture of criminal activities developed by organized criminal groups in Europe and provides a reliable analysis that uses the 'criminal hubs' concept. A criminal hub is a conceptual entity that is generated by a combination of factors including proximity to major destination markets, geographic location, infrastructure, types of organized crime groups and migration processes concerning key criminals and organized crime groups in general. While criminal activities are considered in terms of geographic flows and facilitating factors, organized crime groups are differentiated on the basis of their intentions and operational capabilities. The most recent OCTA report confirmed the existence of five criminal hubs in Europe (Europol, 2009, 13–15). Table 11.2 presents a summary of these findings.

The main illegal operations covered by organized criminal (OC) groups in Europe are drug trafficking (heroin, cocaine, cannabis, and synthetic drugs), crimes against persons (i.e., trafficking in human beings; facilitated illegal immigration/people smuggling), fraud, and counterfeiting (Europol, 2009). Even though the Nordic countries are not part of the geographical center of any of the criminal hubs identified by Europol experts, the region's proximity to distribution centers and criminal markets in northern Europe increases the Nordic countries' vulnerability, especially with regard to drug-related offenses and trafficking in human beings.

Nybakk (2004) noted that drug crime represents the main problem law enforcement agencies face in Norway. The author acknowledged that drug seizures more than doubled from 1996 (13,333 seizures) to 2002 (30,310 seizures). Even though the number of drug seizures reached in 2003 a lower level (13,408 seizures), recent crime statistics (see Table 11.1) show that within the Nordic space, the rate of drug trafficking and drug-related offenses increased in past years and remains relatively high in Norway compared to the other countries in the Nordic region.

The most recent report produced by the United Nations Office on Drug and Crime (UNODC) showed that even though the recent increase in the consumption of synthetic stimulants is a source of concern, particularly in East Asia and the Middle East, drug cultivation (opium and coca) is currently decreasing and major markets for opiates (Europe and South East Asia), cocaine (North America), and cannabis (North America, Oceania, and Europe) are in decline as well. Even though the percentage of the population aged 15–64 using selected illegal drugs by is relatively low in Norway (e.g., in 2004, 0.5% of the population group used ecstasy; 0.8% used cocaine; 0.33% used opiates; 4.6% used cannabis), the 2007 retail prices for illegal drugs in Norway appear to be among the highest in Europe. The typical estimated price for a gram of cocaine was $164.4; the price for a gram of cannabis herb was $27.4; and the retail price per ecstasy tablet was $48, suggesting that the demand for drugs in Norway is also higher than in other European states (UNODC, 2009).

Drug markets in Denmark, Norway, and Sweden are more likely to be impacted by OC groups from the Balkans. In addition, Vietnamese OC

Table 11.2 Criminal Hubs in Europe

Criminal Hubs	North West	South West	North East	Southern	South East
Geographical center	Netherlands Belgium	Spain Portugal	Russian Federation/ Kaliningrad area *St. Petersburg - important logistical nexus	Italy	Located between Asia and Europe
Main role	Distribution center for heroin, cocaine, synthetic drugs, cannabis products	Criminal market for cocaine & cannabis Trafficking in human beings Illegal immigration	Trafficking in women Illegal immigration Cigarette smuggling Counterfeit goods Heroin, synthetic drugs, cannabis products	Criminal market for cocaine & cannabis Illegal immigration Counterfeit goods Cigarette smuggling Production and distribution of counterfeit Euros	Illegal immigration Cocaine traffic Active in producing illicit goods Transit, warehousing, re-packaging area *Romania – significant gateway for facilitation of illegal immigration & cocaine traffic *Bulgaria – role in criminal markets (e.g. synthetic drugs, counterfeit Euros, card fraud)
Destination markets	UK, Ireland, France, Spain, Germany, Baltic states, Scandinavia	Netherlands, France, and other countries	Western Europe, Nordic countries, Baltic states, Russia	E.U. and other countries	E.U.
Presumed location of feeder or transit zone	Middle East *Dubai – key financial & logistical center for OC *Pakistan – growing role in the international trade of opiates to Europe	West, Central & North Africa	Russia, Ukraine, Belarus	OC groups outside the EU	Ukraine, Moldova, Western Balkans, Turkey.

Source: Europol, 2009.

groups tend to be involved in domestic cannabis cultivation and distribution in Norway and Denmark. Lithuanian OC groups tend to traffic synthetic drugs from the Northwest hub to the Nordic markets. Most amphetamine and methamphetamine products found in Nordic markets are produced in Lithuania. Lithuanian OC groups also cooperate and deal with Russian, Belarusian, Estonian, Latvian, and Polish OC groups and frequently make use of outlaw motorcycle gangs to access the Nordic criminal markets (Europol, 2009, 30). In Norway, there are three main criminal motorcycle clubs—Hells Angels, the Bandidos, and the Outlaws. These groups have a different organizational structure and culture and are more likely to be involved in narcotics and torpedo activities. Hells Angels Motorcycle Club members, for instance, tend to launder a part of the proceeds from organized crime in Norway and invest the money in Thailand. In the last decade, the number of criminal motorcycle clubs increased three times in Norway (see Gottschalk, 2010, 164–165).

Europol's OCTA report acknowledged that while the trafficking of women for sexual exploitation is stabilizing in Europe, human trafficking for forced labor in the construction sector, drug production, and begging is increasing. Data also show an increase in the trafficking of children for illegal labor (e.g., domestic slavery) or sexual exploitation (Europol, 2009, 21).

An empirical study of trafficking in human beings in Norway found that prostitution associated with migrant female sex workers was highly organized. In 2003 in Oslo, approximately 600 women representing more than 40 countries were working in prostitution (in massage parlors, on the street, escort services, etc). The largest group of migrant women in prostituion in Norway was from Thailand; the second largest group was from the Dominican Republic. Migrant sex workers from Central and Eastern Europe represented approximately 17% of the total female prostitutes in Norway. At the time the study was conducted, only a third of the sex workers in Norway were Norwegian citizens (Brunovskis & Tyldum, 2004).

In 2003, Norway launched its first Plan of Action to Combat Trafficking in Women and Children. This action plan contained measures to protect and assist the victims, prevent human trafficking, and prosecute the organizers. Norway prohibits all forms of trafficking in persons through its Crimes against Personal Freedom Law of 2004, which prescribes a maximum penalty of five year imprisonment, a punishment commensurate with that given for other serious offenses, such as rape (US Department of State, 2009, 229).

Despite significant changes in Norwegian legislation, trafficking in human beings remains an unsolved problem for Norway's law enforcement. Ambassador Tove Skarstein of the Royal Norwegian Embassy in Bulgaria, who in 2007 participated at a round table concerning organized crime in Bulgaria, acknowledged that Norway could be considered the largest sex market in Northern Europe and a preferred location for trafficking of women for sexual purposes (Center for the Study of Democracy, 2007). Although the Government of Norway fully complies with the minimum standards for the elimination of trafficking in human beings, Norway continues to be a destination country for women and girls trafficked annually worldwide. The main source countries for women trafficked to Norway for commercial sexual exploitation are Nigeria, Bulgaria, Brazil, Estonia, Ghana, Eritrea, Cameroon, Kenya, and the Democratic Republic of Congo. Victims from Africa and Brazil are frequently trafficked through Italy, Spain, Morocco, and the Balkans. Regarding trafficking for labor, it is noted that men and children are trafficked to Norway from Thailand, the United Kingdom, India, Sri Lanka, Romania, and Bulgaria for the purposes of domestic servitude and forced labor in the construction industry. Children in Norwegian refugee centers are particularly vulnerable to human trafficking (U.S. Department of State, 2009, 229).

To avert and reduce trafficking in human beings, the Norwegian government has not only continued its trafficking prevention outreach in key source countries, but also developed awareness efforts in Norway. For instance, from 2003 to 2009, Norway funded anti-trafficking programs by sending trafficking countries grants totaling $7.4 million. The government also improved the victim identification system and in 2008, the immigration law has been amended to forbid the deportation of the victims who testify in court against a trafficker. In recent years, the government has conducted two major campaigns aimed at reducing the demand for commercial sex acts and in January 2009, Norway criminalized the purchase of sexual services. The number of trafficking investigations conducted by the Norwegian police increased from 19 in 2007 to 45 in 2008. Approximately 90% of these were sex trafficking investigations. In addition, the government provided human trafficking briefs to all Norwegian troops prior to deployment overseas on international peacekeeping missions and monitored immigration patterns for evidence of trafficking (U.S. Department of State, 2009, 230).

As Roth, [2010, 381) noted, the Nordic countries are "rarely considered a hotbed of organized crime activity." Several scholars suggested that criminal business enterprises were less lucrative in this European region because the local law enforcement and judiciary were more efficient in preventing the unwanted spread of organized crime in the Nordic space (Johansen, 2005). In addition, it can be argued that Nordic states managed to better control transnational organized crime because they were able to establish strong ties among all national law enforcement agencies in the region and to find ways to extend a good example of interagency cooperation to adjacent geographic areas, where criminal markets started to develop.

Nordic Countries' Cross Border Law Enforcement Cooperation in the Combating and Prevention of Organized Crime

Although it is difficult to distinguish a Nordic identity when discussing international politics, one should acknowledge that the Nordic countries share many common features in their relationships with the world. For instance, during the Cold War the Nordic countries' foreign policies were perceived as having collectively "an unselfish, moral, multilaterist, and internationalist orientation." All five Nordic countries preserved their reputations as active supporters of the United Nations system, were recognized as generous donors of development assistance, and were part of the European Union's peace-building and security efforts (Strömvik, 2006, 199).

Nordic countries were among the first in Europe to encourage the free movement of persons across borders. In 1952, the Nordic Passport Union was created to permit free travel among the Nordic countries and some of their associated territories. Then, in 1958, border controls within the region were eliminated.

Following the Nordic countries' example, in 1985 and in 1990, Belgium, France, Germany, Luxembourg, and the Netherlands formulated two agreements (i.e., the Schengen Convention) to abolish border controls between participating EU countries. Both agreements were integrated into the European Union structure in 1999 by the Amsterdam Treaty (Council of Europe, 2003).

In order to reconcile free movement of people with freedom and security, it was decided that the abolition of border checks would be accompanied by a set of "compensatory" measures. These involved common policies on harmonization of external border controls (coordinated by the EU's FRONTEX agency), temporary entry (under Schengen Visas), cross-border police and judicial cooperation, as well as additional measures meant to combat terrorism and organized crime. The Schengen rules apply in all or part to the 27 EU states and four non-EU members (Iceland, Liechtenstein, Norway, and Switzerland) (Council of Europe, 2003, 6). Even if Norway and Iceland are not EU members, they have been part of the Nordic passport union with Finland, Sweden, and Denmark. In order to preserve this union, they both joined the Schengen area (Gelatt, 2005) in 1996.

Since the 1980s, all the legislative changes that followed the Schengen agreements facilitated international trade, the free movement of persons across Europe, and had multiple additional benefits. However, they also created a more accessible environment for illegal immigrants, transnational criminals, and potential terrorists. As one author (Gelatt, 2005) observed, while Schengen itself did not greatly change European immigration policy, its creation did necessitate policy changes in other arenas, requiring, in particular, a greater interstate collaboration on security issues. In addition, the geopolitical changes that occurred in the early 1990s called for more intense cooperation and improved communication among European law enforcement agencies as well.

For instance, all Nordic countries and other European states participating in the Schengen Agreement Application Convention now have access to the Schengen Information System (SIS), which has been in operation since 1995. SIS is a governmental database that maintains and distributes important information about individuals and property to be used and shared among institutions in participating countries for national security, border control and law enforcement purposes.

Beside the Schengen framework, Interpol and Europol are the other two dominant bodies engaged in matters of police assistance and collaboration in Europe. Created in 1923, the International Criminal Police Organization (Interpol) facilitates cross-border police cooperation and assists all bodies whose mission is to prevent and combat transnational crime. Interpol is an information clearing house for law enforcement and constitutes a very important component of the international criminal justice system (Fichtelberg, 2008, 85). Interpol's member countries can now directly gain access to the organization's central database management system (I-link), speeding investigations and cooperation. All Nordic countries are part of Interpol, which is the world's largest international police organization and currently comprised of 188 member states. Norway joined Interpol in 1931. The liaison officer representing the country at Interpol is posted in France (Interpol, n.d.).

The European Law Enforcement Agency (Europol) handles criminal intelligence. Its main mission is to assist the law enforcement authorities of the EU member states in their fight against serious forms of organized crime. Created in 1999, Europol is in many ways similar to Interpol, but with a more limited mandate and scope. Like Interpol, Europol does not have law enforcement powers. The organization maintains a database that provides information about international and transnational criminal activity. In addition, Europol assists domestic law enforcement to develop, investigate, and prosecute transnational criminal enterprises (Fichtelberg, 2008, 90). On January 1st, 2010, Europol acquired a stronger mandate and new capabilities to fight serious international crime and terrorism. Currently, as a formal EU agency, Europol has increased powers to collect criminal information and has a wider field of competence in supporting investigations of serious offenses. Since 2006, Europol has produced annually a comprehensive assessment of the threat represented by organized crime in Europe.

Although Iceland and Norway, as non-EU member states, do not have Europol membership, both countries established cooperation agreements with Europol. In 2001, Norway signed an operational agreement with

Europol. The agreement applies to unlawful drug trafficking; trafficking in nuclear and radioactive substances; illegal immigrant smuggling; trade in human beings; motor vehicle crimes; crimes committed and likely to be committed in the course of terrorist activities; forgery of money, as well as illegal money laundering activities (Europol, n.d.). Two liaison officers represent Norway at Europol and are posted in the Netherlands.

In November, 2009, Norway signed the Prüm Treaty and joined the EU's decision to maximize cross-border cooperation, in particular to combat terrorism and transnational organized crime. The treaty allows the police forces in participating countries to exchange data more easily. Norway's accession means that EU member states will have access to Norway's DNA, fingerprint and vehicle registers, and vice versa. It also means that Norwegian law enforcement agencies will be able to participate in joint actions and assist EU member states in case of major events, disasters and serious accidents.

In the past, European police officers who wanted to collaborate with their counterparts from other countries could only use Interpol as a formal communication channel. However, during the past decade, policy changes and technological developments have contributed to improvements in interagency cooperation. Currently, police and judicial authorities from different countries have increased access to additional information and communication channels, such as SIS, Europol databases, and extended networks of liaison officers. At the same time, traditional informal communication networks based on personal relationships have diminished in importance, mainly because they appeared to be unstable as a result of frequent staff fluctuations (Council of Europe, 2003, 20).

In the Nordic context, direct law enforcement cooperation has a long tradition. Although many forms of bilateral law enforcement cooperation have been established in the region, the main multilateral forums are the Nordic Police and Customs Cooperation and the Baltic Sea Task Force on Organized Crime.

The Nordic Police and Customs Cooperation (PTN) was established in 1984 and became permanent in 1987 (Nybakk, 2004). Initially, PNT focused solely on combating drug-related crimes, but since 1996 PTN has been involved in the prevention and combating of all types of transnational crime. Norway participates in the Nordic Liaison Project whereby each Nordic liaison officer posted abroad also represents the other Nordic countries. The shared Nordic custom and police liaison officers (36) are assigned to countries considered risk points for the production/distribution of illegal drugs and/or transit countries for illegal enterprises (Nybakk, 2004). Currently, Norway has liaison officers in the Arab Emirates, Bulgaria, Pakistan, Russia, Serbia, Spain, and United Kingdom (Interpol, n.d.).

In 1992, as a response to the geopolitical changes that had taken place in the Baltic Sea region following the end of the Cold War, the region's foreign ministers agreed to establish the Council of Baltic Sea States (CBSS), as an overall political forum for regional intergovernmental cooperation. The members of the Council are the eleven states of the Baltic Sea region (Denmark, Estonia, Finland, Germany, Iceland, Latvia, Lithuania, Norway, Poland, Russia, and Sweden) as well as the European Commission. Since its founding, CBSS has contributed to ensuring positive developments within the Baltic Sea region and has served as a driving force for multilateral cooperation. The presidency of the Council rotates among the member states on an annual basis. The foreign minister of the presiding country is responsible for coordinating the Council's activities and is assisted in this work by the Committee of Senior Officials. (CBSS, 2010).

At the fifth ministerial session of the Council of Baltic Sea States (CBSS) in 1996, the Baltic Sea Region Border Control Cooperation (BSRBCC) was established. The BSRBCC focuses on security-related issues concerning border control in the Baltic Sea region. The most important issues on its agenda include developing practical forms of cooperation, simplifying communication routines between the parties (e.g. the development of the data transmission system COASTNET), and cooperation with FRONTEX (The Schengen Border Control Agency); sea exercises and operations; exchanging information about the tasks and authorities of border services in security control at sea ports, marinas and sea areas; counteracting terrorism; and exchanging experiences and evaluations of existing standards of security controls (CBSS, 2010).

On May 3, 1996, in the presence of the President of the European Council and the President of the European Commission, the heads of the government of Baltic Sea states met in Visby, Sweden. Recognizing the importance of Europe's stability, these government leaders acknowledged immediately after the meeting that CBSS should be the forum for guidance and overall coordination between the Baltic Sea States and the European Commission. Among other tasks, Government leaders also emphasized the urgent need for direct and concerted action to combat organized crime and decided to establish a task force of personal representatives of the heads of government. The aim of the task force on organized crime (TF-OC) is to strengthen the capacities of member states to prevent and combat organized crime by facilitating close cooperation among member-state law enforcement agencies (CBSS, 2010).

The main fields of activity of the TF-OC are improved and increased exchange of information; joint concrete and operative measures; judicial cooperation; special surveys, training, and other cooperation. In addition, TF-OC is responsible for minimizing the duplication of work and for creating a unique channel for the transmission of intelligence information.

To summarize, TF-OC is not a permanent, full-time body, but a network of high-level government representatives who are responsible for operational cooperation in fighting transnational crime. It also includes permanent representatives from Europol, Eurojust (EU body established in 1999 that reinforces the fight against serious organized crime), Interpol, Frontex, and the European Commission (Baltic Sea Task Force, 2010).

Within the task force, a central body, the operative committee (OPC), is in charge of the coordination of inter-country police cooperation. OPC is a multidisciplinary body that includes permanent representatives from police, border/coast guard authorities, customs, and national prosecution offices from participating countries. In addition, OPC includes one representative from both Interpol and Europol. The TF-OC includes five expert groups created to combat illegal immigration, trafficking in women and children, drug trafficking, environmental crime, and trafficking in highly taxed goods and weapons, intellectual property rights, and stolen vehicles (Christensen, 2006).

Although differences in country legislation, dissimilar working methods, variations in the level of training, and the lack of reliable contacts for immediate communication negatively affected the activity of the TF-OC in its first years of operation, more effective cooperation has been established in the last decade between law enforcement authorities in participating countries. By including Russia as a key strategic external partner, the Baltic States Task Force on Organized Crime gained additional power. In addition, bilateral and multilateral collaboration was strengthened by the fact that most states in the region are part of the Schengen space. In December 2007, the Schengen free zone was extended and Estonia, Latvia, Lithuania, and Poland were among the nine countries that successfully met the requirements of the Schengen acquis. With the exception of Russia, all Baltic Sea states now belong to the Schengen area and a higher level of intercountry mutual assistance is anticipated. However, the long term future of the organized crime prevention work in the region remains uncertain because the current mandate of the task force will expire at the end of 2010.

Hämäläinen (2008) suggested the following actions to be considered for inclusion in the EU's strategy regarding the fight against organized crime in the Baltic Sea Region:

Extending the Nordic direct law-enforcement cooperation to cover the entire Baltic Sea Region

Finding stronger political support for the Baltic Sea Task Force on Organized Crime in order to guarantee its stability and permanency

Reinforcing the external dimension, and in particular, cooperation with Russia, which requires a high-level of political commitment

Stronger preventive approaches for combating crime through closer cooperation of all relevant public and private stakeholders (e.g., harbors and shipping companies should be involved in all activities that deter maritime crime);

Creation of a coherent security program that to identify and manage the main crime risks in the region.

Policing Organized Crime in Norway

The organization of the Norwegian police is largely based on the principle of an integrated police (see OSCE, 2010), is subordinate to the Ministry of Justice and the police, and is completely independent from the military forces. There are 27 local police districts, each under the command of a chief of police who has full responsibility for all policing in his district. Each police district has its own headquarters, as well as several police stations. The special agencies of the National Police in Norway are:

The National Criminal Investigation Service (KRIPOS): A central agency whose core function is to prevent and combat organized and other forms of serious crime. The agency provides specialist support to the Norwegian police districts and investigates and prosecutes major and complex cases related to serious organized crime. The unit ensures 24-hour communication with all the international and regional entities Norway cooperates with in combating organized and serious crime. The organization consists of a Central Unit in Oslo, Norway's capital.

The National Authority for Investigation and Prosecution of Economic and Environmental Crime (ØKOKRIM): The agency is both a police unit and a prosecution authority. In addition to cooperating with surveillance authorities, the business sector, and others in combating economic and environmental crime, the agency gathers criminal intelligence and processes suspicious transaction reports, acts as a consultative body for national and supervisory authorities, and participates in international cooperation initiatives.

The Central Mobile Service (UP): This agency's main focus is on traffic safety work.

The National Police Immigration Service (PU): The Norwegian police's expertise center and ancillary body in immigrant cases. This agency's main task is to register and identify asylum seekers arriving in Norway. In addition, the unit coordinates the repatriation of asylum seekers who have had their request for asylum refused. The unit is also responsible for the transportation of the foreign nationals who are to be removed or deported from Norway

The National Police Computing and Material Service (PDMT): The service is responsible for information and computer technology and administration within the police service and the higher prosecuting authority. The unit also provides other agencies within the public administration with certain services and products.

The Norwegian Police University College (PHS): This is the central educational institution for the police service in Norway.

In 2001, the Norwegian Police Directorate in charge of developing and coordinating the central, regional and local organization of the police was established. The directorate was also formed to adjust the organization of the police to the internationalization of criminal networks and has the overall responsibility of coordinating efforts against organized crime including Norway's participation in international police cooperation. The Advisory Council for Combating Organized Crime (ROK) represents a focal point in the coordination of all national entities involved in combating organized crime (Eterno, 2009, 144–145).

In 2007, the directorate developed a national strategy for intelligence and analysis that was to be implemented by all police districts in Norway. The strategy identified three levels of intelligence and analysis—local police districts; cooperation between police districts; and international intelligence and analysis. The main objective of the national strategy is to assist decision makers to prioritize actions, to prepare operations, to plan the efficient use of resources, to collaborate with external partners, to develop prevention plans, and to conduct performance evaluations. The Norwegian model also stresses the importance of organizing responsibilities at national, regional, and local levels. However, as one analyst observed, the document describing the strategy components does not define or operationalize two important concepts—intelligence and analysis. In addition, central law enforcement agencies in Norway did not develop specific implementation procedures. As a result, Norwegian local police districts had to find ways to implement the intelligence strategy themselves. A survey of police districts in 2008 revealed that one year after the strategy's development, implementation varied among districts from zero to 100 percent, with an average rate of 34% (Gottschalk, 2010, 49–51; 72–73).

Worldwide, policing organized crime has become a challenging project. More and more often scholars (see Harfield, 2008) tend to agree that conventional policing appears unable to offer viable solutions to the problem. Harfield (2008), for instance, suggested that governments create a police infrastructure specifically designed to tackle organized crime rather than adapting and adding functions to an existing police infrastructure. Gottschalk (2010, xi) argues that policing criminal business enterprises requires not only police investigations but also police intelligence based on the implementation of a clearly defined intelligence strategy. This brief account shows that this perspective is shared by the Norwegian law enforcement as well. Additional research is, however, required to determine the effect of the Norwegian police intelligence model and evaluate its performance.

Although policing in Norway has undergone significant and positive changes in the last decade, additional improvements could be made. Further developments in Norwegian police activity may include expansion of intelligence-led policing; improved police officers' training in intelligence processes and sharing plans; competence building in partnership with cooperating countries; improved sharing of intelligence with partner countries; a better and more extensive use of liaison officers; improved knowledge of international conventions on privacy and civil rights; expansion of the Internet capabilities of all police units and the creation of websites to be used as important information sources. In addition, a systematic and comprehensive monitoring and impact evaluation of the implementation of the national police intelligence strategy should be conducted. This would enable Norway's central law enforcement agencies not only to establish baselines and assess police performance, but also to identify trends in the fight against organized crime over a longer period of time.

References

Albanese, J. S. 2003. Conclusion: Challenges for the future. In *Organized Crime: World Perspectives*, Eds. J.S. Albanese, D.K. Das, & A. Verma, 438–459. Upper Saddle River, NJ: Prentice Hall.

Baltic Sea Task Force. 2010. Task Force Strategy. www.balticseataskforce.ee/strategy

Brunovskis, A. & Tyldum, G. 2004. *Crossing Borders: An Empirical Study of Transnational Prostitution*. Oslo, Norway: Fafo Institute for Applied International Studies.

Center for the Study of Democracy (CSD). 2007. Round table "Organized Crime in Bulgaria: Markets and Trends." Sofia, Bulgaria, 12/12/2007. http://www.csd.bg/artShow.php?id=9032

Christensen, J. 2006. Task Force on organized crime in the Baltic Sea region. Paper presented at the Chiefs of Police Meeting, Organization for Security and Cooperation in Europe, 11/24/2006, http://www.polis.osce.org/library/f/2657/424/OSCE-BEL-EVT-2657-EN-PresentationbyJaakkoChristensen,BalticSeaTaskForceonOrganizedCrime.pdf.

Council of the Baltic Sea States (CBSS). 2010. Civil Security and the Human Dimension. http://www.cbss.org/Civil-Security-and-the-Human-Dimension.

Council of Europe. 2003. *Cross Border Cooperation in the Combating of Organised Crime*. Organised Crime – Best Practice Survey No. 5. http://www.coe.int/t/dghl/cooperation/economiccrime/organisedcrime/BestPractice5E.pdf

Eterno, J.A. 2009. Interview with Odd Berner Malme, police counsellor, permanent mission of Norway to the United Nations. In *Trends in Policing: Interviews with Police Leaders across the Globe*, Eds. D.K. Das & O. Marenin, 143–154. Boca Raton, FL: CRC Press/Taylor & Francis Group.

Europol. n.d. *Agreement between the Kingdom of Norway and the European Police Office*. http://www.europol.europa.eu/legal/agreements/Agreements/8618.pdf

Europol. 2009. *EU Organized Crime Threat Assessment (OCTA)*. http://www.europol.europa.eu/publications/European_Organised_Crime_Threat_Assessment_OCTA/OCTA2009.pdf

Fichtelberg, A. 2008. *Crime without Borders: An Introduction to International Criminal Justice*. Upper Saddle River, NJ: Pearson Education, Inc.

Gelatt, J. 2005. Schengen and the free movement of persons across Europe. *Migration Fundamentals*. Washington, DC: Migration Policy Institute. www.migrationpolicy.org.

Gottschalk, P. 2010. *Policing Organized Crime: Intelligence Strategy Implementation*. New York, NY: CRC Press, Taylor & Francis Group.

Hämäläinen, E. 2008. Combating Organized Crime. Presented at the Baltic Sea Region Programme – Working meeting, Helsinki, Finland, 09/12/2008.

Harfield, C. 2008. Paradigms, pathologies, and practicalities – Policing organized crime in England and Wales. *Policing* 2(1):63–73.

Institute for Economics & Peace. 2009. Global Peace Index Rankings. http://www.visionofhumanity.org/gpi/home.php

International Monetary Fund (IMF). 2009. *World Economic Outlook Database, April 2009*. http://www.imf.org/external/pubs/ft/weo/2009/01/weodata.

Interpol. n.d. *Norway*. www.interpol.int/Public/Region/Europe/pjsystems/Norway.pdf

Johansen, P.O. 2005. Organised crime, Norwegian style. In *The Organised Crime Economy: Managing Crime Markets in Europe*, Eds. P.C. van Duyne, K. von Lampe, M. van Dijck, and J.L. Newell, 189–208. Nijmegen, the Netherlands: Wolf Legal Publishers.

Kildal, N. and Kuhnle, S. 2005. Introduction. In *Normative Foundation of the Welfare State: The Nordic Experience*, Eds. N. Kildal & S. Kuhnle, 1–10. New York, NY: Routledge, Taylor & Francis.

Nybakk, J.E. 2004. Combating organized crime—The Norwegian experience. Paper presented at the *Center for the Study of Democracy Conference* "Countering the New Security Challenges: the Experience of Norway and Bulgaria," Sofia, Bulgaria, June 23, 2004.

Organization for Security and Cooperation in Europe (OSCE). 2010. *Policing Profiles of Participating and Partner States: Norway*. http://polis.osce.org/countries/details?item_id=41

Roth, M. P. 2010. *Organized Crime*. Upper Saddle River, NJ: Prentice Hall.

Strömvik, M. 2006. Starting to 'think big': The Nordic countries and EU peace-building. In *The Nordic Countries and the European Security and Defense Policy*, Eds.
A.J.K. Bailes, G. Herolf, and B. Sundelius, 199– 214. New York, NY: Oxford University Press.

Tavares, C. & Thomas, G. 2009. Population and Social Conditions: Crime and Criminal Justice. *Eurostat: Statistics in Focus*, 36/2009. http://ec.europa.eu/eurostat/

United Nations Development Programme (UNDP). 2009. *Human Development Report 2009:Norway*. http://hdrstats.undp.org/en/countries/country_fact_sheets/cty_fs_NOR.html

United Nations Office on Drugs and Crime (UNODC). 2009. World Drug Report. http://www.unodc.org/documents/wdr/WDR_2009/WDR2009_eng_web.pdf.
US Department of State. 2009. *Trafficking in Persons Report*. June 2009. http://www.state.gov/g/tip/rls/tiprpt/2009/index.htm
World Bank. 2008. World Development Indicators (WDI): Population data. http://datafinder.worldbank/population_total

The Public Housing Safety Initiative in the Eastern District of New York

12

A Collaborative Researcher and Practitioner Program*

JOHN A. ETERNO

Contents

Introduction

The Public Housing Safety Initiative (PHSI) is a crime prevention program in which the United States Department of Justice joined with Housing and Urban Development (HUD). As described by Correa, Rossman, and Burke-Storer (2008), "The PHSI seeks to: 1) reduce levels of crime—particularly

* This research was made possible by a United States Department of Justice, Office of Justice Programs, Community Capacity Development Office, Public Housing Safety Initiative Grant awarded to the United States Attorney's Office, Eastern District of New York. An earlier version of this paper was presented by the author at the annual meeting of the International Executive Research Symposium, May 12 to May 16, 2008 in Cincinnati, Ohio. The author would like to acknowledge the contribution of Anthony Sciarabba (my research assistant at the time the original draft was written) especially for helping with editing of drafts and with the literature review. The author also thanks the United States Attorney's Office, Eastern District of New York, the New York City Police Department's Housing Bureau, and countless other criminal justice agency personnel for their assistance and cooperation.

involving drugs, guns, or violence—in and around public or federally assisted low-income housing units and 2) strengthen community crime prevention efforts." This manuscript will focus on the Eastern District of New York (EDNY) which received $600,000 in PHSI funding.* The EDNY program is an exercise in criminal justice problem-solving using a proactive strategy indicative of community policing (see especially Goldstein, 1990). Steering committees including a local researcher, law enforcement, prosecutors, and community groups, helped guide the project.

The steering committees developed separate strategies tailored to meet the specific needs of two chosen locations—Far Rockaway, Queens and East New York, Brooklyn. The Hammel House in Far Rockaway contains 14 buildings, 6 and 7 stories tall with a total of 708 apartments. The development was completed on April 20, 1955. Currently, it is home to 1,952 residents and is within the confines of the 100th Precinct in New York City. Crime in this part of the Rockaways has been an issue of enormous concern to law enforcement and residents. For example, Grace (2007, n.p.) states, "The isolated oceanside command saw an 8.5% jump in major crime from January to June, compared to the same period last year...† Far Rockaway is located on a peninsula and, therefore, the community tends to be very closed (i.e., not open to outsiders or strangers). This has important implications for law enforcement.

Cypress Hills development in East New York, Brooklyn has 15 seven-story buildings with a total of 1,441 apartments. The development was completed on May 25, 1955 and is home to 3,473 residents. Cypress Hills is in the confines of the 75th Precinct which is a high-crime command in New York City. In 2008, the precinct saw 17 homicides (NYPD Compstat, 2009). This gives readers a clear idea of the amount of violence present in this precinct. Given these target areas, a comprehensive strategic plan was necessary to properly meet the needs of residents in these public housing developments.

A strategic plan was implemented targeting major issues in the two areas. These plans were based on needs assessment. All partners attended meetings to determine the most effective and reasonable plan based on the specific problems in these target areas, current resources, the amount of money available, and the feasibility of success. These meetings were coordinated by the United States Attorney's Office (USAO) and included federal, state, and local agencies. Discussion also occurred with community leaders, residents, and outreach agencies.

* There are 10 sites in 2004 each receiving $600,000 with an additional 38 sites receiving $50,000. Additionally, in 2005, 10 more sites received $600,000 and 20 sites received $100,000 (Community Capacity Development Office, n.d.).

† While the article is talking about the neighboring 101st Precinct, the Hammel Development is nearby (in the 100th Precinct).

Because of the unique aspects of the two locations, strategies were tailored to the needs of each site. Meetings were very well attended. Generally, larger meetings took place at the county district attorney's offices,although other meetings were held in the communities, at precincts, and other locations. At the outset, the larger steering committee meetings were geared to focus on specific issues. The meetings often involved brainstorming sessions in an attempt to identify problems and come up with possible solutions.

The law enforcement strategy was developed with input from community members. That is, members of the steering committee would talk to residents in the community to identify their needs and then report back to the committee. However, due to the nature of police work, these community members could not attend th strategy sessions since their attendance would compromise the proposed law enforcement operations. Eventually, specific strategies were developed to meet the individual needs of both communities.

In the Hammel Development, it was determined that the most likely success for law enforcement would be based on a program called "Operation Good Neighbor." The Hammel development, isolated in Far Rockaway, can be a challenge for undercover operations. The key is assimilating into the neighborhood. To accomplish this assimilation, officers literally lived there. Officers secured an apartment within close proximity to the Hammel housing development. Then, after making contacts in the community, officers made narcotics buys. This part of the operation was under the command of NYPD, specifically the Queens Narcotics Unit.

Prevention activities were developed to complement the law enforcement work. For the Rockaways, the Center for Court Innovation created a Youth Court. This program helps young people in the Rockaways in several ways. First, respondents are typically youth who were given a formal warning by the local police for an incident in which they were involved. Participation is voluntary. Second, youth from the area are trained in the roles of prosecutor, defense, judge, jury, etc. They experience first-hand what occurs in the criminal justice system. Many can be motivated to continue studies in law or criminal justice and pursue honest careers that will help the community.*

At the Cypress Hills location, the law enforcement strategy dovetailed with existing narcotics investigations. The historic trend of violence and drug sales in and around the development led to a collaborative effort between the NYPD Narcotics Division and the Major Narcotics Investigations Bureau (MNIB) of the Kings County District Attorney's Office. Together, they

* More specifically, training for youth court members focus on skills such as critical thinking, facilitating group decision making, precision questioning, and writing and presentation skills. The content serves teens far beyond their roles on the court. Legal professionals co-facilitate training with the youth court. This informal role modeling impacts participants' educational career goals.

conducted an undercover conspiracy investigation during an 18 month period to identify the scope and structure of a narcotics enterprise. Additionally, a major attempt was made to infiltrate and dismantle it. Evidence establishing the defendants' participation in the conspiracy included the individual sales to undercover officers conducted over the course of the investigation as well as prior convictions for related offenses.

As was done in the Hammels, a prevention program was developed to complement law enforcement efforts. Two programs were specifically targeted to assist with the Cypress Hills PHSI: ComALERT and Gang Prevention. The ComALERT (Community and Law Enforcement Resources Together" program provides substance abuse counseling and other treatment, employment, and housing services to parolees in Kings County, New York. Among a new generation of prisoner reentry programs around the country, ComALERT is unusual in that it provides its clients with a comprehensive array of services shortly after their release from prison. In addition to substance abuse counseling, ComALERT offers transitional housing and employment for up to a year as well as job referral services in an effort to integrate parolees into mainstream social roles. In the overall strategy, it was hypothesized that reentry issues would simply dissipate the results achieved by law enforcement and prosecution. ComALERT helps parolees reenter society such that they no longer pose the risks that they once did.

Gang prevention efforts by the Kings County District Attorney's office also helped to assuage the level of criminal activity in the Cypress Hills Development. Gang workshops were conducted in schools, community centers, and other agencies that deal with at-risk youth. The gang counselor has also been tasked with identifying programs that would accept referrals in criminal cases from gang defendants who were eligible to accept alternative sentences to incarceration.

Literature Review

While the initiative was guided by practical needs, an understanding of past research helps in the analysis and evaluation of the project. Contrary to popular wisdom and even some reports (e.g., Correa, Rossman, and Burke-Storer, 2008), research on the extent of crime in the proximity of public housing is mixed. For example, Santiago, Galster, and Pettit (2003) examined 38 dispersed, small-scale public housing sites in Denver, Colorado during 1992–1995. Their findings revealed that "proximity to public housing was not associated with any increase in reported crime of any type" including violent, property, criminal mischief, disorderly conduct, and other crime. Reported crime rates were provided by the Denver Police Department for the years

1990–1997. Descriptive statistics of the housing units reveal that the public housing population is 9.65% African American and 26% Hispanic.

Additional research conducted by McNulty and Holloway (2000) examined public housing and crime in Atlanta, Georgia from 1990–1992. Using 1990–1992 crime incident data and 1990 Census block group data for the Atlanta area, results indicated that proximity to public housing is related to the highest levels of disadvantage and crime. This included rates of murder, rape, assault, and public order crime. Neighborhood-level crime data was provided by the Atlanta Police Department and consisted of crimes known to the police at the street-level of measurement. The study controlled for the typical social research neighborhood variables including residential stability, vacancy rate, and percentage of youths and young adults (15–24).

Other efforts have been made to determine the success of policies aimed at reducing crime in public housing. Barbrey (2004) examined the effectiveness of public policies and programs designed to reduce crime in the most dangerous public housing developments in Knoxville, Tennessee. The policies and programs studied included the implementation of: "(1) a 'one-strike' eviction policy that was added to the leases of public housing residents; (2) the demolition of one housing project with funding from the HUD's HOPE VI grant program; (3) a 'team-based' approach to policing in the public housing areas which featured several new policing policies; and (4) a new resident screening application process" (Barbrey, 2004, p. 6). Findings indicate that implementation of these policies had very little impact on certain types of crimes, includingcrimes of opportunity and property offenses.

Bowie (2001) examined differences in crime and safety between privately and publically managed urban housing communities in Miami, Florida. A survey of 503 low-income African Americans living in 42 different housing projects, indicated that housing communities operated by private organizations experienced higher rates of breakins and thefts than publicly managed housing communities. However, publicly managed housing communities featured elevated rates of shootings and violence. Additionally, residents living in publicly managed housing reported increased levels of satisfaction with neighborhood police. Similar to other research, all of the public and privately managed housing sites examined were located in socially distressed neighborhoods.

Ireland, Thornberry, and Loeber (2003) examined violence among adolescents living in public housing in Rochester, New York and Pittsburgh, New York. The results of this study indicate that there are negligible difference in the rates of property offending between adolescents who live in public housing and those who do not. Results also indicated that the opposite was true for violent offending as an increased prevalence rate was detected.

Overall, with respect to public housing and crime, findings appear to be mixed at best. Additionally, previous policies instituted in the neighborhoods in the current research had little to no impact on criminal activities in these areas.

Methodology

Several methodological approaches were developed to effectively evaluate the PHSI program. Using several methods allowed the researcher to compare the various methods and compensate for the methodological shortcomings of any single method. One involved collecting official statistics.* Basic crime statistics are kept by the NYPD. Other official statistics include arrests, warrants, number of parolees in ComALERT, etc.

A second comprehensive measure was utilized; an anonymous, self-administered questionnaire (see Appendix for wording of questionnaire). The questionnaire was developed to complement official statistics. It was extensively revised in development.† A key feature of the administration of this survey was anonymity. Residents were advised not to put their names or any identifying information on the questionnaires. In this way, survey respondents were more likely to answer truthfully and not in socially biased ways. Self-administered, anonymous questionnaires are particularly useful for sensitive questions such as the ones asked here (e.g., opinions about law enforcement and the like).‡

With regard to sampling, this research used a nonprobability sampling design.§A contact person was used in both the Hammels and in Cypress Hills to aid in distribution. In the Hammels, distribution took place at a residents'

* Official statistics can be inaccurate measures. For example, crime statistics are based on crimes known to the police. However, from victimization surveys and other sources of information, we can estimate that the majority of crime (about 60%) is not known to the police. That is, many people do not report crimes that occurred to the police. Some crimes have even higher rates of non-reporting such as domestic violence and rape.

† Focus groups examined the questionnaire to determine that it was accurately reflecting what we wanted to measure. The USAO and staff at the Institute of Law and Justice (ILJ) reviewed the questionnaire before it was sent out. Additionally, a review of other survey instruments (e.g., Fort Worth Police Department); utilizing the U.S. Department of Justice's Office of Justice Program's, Bureau of Justice Assistance publication entitled, *A Police Guide to Surveying Citizens and Their Environment*; as well as other research guides (e.g., Maxfield & Babbie,2006) were invaluable tools in helping to produce an accurate and useful survey instrument.

‡ See, for example, Babbie & Maxfield (2006, 2008).

§ There were a number of concerns regarding questionnaire distribution. It was suggested for example, that students hand them out at the front of each of the developments; others suggested knocking on doors of residents and asking them to fill the questionnaire out. Going throughout a development to survey residents about crime may not be a popular endeavor—particularly among drug dealers or other unscrupulous characters. Indeed, knocking on doors or handing out surveys about crime, quality of life, law enforcement, and other activities could be dangerous.

meeting. A few others known to the residents were asked to fill out the questionnaire. The researcher then met with the contact person to pick up the completed questionnaires.

In Cypress Hills, the researcher personally went to a tenants' association meeting. About 30 tenants were present. The researcher directly asked residents to fill out the questionnaire, advising them not to put identifying marks on the survey. The researcher left the room as the residents filled them out and returned later to pick up the completed surveys. In this way, anonymity was maintained at both locations. While this sampling method admittedly has weaknesses, it served the purposes of this evaluation (a purposive sampling design). Overall, 86 questionnaires were completed (59 in the Hammels and 27 in Cypress Hills).

Based on population data collected by the U.S. Census Bureau, the Hammel development and surrounding area consists of 53.35% black, 22.32% Hispanic, 19.21% white and 5.12% other. Our sample of 59 residents in the Hammels is 47.5% black, 25.4% Hispanic, and 6.8% white, with nearly 17% not answering the race question. It may be that those not answering weare whites. If that was the case, this sample, although small and not collected through probability sampling techniques, seems to be somewhat representative of the population— at least based on race and ethnicity data from the Census.

For the Cypress Hills Development, our sample was much smaller—27 respondents. Census population information indicates the area is 62.44% black, 35.12% Hispanic, .9% white and 1.54% other. Survey results indicated that the sample is 77.8% black, 3.7% Hispanic, and 3.7% other. While the sample seems to have an adequate representation of blacks, there was a concern with the small number of Hispanics responding. This can at least partially be attributed to the small sample size and using a tenants' association meeting rather than a probability design. Additionally, the census tract for this development is 99% minority which is very similar to the sample showing at least some representativeness.

Field observations were also utilized. For part of this study, the method was proper, but for other parts, it was not. For example, it was very inappropriate (and even damaging) to observe undercover law enforcement operations. This is because observations could compromise the operations. However, the researcher appropriately attended many of the steering committee and smaller focus group meetings. At these meetings, the researcher took a participant–observer role, advising and recommending, when appropriate, based on experience as an academic and as a criminal justice practitioner. The researcher also observed the youth court in operation.

These three methods (official data; a self-administered, anonymous questionnaire; and field observations) allowed the researcher to triangulate methods. In this way, we could compare the results of the three methods and be more confident that our results were accurate.

The goals for the PHSI were essentially to reduce crime rates (including both violent and non-violent crimes), reduce recidivism, and improve community perceptions. We examined official, questionnaire, and observational data for these goals—first in the Hammels, then in Cypress Hills.

Results

Hammel Development

The long-term Operation Good Neighbor commenced in the Hammels in September 2006. During the course of the operation, undercover officers were able to assimilate into the neighborhood through their initial contacts and successfully make 147 narcotics purchases from 59 subjects. The Good Neighbor operation ended earlier than planned because of the arrest of the main target in a serious case not directly related to this investigation. Nevertheless, the operation resulted in 39 arrests. All but two of these arrests quickly resulted in convictions.

Overall, in the area surrounding the Hammel development, the NYPD arrested 53 persons as a direct result of narcotics purchase. These, included 12 non-arrest warrant identified subjects and 17 additional persons subsequent to the execution of search warrants, none of whom were prior subjects in the case.

Using other official statistics that were available from the NYPD's Housing Bureau's Compstat statistics., we compared the period of September 30 through September 3 for 2006 versus 2007. Based on these statistics, we saw a 5.3% decrease in the total index crime at the Hammel development.* Part of this reduction was due to a decrease in violent crime. The violent crime index (rape, robbery, murder, and felony assault) showed a 7.1% decrease. Notably, there were no rapes or robberies for the entire period of 2007.

While felony assaults were up a bit compared to the previous year, some of the felony assaults were not against members of the public, but against arresting police officers. Thus, the small increase in felony assaults may actually have been due to increased enforcement. Overall, these statistics seemed to indicate an overall drop in crime in the Hammel development.

By the end of the reporting phase of the project (September 30, 2007), the Far Rockaway Youth Court had heard 31 cases. Their goal for the first full year

* Index crime in New York City consists of murder, rape (all degrees are reported in Compstat figures), robbery, felony assault, burglary, grand larceny, and grand larceny auto.

of hearings was 50. and they were on track to exceed that goal. The court had an outstanding sanction completion rate: 87.5% of respondents completed all assigned sanctions. Of the 18 cases closed, 16 respondents completed their hearings and assigned essays, community service, and educational workshops such as conflict resolution and goal setting. The remaining 13 cases were on track for completion.

Based on the survey of 59 residents in the Hammel development, nearly 60% felt at least reasonably safe compared to the previous year (see Table 1).* This was good news and was one indication that the programs were having a positive impact. However, of those who did feel unsafe compared to a year earlier, the difference in responses appeared to be influenced by the resident's age. The "under 20" category felt significantly less safe compared to the other categories. Indeed, examining the under 20 group, we saw that more than 86% felt unsafe compared to a year earlier. The majority of respondents in all other age categories felt safer. Examining the unsafe category only (see Table 12.1), we saw that the under 20 category made up more than half of those feeling unsafe compared to the previous year when 54.5% of the unsafe category were under 20.

Examining the specific issues of violent crime, property crime, gangs, fear of crime, drugs, gun violence, loitering, and graffiti gave us additional insights (see Table 12.2). Except for property crime, the modal response in all of these issues was "much worse." While residents, in general, felt safer, they felt that these issues were getting worse in their neighborhoods compared to the previous year. For violent crime, the gang problem, drugs, gun violence,

Table 12.1 Hammel Residents Perception of Safety Compared to 1 Year Ago

* All analyses are based on valid responses. That is, the number of respondents that answered the questions. Some residents chose not to answer individual questions; they are simply treated as missing values for the question and not figured into any analyses.

Table 12.2 Responses to Crime and Quality of Life Issues (Hammel)

Issue	Percentage Stating Worse or Much Worse
Violence	54.2
Property Crime	37.2
Gang Problem	57.6
Fear of Crime	54.6
Drug Problem	60.4
Gun Violence	55.9
Loitering	52.5
Graffiti	51.7

loitering, and graffiti, more than half of the respondents stated that violent crime was worse or much worse.

The responses to these questions were generally not encouraging. Also, the responses by residents to these crime and quality of life questions, while worse among the under 20 residents, were fairly common across the age categories. Therefore, it was not age that explained these answers. Since the Hammels were chosen because of its narcotics problem, *it may be that while the PHSI was able to meet its law enforcement objectives, additional work and effort will be necessary to change the negative stigma that has developed over time in the neighborhood.* Additionally, due to the undercover nature of the chosen strategy, it is possible that residents were not even aware of many of the law enforcement activities in the area. This theory can be indirectly tested with other information from the questionnaire.

We asked residents about several programs. The majority of residents were not aware of any of them (i.e., Weed and Seed, Drug Education for Youth [DEFY], Project Safe Neighborhoods [PSN], and Youth Court). However, the program the most residents did know about was the PHSI Youth Court initiative (44%), nearly 12% more than the next highest program (Weed and Seed). This indicated that the PHSI was active in the community. Further, it may explain some of the negative responses to the specific crime and quality of life questions; namely, the undercover nature of the strategy may simply have left residents without knowledge. The results from the questionnaire were mixed regarding the success of the PHSI. While generally residents did feel safer compared to the previous year, when asked about specific quality of life and crime issues, they were unabashedly more concerned compared the previous year. This may partially be due to the undercover nature of the chosen law enforcement initiative as well as long term negative feelings (stigmatization) about the neighborhood, an attitudenot likely to dissipate without more work. Residents did, however, feel that key agencies in the area were at least somewhat effective.

The last method utilized was observation. In addition to attending many steering committee meetings, the researcher attended the local youth court in the Rockaways. Students participating as pseudo-members of the court process appeared interested and very intelligent. They handled their assigned tasks with a poise and professionalism not seen in many children of their age. It was clear to this observer, that the youth court concept, using peers to handle minor incidents, is an excellent alternative to the typical criminal justice system response. In my experience, many juveniles are lost in the system. This program seems to provide at least two ways of helping juveniles. First, the students participating in the process learn about law and the courts. Additionally, they learn oral and communication skills which will advance their careers later in life. Second, is the impact on respondents. Rather than the typical police response (juvenile report with minimal follow-up), the youth court offers these kids an alternative—to be judged by their peers. They see that there are good kids out there who are trying to find an honest way and attempting to punish and rehabilitate them with appropriate penalties.

Typical sanctions handed out by the youth court included community service, letters of apology, workshops that focused on goal setting or conflict resolution, and other sanctions such as writing an essay. Also of note is that the program was advertised in the local Far Rockaway newspaper, *The Wave*. This, helped residents become aware of the court. Again, residents were most likely to be aware of the youth court compared to other programs in the area.

As a final observation, while visiting the youth court, the students had a chance to ask questions about going to college and what it takes to get into law school. The students asked articulate questions and were honestly interested. Programs such as the Youth Court are excellent ways to reach inner city youth— a difficult task, at best. Needless to say, I enjoyed the experience and find youth courts to be a healthy, worthwhile response to relatively minor juvenile problems.

Cypress Hills

The NYPD's 75th Precinct's Narcotics Module investigated the illegal sale of narcotics in the Cypress Hills housing development. This case began in October 2005 as a result of the historically high trend of violence and drug sales in the area. The investigation identified three different groups selling crack, heroin, and marijuana in and around the complex. During this investigation, undercover officers made 105 buys and confidential informants made an additional 20 buys. As a result, the NYPD reported that 19 search warrants were executed and 49 arrests were made.

According to the Kings County District Attorney's Office, the takedown of the Cypress Hills investigation began in April. In the initial takedown phase, 31 individuals were arrested. Of those, 28 were indicted on charges of conspiracy in the first degree. This charge was based on their use of juveniles along with other narcotics sale and possession charges and exposed them to sentences of 25 years to life. Of the 31, three were indicted on charges of Conspiracy in the second degree and other related sale and possession of narcotics charges. Nine other individuals were arrested as a result of the execution of search warrants and charged with conspiracy and other related chargesl. Nineteen search warrants were executed resulting in the recovery of 1 firearm (.357 magnum), over 2 ounces of cocaine, over 331 milligrams of heroin, and over 12 ounces of marijuana. Officers advised that 6 other individuals were arrested and several additional individuals who were identified but not yet arrested.

Other official data were also helpful. Using Compstat crime figures supplied by the NYPD's Housing Bureau, we compared index crime for the period of September 30 to September 3 for 2006 versus 2007. In making the comparison, we saw that index crime in the Cypress Hills development was down 28%. Notably, the violent crime index (murder, rape, robbery, and felony assault) decreased 33% during this same period. Felony assaults decreased markedly (down 65%). Overall, based on these official statistics, the PHSI was an overwhelming success, in meeting its goal to reduce the crime rates for both violent and non-violent crime.

According to ComALERT's official statistical report which covered the 73rd and 75th Precincts from October 1, 2006 to September 30, 2007, 116 parolees were accepted into the ComALERT reentry program (see Table 12.3). Of the 116 clients, 28 (38.8%) successfully graduated. The remaining clients were either discharged or were active during the analysis period. All participants of ComALERT receive toxicology testing. Of the 116, 36 tested positive upon initial screening and 26 tested positive during retesting. All 36 clients were placed in intervention groups for clients who have a higher relapse risk. Of these, 8 were still active at the time of analysis and ten were referred to more intense programs. Sixteen of the 116 participants were involved in Doe Fund's Ready Willing and Able Program (see www.doe.org). Forty-one of

Table 12.3 Client Status

Status	Frequency	Percent	Cumulative Percentage
Graduate	28	24.14	24.14
Discharge	44	37.93	62.07
Active	44	37.93	100
Total	116	100	

* Please note, the 38.8% graduation rate is based on the computation of the graduates and discharges frequencies. The active participants are not included because there was no final status as of the end of the period.

Table 12.4 1 year Recidivism Rates of ComALERT Graduates Living in the 73rd/75th Precinct Area

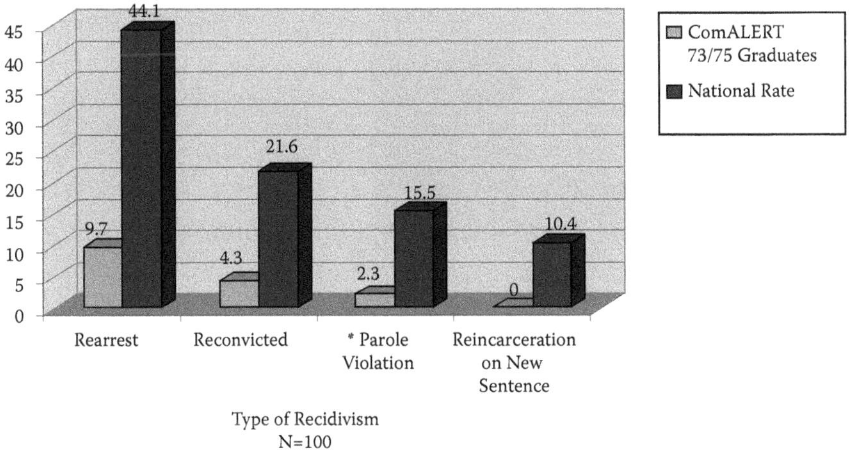

the 116 from the 73rd and 75th precincts were employed prior to coming to ComALERT. Of the 28 ComALERT graduates, 26 were employed at the time of their completion. Of the remaining two, one was receiving job training and the other was enrolled as a student. ComALERT also refers clients to various agencies for housing and other social service needs. Nineteen of the 116 clients needed referrals for either housing or social services.

ComALERT graduates from the 73rd and 75th precincts fared better when compared to the national rate in all four recidivism aspects measured within a one year time frame. As can be seen in Table 12.4, for measures of rearrest, there was a significant difference between the ComALERT graduates and the national rate.

From February through June 2007, the gang counselor and the gang bureau assistant district attorneys of the Kings County District Attorney's Office participated in 18 workshops addressing gang violence, affiliation, and legal consequences for youths as well as Gang awareness workshops for adults. These workshops were conducted in schools, community centers, and other agencies that deal with at-risk youths. Participation in these workshops generated numerous calls from youths and/or parents of youths in gangs seeking assistance in getting out of the gang. Additionally, numerous requests came in for additional gang workshops in other schools and community organizations. Since January of 2007, the gang counselor has been tasked with identifying programs that would accept referrals from gang defendants in criminal cases who are eligible to accept alternative sentences to incarceration. Through August 14, the Gang Counselor had gotten 14 programs to partner in this effort,known as "Project Re-Direct." These agencies varied

Table 12.5 Cypress Hills Residents - Feeling on Safety Compared to a Year Ago

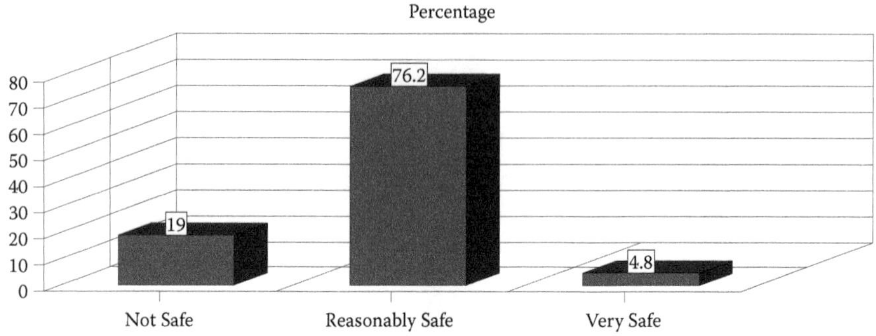

from offering high school equivalency diploma programs, drug testing and counseling to job training as well as personal counseling to help with re-entry into conventional society. The PHSI terminated the end of September. As of mid-August the Gang Counselor hadplaced 9 candidates into Project Re-Direct and the program was in position to service many more defendants in light of the work that had previously been accomplished. Certainly, far more remains to be done here.

Of the 27 surveys filled out for the Cypress Hills development, compared to the previous year, only 4 respondents felt not safe at all (with 6 not responding to this question) which meant that 81% felt at least reasonably safe (see Table 12.5).

There were no significant differences among members responses to this question based on age, ethnicity, marital status, gender, and education level.

Examining the specific issues of violent crime, property crime, gangs, fear of crime, drugs, gun violence, loitering, and graffiti helps us to further understand residents. For this set of questions, residents generally felt that some situations had gotten worse in the last year, namely, drugs, guns, and gangs. However, they seemed to have more positive feeling with respect to crime (both violent and property), fear of crime, graffiti and loitering.

Residents were most concerned about the drug problem. Their responses indicated thatmore than 65% of them felt the problem had gotten worse. Not one respondent stated that the situation was much better. This is an indication that the steering committee was correct in choosing a drug initiative; however, these responses also indicated that far more work was needed to bring the drug problem under control in the Cypress Hills development.

Guns and gangs were the next two problems identified by residents as generally getting worse when compared to the previous year. Responses to the gun question indicated that more than 54% felt the situation was getting worse or much worse, while 21% stated the situation was better or much better. With respect to gangs, the survey indicated that 50% felt the problem was getting worse or much worse, while 14.8% stated it was getting better or much better. One encouraging result from this was that the use of steering committees was a success in choosing the initiatives of most concern to neighborhood residents. Other responses were less discouraging. With respect to crime, more residents were stating it was getting better compared to getting worse, although many felt it was about the same. With respect to property crime, 28.5% of residents felt it was better or much better compared to the previous year; 23.8% felt it was worse or much worse, with the remainder, 47.6% stating it was the same. Concerning violent crime, 29% stated it was better or much better compared to last year; 21% stated it was getting worse and 50% said it was about the same as the previous year. Clearly, however, residents were not as concerned about property or violent crime as they were about illegal drugs.

The survey revealed that residents were divided on the issues of ear of crime, loitering, and graffiti. Starting with fear of crime, 34.7% of residents stated the situation was worse or much worse, while 21.7% stated it was better or much better. The remaining 43.5% were in the middle.* With respect to loitering, 45.8% stated it was worse or much worse, while 25% stated it was better or much better. About 29.2% stated the situation was about the same as last year. Lastly, 36.4% of residents felt that graffiti was worse or much worse, while 22.2% stated it was better or much better with 36.4% stating it was about the same.

ComALERT and gang outreach prevention were direct products of the PHSI. Approximately, 45% of the residents were aware of the ComALERT program and 40% were aware of the gang outreach prevention program. Other programs residents were asked about included Weed and Seed (31.6% were aware of the program), Project Safe Neighborhoods (43.5% were aware), and Drug Education for Youth (nearly 62% were aware).

Conclusions

The scientific literature indicates that those who live in public housing are more likely to experience higher rates of shootings and violence (Bowie, 2001; Ireland, Thornberry, & Loeber, 2003). The PHSI-EDNY was an attempt to decrease crime and, at the same time, increase the quality of life of residents in two specific housing developments—Hammel and Cypress Hills.

The analyses provided the foundation for developing specific conclusions about the impact of the PHSI in the target areas. The cornerstone of the PHSI–EDNY was the use of steering committees. The steering committee

* Some numbers may not add to 100% due to rounding.

concept was demonstrated to be a sound one. The steering committees in both target areas were able to properly discern community need and chose narcotics enforcement to be a major component of the PHSI.

Criminal enterprise activities were reduced in both housing developments. This is clearly supported with the official data on arrests, convictions, and search warrants at each location. The decrease in violent crime at both locations was particularly encouraging (violent crime index decreased 7.1% in the Hammels and 33% in Cypress Hills). However, survey results were not as encouraging. This may be due to the undercover nature of these operations. That is, residents were simply unaware of what enforcement activities were taking place. Nevertheless, the surveys revealed a need to continue enforcement initiatives in these locations in order for long term results to take root. Based on the survey, residents needed to be reassured that law enforcement activities would not dissipate.

The ComALERT program seemed successful. Rearrest and reincarceration rates of ComALERT graduates were particularly revealing. Only 9.7% of the ComALERT graduates in the 73rd and 75th precincts were rearrested compared to the national rearrest rate of 44.1%. Additionally, no ComALERT graduates were reincarcerated compared to a national rate of 10.4%. As a caveat, however, the questionnaire indicates that 45% of those questioned were aware of the ComALERT program. Of the programs residents were asked about, this percentage is not the lowest; however, it could be better. Residents were more aware of the ComALERT program compared to Weed and Seed and Project Safe Neighborhoods (31.6% and 43.5% respectively). However, they were less aware of the ComALERT program compared to Drug Education for Youth (about 62% were aware). Knowledge of these programs helps to reduce levels of fear and allows community participation which helps the programs to be more effective. Therefore, future projects need to consider community outreach in more detail.

With respect to public safety, the official statistics clearly indicated that crime decreased at both target areas (general crime index and violent crime index crimes were reduced). Additionally, survey results at both areas indicated that the majority of residents felt at least reasonably. However, quality of life indicators in the survey showed that the majority of residents did not feel that their quality of life had improved in the last year. At the Hammels, every indicator, including gang problem, fear of crime, drug problem, gun violence, loitering, and graffiti showed that over 50% of residents felt that conditions were getting worse or much worse compared to the previous year. In the Cypress Hills target area, residents were more divided on these quality of life issues indicating slightly more favorable results but still a need for improvement (e.g., concerning fear of crime, 34.7% stated worse or much worse, 43.5% stated no change, and 21.7% stated getting better or much better).

Another issue of importance was the negative stigma that residents associated with their neighborhoods. These areas and programs were identified by both steering committees because they had crime and quality of life issues. Residents seemed to have strong negative feelings about these neighborhoods. Due to these long standing beliefs and cynicism, it was determined that it would take a concerted and consistent effort to reduce that stigma.

In sum, the PHSI–EDNY was truly a problem solving exercise that involved many levels of government as well as private agencies. Under the guidance of USAO, these divergent parties were brought under one umbrella. Considering the limited funding, this was a very successful endeavor. Certainly, proof of concept was demonstrated. Indeed, this is an excellent model for community policing initiatives—even for those with fairly limited funding.

References

Barbrey, J. W. (2004). Measuring the effectiveness of crime control policies in Knoxville's public housing. *Journal of Contemporary Criminal Justice*, 20(1): 6–32.

Bowie, S. L. (2001). The impact of privatized management in urban public housing communities: A comparative analysis of perceived crime, neighborhood problems, and personal safety. *Journal of Sociology and Social Welfare*, 28(4): 67–87.

Bureau of Justice Assistance, U.S. Department of Justice. (1993, October) *A Police Guide to Surveying Citizens and Their Environment*. Washington D.C.: U.S. Government Office.

Community Capacity Development Office (CCDO) "2004 and 2005 Public Housing Safety Initiative Sites." Retrieved on May 8, 2008, from http://www.ojp.usdoj.gov/ccdo/programs/phsi_sites_04_05.pdf.

Correa, V. , Rossman, S. and Burke-Storer, M. R. "The Public Housing Safety Initiative (PHSI): Strategic Crime Reduction and Prevention" *Paper presented at the annual meeting of the American Society of Criminology (ASC)*. 2008-05-07 from http://www.allacademic.com/meta/p126300_index.html

Far Rockaway Youth Court Is Hiring Teens (2007, February 23). *The Wave, Rockaway Beach, N.Y.* : p. 6

Goldstein, Herman (1990). *Problem-Oriented Policing*. New York, McGraw-Hill.

Grace, M. (2007, June 12). Crime spike in Far Rockaway. *New York Daily News.*

Ireland, T., Thornberry, T., & Loeber, R. (2003). Violence among adolescents living in public housing: a two-site analysis. *Criminology and Public Policy*, 3(1): 3–38.

Maxfield, M.G. & Babbie, E. (2006). *Basics of Research Methods for Criminal Justice and Criminology*. Belmont, CA: Thompson.

McNulty, T. L., & Holloway, S. R. (2000). Race, crime, and public housing in Atlanta: Testing a conditional effect hypothesis. *Social Forces*, 79(2): 707–729.

New York City police Department (NYPD) (2009). Compstat. Downloaded from www.nyc.gov/html/nypd/downloads/pdf/crime statistics/cso75pct.pdf on March 26, 2009.

New York City Police Department (NYPD) Housing Bureau (2007). Compstat crime figures. Unpublished Housing Bureau crime statistics.

Santiago, A. M., Galster, G. C., & Pettit, K. L. (2003). Neighborhood crime and scattered-site public housing. *Urban Studies*, 40(1): 2147–2163.

APPENDIX

COMMUNITY SURVEY -FAR ROCKAWAY

The United States Attorney's office has partnered with criminal justice and other agencies in a program called the Public Housing Safety Initiative (PHSI). The PHSI is conducting a survey in your neighborhood to help provide better services. Your participation in the survey is very important. The survey results will be used to help us determine how the current program is working. Your participation in the survey is strictly voluntary and you can stop at any time. **Please do not put your name or other identifying information on this survey**. You indicate your **voluntary consent** to being questioned by filling out the questionnaire. It should only take a **few minutes** to complete the survey.

SIMPLY CIRCLE YOUR ANSWER TO EACH QUESTION.

	1-Not Safe at All 2-Reasonably Safe 3-Very Safe		
1) Rate how you feel about personal safety in this community:	1	2	3
2) Rate how you feel about personal safety in this community now compared with one year ago:	1	2	3

3) In general, within the last year, would you say the issues listed have become much worse, worse, about the same, better, or much better?

	Much Worse	**Worse**	**About the same**	**Better**	**Much Better**
Violent Crime	1	2	3	4	5
Property Crime	1	2	3	4	5
Gangs	1	2	3	4	5
Fear of Crime	1	2	3	4	5
Drugs	1	2	3	4	5
Gun Violence	1	2	3	4	5
Loitering	1	2	3	4	5
Graffiti	1	2	3	4	5

4) In the past year, were you the victim of a violent crime (or an attempted violent crime) such as an assault, robbery, or rape in this neighborhood? **1=Yes** **2=No**

If yes, did you report it to the police? **1=Yes** **2=No**

PLEASE TURN OVER

5) Your gender:	Male	Female			
6) Your age:	under 20	20-40	41-60	61+	
7) Your education level	less than High School	High School	Some College	College Graduate	
8) Your Marital Status	Single	Married	Divorced	Widowed	Other
9) Your Race:	Asian	Black	Hispanic	White	Other

10) I am part of this community because (circle one):

I live here   I work here   I own a business here   I go to school here   Other___________

11) I have been a part of this community for the past (circle one):

less than 1 year   1 to 5 years   more than 5 years

12) Rate the effectiveness of the following agencies :

1-Not effective at all
2-Somewhat effective
3-Very effective

New York City Housing Authority:	1	2	3
New York City Police Department:	1	2	3
Brooklyn/Queens District Attorney's office:	1	2	3

13) Are you aware of the following programs in your area:	**1=Yes**	**2=No**
Weed and Seed	1	2
Drug Education for Youth (DEFY)	1	2
Project Safe Neighborhoods (PSN)	1	2
Youth Court	1	2

If YES, list the programs (if any) that you think are successful: ____________________
____

14) Any additional comments: ____
____
____

COMMUNITY SURVEY - EAST NEW YORK

The United States Attorney's office has partnered with criminal justice and other agencies in a program called the Public Housing Safety Initiative (PHSI). The PHSI is conducting a survey in your neighborhood to help provide better services. Your participation in the survey is very important. The survey results will be used to help us determine how the current program is working. Your participation in the survey is strictly voluntary and you can stop at any time. **Please do not put your name or other identifying information on this survey**. You indicate your **voluntary consent** to being questioned by filling out the questionnaire. It should only take a **few minutes** to complete the survey.

1-Not Safe at All
2-Reasonably Safe
3-Very Safe

1) Rate how you feel about personal safety in this community: 1 2 3

2) Rate how you feel about personal safety in this community now compared with one year ago: 1 2 3

3) In general, within the last year, would you say the issues listed have become much worse, worse, about the same, better, or much better?

	Much Worse	**Worse**	**About the same**	**Better**	**Much Better**
Violent Crime	1	2	3	4	5
Property Crime	1	2	3	4	5
Gangs	1	2	3	4	5
Fear of Crime	1	2	3	4	5
Drugs	1	2	3	4	5
Gun Violence	1	2	3	4	5
Loitering	1	2	3	4	5
Graffiti	1	2	3	4	5

4) In the past year, were you the victim of a violent crime (or an attempted violent crime) such as an assault, robbery, or rape in this neighborhood? **1=Yes** **2=No**

If yes, did you report it to the police? **1=Yes** **2=No**

PLEASE TURN OVER

5) Your gender:	Male	Female			
6) Your age:	under 20	20-40	41-60	61+	
7) Your education level	less than High School	High School	Some College	College Graduate	
8) Your Marital Status	Single	Married	Divorced	Widowed	Other
9) Your Race:	Asian	Black	Hispanic	White	Other

10) I am part of this community because (circle one):

I live here I work here I own a business here I go to school here Other___________

11) I have been a part of this community for the past (circle one):

1 year or less 1 to 5 years more than 5 years

12) Rate the effectiveness of the following agencies :

1-Not effective at all
2-Somewhat effective
3-Very effective

New York City Housing Authority:	1	2	3
New York City Police Department:	1	2	3
Brooklyn/Queens District Attorney's office:	1	2	3

13) Are you aware of the following programs in your area: **1=Yes 2=No**

Weed and Seed	1	2
Drug Education for Youth (DEFY)	1	2
Community and Law Enforcement Resources Together (ComALERT)	1	2
Project Safe Neighborhoods (PSN)	1	2
Gang outreach prevention	1	2

If YES, list the programs (if any) that you think are successful: ____________________
____

14) Any additional comments: ____
____
____

Note:Actual survey used different spacing.

Conclusion

Using the framework of the World Systems Theory as discussed by Peter and Lucille Kratcoski, the information presented in this book centers around the individual differences in theory, style, and practice for many nations in the world. However, each chapter also presents insights and methods that may be used to transfer ideas and strategies from an isolated situation to a piece of a jigsaw puzzle where all countries and jurisdictions are interlocked into a well-designed and complete picture. It is important for each country to recognize both their areas of similarity and difference in relation to other nations and to understand that all of them are able to contribute unique knowledge and history to a global policing system. Collaboration between countries and communication between national and state agencies can make a substantial improvement in the world's policing methodology.

Developing and less-established countries discussed ways that their police agencies are trying to catch up to the global expectation of modern policing ideas and strategies. Representatives from many of these countries talked about their history and explained they are looking to the global community and the more developed nations for guidance and support. Countries with histories of repression and information control are working hard to create new policing systems that incorporate the positive elements of their old society while modifying their agencies to embrace more modern theory and practice. While joining the East and West, democratic and socialist, traditional and modern can be a stressful and difficult process, these chapters demonstrate that the modern theories and practices can be a better, more potent form of policing.

Chapter 2, "Policing Activity and Human Rights" by Kendall, discussed the importance of human rights and ethical and humane police practices in all countries. Kendall used Brazil's problem with drug dealing factions to illustrate the issues and difficulties that emerge when human rights are threatened by a lack of security. Brazil was an especially appropriate choice because while Brazil's police agencies lack control, illegal groups have tremendous power. If a country's citizens do not see the police as powerful allies, those citizens may experience deep feelings of insecurity. Kendall looks toward an international human rights initiative that would enable all countries' citizens to respect and trust police. Chapter 3, "Keeping Order in a Time of Dynamic Change and Exchange: Social Control in Asia and the Pacific" by Shaw, discussed the issues that arise when countries known for a high degree of social control try to become more contemporary in their methods and focus. Shaw described the difficulties in trying to best merge old and new ideas, socialist and capitalist ideals, and Eastern and Western philosophies. He made the point that the most progressive way to move forward is to retain the inherent culture while keeping the best ideas of these contrasting philosophies. He advocated a global ideological consensus so that all nations could benefit from a philosophy of stronger policing through the synthesis of traditional and modern ideas. Shaw called for developed societies to break down technological barriers, to share their knowledge and most effective practices, to offer financial aid and professional training, and to encourage global participation in the profession of policing.

Chapter 5, "On Police and Policing in Slovenia: Obstacles or Challenges" by Mesko and Maver, discussed police professionalism. Mesko and Maver wrote about how Slovenia, a post-socialist country, is facing problems in adapting community policing principles to fit their local culture and legal structure. Current research in Slovenia has revealed that officers and their superiors desperately need training in the areas of community policing and current policing methods. In addition, the curriculum of police ethics, and attempting to reduce the grey (as opposed to black and white thinking) regarding what is the morally correct strategy in various situations. Mesko and Maver write about issues specific to policing in Slovenia including reducing prejudice in and against marginalized groups of citizens by recruiting more citizens from these groups to be police officers. The authors suggest that international support for more ethical practices and increased public pressure may help Slovenia to increase police professionalism and develop progressive leadership. A strong global community involving world-wide police cooperation can aid countries in need of improving their methods and can result in positive changes.

In Chapter 6, "Policing in China" by Wong, the need for national police reform was highlighted. Wong pointed out that much research on Chinese policing has been done by Western criminologists despite the fact that Western methods and ideas are not easily applied to the complex social conditions and political circumstances in China. Wong called for more police research by Chinese researchers, who can better understand and interpret their findings in relationship to China's complex history and culture. Wong discussed the difficulties including having access to limited and "sanitized" data, the prohibition on field survey research, and the need for political correctness in all published research. Wong informed the reader of specialized methods that must be used in China to conduct good police research and obtain the best data. He concluded that it is important to understand the similarities and differences between police agencies across different cultures and between nations and on a global level.

Chapter 7, "Development of Guidance Activities by Police for Prevention of Juvenile Delinquency in Japan" by Yokoyama discussed the cultural implications and the importance of understanding history when describing Japan's juvenile problems and understanding the response of the Japanese police force. Increasing juvenile crime prompted the public opinion that laws were "too soft" on juvenile crime, even in the face of Japan's historical empathy and concern for juveniles who have difficulties with the law. Yokoyama brought his readers' attention to the newer threat of transnational crime and discussed the establishment of an international police force to combat crime committed across borders. He also advocated the idea of establishing a global policy that provided for the return of juveniles to their own country for adjudication when they cross a border and commit a crime.

In Chapter 9, "Nonreturnable Arrest Warrants: A Form of Modern Banishment" by Sorge and Pollard, the importance of returning any criminal to his or her own local province in Canada was highlighted. Sorge and Pollard's research revealed that a substantial number of fugitives wanted for serious offenses are living in jurisdictions other than where the crime was committed. Because of the legal structure in Canada, many of these serious criminals will not be brought to justice. Sorge and Pollard examined Canadian law and determined that there is no law requiring the return of wanted criminals to the original jurisdiction where the crime was committed. They share several methods for modifying existing policy and creating new policy in Canada which would decrease this problem. Although not stated in the chapter, there is validity to the idea that all fugitives should be returned to their own jurisdiction or country because this would increase the global apprehension of criminals who cross borders to avoid justice.

Chapter 4, "Growth and Development of Women Police in India" by Adki, described the historically small and weak role that women play in India's police force. The need for female officers has become more apparent as the number of female offenders and victims has increased, but female officers still represent a minority and occupy mostly lower-level positions in the police force. Adki explained that the goal for the Indian Police is to increase the number and expand the authority of female officers, which is demonstrated by the fact that more female officers are beginning to occupy the upper police ranks. In addition, Adki suggested that India employ and train more women and utilize them as integral and important members of the police force. He further recommended that women be stationed close to their homes so that family responsibilities would not limit their involvement with the job and that daycare centers be provided for their smaller children. Adki also supported the global theme that focuses on the importance of increasing the presence and power of female officers in police agencies worldwide.

The theme of more powerful countries acting as models for less powerful countries, and lending resources, training, money, and technology to less developed nations was woven throughout the book.

Chapter 10, "Spooking the Spooks" by Lowe examined the unique research methodology of covert participation while working as part of a counter intelligence agency. Lowe's methods might have been deadly for a researcher in a less open country than the United Kingdom, but his evaluation of the pros and cons of his delicate strategy in this increasingly important area of policing is provided for other countries to study.

Chapter 11, "The Challenge of Transnational and Organized Crime in the Nordic Countries: The Case of Norway" by Andreescu and Malme, highlights the great need for international collaboration in fighting border-crossing crimes such as human and drug trafficking and cyber fraud. Norway's efforts to work with Europol and Interpol as well as expanding and improving their intelligence analysis provides a model for all countries to emulate.

Chapter 12, "The Public Housing Safety Initiative in the Eastern District of New York: A Collaborative Researcher and Practitioner Program" by Eterno, explained how developing innovative projects to reduce risk and criminal activity in pre-selected high risk developments can reduce both actual criminal acts as well as lessen public perception of criminal activity. The cooperation among local, state, and federal agencies demonstrated that a good idea can be actualized into a reduction in crime. This study should serve as a model intervention for other countries interested in targeting high-risk areas.

Chapter 8, "An Innovative Police Project to Tackle Youth Crime Problems in Hong Kong: Operation Breakthrough" by Li Chi-mei, described how a community policing program borrowed from Southern Australia was implemented in Hong Kong with the cooperation and dedication of police officers who donated their skills and time to a three-day juvenile camp. This project demonstrated how a small donation of time by officers can help at-risk youth increase their self-esteem, develop a wholesome interest in sports, and adopt a healthy lifestyle. Following their camp involvement, the juveniles had adopted more positive values and had greater self-confidence. Other countries can use the proactive methods and ideas presented in Chapters 12 and 8 in order to help decrease their crime rates.

Themes of *Police without Borders: The Fading Distinction Between Local and Global* conclude that more established countries should provide developing countries with information on the best proactive methods for crime reduction and prevention, sharing methods for modifying this information and enabling its use in nations where such techniques were new and unknown. The book also discusses ethical police behavior, professionalism and human rights policies. Methods of community and problem-oriented policing were discussed as areas countries should incorporate in their plans and goals for organizing and developing a more effective national police force. Additionally, the book demonstrates that individual countries need to increase communication and collaboration between local and state or federal agencies within their own borders. Most chapters of the book state or imply that all countries should increase international police cooperation in research, practice, and methodology, which is cited as the best way to fight international crime and bring all criminals to justice.

Only by learning from the successes and failures of other nations can the world create a truly effective police force. Borders must be recognized for what they are—artificial barriers separating nations. Only then can the borders be crossed. Only then will the nations of the world be able to share and adopt ideas and to accept and understand other cultures. Only then will nations be able to create stronger and more capable police agencies.

Jennie K. Singer, Dilip K. Das, and Cliff Robertson

Appendix: Summary of Meeting Presentations

Police without Borders: The Fading Distinction Between Local And Global: The 15th Annual International Police Executive Symposium, Cincinnati, Ohio, USA, May 12–16, 2008

In May 2008, the Cincinnati Police Department and the Ohio Association of Chiefs of Police were hosts of the 15th Annual International Police Executive Symposium (IPES) at the Hilton Netherland Plaza Hotel in downtown Cincinnati. The symposium was organised by IPES and the United Kingdom's Home Office. More than 100 delegates attended from more than 33 nations, representing multinational organisations (such as the United Nations), national and regional police forces, law enforcement organizations, police academies and colleges, security companies, armed forces and university faculties and departments. The symposium provided an unprecedented opportunity for practitioners, professionals, and academics to discuss and debate the theme of "police without borders: the fading distinction between local and global."

The symposium agenda was set in a keynote presentation by Acting Assistant Attorney General Jeffrey Sedgwick from the U.S. Department of Justice. Sedgwick set out clearly the challenges to international policing presented by the globalization of economies and advances in technology and argued that the improved sharing of information would need to provide at least some of the response to these challenges. The impact of new digital technologies also featured in the second presentation of the first day, by James A. Lewis of the Centre for System Security and Information Assurance. Lewis outlined common tools and techniques used by cybercriminals to hack into computer systems and networks. This form of criminal behavior respects neither international boundaries nor jurisdictions.

A panel presentation followed from Foreign Affairs Officer Allison Henry-Plotts (U.S. Department of State), Assistant Director Eric Beinhart (International Criminal Investigative Training Assistance Program [ICITAP], USA), Assistant Director Gary Barr (ICITAP, USA), Professor Richard Mears (University of Maine at Augusta, USA) and Stephen White (European Union

Integrated Rule of Law [UKJUST LEX] Mission) concerning the development of police training within a number of newly emerging democratic countries. In particular, the panel outlined how "democratic policing" is being enhanced through U.S. and E.U. funded programs in Africa, the Middle East, and Central Europe and described the obstacles encountered and how cultural and other barriers were overcome.

The theme of police training in changing times was developed by Dr. Stephen Tong (Canterbury Christ Church University, UK). Dr. Tong analyzed the changes faced by the police service and higher education providers in the United Kingdom when developing initial training for police recruits within a climate of reform and evolving professionalization. Dr. Tong's presentation found echoes in the next paper of the symposium, authored by Professor Dilip Das, the President of IPES, when Dr. Das noted that police leaders, like many other professional practitioners (and unlike their academic colleagues) are not in the habit of writing and sharing their experiences, initiatives, research and thoughts through the medium of peer-reviewed journals. This problem of 'bridging book and badge' was further explored by Professor William P. Bloss, (Department of Criminal Justice, USA). Professor Bloss noted that regardless of the setting, one of the most vexing problems facing policing is determining how to deliver services in an effective and efficient manner.

The use of intelligence is key to enhancing police efficiency, but this intelligence needs to be analyzed into "actionable nuggets." The theme of intelligence was taken up by the next speaker, Dr. Robin Bryant (Canterbury Christ Church University, UK). Dr. Bryant outlined the theoretical foundations to the use of criminal intelligence, particularly in terms of forms of reasoning. His contribution is shortly to be published in *Understanding Criminal Investigation* from John Wiley & Sons.

Professor Gary Cordner's (Kutztown University, Kutztown, Pennsylvania, USA) contribution followed, with a description and analysis of the work of the Commission on Accreditation for Law Enforcement Agencies (CALEA). Of particular note were the reflections on the relevance of CALEA to countries outside of the USA.

The final presentation on the first day of the Cincinnati symposium was offered by Chantal Perras (University of Montreal, Canada). Perras used the example of Colombian trafficking to illustrate the important point that law enforcement agencies might be better employed targeting groups rather than targeting particular forms of illicit trafficking.

Tuesday's keynote address was given by Commissioner Julian Fantino (Ontario Provincial Police, Canada). Commissioner Fantino's presentation emphasized the importance of valuing cultural diversity, not merely tolerating it, "managing" it or simply demonstrating token acceptance. Valuing diversity is not only an important ethical aim in its own right, but also makes good business sense. Valuing diversity featured highly in the presentations by Dr. Sara Charlesworth (Royal Melbourne Institute of Technology [RMIT University], Sydney, Australia) and Detective Sergeant Debra Roberston (Victoria Police, Australia).

The growth and development of women police in India, from Dr. Adki Surender of Vivek Vardhini College, Hyderabad, India was the subject of the next contribution. Dr. Susan Harwood (Curtin University of Technology, Perth, Australia) and Dr. Sara Charlesworth (RMIT) then examined two different but overlapping action research projects within Victoria Police and Western Australia Police; the first project adopted a broad focus on the gendering of police work, the second specifically focused on the quality of part-time work in operational policing. Their observations were complemented by the following input from Dr. Prit Paul Kaur (Minot State University, Minot, North Dakota, USA). in his study of women police in the USA, Germany and India, Prit noted that the division of work based on gender has given rise to two broad conceptual categories of occupations: female oriented and male oriented. This theme was further developed in Dr. Susan Harwood's (Curtin University of Technology, Perth, Australia) paper that followed where examples were given of successfully "crossing the gender border" in policing.

Dr. Jessica Li Chi-Mei's (University of Hong Kong, China) paper followed, analyzing an innovative police project to tackle problems associated with youth crime in Hong Kong (Operation Breakthrough). The final presentation in the morning of the second day of the symposium was from Deputy Commissioner Gary Burns of South Australia Police. Deputy Commissioner Burns examined the theme of police reform and manageralism in South Australia and demonstrated how a focus on underlying causes of crime could minimize the possibility of unhelpful practices regarding crime statistics.

The afternoon session was opened by Dr. Tina Patel (Liverpool John Moores University, UK) who made a presentation about policing racially motivated crime in Northern Ireland. Dr. Frederic Lemieux (from the University of Montreal in Canada) then discussed how to assess the effectiveness of international police cooperation systems. He proposed that, unlike existing attempts to understand police cooperation, alternative analyses would emphasise the significance of understanding supply chains; the practices embedded in task force investigations, and the environmental conditions that either favor or constrain the configuration of the supply chain. Multi-agency attempts to reduce crime were also the subject of the next panel session from Dr. Robin S. Engel (University of Cincinnati), Chief Thomas H. Streicher, Lieutenant Colonel James L. Whalen, and Assistant Police Chief S. Gregory Baker (the latter all from the Cincinnati Police Department).

The Cincinnati Initiative to Reduce Violence (CIRV), which began in 2007, is a multi-agency and community collaborative effort which aims to reduce gun-related violence and homicide. Intelligence has been gathered and analyzed on violent street group networks and the consequences of their actions made clear to the offenders concerned. Initial assessments indicate a significant reduction in the targeted crime types and efforts are currently underway to institutionalize the community, law enforcement, and social service partnerships that have given rise to this initial success.

Professor Kam Wong (Xavier University, Cincinnati) examined how we currently assess professional knowledge and understanding, primarily through the peer review approach. The final presentation on Tuesday was from Professor Minoru Yokoyama (Kokugakuin University, Tokyo, Japan). Minoru described the development of guidance activities for young people by the Japanese Police service since the Second World War, and then discussed whether it is possible to "export" such ideas to other countries and cultures.

The keynote address that opened Thursday's session was from Andrew Carpenter, Chief of the Strategic Policy and Development Section, Police Division, Office of Rule of Law and Security Institutions, Department of Peacekeeping Operations, United Nations. Carpenter examined how concepts, doctrine, policy, and planning for UN police-related activities were developing, with a particular emphasis on peace-keeping activities worldwide. Carpenter was then joined by Colonel Erika Wietinger (Austrian Federal Police, Austria), Deputy Chief Inspector Gwen Boniface (Garda Siochana Inspectorate, Ireland), Detective Sergeant Debra Robertson (Victoria Police, Melbourne, Australia), and Dr. Amy Ramsay (Ontario Police, Canada) to constitute a panel examining gender equality and cultural reform in policing. The panel noted that conservative, incremental, and "modest" approaches to redressing gendered workplace cultures have had only limited success. The panel then discussed, based upon their professional and academic experiences, how a more integrated and gender equitable police organization could be achieved.

The panel presentation was followed by comments from Deputy Chief Inspector Gwen Boniface (Garda Siochana Inspectorate, Ireland) on experiences of police reform and Odd Berner Malme (Norwegian Mission to the UN) on transnational and organized crime (from a northern hemisphere perspective). The morning session concluded with a presentation from Paulo Lino (NDS Americas Inc., Brazil) on intellectual property rights (IPR) crimes. Lino noted that IPR crimes respect no borders, but are often considered to be less serious than many other illegal activities. However, many transborder illegal activities are connected with IPR crimes and Lino suggested possible initiatives to help reduce crime within a borderless Internet-based society.

Thursday afternoon's session was opened with a group presentation from Professor Zelimir Kestovic (University of Belgrade, Serbia), Dr. Nedzad Korajlic and Jasmin Ahic (both from the University of Sarajevo, Bosnia and

Herzegovina) on the emerging private security sector in Serbia, Bosnia, and Herzegovina. The process of privatization, and the arrival of companies from outside the region, has led to an increase in both the quality and extent of supply to the private security market in Serbia.

Captain Michael Doyle (Cleveland Police Division, USA) then described his preliminary findings on the relationship between providing local, national and global security. These preliminary findings point to the ability of local or regional level police departments to realize innovative security practices whereas centralized police organizations are more inhibited by their large scale structures and national bureaucracies.

Next Dr. Bruno Meini (Rutgers University, Italy) explored the connections between HIV/AIDS, law, public safety (particularly interpersonal crimes and property crimes), and policing in South Africa. He produced statistics showing that HIV/AIDS is impacting the availability of experienced police personnel and this, in turn, is likely to diminish the capability of the police to prevent, investigate, and respond to crime.

The risks to police officers from a somewhat different source were examined in the joint presentation by Christer Philipson (Västra Götaland County Police, Sweden) and Jörgen Lundälv (Umea University, Sweden). Although there are examples of studies on the risks that police officers face when driving in a number of countries across the world, research in Sweden on this subject has been somewhat limited. Christer and Jörgen's paper first presented statistics on collision data for 1998–2006 in a county in Sweden and then addressed the need for better driver education.

Their presentation was followed by a contribution from Dr. John A. Eterno (Molloy College, Rockville Centre, New York) on the Public Housing Safety Initiative in the Eastern District of New York. Dr. Mohammed Murad Abdullas (Dubai Police, Dubai) then described Dubai's initiative in the area of drug education of its young people. The final paper of Thursday's session was delivered by Dr. Mile Matijevic (Apeiron University, Bosnia and Herzegovina) and focused on the important role that the police in Bosnia and Herzegovina are playing in the protection of human rights and freedom in the post-conflict society.

The final session of the 2009 symposium was opened with a presentation from Colonel (Ret.) Kenneth Morckel (First Response Solutions Inc., USA) on strategic and tactical approaches to traffic safety. A joint presentation by Professor Gary Cordner (Kutztown University) and Lt. Colonel (Ret.) Cynthia (Cindy) Collins Shain (Eastern Kentucky University, Richmond, Kentucky) then provided the symposium with a summary of a recent conference in Uzbekistan on the themes of human rights, the rule of law, terrorism, and community policing.

Policing in post-1991 Slovenia was the subject of the next presentation from Dr. Darko Maver (University of Maribor, Slovenia). Dr. Catriona (Kate) Storey-Whyte (Audiolex Ltd., UK) then outlined the useful contribution of voice recognition and linguistics to both local and international policing, including suggestions for its handling, analysis, and sharing. Professor Emil Plywaczewski (University of Bialystok, Poland) and Professor Wieslaw Plywaczewski (University of Warmia and Mazury, Poland) followed Dr. Storey-Whyte with a presentation on international police cooperation, from the UK perspective. A particular theme was how to address overlapping responsibilities in terms of police forces themselves and the sharing of information and between law enforcement agencies in the UK.

The final presentation of the symposium was delivered by Brigadier General Zoltan Bolcsik (Veszprem County Police, Hungary). General Bolcsik's presentation reflected the main themes of the conference when he addressed the "explosion" in organized crime activity post-1989. Hungary continues to be a country of transit and destination for trafficking in human beings, drugs and other forms of commodity. A closing ceremony and an invitation to the 2009 IPES symposium (hosted by the Ministry of Interior, Macedonia) concluded the 2008 event.

Robin Bryant
Canterbury Christ Church University, Canterbury, UK.
robin.bryant@canterbury.ac.uk

Index

D

H

J

T

U

INTERNATIONAL POLICE EXECUTIVE SYMPOSIUM
WWW.IPES.INFO

The International Police Executive Symposium was founded in 1994. The aims and objectives of the IPES are to provide a forum to foster closer relationships among police researchers and practitioners globally, to facilitate cross-cultural, international and interdisciplinary exchanges for the enrichment of the law enforcement profession, and to encourage discussion and published research on challenging and contemporary topics related to the profession.

One of the most important activities of the IPES is the organization of an annual meeting under the auspices of a police or educational institution. To date, meetings have been hosted by the Canton Police of Geneva, Switzerland (Police Challenges and Strategies, 1994), the International Institute of the Sociology of Law in Onati, Spain (Challenges of Policing Democracies, 1995), Kanagawa University in Yokohama, Japan (Organized Crime, 1996), the Federal Police in Vienna, Austria (International Police Cooperation, 1997), the Dutch Police and Europol in The Hague, The Netherlands (Crime Prevention, 1998), and Andhra Pradesh Police in Hyderabad, India (Policing of Public Order, 1999), and the Center for Public Safety, Northwestern University, Evanston Illinois, USA, (Traffic Policing, 2000). A special meeting was co-hosted by the Bavarian Police Academy of Continuing Education in Ainring, Germany, University of Passau, Germany, and State University of New York, Plattsburgh, USA, to discuss the issues endorsed by the IPES in April 2000. The Police in Poland hosted the next meeting in May, 2001 (Corruption: A threat to World Order), and thereafter the annual meeting was hosted by the Police of Turkey in May, 2002 (Police Education and Training). The Kingdom of Bahrain hosted the annual meeting in October, 2003 (Police and the Community).

The 2004 meeting in May of that year (Criminal Exploitation of Women and Children) took place in British Columbia in Canada, and it was co-hosted by the University College of the Fraser Valley, Abbotsford Police Department, Royal Canadian Mounted Police, the Vancouver Police Department, the Justice Institute of British Columbia, Canadian Police College and the International Centre for Criminal Law Reform and Criminal Justice Policy. The next meeting (Challenges of Policing in the 21st Century) took place in September, 2005 in Prague, The Czech Republic. The Turkish National Police hosted the meeting in 2006 (Local Linkages to Global Security and Crime). The Fourteenth Annual Meeting was hosted by the Dubai Police on April 8-12, 2007 (Urbanization and Security). In 2008 the 15th Annual Meeting was hosted in Cincinnati (Ohio, USA) by the City of Cincinnati Police and the Ohio Association of Chiefs of Police on the theme of "Police Without Borders: Fading Distinction Between Local and Global." The next annual meeting took place in the Republic of Macedonia in Ohrid on June 9–14, 2009 on the theme of "Policing, Private Security, Economic Development and Social Change". Next year, 2010, we met in Malta for the 17th Annual Meeting on March 14–19 on the theme of "Tourism, Strategic Locations, and Major Events: Policing In An Age of Mobility. Mass Movement and Migration." Negotiations are in progress with several countries in Europe, South America and Asia for hosting of the 2011 Annual Meeting on a topic of interest to the host country.

The majority of participants of the annual meetings are usually directly involved in the police profession. In addition, scholars and researchers in the field also participate. The meetings comprise both structured and informal sessions to maximize dialogue and exchange of views and information. The executive summary of each meeting is distributed to participants as well as to a wide range of other interested police professionals and scholars. In addition, a book of selected papers from each annual meeting is published through Prentice Hall, Lexington Books, Taylor and Francis Group and other reputed publishers.

Police
Practice &
Research
An International Journal

Closely associated with the IPES is the *Police Practice and Research: An International Journal (PPR)*. The journal is committed to highlighting current, innovative police practices from all over the world; providing opportunities for exchanges between police practitioners and researchers; reporting the state of public safety internationally; focusing on successful practices that build partnerships between police practitioners and communities, as well as highlighting other successful police practices in relation to maintaining order, enforcing laws and serving the community. For more information visit our website, www.ipes.info .

IPES Board of Directors

The IPES is directed by a board of directors representing various countries of the world.

The IPES is directed by a board of directors representing various countries of the world (listed below). The registered business office is located at 6030 Nott Road, Guilderland, NY 12064 and Registered Agent is National Registered Agents, 200 West Adams Street, Chicago, Il 60606.

President - Dilip Das
6030 Nott Road
Guilderland, NY 12084, USA
email: dilipdas@ipes.info
Tel (802) 598-3680
Fax (410) 951-3045

Vice President - Tariq Hassan Al Hassan
P.O. Box 13, Manama
KINGDOM OF BAHRAIN
email: Ropac@batelco.com.bh
Tel (973) 17 756777
Fax (973) 17 754302

Treasurer/Secretary - Paul Moore
P.O. Box 1611
West Monroe, LA 71294, USA
email: Paul@ipes.info
Tel (318) 322-5300
Fax (318) 340-1021

Directors

Rick Sarre
P.O. Box 2471, Adelaide, 5001
South AUSTRALIA
email: rick.sarre@unisa.edu.au
Tel 61 8 84314879 (h)
61 8 83020889 Fax 61 8 83020512

Tonita Murray
73 Murphy Street
Carleton Place, Ontario K7C 2B7 CANADA
email: Tonita_Murray@hotmail.com
Tel 613 998 0883 (w)

Snezana (Ana) Mijovic-Das
6030 Nott Road
Guilderland, NY 12084, USA
email: anamijovic@yahoo.com
Tel (518) 452 7845
Fax (518) 456 6790

Andrew Carpenter
The Pier, 1 Harborside Place, Apt 658
Jersey City, NJ 07311, USA
email: carpenter@un.org
Tel (917) 367-2205
Fax (917) 367-2222 Cell (347) 721-1104

Paulo R. Lino
111 Das Garcas St.
Canoas RS, 92320-830, BRAZIL
email: paulino2@terra.com.br
Tel 55 51 8111 1357
Fax 55 51 466 2425

Rune Glomseth
Slemdalsveien5, Oslo, 0369, NORWAY
email: Rune.Glomseth@phs.no

Maximillian Edelbacher
Riemersgasse 16/E/3
A-1190 Vienna, AUSTRIA
email: edelmax@magnet.at
Tel 43-1-601 74/5710
Fax 43-1-601 74/5727

Etienne Elion
Case J-354-V, OCH Moungali 3, Brazzaville
Republic of Congo (Ex French Congo)
email ejeej2003@yahoo.fr
Tel 242 662 1683
Fax 242 682 0293

A.B. Dambazau
P.O. Box 3733
Kaduna, Kaduna State, Nigeria
email adambazau@yahoo.com
Tel 234 80 35012743
Fax 234 70 36359118

For Product Safety Concerns and Information please contact our EU
representative GPSR@taylorandfrancis.com
Taylor & Francis Verlag GmbH, Kaufingerstraße 24, 80331 München, Germany

www.ingramcontent.com/pod-product-compliance
Ingram Content Group UK Ltd.
Pitfield, Milton Keynes, MK11 3LW, UK
UKHW022122190926
475702UK00013B/1584
9780367865030